MICROFINANCE

HANDBOOK

SUSTAINABLE BANKING with the POOR

MICROFINANCE

HANDBOOK

An Institutional and Financial Perspective

Joanna Ledgerwood

THE WORLD BANK

WASHINGTON, D.C.

Copyright © 1999
The International Bank for Reconstruction
and Development/THE WORLD BANK
1818 H Street, N.W.
Washington, D.C. 20433, U.S.A.

Joanna Ledgerwood is consultant to the Sustainable Banking with the Poor Project, World Bank, for Micro Finance International, Toronto, Canada.

Library of Congress Cataloging-in-Publication Data

Ledgerwood, Joanna.
    Microfinance handbook: an institutional and financial perspective/Joanna Ledgerwood.
        p. cm.—(Sustainable banking with the poor)
    Includes bibliographical references and index.
    ISBN 0-8213-4306-8
    1. Microfinance. 2. Financial institutions. I. Title.
II. Series.
HG178.2.L43 1998   98–21754
332.1—dc21   CIP

Contents

Boxes

Figures

Tables

Foreword

The Sustainable Banking with the Poor Project (SBP) began several years ago as a rather unusual joint effort by a regional technical department, Asia Technical, and a central department, Agriculture and Natural Resources. Through the years and the institutional changes, the project has maintained the support of the Asia Region and the Rural Development Department in the Environmentally and Socially Sustainable Development vice presidency and the endorsement of the Finance, Private Sector and Infrastructure Network.

An applied research and dissemination project, SBP aims at improving the ability of donors, governments, and practitioners to design and implement policies and programs to build sustainable financial institutions that effectively reach the poor. While its main audience has been World Bank Group staff, the project has contributed significantly to the knowledge base in the microfinance and rural finance fields at large.

More than 20 case studies of microfinance institutions have been published and disseminated worldwide, many of them in two languages; a seminar series at the World Bank has held more than 30 sessions on microfinance and rural finance good practice and new developments; three regional conferences have disseminated SBP products in Asia and Africa, while fostering and benefiting from exten-

sive discussions with practitioners, policymakers, and donors. SBP also co-produced with the Consultative Group to Assist the Poorest the "Microfinance Practical Guide," today a regular source of practical reference for World Bank Group task team leaders and staff working on microfinance operations or project components that involve the provision of financial services to the poor.

This volume, *Microfinance Handbook: An Institutional and Financial Perspective*, represents in a way a culmination of SBP work in pursuit of its principal aim. A comprehensive source for donors, policymakers, and practitioners, the handbook first covers the policy, legal, and regulatory issues relevant to microfinance development and subsequently treats rigorously and in depth the key elements in the process of building sustainable financial institutions with effective outreach to the poor.

The handbook focuses on the institutional and financial aspects of microfinance. Although impact analysis is reviewed briefly, a thorough discussion of poverty targeting and of the poverty alleviation effects of microfinance is left to other studies and publications.

We are confident that this handbook will contribute significantly to the improvement of policies and practices in the microfinance field.

Mieko Nishimizu
Vice President
South Asia Region

Jean-Michel Severino
Vice President
East Asia and Pacific Region

Ian Johnson
Vice President
Environmentally and Socially Sustainable Development

Masood Ahmed
Acting Vice President
Finance, Private Sector and Infrastructure

Preface

The *Microfinance Handbook*, one of the major products of the World Bank's Sustainable Banking with the Poor Project, gathers and presents up-to-date knowledge directly or indirectly contributed by leading experts in the field of microfinance. It is intended as a comprehensive source for donors, policymakers, and practitioners, as it covers in depth matters pertaining to the regulatory and policy framework and the essential components of institutional capacity building—product design, performance measuring and monitoring, and management of microfinance institutions.

The handbook was developed with contributions from other parts of the World Bank, including the Consultative Group to Assist the Poorest. It also benefited from the experience of a wide range of practitioners and donors from such organizations as ACCION International, Calmeadow, CARE, Women's World Banking, the Small Enterprise Education and Promotion Network, the MicroFinance Network, the U.S. Agency for International Development, Deutsche Gesellschaft für Technische Zusammenarbeit, Caisse Française de Développement, and the Inter-American Development Bank.

Special thanks are due to the outside sponsors of the Sustainable Banking with the Poor Project—the Swiss Agency for Development and Cooperation, the Royal Ministry of Foreign Affairs of Norway, and the Ford Foundation—for their patience, encouragement, and support.

I would like to thank the many individuals who contributed substantially to this handbook. A first draft was prepared by staff members at both the Sustainable Banking with the Poor Project and the Consultative Group to Assist the Poorest. I am grateful to Mike Goldberg and Gregory Chen for their initial contributions. Thomas Dichter wrote the sections on impact analysis and enterprise development services and provided comments on other chapters. Tony Sheldon wrote the chapter on management information systems and provided comments on the first draft. Reinhardt Schmidt contributed substantially to the chapter on institutions.

I wish to thank especially Cecile Fruman for her initial and ongoing contributions, comments, and support. I also appreciate the support and flexibility of Carlos E. Cuevas, which were vital in keeping the process going. Thanks are extended to Julia Paxton and Stephanie Charitonenko Church for their contributions as well as to the many people who reviewed various chapters and provided comments, including Jacob Yaron, Lynn Bennett, Mohini Malhotra, McDonald Benjamin, Jeffrey Poyo, Jennifer Harold, Bikki Randhawa, Joyita Mukherjee, Jennifer Isern, and Joakim Vincze.

I would also like to thank Laura Gomez for her continued support in formatting the handbook and managing its many iterations.

The book was edited, designed, and typeset by Communications Development Inc.

*****

The Sustainable Banking with the Poor Project team is led by Lynn Bennett and Jacob Yaron, task managers. Carlos E. Cuevas is the technical manager and Cecile Fruman is the associate manager. Laura Gomez is the administrative assistant.

Introduction

It has been estimated that there are 500 million economically active poor people in the world operating microenterprises and small businesses (Women's World Banking 1995). Most of them do not have access to adequate financial services. To meet this substantial demand for financial services by low-income microentrepreneurs, microfinance practitioners and donors alike must adopt a long-term perspective. The purpose of this handbook is to bring together in a single source guiding principles and tools that will promote sustainable microfinance and create viable institutions.

The goal of this book is to provide a comprehensive source for the design, implementation, evaluation, and management of microfinance activities.[1]

The handbook takes a global perspective, drawing on lessons learned from the experiences of microfinance practitioners, donors, and others throughout the world. It offers readers relevant information that will help them to make informed and effective decisions suited to their specific environment and objectives.

Microfinance Defined

Microfinance has evolved as an economic development approach intended to benefit low-income women and men. The term refers to the provision of financial services to low-income clients, including the self-employed.

Financial services generally include savings and credit; however, some microfinance organizations also provide insurance and payment services. In addition to financial intermediation, many MFIs provide social intermediation services such as group formation, development of self-confidence, and training in financial literacy and management capabilities among members of a group. Thus the definition of microfinance often includes both financial intermediation and social intermediation. Microfinance is not simply banking, it is a development tool.

Microfinance activities usually involve:

- Small loans, typically for working capital
- Informal appraisal of borrowers and investments
- Collateral substitutes, such as group guarantees or compulsory savings
- Access to repeat and larger loans, based on repayment performance
- Streamlined loan disbursement and monitoring
- Secure savings products.

Although some MFIs provide enterprise development services, such as skills training and marketing, and social services, such as literacy training and health care, these are not generally included in the definition of microfinance. (However, enterprise development services and social services are discussed briefly in chapter 3, as some MFIs provide these services.)

MFIs can be nongovernmental organizations (NGOs), savings and loan cooperatives, credit unions,

---

1. The term "microfinance activity" is used throughout to describe the operations of a microfinance institution, a microfinance project, or a microfinance component of a project. When referring to an organization providing microfinance services, whether regulated or unregulated, the term "microfinance institution" (MFI) is used.

government banks, commercial banks, or nonbank financial institutions. Microfinance clients are typically self-employed, low-income entrepreneurs in both urban and rural areas. Clients are often traders, street vendors, small farmers, service providers (hairdressers, rickshaw drivers), and artisans and small producers, such as blacksmiths and seamstresses. Usually their activities provide a stable source of income (often from more than one activity). Although they are poor, they are generally not considered to be the "poorest of the poor."

Moneylenders, pawnbrokers, and rotating savings and credit associations are informal microfinance providers and important sources of financial intermediation but they are not discussed in detail in this handbook. Rather, the focus is on more formal MFIs.

Background

Microfinance arose in the 1980s as a response to doubts and research findings about state delivery of subsidized credit to poor farmers. In the 1970s government agencies were the predominant method of providing productive credit to those with no previous access to credit facilities—people who had been forced to pay usurious interest rates or were subject to rent-seeking behavior. Governments and international donors assumed that the poor required cheap credit and saw this as a way of promoting agricultural production by small landholders. In addition to providing subsidized agricultural credit, donors set up credit unions inspired by the Raiffeisen model developed in Germany in 1864. The focus of these cooperative financial institutions was mostly on savings mobilization in rural areas in an attempt to "teach poor farmers how to save."

Beginning in the mid-1980s, the subsidized, targeted credit model supported by many donors was the object of steady criticism, because most programs accumulated large loan losses and required frequent recapitalization to continue operating. It became more and more evident that market-based solutions were required. This led to a new approach that considered microfinance as an integral part of the overall financial system. Emphasis shifted from the rapid disbursement of subsidized loans to target populations toward the building up of local, sustainable institutions to serve the poor.

At the same time, local NGOs began to look for a more long-term approach than the unsustainable income-generation approaches to community development. In Asia Dr. Mohammed Yunus of Bangladesh led the way with a pilot group lending scheme for landless people. This later became the Grameen Bank, which now serves more than 2.4 million clients (94 percent of them women) and is a model for many countries. In Latin America ACCION International supported the development of solidarity group lending to urban vendors, and Fundación Carvajal developed a successful credit and training system for individual microentrepreneurs.

Changes were also occurring in the formal financial sector. Bank Rakyat Indonesia, a state-owned, rural bank, moved away from providing subsidized credit and took an institutional approach that operated on market principles. In particular, Bank Rakyat Indonesia developed a transparent set of incentives for its borrowers (small farmers) and staff, rewarding on-time loan repayment and relying on voluntary savings mobilization as a source of funds.

Since the 1980s the field of microfinance has grown substantially. Donors actively support and encourage microfinance activities, focusing on MFIs that are committed to achieving substantial outreach and financial sustainability. Today the focus is on providing financial services only, whereas the 1970s and much of the 1980s were characterized by an integrated package of credit and training—which required subsidies. Most recently, microfinance NGOs (including PRODEM/BancoSol in Bolivia, K-REP in Kenya, and ADEMI/BancoADEMI in the Dominican Republic) have begun transforming into formal financial institutions that recognize the need to provide savings services to their clients and to access market funding sources, rather than rely on donor funds. This recognition of the need to achieve financial sustainability has led to the current "financial systems" approach to microfinance. This approach is characterized by the following beliefs:

- Subsidized credit undermines development.
- Poor people can pay interest rates high enough to cover transaction costs and the consequences of the imperfect information markets in which lenders operate.
- The goal of sustainability (cost recovery and eventually profit) is the key not only to institutional perma-

nence in lending, but also to making the lending institution more focused and efficient.

- Because loan sizes to poor people are small, MFIs must achieve sufficient scale if they are to become sustainable.
- Measurable enterprise growth, as well as impacts on poverty, cannot be demonstrated easily or accurately; outreach and repayment rates can be proxies for impact.

One of the main assumptions in the above view is that many poor people actively want productive credit and that they can absorb and use it. But as the field of microfinance has evolved, research has increasingly found that in many situations poor people want secure savings facilities and consumption loans just as much as productive credit and in some cases instead of productive credit. MFIs are beginning to respond to these demands by providing voluntary savings services and other types of loans.

Size of the Microfinance Industry

During 1995 and 1996 the Sustainable Banking with the Poor Project compiled a worldwide inventory of MFIs. The list included nearly 1,000 institutions that provided microfinance services, reached at least 1,000 clients, and had operated for a minimum of three years. From this inventory, more than 200 institutions responded to a two-page questionnaire covering basic institutional characteristics.

According to the survey results, by September 1995 about US$7 billion in outstanding loans had been provided to more than 13 million individuals and groups. In addition, more than US$19 billion had been mobilized in 45 million active deposit accounts.

The general conclusions of the inventory were:
- Commercial and savings banks were responsible for the largest share of the outstanding loan balance and deposit balance.
- Credit unions represented 11 percent of the total number of loans in the sample and 13 percent of the outstanding loan balance.
- NGOs made up more than half of the sample, but they accounted for only 9 percent of the total number of outstanding loans and 4 percent of the outstanding loan balance.

- Sources of funds to finance loan portfolios differed by type of institution. NGOs relied heavily on donor funding or concessional funds for the majority of their lending. Banks, savings banks, and credit unions funded their loan portfolios with client and member deposits and commercial loans.
- NGOs offered the smallest loan sizes and relatively more social services than banks, savings banks, or credit unions.
- Credit unions and banks are leaders in serving large numbers of clients with small deposit accounts.

The study also found that basic accounting capacities and reporting varied widely among institutions, in many cases revealing an inability to report plausible cost and arrears data. This shortcoming, notably among NGOs, highlights the need to place greater emphasis on financial monitoring and reporting using standardized practices (a primary purpose of this handbook). Overall, the findings suggest that favorable macroeconomic conditions, managed growth, deposit mobilization, and cost control, in combination, are among the key factors that contribute to the success and sustainability of many microfinance institutions.

Why is Microfinance Growing?

Microfinance is growing for several reasons:
1. *The promise of reaching the poor.* Microfinance activities can support income generation for enterprises operated by low-income households.
2. *The promise of financial sustainability.* Microfinance activities can help to build financially self-sufficient, subsidy-free, often locally managed institutions.
3. *The potential to build on traditional systems.* Microfinance activities sometimes mimic traditional systems (such as rotating savings and credit associations). They provide the same services in similar ways, but with greater flexibility, at a more affordable price to microenterprises and on a more sustainable basis. This can make microfinance services very attractive to a large number of low-income clients.
4. *The contribution of microfinance to strengthening and expanding existing formal financial systems.* Microfinance activities can strengthen existing formal financial institutions, such as savings and loan coop-

eratives, credit union networks, commercial banks, and even state-run financial institutions, by expanding their markets for both savings and credit—and, potentially, their profitability.

5. *The growing number of success stories.* There is an increasing number of well-documented, innovative success stories in settings as diverse as rural Bangladesh, urban Bolivia, and rural Mali. This is in stark contrast to the records of state-run specialized financial institutions, which have received large amounts of funding over the past few decades but have failed in terms of both financial sustainability and outreach to the poor.

6. *The availability of better financial products as a result of experimentation and innovation.* The innovations that have shown the most promise are solving the problem of lack of collateral by using group-based and character-based approaches; solving problems of repayment discipline through high frequency of repayment collection, the use of social and peer pressure, and the promise of higher repeat loans; solving problems of transaction costs by moving some of these costs down to the group level and by increasing outreach; designing staff incentives to achieve greater outreach and high loan repayment; and providing savings services that meet the needs of small savers.

What Are the Risks of Microfinance?

Sound microfinance activities based on best practices play a decisive role in providing the poor with access to financial services through sustainable institutions. However, there have been many more failures than successes:

- Some MFIs target a segment of the population that has no access to business opportunities because of lack of markets, inputs, and demand. Productive credit is of no use to such people without other inputs.
- Many MFIs never reach either the minimal scale or the efficiency necessary to cover costs.
- Many MFIs face nonsupportive policy frameworks and daunting physical, social, and economic challenges.
- Some MFIs fail to manage their funds adequately enough to meet future cash needs and, as a result, they confront a liquidity problem.

- Others develop neither the financial management systems nor the skills required to run a successful operation.
- Replication of successful models has at times proved difficult, due to differences in social contexts and lack of local adaptation.

Ultimately, most of the dilemmas and problems encountered in microfinance have to do with how clear the organization is about its principal goals. Does an MFI provide microfinance to lighten the heavy burdens of poverty? Or to encourage economic growth? Or to help poor women develop confidence and become empowered within their families? And so on. In a sense, goals are a matter of choice; and in development, an organization can choose one or many goals—provided its constituents, governance structure, and funding are all in line with those goals.

About This Book

This handbook was written for microfinance practitioners, donors, and the wider readership of academics, consultants, and others interested in microfinance design, implementation, evaluation, and management. It offers a one-stop guide that covers most topics in enough detail that most readers will not need to refer to other sources.

At first glance it might seem that practitioners and donors have very different needs and objectives and thus could not possibly benefit equally from one book.

The objectives of many donors who support microfinance activities are to reduce poverty and empower specific segments of the population (for example, women, indigenous peoples). Their primary concerns traditionally have been the amount of funds they are able to disburse and the timely receipt of requested (and, it is hoped, successful) performance indicators. Donors are rarely concerned with understanding the details of microfinance. Rather, it is often enough for them to believe that microfinance simply works.

Practitioners need to know how actually to operate a microfinance institution. Their objectives are to meet the needs of their clients and to continue to operate in the long term.

Given the purpose of this handbook, it seems to be directed more toward practitioners than toward donors. However, donors are beginning to realize that MFI capacity is a more binding constraint than the availability of funds, making it essential for donors and practitioners to operate from the same perspective if they are to meet effectively the substantial need for financial services. In fact, if we look briefly at the evolution of microfinance, it is apparent that both donors and practitioners need to understand how microfinance institutions operate.

When microfinance first emerged as a development tool, both donors and practitioners focused on the cumulative amount of loans disbursed, with no concern for how well the loans suited borrower needs and little concern about whether or not loans were repaid. Donors were rewarded for disbursing funds, and practitioners were rewarded for on-lending those funds to as many people (preferably women) as possible. Neither was particularly accountable for the long-term sustainability of the microfinance institution or for the long-term effect on borrowers or beneficiaries.

Now that the field of microfinance is more mature, it is becoming clear that effective, efficient, and sustainable institutions are needed to provide financial services well suited to the demands of low-income clients. Both donors and practitioners are beginning to be held accountable for results. The focus is no longer solely on quantity—on the amount disbursed—but on the quality of operations. This view is based on the notion that borrowers will buy microfinance products if they value the service; that is, if the product is right for them. Borrowers are now being treated as *clients* rather than *beneficiaries*. Thus if they are to be effective and truly meet their development objectives, donors must support MFIs that are "doing it right." To do so, they need to understand how to both recognize and evaluate a good microfinance provider.

As it turns out, both donors and practitioners are really on the same side—their joint goal is to make available appropriate services to low-income clients. Therefore, it falls to donors and practitioners themselves to define best practices and to advocate policies that will encourage growth, consistency, and accountability in the field. The intent of this handbook is to provide a basis of common understanding among all stakeholders.

Organization of the Book

The handbook has three parts. Part I, "Issues in Microfinance Provision," takes a macroeconomc perspective toward general microfinance issues and is primarily non-

technical. Part II, "Designing and Monitoring Financial Products and Services," narrows its focus to the provision of financial intermediation, taking a more technical approach and moving progressively toward more specific (or micro) issues. Part III, "Measuring Performance and Managing Viability," is the most technical part of the handbook, focusing primarily on assessing the financial viability of MFIs. (These relationships are shown in figure 1.)

Part I addresses the broader considerations of microfinance activities, including the supply of and demand for financial services, the products and services that an MFI might offer, and the institutions and institutional issues involved. Part I is the least technical part of the handbook; it requires no formal background in microfinance or financial theory. Its perspective is more macro than that of parts II and III, which provide more detailed "how-to" discussions and are specifically focused on the provision of financial services only. Part I will be of most interest to donors and those considering providing microfinance. Practitioners may also benefit from part I if they are considering redefining their market, changing their institutional structure, offering additional services, or implementing different service delivery methods.

Part II, which addresses more specific issues in the design of financial services (both lending and savings

Figure 1. Relationship between Level of Analysis and Technical Complexity in this Book

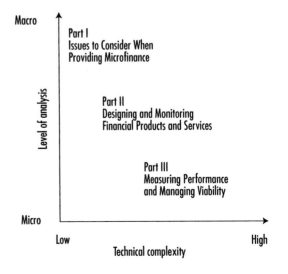

products) and the development of management information systems, will be of most interest to practitioners who are developing, modifying, or refining their financial products or systems, and donors or consultants who are evaluating microfinance organizations and the appropriateness of the products and services that they provide. Part II incorporates some basic financial theory and, accordingly, readers should have a basic understanding of financial management. Readers should also be familiar with using a financial calculator, computer spreadsheet, or both.

Part III provides tools for evaluating the financial health of an MFI and a means of managing operational issues. The material focuses primarily on financial intermediation (that is, credit and savings services, based on the assumption that the main activity of an MFI is the provision of financial services). Social intermediation and enterprise development services are not addressed directly. However, basic financial theory that is relevant to the financial management of MFIs delivering these services is provided as well. The material also underscores the importance of the interrelationship between serving clients well and moving towards institutional and financial self-sufficiency. These two goals serve each other; neither is sufficient on its own.

As the most technical section of the handbook, part III will be of particular interest to practitioners and consultants. Donors will also benefit from part III if they want to understand how MFIs should be adjusting their financial statements and calculating performance indicators. While the technical information is fairly basic, some understanding of financial statements and financial analysis is required.

The overall purpose of part III is to improve the level of financial understanding and management in MFI operations. As donors come to understand both the complexity of microfinance and that it can be delivered in a financially sustainable manner, knowledge of the more technical aspects of microfinance will become increasingly important to them in deciding whether to support institutions and programs.

Each chapter is designed to be used alone or in conjunction with other chapters, depending on the specific needs of the reader. A list of sources and additional reading material is provided at the end of each chapter.

Many of the publications listed at the end of each chapter can be accessed through the following organizations, either by mail or through their Web sites:

ACCION Publications Department
733 15th Street NW, Suite 700
Washington D.C. 20005
Phone: 1 202 393 5113, Fax 1 202 393 5115
Web: www.accion.org
E-mail: publications@accion.org

Calmeadow Resource Center
365 Bay Street, Suite 600
Toronto, Canada M5H 2V1
Phone: 1 416 362 9670, Fax: 1 416 362 0769
Web: www.calmeadow.com
E-mail: resource@calmeadow.com

CGAP Secretariat
Room G4-115, The World Bank
1818 H Street NW
Washington D.C. 20433
Phone: 1 202 473 9594, Fax: 1 202 522 3744
Web: www.worldbank.org/html/cgap/cgap.html
E-mail: CProject@Worldbank.org

Micro Finance Network
733 15th Street NW, Suite 700
Washington D.C. 20005
Phone: 1 202 347 2953, Fax 1 202 347 2959
Web: www.bellanet.org/partners/mfn
E-mail: mfn@sysnet.net

PACT Publications
777 United Nations Plaza
New York, NY 10017
Phone: 1 212 697 6222, Fax: 1 212 692 9748
Web: www.pactpub.com
E-mail: books@pactpub.org

Part I—Issues in Microfinance Provision

Chapter 1–The Country Context provides a framework for analyzing contextual factors. It focuses on issues that affect the supply of microfinance, including the financial sector, financial sector policies and legal enforcement, financial sector regulation and supervision, and economic and social policies.

Chapter 2–The Target Market and Impact Analysis looks at the demand for financial services among low-income populations and presents ways of identifying a target market based on client characteristics and the types of enterprises they operate. It also discusses impact analysis and how the desired impact affects an MFI's choice of target market.

Chapter 3–Products and Services considers the various services that low-income entrepreneurs might demand, including financial and social intermediation, enterprise development, and social services. An overview of well-known microfinance approaches is presented in the appendix.

Chapter 4–The Institution discusses the various types of institutions that can effectively provide and manage the provision of microfinance activities. It addresses issues such as legal structures, governance, and institutional capacity, and also provides information on accessing capital markets for funding.

Part II—Designing and Monitoring Financial Products and Services

Chapter 5–Designing Lending Products provides information on how to design or modify lending products for microentrepreneurs both to meet their needs and to ensure financial sustainability of the MFI.

Chapter 6–Designing Savings Products provides information on the legal requirements to provide savings, types of savings products, and operational considerations for providing savings, including pricing. This chapter focuses on the provision of voluntary savings; it does not address forced or compulsory savings often associated with lending products.

Chapter 7–Management Information Systems (MIS) presents an overview of effective MIS, including accounting systems, loan-tracking systems, and client-impact tracking systems. It also provides a brief discussion on the process of installing an MIS and a summary evaluation of existing software packages.

Part III—Measuring Performance and Managing Viability

Chapter 8–Adjusting Financial Statements presents the adjustments to financial statements that are required to account for loan losses, depreciation, accrued interest, inflation, and subsidies. Adjustments are presented in two groups: standard entries that should be included in the financial statements and adjustments that restate financial results to reflect more accurately the financial position of an MFI.

Chapter 9–Performance Indicators details how to measure and evaluate the financial performance of the MFI, focusing on ratio analysis to determine how successful is the institution's performance and which areas could be improved. In addition, it provides various outreach indicators that can be monitored.

Chapter 10–Performance Management presents ways in which to improve the financial and resource management of microfinance institutions. It discusses delinquency management, staff productivity and incentives, and risk management, including asset and liability management.

A Necessary Caveat

Microfinance has recently become the favorite intervention for development institutions, due to its unique potential for poverty reduction and financial sustainability. However, contrary to what some may claim, microfinance is not a panacea for poverty alleviation. In fact, a poorly designed microfinance activity can make things worse by disrupting informal markets that have reliably provided financial services to poor households over the past couple of centuries, albeit at a high cost.

There are many situations in which microfinance is neither the most important nor the most feasible activity for a donor or other agency to support. Infrastructure, health, education, and other social services are critical to balanced economic development; and each in its own way contributes to a better environment for microfinance activities in the future. Care should be taken to ensure that the provision of microfinance is truly demand driven, rather than simply a means to satisfy donors' agendas.

Sources and Further Reading

Gonzalez-Vega, Claudio, and Douglas H. Graham. 1995. "State-Owned Agricultural Development Banks: Lessons and Opportunities for Microfinance." Occasional Paper 2245. Ohio State University, Department of Agricultural Economics, Columbus, Ohio.

Mutua, Kimanthi, Pittayapol Nataradol, and Maria Otero. 1996. "The View from the Field: Perspectives from Managers of Microfinance Institutions." In Lynn Bennett and Carlos Cuevas, eds., *Journal of International Development* 8 (2): 195–210.

Paxton, Julia. 1996. "A Worldwide Inventory of Microfinance Institutions." Sustainable Banking with the Poor, World Bank, Washington, D.C.

Women's World Banking Global Policy Forum. 1995. "The Missing Links: Financial Systems That Work for the Majority." *Women's World Banking* (April). New York.

Part I–
Issues to Consider When Providing Microfinance

CHAPTER ONE

Understanding the Country Context

The overall political and economic environment of a country affects how microfinance is provided. Government economic and social polices, as well as the development level of the financial sector, influence microfinance organizations in the delivery of financial services to the poor. Understanding these factors and their effect on microfinance is called assessing the country context. This process asks the following questions:

- Who are the suppliers of financial services? What products and services do they supply? What role do governments and donors play in providing financial services to the poor?

- How do existing financial sector policies affect the provision of financial services, including interest rate policies, government mandates for sectoral credit allocation, and legal enforcement policies?

- What forms of financial sector regulation exist, and are MFIs subject to these regulations?

- What economic and social policies affect the provision of financial services and the ability of microentrepreneurs to operate?

As can be seen in figure 1.1, contextual factors affect how suppliers of financial intermediation reach their clients.

This chapter uses a macroeconomic approach to place microfinance in the overall context of a country and so make clear how important macro-level policy and regulation are for developing microfinance providers and microenterprises. Practitioners and donors need to examine the financial system to locate needs and opportunities for providing microfinance services. Analyzing the country context reveals whether changes in policy or in the legal

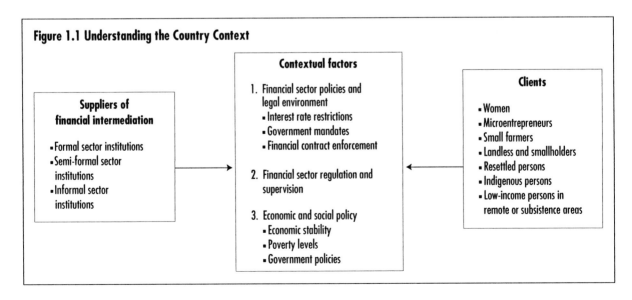

Figure 1.1 Understanding the Country Context

Suppliers of financial intermediation

- Formal sector institutions
- Semi-formal sector institutions
- Informal sector institutions

Contextual factors

1. Financial sector policies and legal environment
   - Interest rate restrictions
   - Government mandates
   - Financial contract enforcement

2. Financial sector regulation and supervision

3. Economic and social policy
   - Economic stability
   - Poverty levels
   - Government policies

Clients

- Women
- Microentrepreneurs
- Small farmers
- Landless and smallholders
- Resettled persons
- Indigenous persons
- Low-income persons in remote or subsistence areas

framework are needed to allow more efficient markets to emerge.

Suppliers of Financial Intermediation Services

The first step in understanding the context in which a microfinance provider operates is to determine who makes up the financial system.

"The *financial system* (or financial sector, or financial infrastructure) includes all savings and financing opportunities and the financial institutions that provide savings and financing opportunities, as well as the valid norms and modes of behavior related to these institutions and their operations. *Financial markets* are the markets—supply, demand, and the coordination thereof—for the services provided by the financial institutions to the nonfinancial sectors of the economy." (Krahnen and Schmidt 1994, 3)

To analyze a country's financial system, it is necessary to look at both the demand for and the supply of financial services. This section focuses on the *supply* of financial services; *demand* will be examined in chapter 2.

Understanding a country's financial system allows microfinance providers to identify areas in which services or products for certain client groups are inadequate or nonexistent. It can also identify institutional gaps and the potential for partnerships between different types of institutions to reach the poor cost effectively.

Intermediaries that provide financial services range from highly formal institutions to informal moneylenders. Understanding the size, growth, number, governance, and supervision of these institutions is an important part of assessing how the financial system works. Financial intermediation varies with the services and products provided and depends to some extent on the type of institution providing the services. Not all markets have access to the same services and products. Determining which financial services are currently being provided to the differing markets is important in identifying unserved or underserved clients.

Financial systems can generally be divided into the formal, semiformal, and informal sectors. The distinction between formal and informal is based primarily on whether there is a legal infrastructure that provides recourse to lenders and protection to depositors. Table 1.1 outlines the wide range of public and private providers that can be found in each group. The dividing lines are not absolute, and regulatory structures vary. For example, credit unions may fall in the formal sector in one country and in the semiformal sector in another.

Formal financial institutions are chartered by the government and are subject to banking regulations and supervision. They include public and private banks, insurance firms, and finance companies. When these institutions serve smaller businesses or farmers (as is often the case with public sector financial institutions), there is potential for them to move into the microfinance sector.

Within the *formal sector,* private institutions generally focus on urban areas, whereas many public institutions provide services in both urban and rural areas. Loans from private sector institutions are often large individual amounts and are usually allocated to large, established, private, and government-owned enterprises in modern industrial sectors. Private formal sector institutions typically mobilize the greatest amount of deposits from the general public. Public sector rural institutions often provide agricultural loans as a means of developing the rural sector. Funding sources include government-distributed and foreign capital, with savings and deposits as secondary sources. Processing of transactions entails detailed paperwork and bureaucratic procedures that result in high transaction costs, reinforcing the bias toward relatively large loans. Box 1.1 describes the operations and problems of rural financial institutions in Mexico.

Semiformal institutions are not regulated by banking authorities but are usually licensed and supervised by other government agencies. Examples are credit unions and cooperative banks, which are often supervised by a bureau in charge of cooperatives. (NGOs are sometimes considered part of the semiformal sector, because they are often legally registered entities that are subject to some form of supervision or reporting requirements.) These financial institutions, which vary greatly in size, typically serve midrange clients associated by a profession or geographic location and emphasize deposit mobilization.

Semiformal institutions provide products and services that fall somewhere between those offered by formal sector and informal sector institutions. The design of their loan and savings products often borrows characteristics from both sectors. In many countries semiformal institutions often receive donor or government support through technical assistance or subsidies for their operations.

Informal financial intermediaries operate outside the structure of government regulation and supervision. They include local moneylenders, pawnbrokers, self-help groups, and NGOs, as well as the savings of family members who contribute to the microenterprise. Often they do not comply with common bookkeeping standards and are not reflected in official statistics on the depth and breadth of the national financial sector. Knowing where and how these financial sources operate helps determine what services are in demand.

These institutions concentrate on the informal sector—on loans and deposits for small firms and households. Often loans are granted without formal collateral on the basis of familiarity with the borrower. Social sanctions within a family, a village, or a religious community substitute for legal enforcement. Credit terms are typically adapted to the client's situation. The total amount lent, as well as the number and the frequency of installments, is fitted to the borrower's expected cash flow. Little if any paperwork is involved in applying for a loan (Krahnen and Schmidt 1994, 32).

Depending on historical factors and the country's level of economic development, *various combinations of these suppliers* are present in the financial sectors of developing countries. Research increasingly shows that the financial sector is complex and that there are substantial flows of funds between subsectors. Identifying the suppliers of financial services in a given country or region leads to a greater understanding of the financial system and also reveals gaps for a microfinance provider to address.

Table 1.1 Providers of Financial Intermediation Services

Formal sector	Semiformal sector	Informal sector
Central bank	Savings and credit cooperatives	Savings associations

Banks
    Commercial banks
    Merchant banks
    Savings banks
    Rural banks
    Postal savings banks
    Labor banks
    Cooperative banks
	Multipurpose cooperatives
	
	Credit unions
	
	Banques populaires
	
	Cooperative quasi-banks
	
	Employee savings funds
		Combined savings and credit associations—rotating savings and credit associations and variants
		
		Informal financial firms
		    Indigenous bankers
		    Finance companies
		    Investment companies

Development banks
    State-owned
    Private
	Village banks
	
	Development projects
		Nonregistered self-help groups
		
		Individual moneylenders
		    Commercial

Other nonbank institutions
    Finance companies
    Term-lending institutions
	Registered self-help groups and savings clubs
	
	Nongovernmental organizations (NGOs)
		Noncommercial
		    (friends, neighbors, relatives)

Building societies and credit unions		Traders and shopkeepers

Contractual savings institutions
    Pension funds
    Insurance companies
		NGOs

Markets
    Stocks
    Bonds		

Source: Food and Agriculture Organization 1995, 5.

Box 1.1 Formal Sector Suppliers in Rural Mexico

IN 1994 AND 1995 A WORLD BANK TEAM CONDUCTED AN
economic and sector study in Mexico to examine the efficiency and fairness of rural financial markets. The team conducted case studies of 96 nonbank lenders, plus a household
survey of 800 rural entrepreneurs and a review of the regulatory framework for the *uniones de crédito* (credit unions) and
the *sociedades de ahorro y préstamo* (savings and loan companies). All forms of formal and informal savings and loan services were analyzed.

The study provided strong evidence about the poor performance of rural financial markets in Mexico. These markets proved to be shallow (only 45 percent of rural
entrepreneurs received a credit transaction during 1992-94),
segmented, noncompetitive, inefficient, and inequitable
(showing strong biases against disadvantaged individuals).
The consequence was a weak supply of credit. The main reasons for this situation were underdeveloped institutional
infrastructure (two-thirds of the municipalities have no bank
offices), inappropriate banking technologies for small markets, and attenuated property rights. Past government intervention characterized by debt forgiveness and subsidized
interest rates had contributed to the bad image of rural
finance. Few bankers from the private sector truly believed
there was a business opportunity in this field. On the
demand side, 75 percent of the households interviewed had
never requested a loan from the formal financial sector.
Rural entrepreneurs felt this would be too risky, given the
excessive amount of collateral required and the noninstitu-
tional techniques used to enforce contracts. Many entrepreneurs admitted that they were afraid of formal institutions
and that they were unwilling to pay high transaction costs.

As a consequence of the inefficiency of rural financial markets, the funds did not flow to the best uses, hindering rural
development in Mexico.

The study convinced the government of Mexico to ask
the World Bank team to propose measures that would help
develop rural financial markets. The first measure proposed
was to expand the distribution network, introduce adequate
financial products and technologies, and carry out organizational reforms, including the introduction of incentives and
internal controls. The second was to improve environmental
conditions by developing better policies and regulations on a
broad range of issues, such as secured transactions and the
regulation of intermediaries (mostly nonbanks) and of related markets such as insurance.

A pilot operation was designed to set up a network of
bank branches in localities of fewer than 20,000 inhabitants
in which no formal financial intermediary was present. The
first step was to convince commercial banks that there is a
business opportunity in rural financial markets. The message
was that profitability is possible if five conditions are met.
First, banks must have a good understanding of their market
and offer simple financial products, such as deposits with
short maturities and small minimum balances, as well as
short-term credit lines. Second, they must keep their fixed
costs low, with minimum investments and two to four
employees. Third, they must lend on the basis of a client's
character and reputation. Fourth, they must develop conducive incentive schemes, encouraging profit sharing and
efficiency wages. Finally, their internal control mechanisms
must be credible, and there must be a credible threat of dis-
missal for nonperforming staff.

Source: Chaves and Sanchez 1997.

Existing Microfinance Providers

Microfinance providers are found in both the public
and the private sectors. To identify market gaps when
providing or considering providing financial services to
microentrepreneurs, it is important to determine who
the existing providers are and how well the needs of
the market are being met. Donors can determine who
is active in microfinance and who might require support or funding. In areas where there is no microfinance activity, practitioners can determine who their
competitors are and the effects they have on the marketplace (such as developing awareness, increasing

demand, oversupplying, saturating or distorting the
market).

**THE EFFECT OF GOVERNMENT PROGRAMS ON PRIVATE PRO-
VIDERS.** Depending on their approach, government-run
microfinance programs can either contribute to or be detrimental to successful microfinance activities. Governments
that operate subsidized, inefficient microfinance programs
through health, social services, or other nonfinancial state-
run ministries or departments (or through a state-run banking system) negatively influence the provision of sustainable
microfinance services (see box 1.2). Governments often
have little or no experience with implementing microfi-

Box 1.2 Do Microfinance Clients Need Subsidized Interest Rates?

MICROFINANCE CLIENTS TEND TO BORROW THE SAME amount even if the interest rate increases, indicating that, within a certain range, they are not interest rate sensitive. In fact, people are often willing to pay higher rates for better service. *Continued* and *reliable* access to credit and savings services is what is most needed.

Subsidized lending programs provide a limited volume of cheap loans. When these are scarce and desirable, the loans tend to be allocated predominantly to a local elite with the influence to obtain them, bypassing those who need smaller loans (which can usually be obtained commercially only from informal lenders at far higher interest rates). In addition, there is substantial evidence from developing countries worldwide that subsidized rural credit programs result in high arrears, generate losses both for the financial institutions administering the programs and for the government or donor agencies, and depress institutional savings and, consequently, the development of profitable, viable rural financial institutions.

Microfinance institutions that receive subsidized funding are less likely to effectively manage their financial performance, since they have little or no incentive to become sustainable. Subsidized interest rates create excess demand that may result in a form of rationing through private transactions between clients and credit officers.

Source: Robinson 1994.

Box 1.3 Credit Institutions as a Political Tool: Debt Forgiveness in India

RURAL FINANCIAL INSTITUTIONS THAT ARE ASSOCIATED WITH governments often become the target of politicians. The influential clientele of these institutions makes them particularly attractive political targets. India's government-appointed Agricultural Credit Review Committee reported in 1989:

> During the election years, and even at other times, there is considerable propaganda from political platforms for postponement of loan recovery or pressure on the credit institutions to grant extensions to avoid or delay the enforcement process of recovery. In the course of our field visits, it was often reported that political factors were responsible for widespread defaults on the ostensible plea of crop failures in various regions.
>
> The "willful" defaulters are, in general, socially and politically important people whose example others are likely to follow; and in the present democratic set-up, the credit agencies' bureaucracy is reluctant to touch the influential rural elite who wield much formal and informal influence and considerable power. Farmers' agitation in many parts of the country can take a virulent form, and banners are put up in many villages declaring that no bank officer should enter the village for loan recovery purposes. This dampens the enthusiasm of even the conscientious members of the bank staff working in rural areas in recovery efforts. The general climate, therefore, is becoming increasingly hostile to recoveries.

Source: Yaron, Benjamin, and Piprek 1997, 102.

---

nance programs and no incentive to maintain long-term sustainability. Also, government microfinance programs are often perceived as social welfare, as opposed to economic development efforts. Some government programs grow too large, without the necessary institutional base, and fail to coordinate efforts with local NGOs or self-help groups.

Governments that forgive existing debts of the poor to state banks can have a tremendous effect on private sector MFIs, whose borrowers may mistakenly understand that their loans need not be repaid either. In general, both donors and practitioners should determine the consequences of existing or past credit subsidies or debt forgiveness (see box 1.3).

Much discussion surrounds the involvement of government in the provision of microfinance. Some people argue that the government's role is to create an enabling environment for the success of both microenterprises and private sector microfinance organizations and that governments should not lend funds directly to the poor. Others argue that the government should provide financial services to microentrepreneurs but must do so on a commercial basis to provide continued access to microfinance and to avoid distorting the financial markets. Some advantages of government involvement include the capacity to disseminate the program widely and obtain political support, the ability to address broader policy and regulatory concerns, and the capacity to obtain a significant amount of funds (Stearns and Otero 1990). A good example of a successfully run government operation is the Bank Rakyat Indonesia, a profitable state bank in Indonesia that serves low-income clients (box 1.4).

Box 1.4 Microfinance in Indonesia

THE BANK RAKYAT INDONESIA, A STATE-OWNED BANK, RAN a program of directed subsidized credit for rice farmers until 1983. The unit desa system was established in 1984 as a separate profit center within the bank.

The unit desa system is a nationwide network of small village banks. The founding objectives were to replace directed agricultural credit with broad-based credit for any type of rural economic activity, to replace subsidized credit with positive on-lending rates with spreads sufficient to cover all financial and operational intermediation costs, and to provide a full range of financial services (savings as well as credit) to the rural population. All these objectives were met within just a few years. The system's phenomenal success in savings mobilization is its distinguishing achievement.

Although the unit desa system forms an integral part of the Bank Rakyat Indonesia, it operates as a separate profit center, and its management has a free hand in determining its interest rates and other operating policies. In the 1980s the Indonesian government implemented financial sector reforms that deregulated certain interest rates and abolished interest rate ceilings. As the unit desa system struggled to become financially self-sustainable, market forces drove its decisionmaking and it became increasingly subject to competition from other financial institutions.

Management has a high degree of autonomy and full accountability for the performance of the unit desa system. This accountability is pushed down the line; every unit is responsible for its own lending decisions and profits. Monetary staff incentives and the prospects of promotion reinforce individual accountability. Reforms to further enhance the unit desa system's autonomy are currently being studied.

Source: Yaron, Benjamin, and Piprek 1997.

THE EFFECT OF PRIVATE MICROFINANCE PROVIDERS ON OTHER SUPPLIERS. Private sector MFIs are often indigenous groups or NGOs operated by local leaders in their communities. They are frequently supported by international donors and international NGOs that provide technical assistance or funding, particularly in the start-up phase. Some private MFIs still subsidize interest rates or deliver subsidized services; others create self-sufficient operations and rely less and less on external donor funds. A few are beginning to access funding through commercial banks and international money markets. In addition to NGOs, both banks and nonbank financial intermediaries may provide financial services to the microsector.

Private sector MFIs that have operated in or are currently operating in the country or region influence the success of new providers by establishing client (or beneficiary) expectations. For example, in Bangladesh the Grameen Bank is so well known within the village population that other microfinance providers routinely adopt the Grameen lending model, and when Grameen Bank changes its interest rate or adds a new product, clients of other MFIs demand the same. Microfinance organizations should be aware of the services offered by other MFIs and the effects they may have on the effective delivery of financial services (see table 1.2).

What Role Do Donors Play in Microfinance?

Donors' interest in microfinance has increased substantially over the past few years. Virtually all donors, including local, bilateral, and multilateral government donors and local and international NGOs, support microfinance activities in some way, providing one or more of the following services:

- Grants for institutional capacity building
- Grants to cover operating shortfalls
- Grants for loan capital or equity
- Concessional loans to fund on-lending
- Lines of credit
- Guarantees for commercial funds
- Technical assistance.

Because donors are the primary funders of microfinance activities (since most MFIs do not collect savings and are not yet financially viable enough to access commercial funding), the approach they take to microfinance and the requirements they set for MFIs to access funding can greatly affect the development of the field of microfinance. Most donors have moved away from subsidized lending and are focusing more on capacity building and the provision of loan capital. However, there is a variety of microfinance providers and a variety of approaches taken by donors. In fact, most MFIs work

---

Table 1.2 Private Institutions in Microenterprise Development

Advantages	*Disadvantages*
Strong methodology based on experience	Limited institutional capacity for scaling-up programs
Committed, trained staff	Low level of technical expertise, especially in financial and information systems
Capacity to reach grassroots associations	
Little or no corruption	Frequent lack of sufficient resources to expand programs
Responsive and nonbureaucratic approach	Isolated manner of operation
Motivation to scale-up programs and aim for self-sufficiency	Little interaction or knowledge about government activity in informal sector
Capacity to associate among many to form a coordinated effort	Limited vision that maintains small programs

Source: Stearns and Otero 1990.

---

with more than one donor, often developing separate products to meet each donor's requirements.

While it is true that donors should avoid duplicating and (especially) contradicting each other's efforts, it is difficult to ensure that donors coordinate their efforts and create perfectly consistent strategies based on market segmentation and comparative advantages. Particularly because microfinance is perceived by some as a panacea for poverty alleviation, donors may want to take on the same kinds of activities, especially lending to the poorest of the poor. Meanwhile, areas in which donors may have real advantages, such as capacity building and policy dialogue, are greatly in need of resources. Indeed, a danger of widespread donor interest in microfinance is an oversupply of funds for on-lending in the face of limited institutional capacity to take on these funds.

Some donors, such as the multilateral organizations, may find their comparative advantage is in *influencing policy reform* and supporting the efforts of finance ministries to strengthen supervisory bodies and create policies that lead to a stable macroeconomy and financial sector (see box 1.5). Donors can also be instrumental in directing governments to various poverty alleviation initiatives that further the development of microenterprises, such as infrastructure development and land transfer programs.

It is helpful for both practitioners and donors to know what other donors are doing. Practitioners need to know which donors support an approach consistent with their own, so that accessing funding does not mean changing the philosophy of their organization. Donors need to avoid duplicating or counteracting each others'

activities. Donors should coordinate their efforts to create a consistent strategy toward microfinance based on market segmentation and the comparative advantages of each. A lack of coordination can quickly undermine the efforts of good microfinance providers, as evidenced by the many cases where donors (and governments) have distorted the entire microfinance market by subsidizing interest rates and consequently making it difficult for other microfinance providers to compete.

Donors can also provide an excellent learning source for microfinance providers. Many donors have worked with specific institutions, in particular regions, and with certain approaches. Sharing these experiences with practitioners and other donors is extremely valuable. In many countries, donors and practitioners have set up informal networks to share their experiences, influence policies, and set industry standards. Box 1.6 describes an important initiative in this direction.

Financial Sector Policies and Legal Enforcement

After determining who is active in microfinance and what the financial system looks like, it is necessary to examine financial sector policies and the legal environment as they pertain to microfinance. Financial sector policy considerations include:

- Interest rate policies
- Government-mandated credit allocations
- Legal enforcement of contractual obligations and the ability to seize pledged assets.

Box 1.5 Multilateral Development Banks' Strategies for Microfinance

BUILDING NATIONAL FINANCIAL SYSTEMS THAT SERVE THE poorest segments of a society requires three essential components: a countrywide, community-based financial services infrastructure; linkages between the grassroots infrastructure of the informal economy and the formal infrastructure of the financial markets; and a favorable regulatory environment that allows microfinance institutions and microentrepreneurs to flourish. The strategy of multilateral development banks should thus comprise three elements: capacity building, formal financial market linkages, and policy reform. The strategy needs to be implemented at all levels in the given country—at the levels of the community, financial intermediaries, and government regulatory bodies.

Multilateral development banks should develop their internal capacity to implement strategy by instituting effective project approval processes, coordinating with other donors, training their staffs in microfinance program design, and providing them with the requisite technical support and financing instruments to implement successful microfinance programs. Multilateral development banks should be cautious about flooding the sector with financial resources until there is appropriate institutional capacity to absorb them.

International donors, including multilateral development banks, should focus on the following interventions:

- *Expanding institutional capacity.* The demand for microfinance is beginning to generate a flood of donor financing for the sector. MFIs need grant funding to build their capacity before they can handle large volumes of financing. They require technical assistance to make the transition from start-up projects to financially sustainable institutions. Some need further assistance in making the transition to a formal financial intermediary.

- *Safeguarding funds.* Existing MFIs are stretching their limits to expand services. MFIs need incentives from donors to maintain high standards of financial prudence while they expand their services.
- *Maintaining a focus on the poor.* MFIs are also striving to meet donor pressures for rapid financial sustainability. This has led some to abandon the poorest of the poor. Donors need to provide incentives for MFIs to guard against upward pressure on their portfolio and keep their focus on the poor—including the very poor—while striving for high levels of financial sustainability.
- *Promoting sectorwide performance standards.* Given the large number of new institutional entrants to the sector, MFIs and donors should work together to promote consistent performance standards.
- *Building a cadre of microfinance technicians and training centers.* Perhaps the most critical obstacle to expanding the microfinance sector today is the lack of knowledgeable microfinance technicians to help institutions develop their management systems. Donors could help ease the shortage by supporting training and technical assistance centers.
- *Promoting sustained linkages to commercial capital.* Multilateral development banks need to provide funding packages that encourage MFIs to move quickly toward commercial sources of financing, to avoid becoming dependent on donated funds.
- *Facilitating an enabling regulatory environment.* MFIs and their clients face a daunting array of regulatory constraints, which the multilateral development banks can address in their policy reform work. MFIs are less inclined to engage in policy advocacy work because they lack both the resources and the experience. Donors need to encourage governments to engage these implementing agencies in policy dialogue.

Source: Yanovitch and Macray 1996.

Interest Rate Policies

Given the cost structure of microfinance, interest rate restrictions usually undermine an institution's ability to operate efficiently and competitively (Rock and Otero 1997, 23). Typically, restrictions do not achieve their public policy purpose of protecting the most vulnerable sectors of the population. Instead, they drive informal lenders underground, so that poor borrowers fail to benefit from the intended low-cost financial services. While

there is reason to question the appropriateness of interest rate limits in any form, financial institutions that can demonstrate services to the poor at a reasonable cost should receive exemptions in countries where usury laws are in effect.

MFIs need to price their loan products to allow for full cost recovery. MFIs operating in countries that impose usury laws often have to establish pricing mechanisms that exceed the usury laws, particularly if they are to become registered formal entities (see box 1.7).

Government Mandates for Sectoral Credit Allocations

In many countries, governments mandate that formal financial sector institutions provide a certain percentage of their portfolio or a certain volume of their assets to the informal or poorer segments of society or to certain economic sectors. Special windows are created in commercial banks or rediscounted lines of credit are provided. For the most part, sectoral allocations do not work well because there are no incentives for commercial banks to participate. Many prefer to pay a penalty rather than meet their obligations.

While some MFIs may benefit from government credit allocations through accessing funding from commercial banks, sectoral mandates almost always distort the market. MFIs participating with banks to access these allocated funds must be aware of imposed conditions that may affect their operational sustainability—for example, below-market interest rates.

MFIs operating in countries in which the government has mandated sectoral credit allocations need to be aware of these mandates, both as possible funding sources and as potential excess supply (often at discounted rates) in the market. Rather than mandating credit allocations, governments should be encouraged to focus their policies on increasing outreach to the poor by creating enabling regulatory environments and building institutional capacity.

Legal Enforcement of Financial Contracts

In some developing countries, the legal framework is unclear or does not allow for effective enforcement of financial contracts. Although the majority of microfinance providers does not require collateral equal to the value of the loans disbursed and hence is not concerned with its ability to legally repossess a client's assets, there are many instances in which laws relating to financial transactions influence the behavior of borrowers. Well-defined property rights and good contract law help to minimize the costs of accomplishing both exchange transactions and production transactions. Minimizing transaction costs frees up resources that can be used to increase overall welfare (USAID 1995).

Some legal systems allow lenders to formally charge borrowers when they fail to repay a loan, which can lead to imprisonment or fines. Usually just the threat of jail or a visit from police can work as an effective deterrent for borrowers who are considering defaulting on a loan. It is useful for microfinance providers to determine the various legal sanctions available when clients do not adhere to their agreements and the ability and effectiveness of the courts to enforce financial contracts.

The Alexandria Business Association provides a good example of the usefulness of an effective legal environment when providing microfinance (box 1.8).

Financial Sector Regulation and Supervision

One of the most important issues in microfinance today is the regulation and supervision of MFIs. As mentioned, most informal and semiformal organizations providing financial services to microenterprises do not fall under the government regulations that are applied to banks and other formal financial institutions. Many nonbank MFIs, especially NGOs, operate on the fringes of existing regulations, especially with regard to deposit mobilization. In some instances they do so with the knowledge of the authorities, who, for political reasons or simply for lack of time and resources, do not interfere. In other instances these nonbank MFIs simply avoid dealing with the issues and proceed with deposit mobilization by calling it something else. All parties involved in microfinance in a particular country need to understand the dynamic of these legally ambiguous operations. One important danger is that as more bank and nonbank MFIs begin operating, authorities who have been disposed to liberal interpretations of the regulations will be forced to invoke a much stricter construction of the laws, thus tipping the balance unfavorably from the point of view of those engaged in microfinance.

The following discussion focuses on issues that must be considered when regulating and supervising

---

Box 1.8 Alexandria Business Association: Legal Sanctions

THE ALEXANDRIA BUSINESS ASSOCIATION IN EGYPT BEGAN operations in 1983 offering loans to individual business owners in amounts ranging from US$300 to US$15,000. When a loan is received, the borrower signs postdated checks for each installment. These checks are enforceable IOUs or promissory notes that use carefully crafted wording that is recognized by the legal system. In addition to a signed check for each installment, one check is signed for the whole amount of the loan. If a client defaults, the Alexandria Business Association can take the client to court and claim the whole amount prior to the maturity date of the loan.

In Egypt it is against the law to bounce a check; the penalty may be imprisonment for three months to three years. If a client has not paid the installment by the end of the month due, the association's lawyers record the case in court. A letter from the court that lists the penalties for nonrepayment according to the law is delivered to the borrower. If payment is still not forthcoming, the lawyer will take one of two routes: send a memo to the police and guide them to the borrower, or—if the lawyer is concerned about bribery of the police by the borrower—direct recourse to the courts to have the borrower taken into custody within two weeks. The lawyer attends the court proceedings, and the process becomes a negotiation between the borrower and the judge.

For association clients, legal pursuit can and does lead to prison. The legal director of Alexandria Business Association says that about 30 people have been jailed since the organization began operations.

Source: Dichter 1997.

MFIs. The information is most useful for governments that are considering regulating the microfinance sector. It is also helpful for both practitioners and donors to understand what is involved if and when an MFI becomes regulated so that they know how the MFI will be affected. Furthermore, if donors and practitioners are aware of the issues involved, they can potentially influence government decisions regarding regulation of the sector and propose self-regulatory measures.

Financial regulation refers to the body of principles, rules, standards, and compliance procedures that apply to financial institutions. Financial supervision involves the examination and monitoring of organizations for compliance with financial regulation.

Prudential regulation and supervision are designed to (Chavez and Gonzalez-Vega 1995):

- Avoid a banking crisis and maintain the integrity of the payments system
- Protect depositors
- Encourage financial sector competition and efficiency.

To create an environment that is conducive to financial intermediation, governments and policymakers must ensure that financial regulation does not result in financial repression—in regulations that distort financial markets and reduce the efficiency of financial institutions. Examples of financial repression are imposed interest rate ceilings, subsidized credit, and tax structures that discourage investment in microfinance. Governments must also ensure that supervisory bodies have the authority and the capacity to implement the regulatory standards (Chavez and Gonzalez-Vega 1994).

Despite some success stories, MFIs probably reach less than 5 percent of the potential clients in the world today. Serving this market will require access to funding far beyond what donors and governments can provide. Thus many MFIs want to expand their outreach by raising funds from commercial sources, including deposits.

Most MFIs are significantly different from commercial banks in institutional structure. Furthermore, managing a microloan portfolio differs in important ways from managing a conventional bank portfolio. MFIs and microloan portfolios cannot be safely funded with commercial sources, especially public deposits, unless appropriate regulation and supervision regimes are developed.

Even MFIs that do not mobilize deposits may benefit from entry rules that ensure the adoption of accepted good practices, as well as adequate recordkeeping and reporting.

When Should MFIs Be Subject to Regulation?

MFIs should be regulated if and when they mobilize deposits from the public. Individual depositors cannot be expected to monitor the financial health of an MFI and necessarily rely on the state to do this. MFIs should also be regulated when standards of good practice are clearly needed, whether because there are no practicing organizations or institutions or because existing practitioners are not operating effectively. The latter commonly occurs when donors push "programs" and target credit, rather than focus on meeting existing demand for financial services.

MFIs should also be regulated when they reach the size at which their failure would have consequences that reach far beyond owners and creditors. Finansol in Colombia is a good example of the importance of regulating growing financial intermediaries (box 1.9).

The Finansol case highlights important lessons regarding the regulation of MFIs created out of NGOs.

"An NGO (nongovernmental organization) is not inherently bound to the same standards of economic performance or financial prudence that may be reasonably expected in the business sector. While this concern is not insurmountable, the NGO parent must ensure that it sets standards appropriate to the financial sector in dealing with its regulated microfinance subsidiary. From the Finansol experience, it is apparent that NGOs should not be owners of MFIs unless they are operated separately, and the only financial link is ownership. This relationship must be transparent, and any financial exchange must include proper transfer pricing. Also, NGOs should not fully control the board and management of an MFI. It would be appropriate for regulators to monitor the financial health of an NGO when it is the majority owner of a regulated financial entity and in some cases to require consolidated financial reporting be presented so that an accurate assessment of the financial health of the regulated financial intermediary may be determined." (Barenbach and Churchill 1997, 47)

Furthermore the Finansol experience shows how regulatory restrictions such as usury laws and limits on asset growth can greatly affect the success of an MFI. It also highlights the importance of having owners with something at risk who are able to monitor their investment and who can help if there is a crisis. And finally, it demonstrates the importance of flexibility on the part of the superintendency.

"When regulation is warranted, it requires coherent prudential guidelines that will further the growth of the microfinance sector while protecting the interest of small savers and supporting the integrity of the financial sector as a whole." (Barenbach and Churchill 1997, 1)

Box 1.9 Regulating MFIs: The Case of Finansol

FINANSOL EMERGED FROM CORPOSOL, A NONGOVERNMENTAL organization (NGO) dedicated to providing services to microentrepreneurs in Colombia's informal sector. In 1992 Corposol determined that it needed access to more capital than its donors were able to provide through grants and guarantee funds in order to finance its impressive growth. It elected to create Finansol by buying the license of an existing finance company in which to book the loans. The license did not allow Finansol to accept general deposits from the public, however. The credit officers remained with Corposol, which also carried out other activities, including training.

Finansol inherited an excellent loan portfolio, a proven lending methodology, and consistent operational profitability. Nevertheless, several factors led to the deterioration of its financial position.

- *Usury law.* To comply with the usury law and cover its full operating costs, Finansol charged a training fee with each loan disbursement. This resulted in incentives for Corposol to disburse loans but not necessarily to collect loans.
- *Rapid expansion of untested new products.* This occurred without the commensurate capacity to manage the diversification.
- *Deviation from basic banking principles.* Corposol borrowed short and lent long. It also refinanced a large portion of its nonperforming portfolio.
- *Management response to banking regulations.* Colombian regulators limited asset growth of regulated financial institutions to 2.2 percent per month. As a nongovernmental organization, Corposol was not affected, so it retained a portion of the loans to permit the combined portfolio to grow at a faster rate.

- *Transparency.* The lack of separation—operationally, financially, and culturally—between the new financial intermediary and the parent nongovernmental organization led to a confusion of purpose, a lack of independence, inadequate management, and a lack of the financial information needed to assess the performance of either the operations or the loan portfolio.

Alarmed by Finansol's growth rate and the deteriorating quality of loans, the bank superintendency increased its supervision. In December 1995 the superintendency required Finansol and Corposol to sever all operational ties. Because Finansol was regulated, it was forced to establish provisions on its portfolio. In 1996 Finansol provisioned for more than US$6 million, which greatly affected its profitability. The effect of the losses eroded Finansol's net worth to such an extent that it violated the superintendency's rule that a regulated financial institution may not lose more than 50 percent of its starting net worth in a given fiscal year. In May 1996 Finansol's equity position fell below this limit, creating a situation in which the superintendency could have intervened.

The potential ramifications of intervention were significant. It could have sent a signal to the market that Finansol's crisis was escalating, rather than reaching a resolution. Not only could this have caused Finansol's collapse due to lack of market confidence, but it could have affected the broader Colombian financial market as well, since Finansol had issued paper amounting to approximately US$30 million. Accordingly, averting this crisis was of utmost concern to all parties, and intense efforts to launch a recapitalization plan were initiated to forestall intervention.

In December 1996 Finansol was successfully recapitalized, and Corposol, the NGO, was forced into liquidation.

Source: Churchill 1997.

RISK FACTORS OF MFIs. While both MFIs and commercial banks are vulnerable to liquidity problems brought on by a mismatch of maturities, term structure, and currencies, the risk features of MFIs differ significantly from those of commercial banks. This is due primarily to the MFIs' client base (low-income, assetless clients requiring small loans), lending models (small, unsecured loans for short terms based on character or group guarantees), and ownership structure (capitalized by donors rather than commercial investors/owners). For a detailed discussion of the risks specific to MFIs, see the appendix to this chapter.

Regulations designed for commercial banks are usually not suitable for MFIs because of MFIs' different

risk profile. An appropriate approach to regulating MFIs must be based on an understanding of the different risks and of the country's legal and institutional framework.

MEANS OF REGULATING MFIs. Regulatory approaches range from self-regulation, in which the industry develops its own supervisory and governance bodies (such as credit cooperatives) to full regulation (either under existing laws or through the establishment of specialized laws specific to MFIs). Another alternative is for MFIs to be regulated by the regulatory authorities, while contracting a third party to perform the supervisory functions.

The challenge facing regulators as they consider appropriate regulatory approaches to the microfinance sector is complicated by the great diversity of MFIs in institutional type, scale of operations, and level of professionalism. To be effective, the regulatory approach in a given country must be consistent with the overall financial sector framework and must consider the variety of institutional types. Flexibility is crucial when regulating MFIs, because many techniques and practices are still experimental when a country is beginning to seriously provide microfinance services (see box 1.10).

Considerations When Regulating MFIs

It is important for regulators to establish minimum standards for MFIs while at the same time remaining flexible and innovative. At a minimum, when regulating and supervising MFIs, five issues need to be considered (adapted from CGAP 1996b):

- Minimum capital requirements
- Capital adequacy
- Liquidity requirements
- Asset quality
- Portfolio diversification.

MINIMUM CAPITAL REQUIREMENTS. Minimum capital requirements are set for all organizations entering the financial sector. This means that financial organizations wanting to formalize must have a minimum amount of capital to support their activities (stated as a currency amount rather than as a percentage of assets). "Capital" refers to the amount of equity an institution holds. (It can also include some subordinated debt, depending on the specific rules of the regulatory board.) Since MFIs rely primarily on donor funds for capital contributions, they may not have sufficient capital to meet these rules, which can limit the formalization of microfinance organizations. While regulators should be encouraged to set minimum capital standards in accordance with their objectives of encouraging competition and low-risk behavior, it is important for them to recognize that MFI owners may consider social objectives over profit maximization goals and that minimum capital requirements may not be as powerful an inducement to sound governance as would generally be the case with standard commercial banking institutions.

Box 1.10 Enhancing the Effectiveness of Oversight

- *Fraud protection.* Experience shows that the altruistic origin of most MFIs does not exempt them from the risk of serious fraud. The first line of defense against such fraud is internal audit procedures carried out by the MFI itself. Superintendencies should develop the capacity to review such procedures, perhaps through mechanisms such as random client-level monitoring of loans.
- *Insolvency.* Regulators must have the authority and will to protect the system by imposing sanctions on insolvent institutions. Having several licensed microfinance providers can reduce the pressure to bail out failures.
- *Internal superintendency structures.* As the microfinance industry develops in individual countries, superintendencies will need to organize themselves to regulate it. Some are creating specialized MFI departments. A less costly alternative might be to contract out reviews to experts familiar with MFI operations.

Source: CGAP 1996b.

CAPITAL ADEQUACY. Capital adequacy refers to the level of capital in an organization that is available to cover its risk. Conventional capital adequacy concepts assume that it is clear what constitutes equity and debt. In nonbank MFIs, it is necessary to distinguish equity and debt by asking such questions as: Do donated funds constitute equity? Do concessional funds provided by donors constitute debt and therefore affect the leverage of the MFI? These questions must be answered before determining the capital adequacy of an MFI.

All financial institutions are required to have a minimum amount of capital relative to the value of their assets. This means that in the event of loss of assets, the organization would have sufficient funds of its own (rather than borrowed from depositors) to cover the loss. Capital adequacy standards refer to the percentage of assets that is funded by debt. Stated differently, capital adequacy standards refer to a maximum level of debt versus equity (degree of *leverage*) that a financial institution can have. (Assets are funded either by debt or equity. Capital adequacy standards limit the proportion of assets that can be funded with debt.) Current international standards outlined in the Basle Accord provide a maximum leverage ratio of 12 to 1 or, stated the other way around, minimum capital of 8 percent of risk-weighted assets.

Assets are risk-weighted between 0 and 100 percent. For example, an unsecured loan to an unknown entity is of high risk and would therefore likely be risk-weighted at 100 percent. A fully secured loan to the government of an industrial country poses little risk and would be risk-weighted at a much lower rate. Once an institution's assets (including off-balance-sheet items) are risk-weighted, the total amount of capital required can be determined. Obviously, the lower the risk, the lower the risk-weighting, the lower the total assets, and, therefore, the lower the amount of required capital. Because capital is generally a more expensive source of funds than debt, banks want to have lower capital requirements and consequently try to have lower risk assets. The result is beneficial for both the banks and the regulators because banks are discouraged from high-risk lending.

Most MFIs are not fully leveraged due to their inability to borrow funds on the basis of their performance and debt capacity. The greater part of the typical MFI's assets is funded with donor contributions that are generally considered capital. Thus almost all MFIs easily meet capital adequacy standards. For example, BancoSol, one of the most leveraged MFIs as of year-end 1995, had a risk-weighted capital adequacy of 17 percent, much higher than is required under the Basle Accord.

There are strong arguments against allowing MFIs to leverage their equity capital (borrow a greater proportion of funds) as aggressively as commercial banks. As most countries are relatively inexperienced with microfinance (there is little empirical data about MFI performance), regulators may wish to begin cautiously in fixing leverage ratios. It is suggested that an initial capital-asset ratio be no lower than about 20 percent for MFIs, subject to downward adjustment as the institution and the industry gain experience.

LIQUIDITY REQUIREMENTS. Liquidity refers to the amount of available cash (or near-cash) relative to the MFI's demand for cash. MFIs are exposed to high levels of liquidity risk: seasonal factors influence many of their clients; MFIs tend to depend on donors, whose funding can be unpredictable; and their nondonor liabilities tend to be short term. If the organization is operating in a stable financial market, it may be able to deal with liquidity risk through short-term borrowings. However, depending on the stability of the market, regulators may find it prudent to set relatively high liquidity standards for MFIs, taking into account the added costs that this implies.

ASSET QUALITY. Asset quality represents the risk to earnings derived from loans made by the organization. In other words, it measures the degree of risk that some of the loan portfolio will not be repaid.

Most MFIs do not require formal collateral and instead base their loan decisions on character, group solidarity, and past repayment history. In many countries, bank regulations limit the percentage of the portfolio that may be extended as nonsecured loans. The types of security available from microentrepreneurs are not usually recognized. Instead of collateral, regulators may consider the best indicators of asset quality to be past performance of the portfolio and the current rate of portfolio at risk (defined as the balance of outstanding loans which have an amount past due). Bank regulators should accept flexible definitions for loan security that enhance repayment incentives. Sufficient experience is now documented to demonstrate that such incentives can result in very low delinquencies and permit the delivery of financial services to sectors of the economy that do not have access to conventional collateral.

Strict loan-loss-provisioning policies should be enforced, commensurate with loan maturities, risk-weighting that considers the quality of security, and standard methods that can be easily and consistently replicated. Regulators should encourage the adoption of standard loan classification procedures to limit management discretion. A focus on staff incentives for dealing with arrears is encouraged.

Regulations like those for commercial banks that require elaborate loan documentation or involved credit approval procedures are not appropriate for MFIs, because the financial viability of MFIs depends on minimizing the processing cost of microloans. Case-by-case loan reviews are impractical.

PORTFOLIO DIVERSIFICATION. Portfolio diversification refers to financial institutions' need to ensure that they have not concentrated their portfolio in one geographic sector or one market segment. Unlike other financial institutions, most MFIs have highly specialized portfolios that consist solely of short-term working capital loans to informal sector clients. Although an MFI may have thousands of loans to diverse industries, externalities could affect the entire market. Regulators should encourage MFIs to diversify their loan portfolios through the development of guidelines that limit sector concentration.

Country Approaches to Regulating MFIs

Although most countries have not yet established an approach to regulating MFIs, Bolivia, Peru, and the West African Economic and Monetary Union have determined that a new type of legal institution was required for MFIs that wanted to begin mobilizing savings (box 1.11 describes Bolivia's initiative). In South Africa and the Philippines local MFIs have formed associations as a first step toward educating regulators and promoting policy dialogue. In Indonesia and Peru a third party has been engaged to perform supervisory functions, either in place of or along with the bank superintendency (Berenbach and Churchill 1997).

In all countries that are considering establishing new types of institutions, one of the main issues is the limited capacity of bank superintendencies to supervise an increasingly large number of small and highly decentralized institutions. This is the case in Ghana (box 1.12).

Box 1.11 Private Financial Funds in Bolivia

THE BOLIVIAN GOVERNMENT RECENTLY CREATED A NEW type of institution, private financial funds, to "channel resources to finance the activities of small businesses and microenterprises in the productive and commercial sectors, as well as to make loans to individuals for soft durable goods purchases. As an additional means of facilitating access to credit for individuals, [private financial funds] may also engage in small-scale consumer credit operations" (from the law setting up the funds).

Incorporation. Private financial funds will be organized as corporations—an ideal form for financial intermediation because of the legal stability of a commercial entity in civil society, and because it allows for timely increases or replenishment of equity when required by the Superintendency of Banks and Financial Institutions.

Minimum operating equity. To incorporate and function private financial funds require the capital equivalent to at least US$1 million. This is significantly less than the US$3.2 million required for incorporating a bank. This start-up capital, together with a strict and prudential framework that establishes credit limits lower than those established for banks and a prohibition on making loans to the private financial fund's own shareholders and managers, represents a reasonable combination of equity backing and spreading of credit risks.

Private financial funds should maintain net worth equivalent to at least 10 percent of their assets and contingencies weighted on the basis of risk; institutions already in operation shall have three years to bring their equity levels into line with this new legal requirement.

Financial operations. Private financial funds hold broad operational powers allowing for financial leasing, traditional lending, certificates of deposit to guarantee performance, and factoring. This diversity of credit instruments will make it possible to adapt credit supply to the specific needs of small borrowers in both the productive and commercial sectors, including wage earners.

Private financial funds may provide for their clients financial services such as drafts and payment orders, foreign exchange operations, and the purchase and sale of foreign currencies. In addition, they may receive savings and time deposits and contract obligations with second-tier banking institutions pursuant to the limits set by these intermediaries.

Limits. To avoid risks that jeopardize their main purpose and are incompatible with the large amount of capital they involve, private financial funds are restricted from several types of banking operations. These include capture of demand deposits, foreign trade operations, trust operations and other charges of fiduciary duty, investments in enterprise capital, participation in the underwriting and placement of securities, and mutual fund management.

A single loan may not exceed 3 percent of the net worth of the private financial fund; credits with personal guarantees may not exceed 1 percent of the fund's net worth; a private financial fund may not maintain a credit relationship with an institution of the national financial system for more than 20 percent of its net worth; and shareholders, statutory auditors, directors and managers, and individuals or entities associated with a private financial fund may not obtain loans from the institution.

Source: Loubiere 1995.

Economic and Social Policy Environment

After examining the supply of microfinance services, financial sector policies and the legal environment, and regulation and supervision issues, the final area to examine within the country context is the economic and social policy environment. Economic and social policies influence both the ability of an MFI to effectively provide financial services and the types of activities microenterprises undertake. For example, economic policies that affect the rate of inflation in a country, the growth of the economy, or the degree of openness to market forces all influence the required interest rate of loans as well as the ability of microentrepreneurs to successfully operate their businesses and thus utilize financial services. The government's investment in infrastructure development, the scale and depth of poverty in a country, and access to social services also affect the way in which a microfinance organization operates. If because of poor roads microentrepreneurs are not able to reach markets, access health care services, or send their children to school, their activities are affected and so, too, is their use of financial services.

Economic and Political Stability

Volatility in all markets affects the risk and hence the choices made by business owners and financial institutions. In general, the stability of financial and other markets makes microenterprises and consequently microfinance services more viable (Yaron, Benjamin, and Piprek 1997).

MFIs should understand how various economic considerations and policies affect the poor. For most countries, there are numerous reports highlighting the economic situation and the various policies that affect the economy. Reports produced by the World Bank, governments, and research institutions should be gathered to develop an overall assessment of the economic situation in a country. Two measures commonly considered are the rate of inflation and the rate of growth of gross domestic product (GDP). These measures provide some indication of the economic stability of a country.

INFLATION. Some degree of inflation is usually present in all economies and must be considered when designing and pricing loan and savings products. Both practitioners and donors should be aware of the inflation rate in countries where they are working, as inflation results in a real

---

Box 1.12 Nonbank Financial Institutions in Ghana

IN 1993 THE GOVERNMENT OF GHANA ENACTED THE Nonbank Financial Institutions Law to create an alternative financial market that would cater to the needs of the broad sector of the Ghanaian economy that was not being served by traditional financial institutions. This was a bold and laudable attempt to introduce diversity in the financial markets by creating an enabling environment for local private participation.

However, the prudential regulations that accompanied the law contained serious mismatches. In Ghana people regularly pay informal savings collectors to provide a daily savings service. Instead of receiving interest on their deposits, customers pay a commission to have their savings collected and kept safe. As a consequence, 60 percent of Ghana's money supply is outside the formal banking sector. However, the original regulations that governed savings and loans institutions limited the frequency of deposits to once a week. To address this issue, regulated institutions lobbied for changes in the legislation to permit unlimited client deposits.

In addition, there was concern by some nonbank financial institutions that the minimum capital requirement—US$100,000—was too low. After advocacy efforts by the financial sector, the capital requirement is being reconsidered. High reserve ratios were also mandated by the superintendency, requiring nonbank financial institutions to place 57 percent of their deposits in first and secondary reserves, leaving the institution with too little to invest in productive activities.

Another issue with the banking regulation involves the reporting format. The superintendency is trying to supervise nine separate categories of financial institutions with an omnibus prudential guideline and reporting format. Since mortgage companies, commercial banks, and savings and loan institutions, for example, provide very different services, they cannot report the same information. To respond to this issue, nonbank financial institutions have created an association to act as an advocate on their behalf.

These observations lead to the following conclusions:
- Bank supervisors need to learn how to supervise the special characteristics of MFIs.
- There is a need for a more involved and active supervisory service provided perhaps by an apex institution or subcontracted to an external body.

Source: Dadson 1997.

cost to MFIs (and their clients) that must be covered by the interest generated on loans.

MFIs can and do operate in countries with high rates of inflation. One possible means of addressing hyperinflation is to index the loan contract to a hard currency such as the U.S. dollar or to a commodity. Other means include maintaining funding and assets in U.S. dollars, utilizing debt rather than equity (if possible), and providing short-term loans (ensuring that they match the clients cash flow needs), which allow for periodic adjustment of interest rates.

If MFIs borrow funds in a currency other than their own (such as U.S. dollars), inflation can result in either foreign exchange gains or losses. Both donors and practitioners need to determine who will benefit from these potential gains or will cover these losses.

GROWTH RATE. A country's annual GDP growth provides an indication of that country's economic stability and future growth prospects. Examining the rate of growth gives both donors and practitioners an indication of the potential opportunities available to microentrepreneurs and hence can affect the forecasted growth and funding requirements of the MFI.

Although positive GDP growth is always preferred, stagnant economies can be potential markets for the provision of microfinance services if unemployment increases and more people become self-employed. However, stagnant or falling GDP levels also result in lower incomes and less demand for products and services, which could result in the failure of microenterprises. Furthermore, volatility in the economy affects the risk and hence choices of financial institutions and microentrepreneurs. In general, the stability of financial and other markets makes microenterprises and consequently microfinance services more viable.

TRANSITION AND POLITICAL UNREST. Transition economies and situations of conflict or political unrest, where existing systems of social networks have broken down and need to be reestablished, pose additional concerns for MFIs (see box 1.13). Transition economies, by definition, are beginning to develop private sector markets and businesses. Often the population is not familiar with business transactions and is generally not entrepreneurial in nature. MFIs need to develop trust among their clients and ensure that borrowers understand the responsibilities associated with financial transactions. This will likely require

additional time spent with borrowers, at least initially, which in turn may increase costs. (For detailed information regarding the provision of microfinance in transition economies, see Carpenter 1996.) Both donors and practitioners should be aware of this.

General instability, corruption, civil war, party or tribal rivalries—all have obvious direct economic effects such as internal migration, outmigration, capital flight, and currency instability. However, there are also less tangible social and psychological effects. How people see their future, where they want to invest, the degree to which they are willing to set up shop on a permanent basis, the very kinds of products they will trade in, and what people are willing to buy with whatever assets they have available will all be affected by the political atmosphere.

During periods of severe political unrest, MFI activities may need to be postponed until a more stable environment ensues, particularly where concern for the safety of both staff and clients exists. Donors must understand the need to postpone activities or slow down growth and not pressure the MFI to continue to meet growth targets during periods of civil unrest (see box 1.14).

Box 1.13 Microfinance in Areas of Political Unrest

IN THE WESTERN PART OF KENYA, MICROFINANCE operations exist, but they seem to be reaching limits of both outreach and sustainability. Initial loan uptake is high, but the market for repeat loans and especially for scaling up enterprise productivity is limited. Part of the reason has to do with the general neglect of the area by the government, which in turn is a function of political and tribal rivalry. As a result, public sector investment and other development efforts go elsewhere, and in these conditions, more and more people enter the informal economy, not with an ambition to become entrepreneurs, but simply as a means of survival. An MFI wishing to operate in this area needs to make strategic decisions that may involve compromising the orthodoxies of sustainability. For example, it would make sense to reduce objectives so that in the medium term, the objectives would be to use microfinance as a means to smooth consumption and alleviate poverty, with the hope that as conditions improve, a more viable market for a true MFI might become possible.

Source: Contributed by Thomas Dichter, Sustainable Banking with the Poor Project, World Bank.

Box 1.14 The Albanian Development Fund

IN LATE 1992, AS ALBANIA ENTERED ITS TRANSITION TO A
market economy, the Albanian Development Fund's rural
credit program began forming village associations for the
purpose of lending. By the end of 1996 the fund was
active in 170 villages in 10 districts and had close to
7,000 outstanding loans totaling more than US$2.4 mil-
lion (243 million lek). In spite of a general lack of understanding of market forces in Albania, the Albanian
Development Fund has achieved commendable loan
repayment, with only one village fund failing to repay.
This success stems from a good understanding of the village networks and from the initial design of the project,
which required full loan repayment before disbursement
of further loans.

In 1992 Albania recorded an inflation rate of 237 percent a year, and its GDP growth was negative –7 percent.
It was during this time that the Albanian Development
Fund began lending. To address such high rates of inflation and their effect on the value of its capital, the fund
set the interest rate at 5 percent per year, with repayment
of principal pegged to the U.S. dollar. In 1995 inflation
had decreased to 6 percent, and the Albanian
Development Fund began charging 10 percent, with loan
repayment no longer pegged to the U.S. dollar.

Beginning in 1997 Albania experienced civil unrest
caused by the collapse of pyramid savings schemes.
Although all borrowing was halted, credit officers continued to maintain contact with borrowers. Repayment of
loans in January and February (when the pyramid schemes
were beginning to collapse) continued to be 100 percent in
rural areas and remained high in urban areas. This
occurred despite an estimated 80 percent participation rate
of farmers in the pyramid schemes and is testimony to the
strength of the Albanian Development Fund system.

Source: Ledgerwood 1997.

Poverty Levels

When examining the country context, it is important
for both practitioners and donors to understand the
depth of poverty in the country in which they are
operating and to determine government and donor
policies that work toward alleviating or reducing
poverty. An understanding of the degree of poverty in
a country helps in estimating the size and needs of the
potential market for microfinancial services and may

also help to clarify or establish an MFI's or donor's
objectives.

Investment in Infrastructure and Human Resource Development

An important consideration when providing microfinance services is the existence of adequate infrastructure
(roads, communications facilities, water and sewer systems) and of affordable social services such as health,
education, and nutrition.

> "Improving rural roads and electricity, or provid-
> ing matching grants for village-determined invest-
> ments such as watershed management, to increase
> the earnings capacity of poor households is often
> more cost-effective than providing financial ser-
> vices, particularly where infrastructure is underde-
> veloped. Similarly, providing or upgrading rural
> primary education and health facilities can achieve
> longer-term benefits for the rural poor, especially
> for the poorest of the poor, by increasing the pro-
> ductivity of labor, the main asset of the poor."
> (Yaron, Benjamin, and Piprek 1997, 42)

A lack of roads, electricity, communication facilities,
and other infrastructure will affect the means by which
an MFI and the microenterprises it supports operate and
should be taken into consideration by both donors and
practitioners.

Identifying the availability of and access to *social services* for an MFI's client base helps to determine whether
clients' needs for services are being met and whether the
objectives of the MFI are suitable (that is, whether the
MFI can provide only financial services while other gov-
ernmental organizations and NGOs provide other needed services). For example, the availability of education
and health services greatly influences the capacity of
microentrepreneurs to increase their enterprise activities.
Any provision of financial services to the poor should
consider the availability of other nonfinancial services
and the environment in which the MFI and the clients
operate.

Some MFIs form relationships with other service organizations to coordinate the provision of financial services,
nonfinancial services, or social services, taking advantage of
the comparative strengths of each organization. However,
it should be noted that the provision of social services such
as health, education, and family planning should not be

directly combined with the provision of financial services (a point discussed in more detail in chapter 3).

Government View of the Microenterprise Sector

It is important to determine the government's position regarding the informal sector and microenterprise development, as this affects policies that may influence the behavior of microentrepreneurs. Some governments recognize the positive contribution of microenterprises to the economy and may actively include informal sector development in the national plan. However, in many countries informal sector issues and their relationship to government policy receive little attention. Most policy frameworks favor large manufacturing sectors and are biased against the informal sector and small enterprises.

Most governments want to encourage the development of businesses in their countries. Some governments supplement general policy goals that apply to business with specific policies and programs aimed at micro and small enterprises. It is helpful if policies are in place that establish a favorable climate for the start-up of new businesses and the growth of existing businesses. Examples are policies that minimize the costs of licensing and registering a business, provide easy access to information about laws and regulations, and facilitate commercial codes, which establish rules to minimize the cost of doing business by defining the rights and responsibilities of all parties to a transaction (USAID 1995).

The decision of governments to become actively involved in microenterprise development through credit programs or other enterprise development services can affect the environment for private microfinance providers, either by negatively distorting the market or by positively contributing to the supply of services. Alternatively, governments can choose to support the informal sector through macropolicies, the allocation of resources that affect microproduction, or work with NGOs that provide services and training.

> "Active collaboration in this sense involves the establishment of a favorable climate to enable these institutions to continue and expand their work with support but no interference from government entities. This can include national recognition of the microenterprise sector, support to discuss the issue, funding research, and scaling up pilot programs." (Stearns and Otero 1990, 27)

Microenterprises and small businesses may be affected by government policies, including excessive regulation, prohibitive levels of taxation, inadequate government protection against cheap imported products, laxity about black markets (which results in unfair competition for the microbusiness sector), harassment by government officials for operating businesses on the streets, and inadequate services and high user fees in public market structures. Many of these regulations work effectively to encourage microenterprises to remain outside the legal or formal mainstream (see the discussion of Argentina's tax laws in box 1.15).

When policies and practices negatively affect clients' businesses, an MFI or donor may choose to undertake environment-level interventions, such as policy and advocacy work, in addition to providing or supporting the provision of financial services. Advocacy can include helping clients organize to protest unfair policies or treatment. MFIs can influence policy by working alone

---

Box 1.15 Tax Laws in Argentina

IN ARGENTINA ALL FORMAL ENTERPRISES MUST BE registered with the Dirección General Impositiva, the tax bureau, and must comply with various tax requirements. The most important tax is the *impuesto al valor añadido*, a 21 percent value-added tax. Businesses must charge this tax on their sales and pay it on all products they buy. The net difference between the two is due to the tax bureau annually.

Small businesses, including small farmers, that are not formalized enterprises are strongly penalized by this system. When purchasing supplies, they must pay the tax up front and are sometimes charged a surtax of 50 percent on purchases as a penalty for not being registered enterprises, raising the effective value-added tax to 31.5 percent. They are then unable to deduct the amount of tax paid from their revenue because, as nonregistered entities, they cannot charge a value-added tax on the sale of their products or services. Buyers purchasing crops from these unregistered businesses (small farmers) offer low prices, arguing that they are taking a risk in buying from them and may be penalized for doing so. The number of buyers willing to work with the informal sector is hence restricted, offering a limited range of channels for commercialization.

Source: Contributed by Cecile Fruman, Sustainable Banking with the Poor Project, World Bank.

or through coalitions of similar organizations to lobby appropriate government or regulatory bodies on behalf of their clients (Waterfield and Duval 1996).

Appendix 1. Risks in the Microfinance Industry

There are four main areas of risk that are specific to MFIs: portfolio risk, ownership and governance, management, and "new industry." Portfolio risk was discussed in the main text of chapter 1. The remaining risks are discussed below. The following discussion is taken from Berenbach and Churchill 1997.

Ownership and Governance

Although effective external regulation and supervision by regulatory bodies are important to the health of the financial system, no amount of external oversight can replace accountability that stems from proper governance and supervision performed by the owners of financial institutions. The following points highlight issues of ownership and governance relative to adequate supervision of MFIs:

- *Adequate oversight of management.* Often, investors in MFIs are motivated by social objectives. As a result, they may not hold this investment to the same standards that they apply to commercial investments. Regulators should encourage meaningful participation of private investors, particularly local business leaders. These private investors are an important source of local governance and a valuable resource if the MFI encounters difficulties. Furthermore, MFIs benefit from the participation of several significant shareholders who bring diverse backgrounds and perspectives to the governance process. In addition to private investors, regulators should encourage investment by other private or public development-oriented institutions with microfinance or related development finance experience.
- *Organizational and ownership structures.* If a social organization, which is funded with public resources and does not have owners, oversees the management and determines the policies of the regulated financial intermediary, social objectives may take priority over financial objectives. This may make it difficult to determine the true performance of the

regulated financial intermediary, hindering bank regulators from gaining an accurate financial profile of the regulated entity. Successful arrangements between the social organization (the nongovernmental organization) and the regulated MFI can be attained if the structure adheres to certain basic principles, including transparency, arm's-length transactions, honest transfer pricing, and operational independence. The regulated MFI must maintain independent management and oversight of its financial services. Regulators can require that the composition of the MFI's board of directors include professional individuals who are prepared to define sound policies and to oversee management. All directors should be held legally liable for the performance of the MFI, as is the case for directors of private sector companies.
- *Sufficient financial depth.* MFIs may be capable of raising the initial capital requirements from their founding shareholders. However, these owners may lack the financial depth or the motivation to respond to additional calls for capital as required. Development institutions may require a lengthy approval process to secure disbursement of funds. Regulators can introduce measures to compensate for the owners' limited capacity to provide additional capital. This can be addressed by the following options: establishing additional reserve funds, limiting dividend distribution until capital benchmarks are reached, and requiring standby financing commitments by MFI owners.

Management Risks

The management risks that apply to MFIs are generated by the specific methods of providing financial services.

- *Decentralized operational systems.* A decentralized organizational structure that permits the provision of financial services directly at the borrower's or saver's location is central to microfinance. Consequently, senior management must train and supervise mid-level management, introduce appropriate reporting systems, and maintain adequate communication systems so that uniform policies and procedures are adopted. Furthermore, decentralized operating methods create an environment that can easily be subject to fraudulent practices. Regulators should require MFIs to maintain strong internal auditing capabilities and aggressive internal auditing procedures. Guidelines should be established for the performance of external audits for MFIs. Finally, adequate measures of internal communications and financial controls are essential.

- *Management efficiency.* MFIs offer a high-volume, repetitive service that operates on very tight margins. If funds are not relent promptly, earnings will suffer. Regulators should ensure a high quality of management to ensure that brisk and timely services are provided.
- *Management information.* Decentralized operating methods, high volume of short-term loans, rapid portfolio turnover, and the requirement for efficient service delivery make accurate and current portfolio information essential for effective MFI management. In general, MFIs have not focused on providing adequate and appropriate financial information for making judgments about their financial viability. Government regulators, donors, potential depositors, and other types of potential creditors all need fairly standard information about financial viability in order to make informed judgments. Reporting requirements for regulated institutions make it necessary for MFIs to be able to produce accurate, useful, and timely management information.

New Industry

A number of the risks that face MFIs stem from the fact that microfinance is a relatively new field. Formal financial services may also be new to the micro market.

- *Growth management.* MFIs that expand into new markets often face little competition. These institutions can experience dramatic growth in their initial years of operation. Regulators should closely monitor MFIs that dramatically surpass the growth projections presented in the license application.
- *New products and services.* Although this industry has made considerable advances in the design of appropriate microfinance products and services, the field remains relatively young and untested. It is difficult to assess when a new product, or service is an ill-conceived deviation from an existing model or a breakthrough in new services for the market. New products and services must be well tested before being

implemented on a broad scale. It may be appropriate to limit the number of new products or services that are introduced at any one time. The challenge facing MFIs is to conduct a large volume of very small transactions and to do so sustainably. Given this challenge, it is most appropriate to limit MFIs to relatively simple products and services that can be easily mastered.

Sources and Further Reading

Basle Committee on Banking Regulations and Supervisory Practices. 1988. "International Convergence of Capital Measurement and Capital Standards." Basle, Switzerland.

Berenbach, Shari, and Craig Churchill. 1997. *Regulation and Supervision of Microfinance Institutions: Experience from Latin America, Asia and Africa.* Occasional Paper 1. Washington, D.C.: MicroFinance Network.

Carpenter, Janney. 1996. *Microcredit in Transitional Economies.* Organisation for Economic Co-operation and Development, Centre for Co-operation with the Economies in Transition, Paris, France.

CGAP (Consultative Group to Assist the Poorest). 1996a. "The Consultative Group to Assist the Poorest—A Microfinance Program." CGAP Focus Note 1. World Bank, Washington, D.C.

———. 1996b. "Regulation & Supervision of Micro-Finance Institutions: Stabilizing a New Financial Market." CGAP Focus Note 4. World Bank, Washington, D.C.

———. 1997. "How CGAP Member Donors Fund Microfinance Institutions." CGAP Focus Note 11. World Bank, Washington, D.C.

Chaves, Rodrigo A., and Claudio Gonzalez-Vega. 1993. "Should Principles of Regulation and Prudential Supervision Be Different for Microenterprise Finance Organizations?" GEMINI Working Paper 38. U.S. Agency for International Development, Washington, D.C.

———. 1994. "Principles of Regulation and Prudential Supervision and their Relevance for Microenterprise Finance Organizations." In Maria Otero and Elisabeth Rhyne, eds., *New World of Microenterprise Finance.* West Hartford, Conn.: Kumarian Press.

———. 1995. "Making the Leap into the Formal Financial System: Structuring Regulation and Prudential Supervision for Microenterprise Finance Organizations." GEMINI Microenterprise Development Brief 19. U.S. Agency for International Development, Washington, D.C.

Chaves, Rodrigo, and Susana Sánchez. 1997. "Formal Sector Suppliers in Rural Mexico." World Bank, Latin America and the Caribbean Region, Finance, Private Sector, and Infrastructure Unit, Washington, D.C.

Christen, Robert P. 1995. "Issues in the Regulation and Supervision of Microfinance." Paper presented at the conference on Regulation and Supervision of Microfinance Institutions, sponsored by ACCION International, November 27–28, Washington, D.C.

Churchill, Craig, ed. 1997. *Regulation and Supervision of Microfinance Institutions Case Studies.* Occasional Paper 2. Washington, D.C.: MicroFinance Network.

Cuevas, Carlos E. 1996. "Enabling Environment and Microfinance Institutions: Lessons from Latin America." *Journal of International Development* 8 (2): 195–210.

Dadson, Christine. 1997. "Citi Savings and Loans, Ghana." Adapted from Craig Churchill, ed., "Establishing a Microfinance Industry." MicroFinance Network, Washington, D.C.

Dichter, Thomas. 1997. "Alexandria Business Association" Case Study for the Sustainable Banking with the Poor Project. World Bank, South Asia Social Development Unit, Washington, D.C.

Drake, Deborah, and Maria Otero. 1992. *Alchemists for the Poor: NGOs as Financial Institutions.* Monograph Series 6. Washington, D.C.: ACCION International.

FAO (Food and Agriculture Organization). 1995. "Safeguarding Deposits: Learning from Experience." FAO Agricultural Services Bulletin 116. Rome.

Gray, Tom, and Matt Gamser. 1994. "Building an Institutional and Policy Framework to Support Small and Medium Enterprises: Learning from Other Cultures." Implementing Policy Change Project. Development Alternatives, Inc., Bethesda, Md.

Krahnen, Jan Pieter, and Reinhard H. Schmidt. 1994. *Development Finance as Institution Building: A New Approach to Poverty-Oriented Lending.* Boulder, Colo.: Westview Press.

Krutzfeldt, Herman. 1995. "The Experience of BancoSol." Paper presented at the MicroFinance Network Conference, November, Manila.

Ledgerwood, Joanna. 1997. "Albania Development Fund." Case Study for the Sustainable Banking with the Poor Project. World Bank, South Asia Social Development Unit, Washington, D.C.

Lobíere, Jacques Trigo. 1995. "Supervision and Regulation of Microfinance Institutions: The Bolivian Experience." Paper presented at the conference on Regulation and Supervision of Microfinance Institutions, sponsored by

ACCION International, November 27–28, Washington, D.C.

Rhyne, Elisabeth. 1995. "Major Issues in Supervision and Regulation." Paper presented at the MicroFinance Network Conference, November, Manila.

Robinson, Marguerite. 1994. "Savings Mobilization and Microenterprise Finance: The Indonesian Experience." In Maria Otero and Elisabeth Rhyne, eds., *The New World of Microenterprise Finance.* West Hartford, Conn.: Kumarian Press.

Rock, Rachel, and Maria Otero, eds. 1997. *From Margin to Mainstream: The Regulation and Supervision of Microfinance.* Monograph Series 11. Washington, D.C.: ACCION International.

Rosenberg, Richard. 1994. "Beyond Self-Sufficiency: Licensed Leverage and Microfinance Strategy." U.S. Agency for International Development, Washington, D.C.

Stearns, Katherine, and Maria Otero, eds. 1990. *The Critical Connection: Governments, Private Institutions, and the Informal Sector in Latin America.* Monograph Series 5. Washington, D.C.: ACCION International.

USAID (U.S. Agency for International Development). 1995. "Policy Goals, Reform, and Microenterprise Development." Microenterprise Development Brief 25. GEMINI Project, Washington, D.C.

———. 1998. *Microenterprise Development Policy Paper.* Washington, D.C.

Vogel, Robert C. 1994. "Other People's Money: Regulatory Issues Facing Microenterprise Finance Programs." International Management and Communications Corporation, Washington, D.C.

Waterfield, Charles, and Ann Duval. 1996. *CARE Savings and Credit Sourcebook.* Atlanta, Ga.: CARE.

Women's World Banking Global Policy Forum. 1995. "The Missing Links: Financial Systems That Work for the Majority." *Women's World Banking* (April).

Yanovitch, Lawrence, and Dennis Macray. 1996. "The Multilateral Development Banks and the Microfinance Sector: Opening Financial Markets to the World's Self-Employed Poor." Paper prepared for the Congressional Task Force on the U.S. and Multilateral Development Banks and the Center for Strategic and International Studies. Foundation for International Community Assistance, Washington, D.C.

Yaron, Jacob, McDonald P. Benjamin, Jr., and Gerda L. Piprek. 1997. *Rural Finance; Issues, Design, and Best Practices.* Environmentally and Socially Sustainable Development Studies and Monographs Series 14. Washington, D.C.: World Bank.

CHAPTER TWO

The Target Market and Impact Analysis

A target market is a group of potential clients who share certain characteristics, tend to behave in similar ways, and are likely to be attracted to a specific combination of products and services. A target market represents a defined market segment that contains identifiable clients who demand or represent a potential demand for microfinance services. In selecting a target market for microfinance services, MFIs need to determine their own objectives, understand what motivates a group of clients, and assess whether the target market can be reached in a way that will eventually be financially sustainable. Most important, the market must be chosen based on effective demand for financial services and the capacity within that market to take on debt.

Organizations that do not define their objectives, and hence their target market, or that fail to design their products to meet the needs of this market often have difficulty managing their operations and staying focused. For example, an organization that simply wants to provide financial services to the poor without defining who the poor are and which level of the poor it wants to reach often ends up operating with different credit models, trying to serve different groups and satisfy different donors. Both donors and practitioners should be clear about appropriate target markets for particular MFIs and must continually focus on meeting those markets' needs. Specifically, donors should not encourage MFIs to operate in areas or market segments where they have no experience, expertise, or resources.

Target markets can be identified by the characteristics of the clients (poverty level, gender, ethnicity, caste, religion, and so forth) the MFI wants to serve and the type or level of business activity (existing businesses, growth-oriented businesses, or specific economic sectors) it wishes to support. Furthermore, the clients' cash flow and capacity for debt must match the services being offered.

Once a target market is selected, it is important to determine *if* that market is in fact being reached and what *impact* the provision of financial services has on that market. This is done by carrying out impact analysis, discussed in the second half of this chapter.

Chapter 1 examined the *supply* of financial services; this chapter focuses on *demand* and on how to determine the *impact* of meeting that demand on the target market. It summarizes what stakeholders need to know to determine whom they want to provide services to (practitioners) or support the provision of services to (donors) and whether they achieve the desired outcomes.

This chapter covers two main topics: identifying a target market, and analyzing the impact of services on that market.

Objectives of the Microfinance Institution

Selecting a target market depends on the objectives of the microfinance service provider and the perceived demand for financial services. In any country there are unserved or underserved enterprises and households, ranging from the ultra-poor, who may not be economically active, to small growing enterprises that provide employment in their communities. This range or continuum constitutes the demand side for microfinance services. Often the supply side does not offer a corresponding continuum of services. MFIs need to supply services that fill the gaps and integrate the unserved groups into the market.

The goal of MFIs as development organizations is to service the financial needs of unserved or underserved markets as a means of meeting development objectives. These development objectives generally include one or more of the following:

- To reduce poverty
- To empower women or other disadvantaged population groups
- To create employment
- To help existing businesses grow or diversify their activities
- To encourage the development of new businesses.

In a World Bank study of lending for small and microenterprise projects, three objectives were most frequently cited (Webster, Riopelle, and Chidzero 1996):

- To create employment and income opportunities through the creation and expansion of microenterprises
- To increase the productivity and incomes of vulnerable groups, especially women and the poor
- To reduce rural families' dependence on drought-prone crops through diversification of their income-generating activities.

Given the large number of conditional variables in each country context, every organizational decision to enter or serve a target market will involve balancing the conditions in that market. This decisionmaking process must keep in mind the two long-term goals of microfinance: *outreach,* serving those who have been consistently underserved by financial institutions (such as women, the poor, and indigenous and rural populations), and *sustainability,* generating enough revenue to cover the costs of providing financial services. Depending on which target market is selected, there are consequences to the MFI's financial position, because costs will be affected. In short, there are trade-offs involved in the decisions about objectives and how to reach them. The central calculus for an MFI concerns which objectives it can *afford* to set and for how long.

MFIs need to determine where there is unmet demand for microfinance services and which target group matches their objectives. For example, if an MFI's objective is to reach the very poor with financial and other services, its target market will differ from an MFI that wishes to serve the economically active poor with only financial services. In addition, some MFIs may wish to focus on a particular economic sector or level of business activity as a means of achieving their objectives.

Direct and Indirect Targeting

Before discussing how MFIs identify their target markets, it is worthwhile to clarify the meanings of and differences between direct and indirect targeting and to explain why indirect targeting (or "identifying" the market) is the preferred means of reaching a target market with financial services.

Direct targeting generally refers to the allocation of a specific amount of funds to provide credit to a particular sector of the economy or population. Direct targeting is founded on the belief that because certain groups (the poor, specific castes) or sectors (agriculture, fisheries) are unable to access credit (or to access it at affordable prices), credit must be made accessible through a government or donor mandate. In some cases the government or donor also subsidizes the clients' cost of borrowing.

In spite of the good intentions of such a strategy, one should be skeptical about its usefulness (see box 2.1). First, due to the fungibility (exchangeability) of money, it is almost always impossible to know what any given loan "really" finances. Second, it is highly doubtful that anyone knows better than the recipients themselves what is good for them. Third, the strategy rests on the idea that "commerce" and "consumption" are less valuable

---

Box 2.1 Targeted Credit Activities

IN MOST DEVELOPING COUNTRIES THERE HAS BEEN extensive government intervention in the allocation of credit. Although a degree of intervention may have been useful during the early stages of development, many countries have come to recognize that this policy has had an adverse effect on industrial and financial development. The evidence suggests that direct targeted credit programs have been an inefficient way of redistributing income and dealing with imperfections in the goods market. However, some programs that were well designed and narrowly focused have been reasonably successful in dealing with specific imperfections in the financial markets (for example, the lack of risk capital). In the future governments should attack the conditions that made direct credit appear desirable—imperfections in markets or extreme inequalities in income—instead of using directed credit programs and interest rate subsidies.

Source: Pederson 1997.

socially than "production" and "income generation" and should therefore not be financed. This naively transfers notions from industrialized to developing countries and from the world of the wealthy to the world of the poor. For example, if people are engaged in trade, this is likely to be a better line of business for them. However, consumption by a poor household is very often a way of strengthening income-generation capabilities through improved education and nutrition.

Direct targeting generally leads to credit diversion and low repayment. It also results in substantial costs of monitoring eligibility and compliance. Furthermore, potential clients who have profitable but unfinanced or underfinanced businesses may be excluded because they do not fit the profile. Alternatively, people who do match the qualifications and receive credit may not have entrepreneurial skills or a profitable venture in need of financing.

Indirect targeting means that products and services are designed for and aimed at people who are beyond the normal frontiers of formal finance, instead of mandating specific funds to particular groups who fit a narrowly defined profile. Indirect targeting focuses on those who cannot take advantage of income-generating opportunities because of market imperfections or other barriers to financial services. With indirect targeting, self-selection takes place by virtue of the design of microfinance services. Economists refer to this as "incentive compatibility"—the terms and conditions are such that unwanted clients will not be interested, both because the products are less attractive and because the set of requirements imposed to access the services will seem too burdensome. This happens because populations outside of the target group have other alternatives for financial services that the target group does not have.

For example, an MFI that seeks to provide the very poor with credit should design its loan products so that the relatively high interest rates and small size of loans are attractive only to the very poor. The MFI may also require group guarantees and weekly attendance at group meetings. More affluent clients usually see this as an inconvenience, which makes the credit attractive only to poorer clients.

The primary difference between direct and indirect targeting lies in the means that the MFI uses rather than in the target group. Both direct and indirect targeting may reach the same population groups or economic sectors, but direct targeting imposes eligibility criteria, while indirect targeting designs appropriate products and services.

The Importance of Adequate Cash Flow and the Capacity to Service Debt

Debt capacity is an important consideration in determining the demand for financial services. When identifying their target market, MFIs must consider clients' and potential clients' cash flow as well as their ability to repay loans. Cash flow is the comparison of cash inflows and outflows. Debt capacity is the amount of additional debt a client can take on without running the risk of inadequate cash flow and consequent loan default.[1]

MFIs need to consider *debt capacity* as opposed to basing credit decisions on a "credit need" approach that risks future trouble for both lenders and borrowers. A credit-need assessment yields unreliable information because self-reported credit need involves "wishing." By focusing on credit need rather than debt capacity the lender risks not getting the money back, and the borrower risks serious debt. This is because the need for credit and the ability to repay debt cannot be assumed to match.

No matter how the target market is identified, it is imperative for MFIs to ensure that each client and target group can generate enough cash to repay the loan on time. This in turn determines the *size* of the potential target market (differentiating between "credit need," or what borrowers say they want, and "effective demand," or what borrowers can and are willing to borrow and repay).

"Lenders are able to recover loans on schedule only when the repayment capacity of the borrower equals or exceeds debt service, which consists of principal and interest due for payment. Borrowers are able to repay their loans on time without suffering hardship only when their repayment capacity equals or exceeds the debt service due according to the loan contract. These simple, self-evident relationships define the role that credit plays in development and influence the fate of efforts to expand the frontier of formal finance." (Von Pischke 1991, 277)

---

1. This discussion is drawn from Von Pischke (1991).

To determine potential clients' debt capacity, the first consideration is their cash flow. It is then necessary to assess the degree of risk associated with this cash flow and other claims that may come before repaying the MFI loan. Adjusting the debt capacity of a borrower for risk should reflect reasonable expectations about adverse conditions that may affect the borrower's enterprise. Adjustment for *adversity* should reflect the lender's willingness to assume the risks of borrowers' inability to repay. The greater the MFI's capacity to assume risk, the higher the credit limits the lender can offer.

Other claims that need be considered are debts to other lenders (claims by informal lenders generally rank ahead of those of formal credit institutions) and household expenses such as food and fuel, taxes, school fees, and expenditures for emergencies, important social obligations, and ceremonies.

MFIs need to be conservative when estimating the debt capacity of a potential target market, because determining clients' debt capacity is an important part of identifying a target market and designing appropriate products and services for this market. For the most part, borrowers do not go into debt to the full extent of their debt capacity. Economists refer to this as "internal credit rationing." If borrowers attempt to fully exhaust their debt capacity, they are usually behaving opportunistically and are at risk of not being able to manage debt.

Minimal Equity Requirement

In addition to assessing clients' debt capacity, MFIs should consider clients' ability to contribute a minimum amount of equity. In other words, loans should not finance the entire business activity. Some MFIs set a certain percentage of equity as one of the loan conditions. Even when the target group is start-up businesses owned by the very poor, where equity contributions in the strict sense are not possible, some MFIs require the pledging of a household asset before granting the loan. Other forms of equity can be compulsory savings or an amount contributed by the borrower to the project in the form of a "membership fee" or "loan application fee." While these fees or contributions are financially insignificant from the lenders' point of view, they carry financial and psychological weight for the prospective borrowers.

In banking terms, minimal equity requirements reduce the lender's risk. However, in microfinance it is equally important to invoke the underlying psychological basis for a minimal equity contribution. People care about an asset if they have worked for it or own it. This seems to be a universal trait of human nature. If the MFI lends 100 percent of the cost of projects or assets, borrowers have little or no risk since their own money is not at stake. By requiring a contribution by the borrower (even if it is in fact a token from the lender's viewpoint), MFIs hope to increase responsible behavior among borrowers and thereby reduce the chances of loan default.

However, MFIs need to monitor where their clients are accessing the capital for this minimal equity contribution. If clients need to borrow funds from another source (at potentially higher interest rates) to contribute equity, they may be increasing the risk of default.

Moral Hazard

Managing debt capacity and ensuring a minimal equity requirement offset moral hazard. Moral hazard is defined as "the incentive by someone (an agent) who holds an asset belonging to another person (the principle) to endanger the value of that asset because the agent bears less than the full consequence of any loss" (Chaves and Gonzalez-Vega 1994). For example, a borrower's efforts to repay may be largely unobservable by an MFI; it cannot readily determine what is attributable to the lack of effort by the client as opposed to bad luck or external forces. An MFI that could observe the borrower could relate the terms of the loan contract to the effort put in by the borrower, but because it costs too much to do this, the best the MFI can do is to ensure that the cash flow and debt capacity of the borrower are sufficient to service the debt. MFIs must also set terms of the loan that are acceptable to the borrower and result in behavior that the MFI prefers. This usually means giving the borrower more risk (by being less willing to forgive loans when things go wrong) than the MFI would be ready to assume if it had better information (Yaron, Benjamin, and Piperk 1997).

Market Size

MFIs should estimate the size of the market for microenterprises that can benefit from financial services, lest self-reported credit need be confused with debt capacity and effective demand. Obviously, since there are costs involved in starting the delivery of financial services in a given area, it is important to know:

- What kind of financial service will both benefit households or enterprises and have a high likelihood of good repayment to the lender?
- How much effective demand for the product(s) will there be initially, and how expandable will that market be?

These questions can be answered by undertaking limited survey work, preferably in-depth interviews with selected potential clients supplemented by some quantitative work, or, alternatively, by undertaking a full constraints analysis and a large-scale survey to estimate the full range of possibilities. Whichever method is selected, it is important to estimate the market size to ensure that, in the long term, enough demand exists to justify the MFI's continued existence.

Identifying the Target Market

Profit-oriented companies either invest in identifying specific segments of the market for a product they want to sell or design products specifically with a market segment in mind. For donors or development organizations that want to achieve development goals (rather than profit), market identification serves a somewhat different purpose. In this case, the target market is identified because it is underserved and disadvantaged in some way that slows development. The goal is not simply profit, but rather a more equitable distribution of financial services to groups that can make productive use of them (Bennett 1997).

Nevertheless, even though the goals may differ, development organizations still need to use the approach of profit-oriented companies to identify what the chosen clients want and what they can afford to pay, so that appropriate products and services can be offered. The question is not whether to identify a target market, but how to identify it.

Understanding the characteristics of the target market helps MFIs design products and services that *attract* different groups (as opposed to targeting them directly). This becomes an iterative process as the MFI learns more about the target market and its needs.

While it is usual to broaden the client base over time, most successful microfinance projects begin with a narrowly defined group of clients to establish a market niche and develop a thorough understanding of this client base.

The target market for MFIs generally takes into consideration a combination of two factors:

- Characteristics of the population group, including the level of poverty
- The type of microenterprises being financed.

Characteristics of the Population Group

In many countries, people operating in the informal sector are illiterate. An MFI needs to understand the level of literacy (including financial literacy) of its client base to design appropriate interventions. Some MFIs require illiterate borrowers to use their thumbprint or fingerprint as a means of formally agreeing to a financial contract. Others have spent time teaching the borrowers how to sign their names and read numbers to be able to verify the contracts they sign. Literacy and numeracy are not necessary prerequisites for accessing financial services from many MFIs; however, they must be taken into account when designing credit and savings transactions.

Based on their objectives, microfinance providers may want to select a target market to address a specific client population. Characteristics of the population group take into account various socioeconomic characteristics, including gender, poverty level, geographic focus, and ethnicity, caste, and religion (figure 2.1).

FOCUSING ON FEMALE CLIENTS. The objective of many MFIs is to empower women by increasing their economic position in society. The provision of financial services directly to women aids in this process. Women entrepreneurs have attracted special interest from MFIs because they almost always make up the poorest segments of society; they are generally responsible for child-rearing (including education, health, and nutrition); and they often have fewer economic opportunities than men.

Women face *cultural barriers* that often restrict them to the home (for example, Islamic purdah), making it difficult for them to access financial services. Women also have more traditional roles in the economy and may be less able to operate a business outside of their homes. Furthermore, women often have disproportionally large household obligations.

Figure 2.1 Client Characteristics

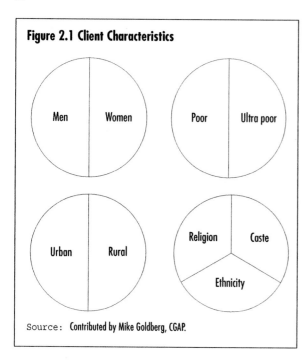

Source: Contributed by Mike Goldberg, CGAP.

monitoring repayment data reported a higher rate of repayment of loans in projects focused on women than in companion nontargeted projects (Rhyne and Holt 1994).

The *characteristics* of women's businesses differ from those of men's in important ways. In general, women tend to weigh household maintenance and risk reduction more heavily in their business strategies. Women also tend to give less emphasis to enterprise growth, preferring to invest profits in their families rather than in expanding the enterprise. Other characteristics include:

- A concentration in trade, services, and light manufacturing (particularly in subsectors using traditional technologies)
- A tendency to start smaller and stay smaller throughout their lifetimes, although women's businesses last as long (if not longer) than those of men
- The frequent use of family labor and the location of their businesses in the household.

In both urban and rural settings, women tend to engage in activities that offer easy entry and exit and do

In some instances, commercial banks are unwilling to lend to women or mobilize deposits from them. This is based on their perception that women are unable to control household income. Moreover, because women's access to property is limited and their legal standing can be precarious, women also have fewer sources of collateral. Finally, in many countries women have lower literacy rates, which makes it more difficult for them to deal with financial systems that depend on written contracts.

Experience has shown that women generally have a *high sense of responsibility* and are affected by social pressure (although, like men, they often fail to repay subsidized loans from government or other programs that they perceive as charity rather than business). It has been argued that an increase in women's income benefits the household and the community to a greater extent than a commensurate increase in men's income. Women have also demonstrated higher repayment and savings rates than male clients (box 2.2). Anecdotal evidence suggests that arrears rates are slightly higher among men; however, since many generally accepted ideas about women and microfinance are based on the Grameen Bank's experience, which lacks a control group of men, it is difficult to generalize conclusively about the repayment behavior of males and females. However, a review of World Bank projects supporting enterprise development for women found that the majority of projects

---

Box 2.2 U.S. Agency for International Development Findings on Female Borrowers

In a U.S. Agency for International Development (USAID) study of 11 successful MFIs, findings indicate that the organizations studied do in fact reach large numbers of women, either because of direct policy decisions (Grameen Bank, Association Dominicana para el Desarrollo de la Mujer, or ADOPEM) or because of a commonly held belief that women demonstrate stronger repayment performance and are more willing to form groups (the Kenya Rural Enterprise Programme).

Among programs concentrating on women, motivations generally include the belief or experience that women are good credit risks and are more likely to have poor access to resources and services. Female participation rates in programs without gender preference are determined by the prevalence of women in client groups served and by features not studied that may impede or facilitate women's access. Some correlation exists between programs offering smaller loans and programs serving more women, but the correlation is far from perfect. For example, BancoSol has a relatively high average outstanding loan size, yet 71 percent of its clients are women.

Source: Christian and others, 1995.

not require large amounts of working capital, fixed assets, or special skills (beyond those already acquired in the household). Such activities offer the flexibility regarding time commitments that enables women to balance their work and family obligations. The activities are often seasonal, geographically portable, and fit household conditions and space limitations. The market is usually limited to local consumers. These characteristics imply that women's household duties limit their choice of business activity, which is an important consideration when providing financial services specifically for women.

MFIs need to be proactive in identifying female clients. They need to look beyond areas with high concentrations of manufacturing enterprises to promoting services through existing women's networks and by word of mouth. The gender of loan officers may also affect the level of female participation, depending on the social context. In such cases, if female credit officers are not available (because they lack educational opportunities or are unable to walk on the streets alone or at night), it may be more acceptable for male credit officers to work with women in groups.

A study by the World Bank's Sustainable Banking with the Poor project titled "Worldwide Inventory of Microfinance Institutions" (Paxton 1996) found that predominately female programs are typically group-based, with small loan sizes and short loan terms. "The median loan size for female-based programs is US$162, compared to US$768 for the predominately male programs" (Paxton 1996, 13). However, this finding does not definitively support smaller loan sizes for women, because it is based on the identification of MFIs simply as having more than 50 percent women (rather than an actual percentage of women clients).

THE LEVEL OF POVERTY. Because the objective of many MFIs is poverty reduction, they often wish to focus on the poorest segments of the population. In most countries many people do not have access to financial services, from the poorest of the poor, who may not be economically active, to small business operators, who may not qualify for formal financial sector services. MFIs commonly measure their *outreach* of services in terms of scale, or the number of clients they reach, and *depth,* or the level of poverty of their clients. An MFI's products and services will vary with the extent of outreach.

There is much debate in the field of microfinance as to whether access to financial services benefit the "poor-

est of the poor." While there are now many examples of programs and institutions serving the working poor with financial services in a self-sustainable manner, there is less experience of successfully serving the very poor, the destitute, and the disabled. Many donors, practitioners, and academics believe they ought to be beneficiaries of transfer programs that do not entail an additional liability for the recipient (Hulme and Mosley 1996).

One of the most important studies on whether microfinance is appropriate for the poorest of the poor is that by Hulme and Mosley in their book *Finance against Poverty.* Using data from MFIs in seven countries, they compare increases in borrowers' income with those in a control group. Their findings suggest that successful institutions contributing to poverty reduction are particularly effective in improving the status of the middle and upper segments of the poor. However, clients below the poverty line were worse off after borrowing than before. Furthermore, the impact on the client's income seems to be directly related to the level of income, which would reinforce the tendency of those MFIs wishing to preserve their viability to concentrate on the less-poor. A related consequence is that the development and refinements of microfinance products remain focused on the middle and upper segments of the poor, leaving the poorest behind.

Hulme and Mosley suggest that recognizing the heterogeneity of the poor should lead to more innovation and experimentation, which deepens the downward reach of financial services. However, there is still a large unsatisfied demand for financial services among the bankable poor (those with the capacity for debt), which could be met by mainstreaming the known successful approaches. This debate will likely continue for some time. The "depth" of outreach achieved by an MFI will depend to a great extent on its objectives and its ability to design products and services suitable to the level of poverty it is targeting.

In light of the need for most MFIs to reach financial sustainability, consideration must be given to the trade-off between minimizing costs and focusing on the poorest clients. While serving the ultra-poor may indeed be possible in a financially sustainable way, it is likely that the time frame to reach financial self-sufficiency will be shorter for MFIs serving the economically active poor. If the target market identified is the poorest of the poor, donors and practitioners alike need to be committed to supporting the institution over a longer period.

GEOGRAPHIC FOCUS. One of the most important considerations for an MFI is whether it will serve urban or rural clients. This decision greatly affects the development of products and services, and it should be based on both the activities characteristic of different geographical settings and the varying levels of infrastructure development in urban and rural areas.

Choosing a target market that is based in urban areas has both advantages and disadvantages. It is highly dependent on the objectives of the MFI. The advantages of focusing on an urban market may include:

- Lower transaction costs (shorter distances) for clients
- Greater chance that clients will be literate
- Potential higher chance of repayment, since interactions with clients can be more frequent
- Possible leveraging through relationships with formal financial institutions, since urban clients may be physically closer to formal sector banks and more comfortable with visiting banks
- More developed local infrastructure and more varied markets.

However, urban clients may be more transitory, resulting in a higher risk of potential default. Character-based lending may be more difficult. In addition, covariance risk can exist if most clients are active in the same economic sector; in other words, if they are all traders in the same area or manufacturers of the same products. When the loan portfolio of any financial institution is heavily concentrated in a few activities, risks can increase substantially. The same thing happens in all markets if the region has one principal economic sector that enters into decline. Financing larger clients in these environments does not effectively diversify risks.

Some MFIs provide financial services in *rural areas* only, based on a general lack of supply of services outside urban centers and the fact that in some countries poverty is largely a rural phenomenon. Providing services to rural clients can therefore be an effective means of reaching a large number of poor households. Furthermore, there are often local informal organizations that can be used to deliver financial services. For example, the Kenyan *chikola* system, a form of village rotating savings and credit system, has become the mainstay of the Kenya Rural Enterprise Programme (K-REP; box 2.3).

However, rural markets may also have disadvantages:

- There may be a long history of poorly designed rural credit programs (with subsidized credit, no savings

mobilization, or credit tied to specific activities or purchases).

Box 2.3 The Kenya Rural Enterprise Programme

THE KENYA RURAL ENTERPRISE PROGRAMME (K-REP) WAS established in 1984 as a development NGO that provides credit for on-lending and technical assistance to other NGOs. To promote growth and generate employment in the microenterprise sector, K-REP lends indirectly through NGOs and directly to groups that would otherwise find it extremely difficult to access credit from commercial banks and other formal financial intermediaries.

K-REP offers credit directly to groups through its Juhudi and Chikola loan products. Juhudi, initiated in 1989, provides loans based on a modification of the group lending methodology used by the Grameen Bank in Bangladesh. K-REP facilitates the formation of five to seven member groups called *wantanos*. Up to six wantanos confederate into a *kiwa,* which is registered by the Kenyan Ministry of Culture and Social Services as a self-help group. The Chikola program, initiated in 1991, provides credit to individual entrepreneurs through existing rotating savings and credit associations. Under the Chikola program, K-REP provides a single loan to an established group, which then retails the loan to its individual members. To be eligible the group must be registered as a self-help group, be in existence for at least one year, and have an average membership of 20. The Chikola must be operating or must intend to operate a revolving loan fund and must have a group savings account. The qualifying level of savings is not less than 10 percent of the requested loan amount.

A K-REP credit officer appraises the loan application and makes the disbursement by bank check to the group. Each group must meet at least once a month to conduct group activities, including collection of savings and loan repayments. Scheduled group loan repayments are made (due to regulation) by transfers from the group savings account to K-REP's bank account. The loan limit is 25,000 Kenyan shillings (about US$450) per member for the first loan, with subsequent loans varying in size according to the needs of the group and its members. The savings of the group serve as collateral for the loan, and each member agrees to forfeit his or her savings in the event of default by a group member.

Source: Contributed by Stephanie Charitonenko Church, Sustainable Banking with the Poor Project, World Bank.

- There may be a less diversified economic base.
- Covariance risk can be significant. For example, if the MFI is engaged in agricultural lending, many farmers may grow the same crop or raise the same type of animals, resulting in higher risk in case of drought or other climate disorder.
- There may be no branches of formal financial institutions in the area. This can create problems when clients need access to a branch network for savings deposits or loan repayment.
- It may be more difficult to reach the minimal scale required to break even.
- There is likely to be a poorly developed infrastructure and a more dispersed population.

Whether microentrepreneurs are based in a rural or urban area, they need access to markets and supplies. Rural areas are often isolated from markets. Furthermore, an inability to produce and deliver goods due to a lack of infrastructure may limit microentrepreneurs' success and growth possibilities, thus limiting the demand for financial services. A good transportation system reduces transaction costs for both clients and MFIs. Some MFIs, such as the Grameen Bank, operate branches in the same geographic areas as their clients, reducing the barrier to accessible financial services due to poor roads and inadequate transportation services.

MFIs depend on attaining a certain scale of operations to achieve sustainability. Providing services to populations that are widely dispersed incurs greater transaction costs. However, while less densely populated areas are harder to service, new methods, such as self-managed village banks, are being developed to overcome this problem by decentralizing most of the financial transactions at the village level, thus limiting transportation costs.

ETHNICITY, CASTE, AND RELIGION. In most countries there are ethnically or traditionally defined groups that are unserved or underserved by existing formal financial institutions. There are cases in which a certain group within a community cannot or will not take part in a financial services project due to a religious, ethnic, or other social influence. It is important to understand these restrictions when identifying a target market, so that products and services can be developed that take into account the limitations on some groups.

Building and maintaining a level of trust when different ethnic or religious groups are involved can make pro-

viding microfinance services more difficult. (Caste, while not solely an ethnic factor, can pose cultural barriers similar to ethnic differences.) Societies differ in their stock of "social capital—those features of social organization such as *networks, norms,* and *trust* that facilitate coordination and cooperation for mutual benefit" (Putnam 1993, 36). These structures depend on traditions of collaboration and a certain level of trust between members of society. In societies with high social capital, where systems and structures have been developed to build trust and foster social and economic transactions beyond the family and kingroup, it will be easier and less costly to build sustainable systems for financial intermediation (Bennett 1997).

When identifying a target market, MFIs must ensure that they are able to *communicate* with their clients clearly. If serious language barriers exist, it may make financial services to certain clients too costly. In addition, legal or financial jargon, even when in the client's language, may create a communication barrier. MFIs must ensure that communication with clients is appropriate to their level of understanding, particularly if clients are anxious to access financial services and do not fully understand the implications and responsibilities of doing so (box 2.4).

Box 2.4 The Influence of Ethnicity and Language in Microfinance

DOGON VILLAGES IN MALI HAVE REMAINED VERY secluded over the years because of their physical isolation and the poor condition of communication networks. As a result, the Dogon culture is relatively homogeneous and traditions have remained very strong. In addition, villages have maintained their own linguistic identity. Dialects differ from one village to another, even though they are only a few miles away, making communication difficult. The total Dogon population amounts to only 600,000 people speaking at least 30 different dialects.

For a local MFI, the multitude of dialects has three important effects. First, all staff have to be hired locally, taking into consideration their ability to master several dialects. Second, training activities and documents for villagers on bank management have to be adapted into several dialects. Third, networking among village banks involves many translations.

Source: Contributed by Cecile Fruman, Sustainable Banking with the Poor Project, World Bank.

Some religious groups do not allow their members to enter into financial transactions. Both donors and practitioners should be aware of religious practices that might affect the delivery of financial services and consequently the objectives and goals of the MFI. Islamic banking provides an example of financial markets directly affected by religious practices (box 2.5).

Types of Microenterprises

In addition to determining the characteristics of the population group to be served by the MFI, it is also impor-

tant to consider the types of activities in which the target market is active and the level of development of the enterprise being financed. This will further define the types of products and services suitable for the MFI's market.

Enterprises vary by whether they are existing or start-up businesses; unstable, stable, or growing; and involved in production, commercial, or service activities (figure 2.2).

EXISTING OR START-UP MICROENTERPRISES. When identifying a target market, an MFI needs to consider whether it will focus on entrepreneurs already operating a microenterprise or on entrepreneurs (or potential entrepreneurs) who need financial services to start a business and possibly some form of business training.

Working capital is the most common constraint identified by entrepreneurs of *existing microenterprises*. To access working capital, microentrepreneurs often borrow from informal financial sources, such as family or friends, suppliers, or a local moneylender. Usually moneylenders charge relatively high interest rates and may not offer loan products or terms suited to the borrower. The ability to both borrow and save with an MFI may increase microentrepreneurs' profits (through lower interest rates and access to appropriately designed loan products) and improve their ability to manage working capital needs (through borrowing and saving at different times as required).

Box 2.5 Islamic Banking

FINANCIAL PROVIDERS IN ISLAMIC COUNTRIES ARE subject to specific banking laws. The primary difference between Islamic and conventional banking products is that in Islamic banking, *money cannot be treated as a commodity*. Money must be used productively (like labor or land), with the return based solely on actual profit or loss. The bank and the entrepreneur share the risk of a project. Islamic banks can neither charge nor pay interest *(riba)*, nor can they require specific provisions for inflation. Islamic banks tend to make their profits through fees and non-interest-bearing investments (that is, through project profits). It should be noted, however, that due to the competitive nature of the banking field in general, returns on Islamic banking products are close to those of similar products developed by conventional banks.

Islamic banks are governed by *sharia* (Islamic law and councils of advisers), which dictate the products and services that are Islamically correct. Sharia and their interpretations of the religious commentary vary from country to country, making it difficult to develop standard products. This complicates efforts to establish an adequate regulatory environment.

In some ways Islamic banking is well suited to microfinance. In many cases collateral is not required. Instead, emphasis is placed on the profitability of the project. However, because the nature of Islamic banking often requires the bank to share project risks with the client, a more detailed study of the project is required than a conventional bank would carry out. Consequently, some Islamic banks maintain staff with technical backgrounds in addition to more conventional financial staff.

Source: Khayat 1996.

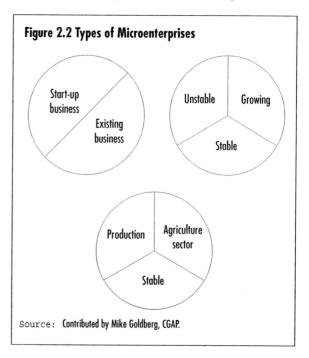

Figure 2.2 Types of Microenterprises

Source: Contributed by Mike Goldberg, CGAP.

Profits can also be increased through the acquisition of capital assets, such as sewing machines or rickshaws. Access to continued financial services, including loans for capital purchases and savings services to build up reserves, allows microentrepreneurs to increase their asset base and improve their ability to generate revenue.

There are many advantages to working with existing microentrepreneurs. Active businesses have a history of success, which greatly reduces the risk to the MFI. Furthermore, existing microentrepreneurs have the potential to grow and create employment opportunities. However, some may have other debts (to moneylenders, suppliers, family, or other MFIs), which they may pay off with the proceeds of new loans, thereby increasing the risk of default to the new lender (box 2.6).

MFIs that target potential entrepreneurs often have poverty alleviation as an objective. The belief is that by aiding potential entrepreneurs to *start up* their own businesses, they will increase their incomes and consequently reduce their level of poverty.

However, potential entrepreneurs often need more than financial services. Many need skills training or other inputs to make their enterprises a success. When there are significant barriers to entry into certain fields (due to minimum investment requirements, technology levels, and market contacts), an integrated approach can prepare potential entrepreneurs prior to taking on debt. However, the impact of training courses and technical assistance is not clearly linked to increased production, profitability, job creation, and reinvestment. If services are subsidized, it can be difficult to remove these subsidies and put the enterprise on an equal footing with local competitors. Also, training programs often assume that anyone can become an entrepreneur, which is not the case, because not everyone is willing to take the risks inherent in owning and operating a business (although social intermediation services can help—see chapter 3). Furthermore, training courses linked to credit access sometimes assume that entrepreneurs cannot contribute their own equity and that credit should be arranged for 100 percent of the investment.

Most MFIs prefer to focus on existing businesses, with perhaps a small portion of their portfolio invested in start-up businesses, thereby reducing their risk. This is again dependent on their objectives and the trade-off between increased costs (and lower loan sizes) for start-

---

Box 2.6 The Association for the Development of Microenterprises' Work with Existing Microenterprises

THE ASSOCIATION FOR THE DEVELOPMENT OF Microenterprises (ADEMI) has developed an effective lending methodology to meet the needs of low-income urban clients in the Dominican Republic. As of June 1997 it had a network of 25 branches serving over 16,300 clients. Its assets totaled RD606 million (US$43 million) and its equity was RD242 million (US$17 million). ADEMI has served more than 40,000 small and micro enterprises during the past 15 years and had a direct impact on the jobs of more than 200,000 owners and employees of micro and small-scale enterprises.

Objectives. Job creation and delivery of sustainable financial services.

Target clients. Established microenterprises with at least one year of experience and the potential to create new jobs. Clients must be over 18 years old, show initiative, and have a minimum level of business aptitude to ensure their success and growth.

Services. Loans for working capital or the acquisition of equipment and machinery (fixed assets); and ADEMI Mastercard; home improvement loans; and minimal savings services. ADEMI does not make consumption loans.

Method. Individual loans; no formal collateral, although ADEMI does encourage the use of guarantors and will repossess equipment or seize other assets if a client defaults. All borrowers must sign a legal contract and promissory note, stating their obligation to repay funds at specified terms. Loan terms are on average between 10 and 34 months; repayment is monthly; average loan sizes vary from US$1,000 to US$10,000 for microenterprises; interest rates range from 2.2 percent to 3 percent a month.

Source: Benjamin and Ledgerwood 1998.

---

up businesses, on the one hand, and sustainability, on the other.

LEVEL OF BUSINESS DEVELOPMENT. The level of business development is another consideration when identifying the types of microenterprise to which an MFI wishes to provide financial services. This is closely linked with the level of poverty existing in a potential target market. There are typically three levels of business development of microenterprises that benefit from access to financial services:

- *Unstable survivors,* with operators who have not found other employment and tend to have very unstable enterprises for a limited time
- *Stable survivors,* with operators for whom the microenterprise provides a modest but decent living while rarely growing
- *Growth enterprises,* or businesses that have the potential to grow and become genuinely dynamic small enterprises.

Unstable survivors comprise the group most difficult to provide financial services to in a sustainable fashion, because loan sizes tend to remain small and the risk of business failure is high. Focusing on unstable survivors as a target market can result in a great deal of time spent with the clients just to ensure that their businesses will survive and that they will continue to be able to make loan payments. Some technical assistance may also be required, resulting in further time and cost increases. Also, unstable survivors often need credit for consumption-smoothing rather than income-generating activities. Depending on the objectives of the MFI, these stopgap loans may or may not be appropriate.

Generally, the debt capacity of unstable survivors does not increase. Accordingly, the MFI is limited in its attempts to reduce costs or increase revenue, because loan sizes remain small. While not all MFIs have the immediate goal of reaching financial self-sufficiency, over the long term the choice to focus on unstable survivors will likely be a time-bound strategy, because access to donor funding may be limited.

Stable survivors comprise the group that many MFIs focus on and for which access to a permanent credit supply is vital. This is the group that benefits from access to financial services to meet both production and consumption needs, while not necessarily requiring other inputs from the MFI.

Stable survivors are targeted by microfinance providers with poverty reduction objectives. For these businesses, returns on labor are relatively low, and market imperfections and near monopsony conditions may result in uneven bargaining positions. Stable survivors are often women who simultaneously maintain family-related activities (providing food, water, cooking, medicine, and child care) while engaging in income-generating activities. Seasonal changes and household life cycles often force such people to consume rather than invest in the business.

Generally, profits are low, leading to low reinvestment, low output, and a high level of vulnerability. Profits remain low due to:

- The unspecialized nature of the product
- The lack of timely and complete market information (beyond the local market)
- Underdeveloped infrastructure facilities
- The lack of value-added services (such as packaging)
- The number of producers with similar products.

Experiences with this target group have demonstrated both advantages and disadvantages. Advantages may include:

- The high poverty impact of a financial services project, since these enterprises are run by poor households
- High repayment, due to limited access to alternative sources of credit and the economic, social, and financial costs of those alternatives
- Effective savings services, since there are rarely secure, liquid alternative forms of savings that offer a return for the operators of these enterprises (they also help to smooth consumption for poor households)
- A general willingness to work with new credit technologies (such as groups) as an alternative to tangible collateral.

Disadvantages may include:

- Little or no new job creation resulting from support to these enterprises
- Limited growth potential or high covariance risk, because many entrepreneurs are active in the same businesses (financing them may create excess competition, meaning that the loan portfolio has to grow by increasing the number of clients rather than increasing loan amounts to good clients)
- Difficulty in mobilizing long-term savings, since households are accustomed to seasonal savings build-up and liquidation cycles.

Growth enterprises are often the focus of MFIs whose objective is job creation and whose desire is to move microentrepreneurs from the informal sector to a progressively more formal environment. These MFIs often establish linkages with the formal sector and provide additional products and services. Growth enterprises represent the upper end of the poverty scale: they usually pose the least risk to the MFI. While generally a heterogeneous collection of enterprises, they tend to share some characteristics and face similar problems. Most have both production and risk-taking experience, keep minimal accounting records, and usually do not pay taxes. In addition, they often have little or no formal management experience. Other similarities include:

- *Product line and labor.* Firms that produce a single product or line of products serving a narrow range of market outlets and clients tend to use labor-intensive production techniques and rely on family and apprentice labor.
- *Working capital and fixed asset management.* These firms build their asset base slowly, in an ad hoc manner. They depend largely on family credit for initial investment capital and on informal sector loans for working capital. Cash flow is a constant concern, and they are very sensitive to output and raw material price changes. They often use second-hand equipment.

Growth-oriented microenterprises may be an attractive target group, because they offer potential for job creation and vocational training within the community. They can resemble formal sector enterprises in terms of fixed assets, permanence, and planning, which offers the potential for physical collateral and more thorough business analysis. All these offset risk for the MFI.

However, selecting growth-oriented microenterprises can require a more involved approach on the part of the MFI. Growth-oriented businesses may need some or all of the following services:

- Assistance in choosing new product lines and value-added services
- Working capital and sometimes longer-term investment credit
- Accounting systems to track costs
- Marketing advice to help find new markets.

TYPE OF BUSINESS ACTIVITY. While the level of business development is an important consideration when iden-tifying a target market, the economic sector of activities is also important. Enterprises can generally be divided among three primary sectors: production, services, and agriculture. Each sector has its own specific risks and financing needs, which directly influence the choices made by the MFI and the products and services provided. Table 2.1 identifies the loan purpose, the loan term, and the collateral available for each of the three primary sectors.

There are several advantages to focusing on one economic sector:

- Credit officers can focus their learning on one sector, thereby developing an understanding of the characteristics and issues that their borrowers face. Consequently, they may be able to provide technical assistance more easily if it is required.
- One loan product may be sufficient for all, thereby streamlining operations and reducing transaction costs.

However, MFIs are subject to covariance risk when selecting a target market active in only one economic sector.

Not all MFIs target a single economic sector. Many provide financial services for a combination of sectors, designing loan or savings products or both for each. However, it is generally recommended that MFIs focus on one sector until they have developed a sustainable approach before developing new products (bearing in mind the higher covariance risk).

Depending on the MFI's objectives, selecting a target market based on the business sector allows it to clearly differentiate its products and influence the type of activities in a given area. This is evidenced by the Foundation for Enterprise Finance and Development in Albania (box 2.7).

Once a target market has been identified, the MFI needs to design its products and services to meet the

---

Table 2.1 Enterprise Sector Credit Characteristics

Criterion	Agriculture	Production	Services
Use of loan proceeds	Working capital, some fixed assets	Working capital, fixed assets, infrastructure	Working capital, some fixed assets
Loan term	Growing season	6 months–5 years	4 months–2 years
Amount of collateral available	Minimal	Good	Minimal

Source: Waterfield and Duval 1996.

needs of that market (see chapter 3). However, before doing this, it is important to consider the type of impact that the MFI hopes to achieve. This will help develop products and services and should be considered part of the design process. This is particularly relevant if the MFI wishes to maintain a database on the target market to see the impact of financial services over time.

Impact Analysis

Analyzing the impact of microfinance interventions is especially important if the interventions are ultimately aimed at poverty reduction (as most are).[2] If microfinance practitioners do not make efforts to determine who is being reached by microfinance services and how these services are affecting their lives, it becomes difficult to justify microfinance as a tool for poverty reduction.

In the most generic sense, impact analysis is any process that seeks to determine if an intervention has had

the desired outcome. If the intervention is, for example, an immunization program and the desired outcome is to prevent polio, the impact analysis would focus on polio rates. If it could be shown that polio rates went down as a result of the immunizations, the program's impact could be deemed successful. In other words, the impact analyzed should correspond to the desired outcome.

Microfinance impact analysis is the process by which one determines the effects of microfinance as an intervention. The effects examined depend on the outcomes that were sought (the objectives of the MFI). Generally, the narrower the goals of the intervention, the less problematic the impact analysis.

Decisions about the degree, frequency, and depth of impact analysis involve consideration of the following factors:

- The time and cost
- The disruption to the institution and its clients
- The way the results will be used (the fear of bad news).

All interventions can have unintended consequences. It is optional to seek and investigate unintended impacts, but the analysis is more complete to the extent that these unintended consequences can be illuminated.

Some likely users of microfinance impact analysis are:

- Microfinance practitioners
- Donors
- Policymakers
- Academics.

Both practitioners and donors are usually concerned about improving their institutions or those that they support, as well as learning if their interventions are having the desired impact. Thus they may also be interested in impact analysis as a form of market research through which they can learn more about their clients' needs and how to improve their services. Impact assessment can also contribute to budget allocation decisions.

Policymakers and academics are solely concerned with attributing impact effects to microfinance interventions. They can use impact assessment information to influence policy changes and budget allocation decisions and to address questions suited to academic research.

2. This section was written by Thomas Dichter. It assumes a basic knowledge of statistics, sampling techniques, and the broad spectrum of field methods of assessment. If there are terms with which readers are unfamiliar, they should read some of the sources listed at the end of this chapter to understand better the skills and resources needed to conduct microfinance impact analysis.

Impacts to be analyzed should correlate with impacts that are intended. Most MFIs see microfinance as a cost-effective means of poverty reduction or poverty alleviation, but the detailed intentions and expectations of microfinance programs can differ considerably. A good starting point for impact analysts is the MFI's mission or goal.

Kinds of Impacts

Broadly, impacts of microfinance activities fall into three categories:
- Economic
- Sociopolitical or cultural
- Personal or psychological.

Within each of these categories there are different levels of effect and different targets.

ECONOMIC IMPACTS. Economic impacts can be at the level of the economy itself. A large MFI reaching hundreds of thousands of clients may expect or aim at impact in terms of changes in economic growth in a region or sector.
- One MFI may seek outcomes at the level of the enterprise. If so, it will look for business expansion or transformation of the enterprise as the primary impact.
- Another may seek net gains in the income within a subsector of the informal economy (for example, the operators and owners of tricycle rickshaws).
- Another may seek impact in terms of aggregate accumulation of wealth at the level of the community or household.
- Another may seek positive impacts in terms of income or economic resource "protection" (reducing the vulnerability of poor people through what has come to be called consumption smoothing).

SOCIOPOLITICAL OR CULTURAL IMPACTS. An MFI may seek a shift in the political-economic status of a particular subsector.
- A project aimed at credit for tricycle rickshaw drivers may hope that the drivers' increased business will enable them to move collectively to formal status, either by forming an association or by being able to change policy in their favor.
- An MFI in a remote rural area may expect to help shift rural people from a barter to a monetarized economy.
- Another may hope for changes in power (and status) relationships. For example, an MFI that targets a minority ethnic group may seek impact in terms of

---

Box 2.8 The Impact of Finance on the Rural Economy of India

A RECENT STUDY OF RURAL FINANCE IN INDIA ANALYZES data for 1972 to 1981 for 85 rural districts. The study found that the Indian government had pursued a policy of rapid, forced expansion of commercial banks into rural areas. This expansion resulted in a rapid increase of nonagricultural rural employment and a modest increase in the rural wage rate. By inference the study concludes that the policy must have significantly increased the growth of the nonagricultural rural sector. These findings suggest that the expansion of commercial banks into rural areas eliminated severe constraints in rural financial markets and led to significant deepening of rural finance.

The Indian government also pursued a policy of directing commercial banks and the cooperative credit institutions to lend specifically for agriculture. The study found that the expansion of rural and agricultural credit volumes had a small positive impact on aggregate crop output. This small increase is accounted for by a large increase in fertilizer use and by increased investments in animals and irrigation pumpsets. At the same time, agricultural employment declined. This implies that the policy of forced lending to agriculture had more impact on the substitution of capital for labor than on agricultural output, a clearly counterproductive outcome when the abundance of labor in India is considered.

The study compares the modest increase in agricultural output with the costs to the government of the directed and modestly subsidized credit to agriculture. The government costs include rough estimates of the transaction costs, interest subsidy, and loan losses in the system. Assuming a default rate of 10 percent, the findings suggest that the value of the extra agricultural output triggered by the targeted credit almost covered the government's cost of providing it. Of course, farmers have additional costs in making their investments that are not included in the government's costs.

These findings indicate that deepening the system of rural financial intermediation in India had high payoffs in rural growth, employment, and welfare, but that specifically targeting credit to agriculture was of doubtful benefit.

Source: Binswanger and Khandker 1995.

---

changing the balance of power between that group and the local majority group.

- Another may seek, as a primary impact, the redistribution of assets (and power or decisionmaking) at the household level (for example, shifting part of economic decisionmaking from men to women).
- Another may seek changes in children's nutrition or education as the result of a microfinance activity aimed at their mothers.

PERSONAL OR PSYCHOLOGICAL IMPACTS. Microfinance can have impacts on the borrower's sense of self.

These impacts are the other half of empowerment effects. The first half is in a sense political—people achieve more power in the household or community as the result of financial services. The second half is internal and has to do with the person's changed view of self. Such a change, if positive, can prepare the way for other changes. For example, a person who feels more confident may be willing to take new kinds of risks, such as starting or expanding a business.

Of course, all three general impact categories (as well as the different levels and targets) can shift in terms of which are primary and which are secondary effects. Finally, an impact from one of these categories can in itself cause an impact in one or more of the others.

What Kinds of Impacts Have We Seen with Microfinance?

In the short history of microfinance impact analysis, we have seen relatively little impact on a macro level. However, few MFIs aim for impacts at the level of the economy as a whole.

With regard to impacts at the level of microenterprises in the informal economy, the body of evidence suggests that microenterprise credit does not result in significant net gains in employment, but it can and does lead to increased use of family labor. We can state that there is as yet no solid evidence of business growth and transformation as the result of microenterprise credit, but there is evidence of credit enabling enterprises to survive (remain in business) in crises.

The microfinance field has not yet amassed a large body of well-researched impact analyses. In recent years there have been reviews of existing impact studies, and these as well as other research into the nature of poverty at the grassroots have begun to interact with the discipline of impact analysis. As a result, the questions have

begun to change. New empirical evidence makes it possible to redirect some of the impact questions and with them microfinance itself.

Johnson and Rogaly (1997), for example, provide a useful distinction between three sources of poverty:
- Lack of income
- Vulnerability to income fluctuations
- Powerlessness (few choices and little control).

Interventions can therefore promote income, protect income, or empower people. They point out that most MFIs, especially those run by NGOs, measure (or more often estimate) only the first of these. Thus they look only at income changes as the result of credit (Johnson and Rogaly 1997) This is gradually changing.

AT THE HOUSEHOLD LEVEL. While many MFIs still direct credit to preexisting informal sector microenterprises, many others now direct credit specifically to women who are engaged in what could be called an income-generating activity rather than a business. These MFIs are less concerned about whether the credit is used for "business purposes." A few MFIs also explicitly lend for consumption and seek impacts at the household level.

Making households and the household economy the targets of microfinance is increasing as research shows how important it is to reduce the economic insecurity of poor people, not by raising their income, but by "protecting" what little they do have and reducing their vulnerability (Corbett 1988).

A recent review of research on impact discusses the concept of the "household economic portfolio" as the sum total of human physical and financial resources, which is in a dynamic relationship to the sum total of household consumption, production, and investment activities (Dunn 1996). This very realistic approach to the way in which credit is used by many poor borrowers helps us to understand that the categories of "borrowing for production" and "borrowing for consumption" are not always useful in practice.

AT THE INDIVIDUAL LEVEL. Similarly, as the household—seen as a tiny economy in itself—became a guiding concept in impact analysis, formal economic models of household decisionmaking have entered into economic thinking. For example, "the role of individual preferences, resources and bargaining power in intra-household deci-sion making" is now recognized as important (Chen and Dunn 1996). Such concepts are coming into use as ways to map changes at both the household level (as a social and economic unit) and among the persons living in the household. Thus, while the evidence of significant impacts on health and nutrition are negligible and the results on education are mixed as a result of microfinance interven-tions, we are now able to see "empowerment" outcomes for women that are significant. (It should be emphasized that we are referring to changes attributable to credit only. There are studies indicating that when credit services are combined with health education or nutrition education services to groups, they do result in improvements to health, nutrition, and education.)

Impact Proxies

Doing impact analysis well (and therefore credibly) can be difficult and expensive. Addressing this dilemma, there is a school of thinking that advocates certain "proxies" for impact. Otero and Rhyne have summarized recent micro-finance history by saying that there has been an important shift from focusing on the individual firm or client of financial services to focusing on the institutions providing services. This financial systems approach "necessarily relax-es its attention to 'impact' in terms of measurable enter-prise growth and focuses instead on measures of increased access to financial services" (Otero and Rhyne 1994).

Willingness to pay is sometimes viewed as a proxy for impact. Essentially, this view derives from a market eco-nomics paradigm—the clients are customers; if the prod-uct or service is made available to them and they buy it, then there is value. Therefore, microfinance impact analysis should concentrate on evidence of good outreach and evidence of willingness to pay.

The rational for the willingness-to-pay test of impact is that financial services usually require clients to pay the cost of acquiring the service in the form of interest pay-ments and fees as well as the transaction and opportunity cost of the time required to come to group meetings or to deal with other aspects of the loan process. If clients use the services (credit) repeatedly and, therefore, pay for them repeatedly (and on time), it is evident that they value the services more than the cost. One can surmise, therefore, that the client believes that the benefits (impact) of the service on their lives exceeds the cost.

High repayment rates and low arrears can be taken as prima facie evidence of willingness to pay. (This can also be applied to savings services; if people continue to uti-lize the savings services on an MFI, it can be assumed that the service is valued.)

But there are some caveats to this test. For example, when a client uses a service only once (and drops out) or if the service is priced below its market value (for example, through subsidized interest rates), it is unclear whether this service would still be valued if the cost were raised to a sustainable amount. The willingness-to-pay test may also provide unclear results if a single service is linked to other services (such as nutrition edu-cation), if coercion is involved (as when a woman is forced by her husband to take out a loan), or if the intrahousehold effects are mixed (for example, a decline in girls' school attendance due to increased labor demands at home).

Thus while willingness to pay is a low-cost, simple proxy for impact, the weaknesses are substantial and include the following considerations:

- The magnitude of impact is hard to determine.
- Intrahousehold effects are not captured.
- Long-term development impact (poverty reduction) is unclear.

Perhaps the biggest argument against market-deter-mined proxies such as willingness to pay is that they pre-sume that microfinance is a product for the marketplace like any other. If microfinance were merely a product there would be little concern to look beyond willingness to pay, just as the sellers of cigarettes construe their prof-its as sufficient evidence of the success of their product. Microfinance, however, is intended as a tool for poverty reduction, which is why many experts argue that analyz-ing its impact on poverty is an unavoidable task (see Hulme 1997, who states clearly that monitoring MFI performance in not enough).

Client-Oriented Impact Analysis

The other school of thought about impact analysis consists of those who believe that attempts must be made to assess, analyze, and measure direct impacts. Unfortunately, the dilemma of cost and the inherent difficulty of conducting such an analysis well have been persistent problems, which have led to a general avoidance of the task. Few MFIs invest much in impact analysis, and the literature on microfinance and microenterprise development has been remarkably short on discussions of the subject. (for example, the *Small Enterprise Development Journal* has had very few articles on the subject in the past seven years). One exception is PRODEM in Bolivia (box 2.9).

We stated earlier that what one measures is related to an MFI's mission and goals. If, for example, the MFI's mission is poverty reduction, a further question to be asked is: How does the MFI intervene on behalf of the poor? If the provision of credit is the main instrument, then regardless of whether the focus is on increasing income or household economic portfolio effects or empowerment outcomes, the ultimate subject for any impact research will of necessity be human beings. This is where most of the methodological dilemmas begin.

THE DILEMMA OF THE HUMAN SUBJECT AS A "DYNAMIC TARGET." If an MFI wants to effect positive change in the lives of poor people, the more the expected impact is the result of a direct intervention, the more the analysis will encounter the complexity of human dynamics. For microfinance aimed at poverty reduction, the heart of the impact measurement problem is that the subjects are human beings. As such they are unique and also embedded in a culture and a society. And as if it were not enough to deal with these three variables (the culture, the society, and the person), all three can and do change at different rates of speed.

If the mission of a development project were to build a dam to irrigate thousands of acres of previously non-arable land, the impact of such goals could be assessed with some confidence. The impact of the dam on the land could be accurately measured. There could be little doubt of findings that pointed to a specific number of hectares of improved soil and a resulting number of tons of food produced where none had grown before. There would, of course, be impacts on people's lives, and these would be more difficult to measure, but then they were not the stated objectives of the project.

Box 2.9 PRODEM's Impact and Market Anaylsis Project

PRODEM IS A BOLIVIAN NONPROFIT ORGANIZATION THAT provides support to the microenterprise sector with the aim of improving the quality of life for informal sector entrepreneurs. In 1995 Calmeadow, a Canadian nonprofit organization working in the field of microfinance, developed an impact study for PRODEM. Unlike traditional approaches to impact analysis, which aim to link changes in borrowers' quality of life to their use of financial services, this impact study was designed to provide direct feedback on not only the changes that may occur in the lives of PRODEM's clients during the period that they are associated with PRODEM, but also on their changing credit needs and the evolving nature of their productive activities. It was anticipated that the information generated would help PRODEM to further develop its lending products to enhance the services it offers as a rural microlender.

The study was designed to analyze the systems of relationships that make up the productive lives of PRODEM's clients (suppliers, traders, transporters, and buyer markets) and to give insight to PRODEM's current and potential role as part of the financial strategies (for both production and household consumption) of these clients.

The study was based on six objectives:

- Evaluate indicators of socioeconomic change for clients and their households over a three-year period, which can be linked to their use of PRODEM credit services.
- Assess changes in PRODEM client businesses and productive activities resulting from access to PRODEM credit services.
- Evaluate the impact of PRODEM credit services in selected economic subsectors to provide insight into the operating context of PRODEM clients' businesses.
- Gain enhanced understanding of rural clients' markets to assess credit needs and market opportunities.
- Use the data collection and analytical processes as a staff development opportunity for both field officers and head office staff through exposure to new methodological approaches.
- Contribute to the field of impact assessment generally by developing an innovative study model that incorporates analysis of the impact of new credit on local markets and ties impacts at the household and business levels with changes occurring in the markets on which they depend.

The study used data collected through surveys and in-depth interviews in two areas in which PRODEM operates and in one control community.

Source: Burnett 1995.

In the case of microfinance we see a similar dilemma, but with a difference. If an MFI aims at providing financial services to the poor to reduce their poverty, then the institution cannot take refuge in simply measuring how well it made services available (which is analogous to how well the dam was constructed). Because the stated end result—reducing poverty—is fully measurable only in direct relationship to the lives of human beings, the number of possible effects, distortions, and permutations of those effects is, to put it mildly, far greater than in the case when a project's direct impact is intended to be an increase in arable land as the result of building a dam.

The dynamic interaction of individual humans, their local society, and their culture can produce surprising results and can spoil a positive impact. Yaqub (1995) describes a group-based microcredit scheme operated by BRAC in Bangladesh. The scheme was deemed successful—as measured by increases in aggregate wealth of the members. But it is precisely because of aggregate wealth that the nature of the relationships in the group and its culture began to change. Because neither all persons in the group nor their "life chances" are the same, some gradually became better off than others. As Yaqub showed, some members with new wealth began to feel that they had less to lose by ignoring group pressure to repay and thus became defaulters. This was a function of the new power of their wealth rather than their inability to repay. If the defaults caused by the successful use of credit resulted in the dissolution of the group and the subsequent ineligibility of other members for future loans, even *their* gains might be in jeopardy. Simply put, if the impact analysis story stopped at aggregate wealth accumulation, it would miss a very important sequel.

However, even before one gets to these unintended consequences and feedback loop effects, there are other practical problems involved in dealing with human subjects.

CLIENT TRANSPARENCY AND HONESTY. It is commonly understood that money is fungible—that is, someone may take a loan for the stated purpose of starting or financing a business and then put the loan proceeds into the business, or they may use it to pay for their child's education or wedding and then use other household income to put into the business. If clients feel that they will not receive another loan if they have not actually used the preceding loan for the stated purpose, they may not accurately report the use of the loan.

In addition, there are many other reasons not to report accurately, including:

- Embarrassment
- Fear of taxation
- Not wanting others in the community to know
- Wanting to impress the person asking the question
- Wanting to please the person asking the question
- A different way of calculating things than the questionnaire—that is, the respondent genuinely may not know the answers to the questions.

THE VESTED INTEREST OF THE ASSESSMENT TEAM. Those conducting the impact assessment may have an interest in the outcome of the study and thus consciously or unconsciously may distort some responses. Anyone who is paid to do something may have a concern to please the agency paying them, especially when they are being paid to conduct an impact assessment for the agency whose project is being evaluated. Such an interest can be expressed unconsciously, even in the very design of the survey instrument or the sample selection. At the level of data collection, it is possible that enumerators, interviewers, or translators may subtly avoid, ignore, or not notice data that may be offensive to the agency sponsoring the evaluation.

THE ATTRIBUTION DILEMMA. Attributing an income change to the credit taken by someone requires knowing in detail all the sources and uses of funds by the client (which in turn is related to the fungibility issue). Finding out the client's sources and uses of funds is made difficult by the challenge of respondent honesty and transparency as well as the fundamental fact that the livelihood strategies of most people, especially poor people, are complex, involving daily judgments about (and juggling of) new opportunities and obstacles as well as new costs and old obligations.

Attribution further requires knowing all the other events and influences that occurred while the credit intervention was undertaken and separating them from the specific impacts of the credit and savings program.

There are other dynamic interactions that are functions of microfinance itself. The use of one financial service can affect or influence the demand and usefulness of others. These, too, are difficult to trace.

HYPOTHETICAL IMPACTS IN THE ABSENCE OF SERVICES. A different facet of the attribution dilemma is the difficulty in determining how outcomes might have been different if no intervention had been made. To determine this requires, at the least, the establishment of baselines and control groups. These are tasks that are not only costly but in some sense impossible to do perfectly, since it is extremely unlikely that one can find a sample of people who are similar in every way to another sample of people, other than they did not receive a loan and others did. Moreover, estimating those similarities and conducting baseline surveys is subject to the same kinds of reporting errors as we have already noted. Still, one can get a sense of what might have happened in the absence of the services by looking at how many other financing options exist, how accessible they are to the same clientele, and how attractively they are priced (including pricing the social transaction costs).

Similar to the question of what would have happened if the loan had not been made, one must also consider what other options for interventions were available and what resources could have been used for interventions, other than the provision of financial services.

TEMPORARY IMPACTS. An additional dilemma is the question of the ultimate value of the finding. Assume that one finds that an intervention was or appeared to be successful in raising people's incomes or reducing their powerlessness. Have they moved across the poverty line? Have the local structures in which their lives have been embedded in the past altered in significant ways? In short, how lasting are the changes? It is empirically evident that small changes can be undone very quickly. Small incremental moves upward in income or nutrition levels or changes in power relationships within the family can be reduced or wiped out by other reactions and forces, some of which are environmental, macroeconomic (even related to world trade), or political.

The usefulness of a loan obviously depends on circumstances, which can change. If, for example, poor women take loans repeatedly through several cycles, this simply says that they have been able to find ways to ensure repayment. Especially in cases where women do not have regular and direct access to income, field studies have shown that they borrow money from others in the family, take from remittance income, or even take from their own stocks of food to repay the loan. There are highly variable reasons why they may make an effort that can appear to be a sign of how much they value the service. They may borrow

because the loan comes at a time of particular need, because someone else has asked them to take the loan on his or her behalf, because they fear loss of face in their group, because they are hedging their bets in the belief that they may get a larger loan in the future, or even because they are counting on being able to default later on (when loan follow-up eventually slacked off), based on experience with past credit interventions. In the case research for the Sustainable Banking with the Poor project, dropout rates have been increasing, particularly among target groups in which the prospects for sustained income growth are not promising.

When Should Impact Be Assessed?

The question of when to conduct an impact assessment is not just a practical matter of cost and methodological advantage. As with the other aspects of impact, this question also relates to each MFI's mission and purpose.

IMPACT ASSESSMENT BEFORE INTERVENTION. If the mission contains an absolute commitment to reach directly the poorest segment of the population (as is the case for Credit and Savings for the Hard-core Poor Network (CASHPOR) in the Philippines) then conducting a baseline impact assessment prior to the initiation of financial services is essential to finding out who is going to be the main beneficiary of the loans in terms of relative wealth. This does not have to be expensive. In many villages in Asia, for example, the material used in people's roofs can be a reliable indicator of relative poverty. CASHPOR therefore advocates a house index based simply on comparative measurements of the three dimensions of the house and notation of the roof material (Gibbons 1997b).

IMPACT ASSESSMENT AFTER INTERVENTION. The conventional approach to impact assessment and analysis is to conduct the research after the MFI has been operating for a set period of time, such as three years (a period often imposed by donors). In this approach there are often three phases: first, a baseline study establishing some controls at the beginning of the MFI's operations, then an interim or midterm impact assessment, followed 18 months or 2 years later by the final assessment. Increasingly, this approach is being viewed as inadequate.

IMPACT ASSESSMENT DURING INTERVENTION. Those who are most concerned with human and social dynamics and the methodological problems they present recommend that impact assessment be done on a continuous basis and that someone from the MFI remain involved with a representative cross section of clients over time. This is coming to be called "impact monitoring." Obviously, this approach will likely involve keeping someone on the MFI staff full-time for this purpose.

Methods of Impact Assessment

In assessing the reviews of microfinance impact studies conducted in recent years (for example, Gaile and Foster 1996) and recalling the dilemmas outlined above, it is tempting to conclude that the number of problems unearthed is so great that the prospects of overcoming them are slim. However, the opposite seems to be the case. The consensus seems to be that *multiple methods* (as opposed to a single method) *must be used* and that combining qualitative and quantitative approaches may be the only way to overcome these dilemmas (Hulme 1995; Carvalho and White 1997).

The growing literature on microfinance impact assessment is replete with details on the pitfalls of various approaches. For example, Gaile and Foster reviewed 11 studies and concluded that "some form of quasi experimental design is appropriate" along with multivariate statistical analysis. Their recommendations include an overall sample size of about 500, "which should allow for effective use of control variables and for dealing with problems associated with longitudinal analysis; longitudinal studies should have an interval of 18 to 24 months between data collection rounds." At the same time, their review concluded that "none of the reviewed studies successfully controlled for the fungibility of resources between household and enterprise."

They recommend that control methods include:
- "Statistically equated control methods," which they feel are sufficient to address most control issues
- Gender, which is a critical control variable
- Continued efforts to control for fungibility
- Control methods that are a function of the data available.

Among other lacunae in the studies they reviewed were:
- Minimal consideration as to the location of the MFI, which is a major determinant of success.
- Too little attention to alternative methodologies, such as qualitative methods and counterfactual analysis

- Scant notice to questionnaire concerns, such as survey fatigue and the need for back translation.
- Infrequent inclusion of issues, such as politics, favoritism, corruption, accountability, and leakages, as part of the design.

Measuring asset accumulation at the *household level* is an approach that is also increasingly recommended as a focus of impact study, especially as a way to get around the inherent difficulties in measuring income changes accurately.

Barnes (1996) identifies six approaches to measuring assets in the microenterprise literature:
- Attaching a current monetary value to assets and liabilities
- Specifying whether or not a specific asset is held, which may be used to discuss the structure of the holding or other qualitative dimensions
- Computing the flow value from productive assets
- Ranking assets based on their assumed monetary value of other qualities
- Constructing an index that is a composite of measures
- Determining the meaning of the assets to the owners and the social effects of the assets.

Barnes also notes that the biggest quantitative problem with respect to asset accumulation involves depreciating and valuing physical assets.

It is because these pitfalls are unavoidable that there is a convergence of opinion that a mix of methods needs to be used. The basics of both quantitative and qualitative methods are reviewed briefly below.

Fundamental Characteristics of Qualitative Approaches

The most commonly prescribed alternatives to quantitative instruments and measures of impact fall within the fields of sociology and anthropology. The most recent approach is the rubric of participant observation, which is the classic mode of anthropological fieldwork. Participant observation is not so much a single method as a combination of methods and techniques used to deal with the problems posed by the complexity of social organizations. (As noted above, lone humans are complex enough, and in reality humans are almost never alone. They are always part of a social unit, with levels of complexity all the greater.) As one textbook on the subject of participant observation puts it, "this blend of techniques …involves some amount of genuine social interaction in the field with the subjects of the study, some direct observation of relevant events, some formal and a great deal of informal interviewing, some systematic counting... and open-endedness in the directions the study takes." (McCall and Simmons 1969).

The important general characteristics of such approaches usually include the following:

- *Intensivity* (a continuous or regular presence among clients over time). This enables the researcher to deepen his or her understanding of what is going on and in turn enables trust to develop on the part of the respondent. Naturally, one cannot be present among people over time without social interaction—hence the word "participant" in the term "participant observation."
- *Structured observation.* Observation is not as passive a function as it might seem. The researcher studying microfinance impacts has in mind some hypotheses about indicators and will naturally pay close attention to them. They are thus part of a structured observation plan. The actual activity in the field may include formal interviewing, using a questionnaire or interview guide. The observation part comes into play as a form of research control. As a simple example, in asking about household assets a respondent may mention having recently purchased a radio or mirror. If the interview takes place in the respondent's home, the trained (observant) interviewer will look around to see if the radio or mirror is in sight. If it is not, the interviewer may then ask where it is.
- *Triangulation.* Triangulation involves checking data with respondents and cross-checking with others to get different points of view of the same phenomenon. Careful use of triangulation helps to deal with the problems of the inherently untrustworthy respondent and causality.
- *Open-endedness.* This is the characteristic that causes some methodological distress, because it implies that there may be no closure to the effort or that it has no methodological rigor. In fact, the notion of open-endedness is a response (again) to human dynamism and complexity. It is another way of saying that the impact assessment process must be prepared to go where the data lead. Often findings or indications of findings are a surprise and may not fit a prior hypothesis. In many cases these findings, especially if not numerically significant, are dismissed. In participant observation the objective is to *make use* of such findings by following their "tracks" as it were, to see what significance they may have.

Translated into the technique of "sampling" (the process of selecting those with whom to interact), open-endedness means using what is called "nonprobability" sampling. This begins with common sense—ensuring diversity by choosing a range of people in a range of situations. But it also means being in position to take advantage of an accidental meeting with someone or to follow a lead.

Rapid rural appraisal methods are derivative of classic sociological and anthropological approaches in that they also involve the use of semistructured interviews with key informants, participant observation, and the methodological principles of triangulation and open-endedness. But rapid rural appraisal is more interactive and aims at a shorter duration. It also employs such new techniques as (Robert Chambers work in Carvalho and White 1997):

- *Focus groups* with 5 to 12 participants from similar backgrounds or situations (these may be observants or the subjects under analysis)
- *Social mapping and modeling* drawn by participants (often on the ground) to indicate which institutions and structures of their community are important in their lives
- *Seasonality maps* or calendars on which communities show how various phenomena in their lives vary over the course of a year
- *Daily time-use analysis*
- *Participatory linkage diagramming* showing chains of causality
- *Venn diagrams* showing the relative importance of different institutions or individuals in the community
- *Wealth ranking.*

Fundamental Characteristics of Quantitative Approaches

By definition quantitative approaches (the word "quantitative" derives from the Latin "quantus," meaning "of what size") involve quanta (units) or things that can be counted, including income, household expenditures, and wages. Because conclusions must be drawn from these numbers, the rules of statistics must be rigorously applied. Probability is one of the most important of these rules, and thus sampling (choosing which persons, households, or enterprises to survey) is extremely important and has to be done carefully to ensure that randomness is achieved (that is, that every unit in the population to be studied has an equal chance of being selected). Probability theory demands that the numbers of units to be studied be relatively large and widespread to have statistical validity.

Quantitative approaches to microfinance impacts rely on predesigned and pretested questionnaires. These are formal rather than unstructured, because the responses must be comparable and easy to count. Because survey questionnaires are structured and relatively fixed, little interactivity is likely between surveyor and respondent. As a result, survey questionnaires rely almost totally on respondent recall. This may be unreliable if the events being recalled are far back in time.

Because of the widespread coverage necessary, the cost of designing, testing, and administering quantitative approaches is usually greater than that of qualitative approaches.

The reason quantitative approaches have traditionally been attractive to policymakers, however, derives from the notion that there is strength in numbers. Numbers offer confidence and reliability precisely because they are presumed to represent true measures. If the methods used have been applied with rigor, the precision of the results can be verified.

Appendix 1 provides a matrix comparing some of the major quantitative methods used in microfinance impact analysis.

In general, the available quantitative methods fall into three categories:

- Experimental methods
- Quasi-experimental methods
- Nonexperimental methods.

Experimental methods involve a natural or devised experiment in which some randomly chosen group is given the "treatment" or, in development terms, the "intervention" (here, microfinance services). The results are then compared to a randomly selected group of controls from whom the treatment is withheld. The randomization guarantees that there are no differences—neither observable nor unobservable—between the two groups. Consequently, in theory, if there is a significant difference in outcomes, it can only be the effect of the treatment. Although the role of experimental methods has been expanded in recent years, there are many cases in which such experiments are difficult or impossible because of the cost or the moral or political implications (Deaton 1997, 92).

Quasi-experimental methods attempt to mimic the analysis of controlled experiments, with treatment and control groups created from different people. The differences between the treatment and control groups may be observable or unobservable due to their nonrandom selection.

Nonexperimental methods use nonexperimental (nonrandom) survey data to look at the differences in behavior between different people and relate the degree of exposure to the treatment to variations in outcomes. The absence of a control group separates such methods from quasi-experimental methods.

Econometrics is an analytical technique that applies statistical methods to economic problems. Econometric techniques have been used extensively to analyze data gathered using quasi- and nonexperimental methods. Economists and econometricians have been studying statistical methods for program evaluation for at least 25 years (see Moffitt 1991, 291). During this time many econometric techniques have been developed to mitigate the various problems associated with nonrandom data selection. Some of the techniques available for performing econometric analysis are described below, along with their advantages and disadvantages.

Perhaps the most fundamental choice in an econometric analysis is to select a model. Every analysis of an economic, social, or physical system is based on some underlying logical structure, known as a model, which describes the behavior of the agents in the system and is the basic framework of analysis. In economics, as in the physical sciences, this model is expressed in equations describing the behavior of economic and related variables. The model that an investigator formulates might consist of a single equation or a system involving several equations.

In single-equation specification (regression analysis), the analyst selects a single (dependent) variable (denoted as Y) whose behavior the researcher is interested in explaining. The investigator then identifies one or a number of (independent) variables (denoted by X) that have causal effects on the dependent variable. In some econometric studies the investigator may be interested in more than one dependent variable and hence will formulate several equations at the same time. These are known as simultaneous equation models (Ramanathan 1997, 6)

To estimate the econometric model that a researcher specifies, sample data on the dependent and independent variables are needed (Hulme 1997, 1). Data are usually drawn in one of two settings. A cross section is a sample of a number of observational units all drawn at the same point in time. A time series is a set of observations drawn on the same observational unit at a number of (usually evenly spaced) points in time. Many recent studies have been based on time-series cross section, which generally consist of the same cross section observed at several points in time. Since the typical data set of this sort consists of a large number of cross-sectional units observed at a few points in time, the common term "panel data set" is more fitting for this type of study (Greene 1997, 102).

Comparisons of Quantitative and Qualitative Approaches

The major underlying difference between quantitative and qualitative approaches is their philosophical position on "reality." The qualitative approach essentially says there are multiple forms of reality and which "reality" is in play depends on whose point of view one takes. Advocates of the qualitative approach say, for example, that poverty cannot be defined only by the donor or project personnel but must also be defined by the poor themselves, because poverty is more than simply lack of income. The quantitative approach essentially assumes that there is only one reality that can be counted. In the case of poverty, the quantitative approach would think it appropriate to have external surveyors determine adequate poverty indicators such as amount of income, assets, access to basic services, health, nutrition, potable water, and other measurable variables, either by yes or no answers or actual counting.

These basic differences have been summed up in the commonly held notion that quantitative impact analysis is more of a "science," while qualitative approaches are more of an "art" (Hulme 1997, 1).

Whereas for *data* in quantitative methods the variables (for example, food expenditure) must be countable, in qualitative methods only the responses to questions or the number of times a phenomenon was observed can be counted, since the variables are attitudes, preferences, and priorities. As a result, while quantitative approaches are not prone to errors involving the representativeness of the sample, they are highly prone to what is called "nonsampling error." The opposite is the case with qualitative approaches.

The *processes* by which *both* quantitative and qualitative methods are implemented necessarily depends on field workers, whether employed as enumerators, surveyors,

interviewers, participant observers, translators, or focus group facilitators. A large potential weakness in both quantitative and qualitative methods is that the quality of these personnel can vary greatly. Consequently, if impact analysis is to be done, those paying for it should invest up front in high-quality field personnel. This implies careful recruiting, training, and supervision, as well as a sensible remuneration policy.

Integrating Methodologies

"The key is to tap the breadth of the quantitative approach and the depth of the qualitative approach. The exact combination of qualitative and quantitative work will depend on the purpose of the study and the available time, skills, and resources. In general, integrating methodologies can result in better measurement; confirming, refuting, enriching, and explaining can result in better analysis; and merging the quantitative and qualitative findings into one set of policy recommendations can lead to better action." (Carvalho and White 1997)

Carvalho and White (1997) recommend specific types of integration such as:

- Using the quantitative survey data to select qualitative samples
- Using the quantitative survey to design the interview guide for the qualitative work
- Using qualitative work to pretest the quantitative questionnaire
- Using qualitative work to explain unanticipated results from quantitative data.

The Choice of Unit of Analysis

Regardless of the unit of analysis (the individual client, the enterprise, the household, or the community), it is important to investigate, get to know, and interview nonusers as well as users of the financial service. Nonusers can be of two types: those who were and ceased to be users (dropouts) and those who were never users.

THE CLIENT AS A CLIENT. This unit of analysis focuses on the individual client as a client of the microfinance services. The main purpose of such an analysis is for market research—to gather the clients' perceptions of the services so as to improve them. This has validity if concerns about outreach have come up or if there are dropouts.

THE CLIENT AS AN INDIVIDUAL. Both quantitative and qualitative methods can focus on the client as an individual (also called intrahousehold impact analysis when it extends to members of the client's household). The advantage of this level of investigation is that individual clients are easily defined and identified. They can be surveyed or interacted with in focus groups through interviews or participant observation.

Among the impacts to be sought at this level are changes in income, allocation of income (to pay for girls' schooling, for example), changes in behavior (such as willingness to take risks), changes in status or sense of self, and so on.

The disadvantages of focusing on the client as an individual is that estimations of the magnitude of impact can be highly subjective and are likely to go beyond the person or persons looked at. Thus it becomes difficult to disaggregate the impacts on the primary subjects and those that extend to others.

THE ENTERPRISE. Using the enterprise as the unit of analysis assumes that the goal of the MFI is largely economic: a change in the overall prospects of the enterprise (growth, greater profits, increase in production, higher sales, acquisition of a productive asset, general increase in competitiveness, or some evidence of business transformation, such as moving to a fixed location).

The main methodological advantage of this unit of analysis is the availability of well-understood analytical tools, such as profitability and return on investment (Hulme 1997, 6). One disadvantage lies in defining the enterprise clearly enough for comparability with other enterprises. Many microenterprises are survivalist activities rather than businesses in the conventional sense. Thus the information needed for analysis will often be lacking. The main disadvantage, however, is the problem of fungibility: the fact that there is no sure way to tell whether loan money has gone to benefit the enterprise or the household (especially when this distinction is not clear to the entrepreneur).

THE SUBSECTOR. This unit and level of analysis is rarely if ever used in microfinance impact analysis. It is brought to the reader's attention to recall that the level of analysis depends on the nature of the intervention and the intended outcomes. It is possible that a microfinance program is designed to focus on one subsector of the economy. Thus besides using the enterprises in that subsector (for example, all basket weavers) as units of analysis, the entire subsector would also be looked at in the aggregate. Indicators could include jobs created; aggregate output; changes in subcontracts with other subsectors; alleviating constraints affecting the whole subsector, such as input supply; and price changes brought about by changes in the subsector. Needless to say, this level of analysis is highly research-oriented and requires significant time and resources.

THE HOUSEHOLD ECONOMIC PORTFOLIO. This approach looks at the household, the individual, his or her economic activity, and the local society in which he or she is embedded and traces interactions among them. Such an analysis is difficult and costly and usually requires both a high degree of technical specialization and a good knowledge of local contexts. It can involve living on site for a period of time. The payoff, however, is that it provides a more comprehensive picture of the impacts and the linkages between different parts of the whole.

In summary, impact analysis is not easy or without real costs. At a time in microfinance when institutional sustainability is an almost universal goal, finding ways to pay for impact analysis poses serious challenges. However, the future of microfinance may be at stake as a deliberate tool for poverty reduction. It is probably best if provisions for impact analysis are made part of MFI activities from the beginning and the subject is given the same priority as financial sustainability. Impact analysis, for all its difficulties—and they are daunting—can be done well. The current consensus seems to be that the first step is to take the task seriously so that appropriate care and talent are devoted to carrying it out.

Appendix 1. Quantitative Impact Assessment

Most Common Impacts Analyzed with Quantitative Methods

Enterprise level	Household level	Individual level
Output	Income	Women's empowerment
Asset accumulation	Specialization	Control over finances and other resources
Risk management	Diversification	Contraceptive use
Technology	Asset accumulation	Children
Employment	Savings	Survival rates
Management	Consumption	Health and nutrition
Market	Food	Education
Income	Nonfood	Exploitation

Most Common Quantitative Methods Used to Analyze Impacts

Quantitative method	Advantages	Disadvantages
Experimental	▪ Easiest to identify the effect of the program since treatment and control groups are randomized	▪ Often difficult to find or create situation where a true experiment exists.
Quasi-experimental	▪ Can solve some problems plaguing nonexperimental data by simulating a true control group	▪ Hard to create a control group without bias ▪ Some assumptions regarding the data are required
Nonexperimental	▪ Assumptions made are rarely case-specific and can lead, therefore, to generalizable results	▪ Most complicated method for separating the effects of program participation from other factors ▪ Many assumptions are required of the data, which may not be met

Econometric Options

Quantitative method	Advantages	Disadvantages
Choice of model		
Simple linear regression (two-variable regression)	▪ Simplest of models ▪ Can be used to handle nonlinear relationships provided the model is linear in parameters	▪ Assumptions required are often unrealistic for most applications (estimates are unbiased, consistent, and efficient)
Mulitvariate regression	▪ The assumptions of the simple linear regression model can be relaxed somewhat, allowing for a more generalized application ▪ Can accommodate nonlinearities ▪ Allows for the control of a subset of independent (explanatory) variables to examine the effect of selected independent variables	▪ Inclusion of too many variables can make the relative precision of the individual coefficients worse ▪ Resulting loss of degrees of freedom would reduce the power of the test performed on the coefficients
Simultaneous equation	▪ Allows for the determination of several dependent variables simultaneously	▪ Must consider additional problems of simultaneity and identification

Choice of data set

Single cross section	■ Provides a relatively quick, inexpensive snapshot of a representative group at a given point in time	■ Cannot gauge the dynamics (magnitude or rate) of change at the individual level
Repeated cross section	■ Can track outcomes or behaviors for groups of individuals with less expense and time	■ Cannot gauge the dynamics (magnitude or rate) of change at the individual level
Longitudinal or panel	■ Allows analysis of dynamic changes at the individual level ■ Can be used to measure dynamic changes of the representative group over time	■ Attrition of and change in original panel over time ■ Measurement periods are usually long with high associated costs

Source: Contributed by Stephanie Charitonenko-Church, Sustainable Banking with the Poor Project, World Bank.

Sources and Further Reading

Almeyda, Gloria. 1996. *Money Matters: Reaching Women Microentrepreneurs with Financial Services.* Washington, D.C.: United Nations Development Fund for Women and Inter-American Development Bank.

Barnes, Carolyn. 1996. "Assets and the Impact of Microenterprise Finance Programs." AIMS (Assessing the Impact of Microenterprise Services) Brief 6. U.S. Agency for International Development, Washington, D.C.

Benjamin, McDonald, and Joanna Ledgerwood. 1998. "The Association for the Development of Microenterprises (ADEMI): 'Democratising Credit' in the Dominican Republic." Case Study for the Sustainable Banking with the Poor Project, World Bank, Washington, D.C.

Bennett, Lynn. 1993. "Developing Sustainable Financial Systems for the Poor: Where Subsidies Can Help and Where They Can Hurt." Talking notes for the World Bank AGRAP Seminar on Rural Finance, May 26, Washington, D.C.

———. 1997. "A Systems Approach to Social and Financial Intermediation with the Poor." Paper presented at the Banking with the Poor Network/World Bank Asia Regional Conference on Sustainable Banking with the Poor, November 3–7, Bangkok.

Bennett, Lynn, and Mike Goldberg. 1994. *Enterprise Development and Financial Services for Women: A Decade of Bank Experience.* World Bank, Asia Technical Department, Washington, D.C.

Binswanger, Hans, and Shahidur Khandker. 1995. "The Impact of Formal Finance on the Rural Economy of India." *Journal of Development Studies* 32 (2): 234–62.

Blair, Edmund. 1995. "Banking: MEED Special Report." *Middle East Business Weekly* 39 (June): 23–38.

Burnett, Jill. 1995. "Summary Overview of PRODEM Impact and Market Analysis Project." Calmeadow, Toronto, Canada.

Berger, Marguerite, Mayra Buvinic, and Cecilia Jaramillo. 1989. "Impact of a Credit Project for Women and Men Microentrepreneurs in Quito, Ecuador." In Marguerite Berger and Mayra Buvinic, eds., *Women's Ventures: Assistance to the Informal Sector in Latin America.* Hartford, Conn.: Kumarian Press.

Bolinick, Bruce R., and Eric R. Nelson. 1990. "Evaluating the Economic Impact of A Special Credit Programme KIK/KMKP in Indonesia." *Journal of Development Studies;* 26 (2): 299–312.

Carvalho, Soniya, and Howard White. 1997. *Combining the Quantitative and Qualitative Approaches to Poverty Measurement and Analysis: The Practice and Potential.* World Bank Technical Paper 366. Washington, D.C.

CGAP (Consultative Group to Assist the Poorest). 1996. "Financial Sustainability, Targeting the Poorest and Income Impact: Are There Trade-offs for Micro-finance Institutions?" CGAP Focus Note 5. World Bank, Washington, D.C.

Chambers, Robert. 1992. "Rural Appraisal: Rapid, Relaxed and Participatory." Discussion Paper 311. University of Sussex, Institute of Development Studies, United Kingdom.

Chaves, Rodrigo A., and Claudio Gonzalez-Vega. 1994. "Principles of Regulation and Prudential Supervision and Their Relevance for Microenterprise Finance Organizations." In Maria Otero and Elizabeth Rhyne, eds., *The New World of Microenterprise Finance.* W. Hartford, Conn.: Kumarian Press.

Chen, Martha, and Elizabeth Dunn. 1996. "AIMS Brief 3." U.S. Agency for International Development, Washington, D.C.

Christen, Robert Peck, Elisabeth Rhyne, Robert C. Vogel, and Cressida McKean. 1995. *Maximizing the Outreach of Microenterprise Finance: An Analysis of Successful Microfinance Programs.* Program and Operations Assessment Report 10. Washington, D.C.: U.S. Agency for International Development.

Corbett, Jane. 1988. "Famine and Household Coping Strategies." *World Development* 16 (9): 1099–112.

Deaton, A. 1997. *The Analysis of Household Surveys: A Microeconomic Approach to Development Policy.* Baltimore, Md.: The Johns Hopkins University Press.

Downing, Jeanne, and Lisa Daniels. 1992. "Growth and Dynamics of Women Entrepreneurs in Southern Africa." GEMINI Technical Paper 47. U.S. Agency for International Development, Washington, D.C.

Dunn, Elizabeth. 1996. "Households, Microenterprises, and Debt." AIMS Brief 5. U.S. Agency for International Development, Washington, D.C.

Gaile, Gary L., and Jennifer Foster. 1996. "Review of Methodological Approaches to the Study of the Impact of Microenterprise Credit Programs." AIMS (Assessing the Impact of Microenterprise Services project) paper, Management Systems International, Washington, D.C.

Garson, José. 1996. "Microfinance and Anti-Poverty Strategies. A Donor Perspective." United Nations Capital Development Fund Working Paper. UNDCF, New York.

Gibbons, David. 1997a. "Targeting the Poorest and Covering Costs." Paper presented at the Microcredit Summit, February 3, Washington, D.C.

———. 1997b. Remarks made at the Microcredit Summit, February, Washington, D.C.

Goetz, Anne Marie, and Rina Sen Gupta. 1993. "Who Takes Credit? Gender, Power, and Control over Loan Use in Rural Credit Programmes in Bangladesh." Institute of Development Studies, University of Sussex, and Bangladesh Institute of Development Studies, Dhaka.

Goldberg, Mike. 1992. *Enterprise Development Services for Women Clients.* Population and Human Resources, Women in Development. Washington, D.C.: World Bank.

Greene, W.H. 1997. *Econometric Analysis.* Upper Saddle River, N.J.: Prentice Hall.

Hulme, David. 1995. "Finance for the Poor, Poorer, or Poorest? Financial Innovation, Poverty, and Vulner-

ability." Paper presented at the Finance against Poverty Seminar, March 27, Reading University, United Kingdom.

———. 1997. "Impact Assessment Methodologies for Microfinance: A Review." Paper prepared for the CGAP Working Group on Impact Assessment Methodologies, Washington, D.C.

Hulme, David, and Paul Mosley. 1996. *Finance Against Poverty.* London: Routledge.

Johnson, Susan, and Ben Rogaly. 1997. *Microfinance and Poverty Reduction.* London: Oxfam and ActionAid.

Khayatt, Djenan. 1996. *Private Sector Development.* Washington, D.C.: World Bank.

Lapar, Ma. Lucila A., Douglas H. Graham, Richard L. Meyer, and David S. Kraybill. 1995. "Selectivity Bias in Estimating the Effect of Credit on Output: The Case of Rural Non-farm Enterprises in the Philippines." Ohio State University, Department of Agricultural Economics and Rural Sociology, Columbus, Ohio.

Lawai, Hussain. 1994. "Key Features of Islamic Banking." *Journal of Islamic Banking* 11 (4): 7–13.

Ledgerwood, Joanna. 1997. "Albanian Development Fund." Case Study for the Sustainable Banking with the Poor Project. World Bank, Washington, D.C.

Liedhom, Carl, and Donald C. Mead. 1987. "Small Scale Industries in Developing Countries: Empirical Evidence and Policy Implications." International Development Paper 9. Michigan State University, East Lansing, Mich.

Mahajan, Vijay, and Bharti Gupta Ramola. 1996. "Financial Services for the Rural Poor and Women in India: Access and Sustainability." *Journal of International Development* 8 (2): 211–24.

Malhotra, Mohini. 1992. "Poverty Lending and Microenterprise Development: A Clarification of the Issues." GEMINI Working Paper 30. U.S. Agency for International Development, Washington, D.C.

McCall, George J., and J.L. Simmons. 1969. *Issues in Participant Observation.* Reading, Mass.: Addison-Wesley.

McCracken, Jennifer A., Jules N. Pretty, and Gordon R. Conway. 1988. *An Introduction to Rapid Rural Appraisal for Agricultural Development.* London, U.K.: International Institute for Environment and Development, Sustainable Agriculture Programme.

Moffit, R. 1991. "Program Evaluation with Nonexperimental Data." *Evaluation Review* 15 (3): 291–314.

Naponen, Helzi. 1990. "Loans to the Working Poor: A Longitudinal Study of Credit, Gender, and the Household

Economy." PRIE Center for Urban Policy Research, Rutgers University, New Brunswick, N.J.

O'Sullivan, Edmund. 1994. "Islamic Banking: MEED Special Report." *Middle East Business Weekly* 38 (August): 7–13.

Otero, Maria, and Rhyne, Elizabeth, eds. 1994. *The New World of Microenterprise Finance.* West Hartford, Conn.: Kumarian Press.

Parker, Joan, and C. Aleke Dondo. 1995. "Kenya: Kibera's Small Enterprise Sector—Baseline Survey Report." GEMINI Working Paper 17. U.S. Agency for International Development, Washington, D.C.

Paxton, Julia. 1996. "Worldwide Inventory of Microfinance Institutions." Sustainable Banking with the Poor Project, World Bank, Washington, D.C.

Pederson, Glen D. 1997. "The State of the Art in Microfinance. A Summary of Theory and Practice." Sustainable Banking with the Poor Project, World Bank, Washington, D.C.

Pitt, Mark, and Shahidur R. Khandker. 1996. *Household and Intrahousehold Impact of the Grameen Bank and Similar Targeted Credit Programs in Bangladesh.* World Bank Discussion Paper 320. Washington, D.C.

Putnam, Robert D., with Robert Leonardi, and Raffaella Y. Nanetti. 1993. *Making Democracy Work: Civic Traditions in Modern Italy.* Princeton, N.J.: Princeton University Press.

Ramanathan, R. 1997. *Introductory Econometrics with Applications.* Baltimore, Md.: Academic Press.

Rhyne, Elisabeth, and Sharon Holt. 1994. "Women in Finance and Enterprise Development." ESP Discussion Paper 40. World Bank, Washington, D.C.

Schuler, Sidney Ruth, and Syed M. Hashemi. 1994. "Credit Programs, Women's Empowerment and Contraceptive Use in Rural Bangladesh." *Studies in Family Planning* 25 (2): 65–76.

Sebstad, Jennifer, Catherine Neill, Carolyn Barnes, with Gregory Chen. 1995. "Assessing the Impacts of Microenterprise Interventions: A Framework for Analysis." Managing for Results Working Paper 7. U.S. Agency for International Development, Office of Microenterprise Development, Washington, D.C.

Sharif bin Fazil, Muhammad. 1993. "Financial Instruments Conforming to Shariah." *Journal of Islamic Banking* 10 (4): 7–20.

Von Pischke, J.D. 1991. *Finance at the Frontier.* World Bank, Economic Development Institute. Washington, D.C.

Waterfield, Charles, and Ann Duval. 1996. *CARE Savings and Credit Sourcebook.* Atlanta, Ga: CARE.

Webster, Leila, Randall Riopelle, and Anne-Marie Chidzero. 1996. *World Bank Lending for Small Enterprises, 1989–1993.* World Bank Technical Paper 311. Washington, D.C.

Weidemann, Jean. 1993. "Financial Services for Women." GEMINI Technical Note 3. U.S. Agency for International Development, Washington, D.C.

Yaqub, S. 1995. "Empowered to Default? Evidence from BRAC's Microcredit Programmes." *Journal of Small Enterprise Development* 6 (4) December.

Yaron, Jacob, McDonald P. Benjamin, Jr., and Gerda L. Piprek 1997. "Rural Finance: Issues, Design, and Best Practices." Environmentally and Socially Sustainable Development Studies and Monographs Series 14. World Bank, Rural Development Department. Washington, D.C.

CHAPTER THREE

Products and Services

In chapter 1 we examined various contextual factors that affect the supply of *financial services* to low-income women and men. In chapter 2 we looked at the objectives of MFIs and ways to identify a target market and assess impacts. In this chapter we look at the range of products and services that an MFI might offer, taking into account the supply and demand analysis outlined in the previous two chapters.

MFIs can offer their clients a variety of products and services. First and foremost are financial services. However, due to the nature of an MFI's target clients—poor women and men without tangible assets, who often live in remote areas and may be illiterate—MFIs cannot operate like most formal financial institutions. Formal financial institutions do not generally regard the tiny informal businesses run by the poor as attractive investments. The loan amounts the businesses require are too small, and it is too difficult to obtain information from the clients (who may communicate in local dialects that the lender does not know). The clients are also often too far away, and it takes too long to visit their farms or businesses, especially if they are located in the urban slum. All of this means that the costs per dollar lent will be very high. And on top of that, there is no tangible security for the loan (Bennett 1994).

This means that low-income men and women face formidable barriers in gaining access to mainstream financial service institutions. Ordinary financial intermediation is not usually enough to help them participate, and therefore MFIs have to create mechanisms to bridge the gaps created by poverty, illiteracy, gender, and remoteness. Local institutions must be built and nurtured, and the skills and confidence of new clients must be developed. In many cases clients also need specific production and business management skills as well as better access to markets if they are to make profitable use of the financial services they receive (Bennett 1994).

Providing effective financial services to low-income women and men therefore often requires *social intermediation*—"the process of creating social capital as a support to sustainable financial intermediation with poor and disadvantaged groups or individuals" (Bennett 1997). Most MFIs provide some form of social intermediation, particularly if they work with groups. In some cases social intermediation is carried out by other organizations working with MFIs.

In addition, some MFIs provide *enterprise development services* such as skills training and basic business training (including bookkeeping, marketing, and production) or *social services* such as health care, education, and literacy training. These services can improve the ability of low-income men and women to operate microenterprises either directly or indirectly.

Deciding which services to offer depends on the MFI's objectives, the demands of the target market, the existence of other service providers, and an accurate calculation of the costs and feasibility of delivering additional services.

This chapter will be of interest to donors who are considering supporting a microfinance activity or existing MFIs that are considering adding new services or changing the way in which they operate. In particular, the overview of the products and services an MFI might offer its clients enables the reader to determine the level at which it meets the needs and demands of the target market.

The Systems Framework

Providing microfinance services to marginal clients is a complex process that requires many different kinds of skills and functions. This may require more than one institution. Even MFIs taking an *integrated* approach do not often provide all of the services demanded by the target group (see below). Thus understanding how the process of financial and social intermediation takes place requires a *systems analysis* rather than a simple institutional analysis.[1]

The systems perspective is important not only because there may be a number of different institutions involved, but also because these institutions are likely to have very different institutional goals or "corporate missions." Thus if a commercial bank is involved, its goal is to build its equity and deliver a profit to its owners. In contrast, both government agencies and nongovernmental organizations (NGOs), despite their many differences, are service organizations rather than profit-making institutions. Credit and savings clients themselves, if formed as a membership organization, have their own corporate mission: to serve its members who are both clients and owners.

The systems approach is useful for both donors and practitioners, because it makes the issue of *subsidies* much easier to understand and deal with honestly. It allows us to see each institution involved in the intermediation process as a *separate locus of sustainability* when we are assessing the commercial viability of the whole system. When it comes to covering the costs of providing services within the systems framework, each institution may have a different perspective. For formal financial institutions and membership organizations, financial sustainability is an essential goal. NGOs although expected to operate efficiently and to cover as much of their costs as possible, are not expected to generate a profit. Typically they work to deliver financial services to a target group for whom "the market" has failed. For many NGOs financial self-sustainability as an institution is not a goal consistent with their corporate missions.

If we consider the system as a whole, we can be much clearer about where the subsidies are. If a given institution is solely involved in providing social intermediation, then we can make an informed decision to provide ongoing subsidy for this work. The systems approach allows us to deal with the fact that microfinance involves a mix of "business" and "development." Instead of trying to force formal banks to become NGOs worrying about social intermediation, empowerment, and participation, and instead of urging NGOs to transform themselves into banks that must make a profit, we can encourage institutions to form *partnerships* in which each does what it does best, pursuing its own corporate mission while combining different skills to provide a lasting system that provides the poor with access to financial services.

(However, it is important to note that a new breed of NGOs, called "business NGOs," have begun to emerge. In the discourse currently surrounding microfinance, there seems to be an expectation that all NGOs involved in microfinance will basically transform themselves into financial institutions to achieve the goal of financial self-sustainability. Because not all NGOs are the same, considerable caution is required before drawing this conclusion. Before encouraging an NGO to become a formal financial institution, it is important to be very clear about the organization's institutional goals, management capacity, and experience. Not all NGOs can—or should—become banks. Indeed, there are many valid roles for NGOs to play within a sustainable system of financial intermediation—even if they themselves are not able to become financially self-sustainable in the way that a well performing bank or cooperative can.)

Within the systems framework there are four broad categories of services that may be provided to microfinance clients:

■ *Financial intermediation,* or the provision of financial products and services such as savings, credit, insurance, credit cards, and payment systems. Financial intermediation should not require ongoing subsidies.

■ *Social intermediation,* or the process of building the human and social capital required by sustainable financial intermediation for the poor. Social intermediation may require subsidies for a longer period than financial intermediation, but eventually subsides should be eliminated.

■ *Enterprise development services,* or nonfinancial services that assist microentrepreneurs. They include business training, marketing and technology services, skills

---

1. This discussion is taken from Bennett (1997).

development, and subsector analysis. Enterprise development services may or may not require subsidies, depending on the willingness and ability of clients to pay for these services.

- *Social services,* or nonfinancial services that focus on improving the well-being of microentrepreneurs. They include health, nutrition, education, and literacy training. Social services are likely to require ongoing subsidies, which are often provided by the state or through donors supporting NGOs.

The degree to which an MFI provides each of these services depends on whether it takes a "minimalist" or "integrated" approach.

Microfinance Institutions—Minimalist or Integrated?

MFIs by definition provide financial services. However, an MFI may also offer other services as a means of improving the ability of its clients to utilize financial services. There is much debate in the field of microfinance as to whether MFIs should be *minimalist*—that is, offering only financial intermediation—or *integrated*—offering both financial intermediation and other services (figure 3.1). Most MFIs offer social intermediation to some extent. The decision to offer nonfinancial services determines whether an MFI is minimalist or integrated.

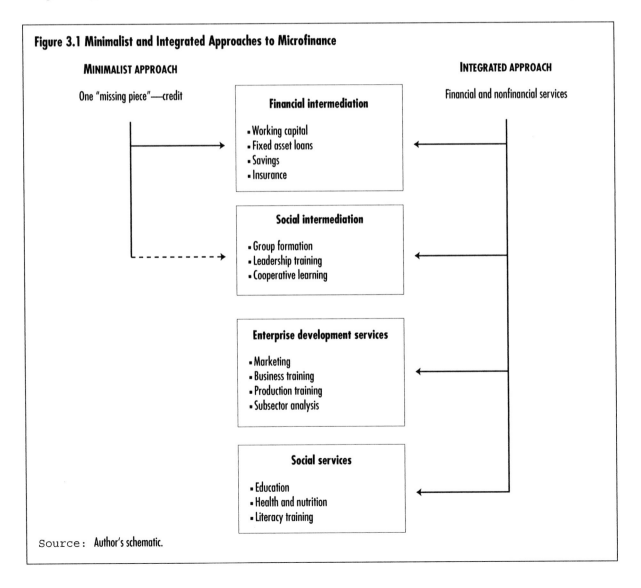

Figure 3.1 Minimalist and Integrated Approaches to Microfinance

MINIMALIST APPROACH

One "missing piece"—credit

INTEGRATED APPROACH

Financial and nonfinancial services

Financial intermediation
- Working capital
- Fixed asset loans
- Savings
- Insurance

Social intermediation
- Group formation
- Leadership training
- Cooperative learning

Enterprise development services
- Marketing
- Business training
- Production training
- Subsector analysis

Social services
- Education
- Health and nutrition
- Literacy training

Source: Author's schematic.

MFIs using the *minimalist approach* normally offer only financial intermediation, but they may occasionally offer limited social intermediation services. Minimalists base their approach on the premise that there is a single "missing piece" for enterprise growth, usually considered to be the lack of affordable, accessible short-term credit, which the MFI can offer. While other "missing pieces" may exist, the MFI recognizes its comparative advantage in providing only financial intermediation. Other organizations are assumed to provide other services demanded by the target clients. This approach offers cost advantages for the MFI and allows it to maintain a clear focus, since it develops and provides only one service to clients.

The *integrated approach* takes a more holistic view of the client. It provides a combination or range of financial and social intermediation, enterprise development, and social services. While it may not provide all four, the MFI takes advantage of its proximity to clients and, based on its objectives, provides those services that it feels are most needed or that it has a comparative advantage in providing.

An MFI chooses a minimalist or more integrated approach depending on its objectives and the circumstances (demand and supply) in which it is operating. If an MFI chooses to take an integrated approach, it should be aware of the following potential issues:

- Providing financial and nonfinancial services are two distinct activities, which may at times lead an institution to pursue conflicting objectives.
- It is often difficult for clients to differentiate "social services," which are usually free, from "financial services," which must be paid for, when they are receiving both from the same organization.
- MFIs offering many services may have difficulties identifying and controlling the costs per service.
- Nonfinancial services are rarely financially sustainable.

Financial Intermediation

The primary role of MFIs is to provide financial intermediation. This involves the transfer of capital or liquidity from those who have excess at a particular time to those who are short at that same time. Since production and consumption do not take place simultaneously, something is needed to coordinate these different rhythms.

"Finance in the form of savings and credit arises to permit coordination. Savings and credit are made more efficient when intermediaries begin to transfer funds from firms and individuals that have accumulated funds and are willing to shed liquidity, to those that desire to acquire liquidity" (Von Pischke 1991, 27).

While virtually all MFIs provide credit services, some also provide other financial products, including savings, insurance, and payment services. The choice of which financial services to provide and the method of providing these services depends on the objectives of the MFI, the demands of its target market, and its institutional structure.

Two key imperatives that must be considered when providing financial services are:

- To respond effectively to the *demand* and preferences of clients
- To design products that are *simple* and can be easily understood by the clients and easily managed by the MFI.

The range of products commonly provided includes:

- Credit
- Savings
- Insurance
- Credit cards
- Payment services.

The following section provides a brief description of the products MFIs offer their clients. This overview is provided to familiarize the reader with the unique ways that financial services are provided to microentrepreneurs. Specific information on how to design credit and savings products can be found in chapters 5 and 6. Appendix 1 summarizes the main approaches to financial intermediation.

Credit

Credit is borrowed funds with specified terms for repayment. When there are insufficient accumulated savings to finance a business and when the return on borrowed funds exceeds the interest rate charged on the loan, it makes sense to borrow rather than postpone the business activity until sufficient savings can be accumulated, assuming the capacity to service the debt exists (Waterfield and Duval 1996).

Loans are generally made for productive purposes—that is, to generate revenue within a business. Some MFIs also make loans for consumption, housing, or special occasions. While many MFIs insist that only productive loans be made, any loan that increases the liquidity of the household frees up enterprise revenue, which can be put back into the business.

Most MFIs strive to reach sustainability (which may or may not include financial sustainability—see chapter 9) by ensuring that the services offered meet the demands of clients, that operations are as efficient as possible and costs are minimized, that interest rates and fees are sufficient to

cover costs, and that clients are motivated to repay loans. MFIs can be sustainable providing they have enough funds to continue operating in the long term. These funds can be obtained solely through operational revenue or through a combination of grants and operating revenue. As microfinance develops, clear principles are being established that lead to *financially viable lending* (box 3.1).

Methods of credit delivery can generally be divided into the two broad categories of individual and group

---

Box 3.1 Principles of Financially Viable Lending to Poor Entrepreneurs

Principle 1. Offer services that fit the preferences of poor entrepreneurs.

These services might include:

- *Short loan terms, compatible with enterprise outlay and income patterns.* ACCION International programs typically lend for three-month terms, and Grameen Bank for one year.
- *Repeat loans.* Full repayment of one loan brings access to another. Repeat lending allows credit to support financial management as a process rather than as an isolated event.
- *Relatively unrestricted uses.* While most programs select customers with active enterprises (and thus the cash flow for repayment), they recognize that clients may need to use funds for a mixture of household or enterprise purposes.
- *Very small loans, appropriate for meeting the day-to-day financial requirements of businesses.* Average loan sizes at Badan Kredit Kecamatan in Indonesia and Grameen are well under $100, while most ACCION and Bank Rakyat Indonesia activities feature average loans in the $200 to $800 range.
- *A customer-friendly approach.* Locate outlets close to entrepreneurs, use extremely simple applications (often one page), and limit the time between application and disbursement to a few days. Develop a public image of being approachable by poor people.

Principle 2. Streamline operations to reduce unit costs.

Develop highly streamlined operations, minimizing staff time per loan.

Standardize the lending process. Make applications very simple and approve on the basis of easily verifiable criteria, such as the existence of a going enterprise. Decentralize loan approval. Maintain inexpensive offices—Badan Kredit Kecamatan operates its village posts once a week from

rooms in local government buildings, paying little or no overhead while reaching deep into rural areas. Select staff from local communities, including people with lower levels of education (and hence lower salary expectations) than staff in formal banking institutions.

Principle 3. Motivate clients to repay loans.

Substitute for preloan project analysis and formal collateral by assuming that clients will be *able* to repay. Concentrate on providing *motivation* to repay. These motivations might include:

- *Joint liability groups.* An arrangement whereby a handful of borrowers guarantees each other's loans is by far the most frequently used repayment motivation. This technique is employed by Grameen and in a slightly different form by ACCION affiliates. It has proved effective in many different countries and settings worldwide. Individual character lending can be effective when the social structure is cohesive, as has been demonstrated throughout Indonesia's array of credit programs.
- *Incentives.* Incentives such as guaranteeing access to loans motivate repayment, as do increases in loan sizes and preferential pricing in exchange for prompt repayment. Institutions that successfully motivate repayments develop staff competence and a public image that signals that they are serious about loan collection.

Principle 4. Charge full-cost interest rates and fees.

The small loan sizes necessary to serve the poor may result in costs per loan requiring interest rates that are significantly higher than commercial bank rates (though significantly lower than informal sector rates). Poor entrepreneurs have shown a willingness and an ability to pay such rates for services with attributes that fit their needs.

Source: Rhyne and Holt 1994.

approaches, based on how the MFI delivers and guarantees its loans (adapted from Waterfield and Duval 1996).

- *Individual loans* are delivered to individuals based on their ability to provide the MFI with assurances of repayment and some level of security.
- *Group-based approaches* make loans to groups—that is, either to individuals who are members of a group and guarantee each other's loans or to groups that then subloan to their members.

INDIVIDUAL LENDING. MFIs have successfully developed effective models to lend to individuals, which combine formal lending, as is traditional in financial institutions, with informal lending, as carried out by moneylenders.

Formal financial institutions base lending decisions on business and client characteristics, including cash flow, debt capacity, historical financial results, collateral, and character. Formal sector lenders have also proven the usefulness of personal guarantors to motivate clients to repay loans. They have demonstrated the value of a businesslike approach and the importance of achieving cost recovery in their lending operations. Finally, they have established the importance of external regulation to safeguard client savings and the institution itself. However, formal sector lending practices are often not suitable for microfinance institutions, as many microbusinesses or business owners do not have many assets or adequate financial reporting systems.

Informal sector lenders approve loans based on a personal knowledge of the borrowers rather than on a sophisticated feasibility analysis, and they use informal collateral sources. They also demonstrate the importance of responding quickly to borrowers' needs with a minimum of bureaucratic procedures. Perhaps most important, moneylenders demonstrate that the poor do repay loans and are able to pay relatively high interest rates. However, loans from moneylenders are often not taken for productive purposes but rather for emergency or consumption smoothing. They are usually for a relatively short period of time.

Characteristics of individual lending models include (Waterfield and Duval 1996, 84):

- The guarantee of loans by some form of collateral (defined less stringently than by formal lenders) or a cosigner (a person who agrees to be legally responsible for the loan but who usually has not received a loan of her or his own from the MFI).

- The screening of potential clients by credit checks and character references.
- The tailoring of the loan size and term to business needs.
- The frequent increase over time of the loan size and term.
- Efforts by the staff to develop close relationships with clients so that each client represents a significant investment of staff time and energy.

Individual lending requires frequent and close contact with individual clients. It is most often successful in urban areas where client access is possible. Individual lending can also be successful in rural areas, particularly through savings and credit cooperatives or credit unions. In both urban and rural areas individual lending is often focused on financing production-oriented businesses, whose operators are generally better off than the very poor.

The Fédération des Caisses d'Epargne et de Crédit Agricole Mutuel in Benin provides an example of effective individual lending in rural areas (box 3.2).

Because credit officers need to spend a relatively long period of time with individual clients, they usually serve between 60 and 140 clients. Loans to individuals are usually larger than loans to members in a group. Accordingly, given an equal number of loans, these loans to individuals provide a larger *revenue base* to cover the costs of delivering and maintaining the loans than group loans. The revenue base is the outstanding amount of a loan portfolio that is earning interest revenue. Because interest revenue is based on a percentage of the amount lent, the larger the amount lent the greater the revenue and hence the more funds available to cover costs, even though costs may not be that much higher than for loans of smaller amounts (see chapter 9). Furthermore, individual lending models may be less costly and less labor-intensive to establish than group-based models.

The Association for the Development of Microenterprises in the Dominican Republic provides an excellent example of a successful MFI that provides individual loans (box 3.3).

GROUP-BASED LENDING. Group-based lending involves the formation of groups of people who have a common wish to access financial services. Group-lending approaches frequently build on or imitate existing informal lending and savings groups. These groups exist in virtually every

---

Box 3.2 Individual Loans at Fédération des Caisses d'Epargne et de Crédit Agricole Mutuel, Benin

THE FÉDÉRATION DES CAISSES D'EPARGNE ET DE CRÉDIT Agricole Mutuel (FECECAM) is a large network of savings and credit cooperatives with more than 200,000 clients. Most of the loans are provided to individuals. Loan analysis is conducted by a credit committee composed of representatives from the villages to which the local savings and credit cooperative provides financial services. Loans are therefore character-based, although some form of collateral is also required. Borrowers must also have a savings account with the cooperative, and the loan amount they receive is related to their volume of savings. Savings cannot be drawn on until the loan is paid back in full. In the case of agricultural loans, the village farmers group participates in the credit analysis and acts as a guarantor.

Individual lending has been very much geared toward men because they have the most assets (and hence collateral) and as heads of households receive support from the farmers group. For women this approach has been rather ineffective. In 1993 the federation introduced group lending for female clients. The goal is to help women become familiar with the savings and credit cooperatives and build up enough savings to become individual borrowers after taking two or three loans with the backing of their group.

Source: Fruman 1997.

---

country and are called by various names, the most common being rotating savings and credit associations (box 3.4).

Group-lending approaches have adapted the model of rotating savings and credit associations to provide additional flexibility in loan sizes and terms and generally to allow borrowers to access funds when needed rather than having to wait for their turn. More well-known group-lending models include the Grameen Bank in Bangladesh and ACCION International's solidarity group lending, both of which facilitate the formation of relatively small groups (of 5 to 10 people) and make *individual* loans to group members. Other models, such as the Foundation for International Community

---

Box 3.3 The Association for the Development of Microenterprises

THE ASSOCIATION FOR THE DEVELOPMENT OF MICRO-enterprises (ADEMI) provides credit and technical assistance to microenterprises and small enterprises. The credit service has the following characteristics:

- Emphasis on providing credit to microenterprises, followed by appropriate amounts of noncompulsory, complementary, direct technical assistance.
- Initial, small, short-term loans provided for working capital and later increased in successively larger amounts and longer terms to purchase fixed assets.
- Use of commercial banks for loan disbursements and collection.
- Positive real rates of interest charged on the loans.
- Caution in disbursements, so that the timing of the loan and the amount are appropriate.

The size and terms of each loan provided by the association are set individually by the loan officer based on the client's needs and capacity to repay. Loans are approved by management. Most loans to microenterprises are for up to one year, although the term may be longer for fixed asset loans.

ADEMI uses a combination of collateral and guarantors to secure its loans. All borrowers are required to sign a legal contract stating their obligation to repay funds at specified terms. Most clients also have a guarantor or cosigner who assumes full responsibility for the terms of the contract in case the client is either unable or unwilling to repay the loan. When feasible, borrowers are also required to sign deeds for property or machinery as loan guarantees. In some case guarantors may be asked to pledge security on behalf of the borrower.

However, ADEMI strongly recommends that if applicants are not able to provide collateral they should be limited in their ability to access the association's credit. When first-time borrowers are unable to provide security, loan officers rely heavily on *information* as a collateral substitute. In these situations the loan officer will investigate the reputation of the applicant in much the same way that an informal moneylender might. Visits are made to neighboring shops and bars. Applicants may be asked to produce financial statements if possible or receipts for utility payments. Each application is considered on a case-by-case basis.

Source: Ledgerwood and Burnett 1995.

Box 3.4 Rotating Savings and Credit Associations

ROTATING SAVINGS AND CREDIT ASSOCIATIONS (ROSCAs) are informal groups developed by their members at the grass-roots level. They bear different names in different countries. For example, in West Africa they are *tontines, paris,* or *susus;* in South Africa they are *stokvels;* in Egypt they are *gam'iyas;* in Guatemala they are *cuchubales;* and in Mexico they are *tandas.*

Individuals form a self-selected group and all members agree to contribute a regular fixed amount every week or month. Members then take turns receiving the full amount collected in the period until all members have had a turn to receive funds. The order in which members receive funds is determined by lottery, mutual agreement, or need or personal emergencies of the group members. Often the person who initiated the formation of the association receives the funds first.

Interest is not directly charged but is implicit. Those who benefit from the loan early are privileged over those who receive it in the late stages. Rotating savings and credit associations also play an important social role. Members might

switch turns if someone is in need, and some associations build up security funds for mutual assistance. Variations exist in the size of groups, the amounts "saved," the frequency of meetings, and the order of priority in receiving loans. In Latin America commercial associations (tandas) are used to buy expensive consumer durables such as cars or machinery. Some people belong to several associations. The rotating savings and credit associations can be rural or urban and include men and women, usually in separate groups, sometimes jointly. Members can be at any income level; many civil servants or office employees participate.

However, rotating savings and credit associations are limited due to their lack of flexibility. Members are not always able to receive a loan when needed or in the amount required. Also, membership in some associations involves high social and transaction costs, such as regular meetings and providing refreshments for group members. Rotating savings and credit associations also imply risk in the form of the chance that some members will drop out before everyone has had a turn at receiving the contributions.

Source: Krahnen and Schmidt 1994.

Assistance (FINCA) village banking model, utilize larger groups of between 30 and 100 members and lend to the *group* itself rather than to individuals.

Several *advantages* of group-based lending are cited frequently in microfinance literature. One important feature of group-based lending is the use of peer pressure as a substitute for collateral. Many group-based lending programs target the very poor, who cannot meet the traditional collateral requirements of most financial institutions. Instead, group guarantees are established as collateral substitutes. While many people presume that group guarantees involve the strict joint liability of group members, members are seldom held responsible. Instead, the default of one member generally means that further lending to other members of the group is stopped until the loan is repaid. The financial and social grouping elicits several types of group dynamics that may increase repayment rates. For example, peer pressure from other group members can act as a repayment incentive, since members do not want to let down the other members of their group or suffer any social sanctions imposed by the group as a result of defaulting. In other cases, the group may recognize a legitimate reason for the arrears of a certain

member and offer to help until the problem is resolved. In still other cases, the mandatory savings of group members may be used to pay off the loan of a defaulter.

Another advantage of group lending is that it may reduce certain institutional transaction costs. By shifting screening and monitoring costs to the group, an MFI can reach a large number of clients even in the face of asymmetric information through the self-selection of group members. One of the reasons that self-selection is so important is that members of the same community generally have excellent knowledge about who is a reliable credit risk and who is not. People are very careful about whom they admit into their group, given the threat of losing their own access to credit (or having their own savings used to repay another loan). Hence group formation is a critical component of successful group lending. In addition to cost reduction through internal group monitoring and screening of clients, MFIs using group-based lending also can save by using a hierarchical structure. Typically, loan officers do not deal with individual group members but rather collect repayment from a group or village leader, thereby reducing transaction costs. Puhazhendhi (1995) found that microfinance banks that use intermediaries such as self-help groups reduce transaction costs more successfully than banks that work directly with clients.

While numerous potential advantages of group lending have been reported, several *disadvantages* exist as well. Bratton (1986) demonstrates how group lending institutions have better repayment rates than individual lending programs in good years but worse repayment rates in years with some type of crisis. If several members of a group encounter repayment difficulties the entire group often collapses, leading to a domino effect. This effect was a strong and significant determinant of group loan repayment in a study in Burkina Faso (Paxton 1996b) and signals the inherent instability of group lending in risky environments (box 3.5).

Some critics question the assumption that transaction costs are indeed lower with group lending (for example, Huppi and Feder 1990). Group training costs tend to be quite high, and no individual borrower-bank relationship is established over time. Not only are institutional transaction costs high, but client transaction costs are quite high as well as more responsibility is shifted from the MFI to the clients themselves.

Finally, while it appears that some people work well in groups, there is the concern that many people prefer to have individual loans rather than being financially punished for the irresponsible repayment of other group members. Given the presence of opposing advantages and disadvantages associated with group lending, it is not surprising to see group lending work well in some contexts and collapse in others (see box 3.6).

Savings

Savings mobilization has long been a controversial issue in microfinance. In recent years there has been increasing awareness among policymakers and practitioners that there is a vast number of informal savings schemes and MFIs around the world (in particular, credit union organizations) have been very successful in mobilizing savings. These developments attest to the fact that *low-income clients can and do save.* The World Bank's "Worldwide Inventory of Microfinance Institutions" found that many of the largest, most sustainable institutions in microfinance rely heavily on savings mobilization. "In 1995, over $19 billion are held in the surveyed microfinance institutions in more than 45 million savings accounts compared to nearly $7 billion in 14 million active loan accounts. Often neglected in microfinance, deposits provide a highly valued service to the world's poor who seldom have reliable places to store their money or the possibility to earn a return on savings" (Paxton 1996a, 8).

The survey also found that the ability to effectively mobilize deposits depends greatly on the macroeconomic and legal environment. "Statistical analysis of the surveyed institutions reveals a positive correlation between the amount of deposits mobilized and the average growth in per capita GNP of the country from 1980 to 1993. Likewise, higher deposit ratios are negatively correlated with high levels of inflation. Finally, the amounts of deposits are positively correlated with high levels of population density" (Paxton 1996a, 8). Furthermore, institutions operating with donor

---

Box 3.5 Repayment Instability in Burkina Faso

A 1996 STUDY OF GROUP LENDING EXAMINED THE INFLU-ences of group dynamics on loan repayment in 140 lending groups of Sahel Action. Several variables were shown to have a positive influence on successful loan repayment, including group solidarity (helping a group member in need), location (urban outperformed rural), access to informal credit, and good leadership and training. Nevertheless, other variables led to repayment instability.

The variable that had the most destabilizing effect on loan repayment was the domino effect. Joint liability existed not only at the group level but also at the village level, in the sense that if any group in the village defaulted on its loan then no other loans would be issued in the village.

Thus an incentive existed for correctly paying groups to default if any default existed within the village. In addition, groups tended to default after several loan cycles. A possible explanation for this phenomenon is that the terms and conditions of the group loan no longer fulfilled the demand of *each* group member in consecutive loan cycles, leading one or more members to default.

Positive and negative externalities exist within any group-based lending program. However, given the importance and delicacy of maintaining strong repayment rates, a thorough understanding of the factors leading to repayment instability is critical to reduce the causes of widespread default.

Source: Paxton 1996b.

Box 3.6 The Role of Groups in Financial Intermediation

Guidelines for effective use of groups:

- Groups are more effective if they are small and homogeneous.
- Imposing group penalties and incentives (such as no access to further loans while an individual is in default) improves loan performance.
- Loan sizes that increase sequentially appear to allow groups to screen out bad risks.
- Staggered disbursements to group members can be based on the repayment performance of other members.

Possible advantages of using groups:

- Economies of scale (a larger clientele with minimal increases in operating costs).
- Economies of scope (an increased capacity to deliver multiple services through the same group mechanism).
- Mitigation of information asymmetry related to potential borrowers and savers through the group's knowledge of individual members.
- Reduction of moral hazard risks due to group monitoring and peer pressure.
- Substitution of joint liability for individual collateral.

- Improved loan collection through screening and selecting, peer pressure, and joint liability, especially if group penalties and incentives are incorporated in the loan terms.
- Improved savings mobilization, especially if incentives are incorporated in a group scheme.
- Lower administrative costs (selection, screening, and loan collection) once the initial investment is made in establishing and educating the groups.

Risks associated with using groups:

- Poor records and lack of contract enforcement.
- Potential for corruption and control by a powerful leader within the group.
- Covariance risk due to similar production activities.
- Generalized repayment problems (domino effect).
- Limited participation by women members in mixed-gender groups.
- High up-front costs (especially time) in forming viable groups.
- Potential weakening of group if group leader departs.
- Increased transaction costs to borrowers (time for meetings and some voluntary management functions).

Source: Yaron, Benjamin, and Piprek 1997.

---

funds generally were found to have a high rate of loan portfolio growth, while deposit-based programs grew more slowly (probably due to a lack of funds). Also, institutions that mobilized deposits were found to have higher average loan sizes and were more likely to work in urban areas than institutions providing only credit. This latter finding relates to the fact that most institutions that collect savings must be regulated to do so. Larger urban institutions tend to be regulated more often than smaller MFIs, and they often reach a clientele at a higher income level.

Bank Rakyat Indonesia and the Bank for Agriculture and Agricultural Cooperatives in Thailand are well-known examples of established MFIs with fast-growing savings mobilization. The Caisses Villageoises in Pays Dogon, Mali, provides another less well-known example (box 3.7).

COMPULSORY SAVINGS. Compulsory savings differ substantially from voluntary savings. Compulsory savings (or compensating balances) represent funds that must be contributed by borrowers as a condition of receiving a loan, sometimes as a percentage of the loan, sometimes as

a nominal amount. For the most part, compulsory savings can be considered part of a loan product rather than an actual savings product, since they are so closely tied to receiving and repaying loans. (Of course, for the borrower compulsory savings represent an asset while the loan represents a liability; thus the borrower may not view compulsory savings as part of the loan product.)

Compulsory savings are useful to:

- Demonstrate the value of savings practices to borrowers
- Serve as an additional guarantee mechanism to ensure the repayment of loans
- Demonstrate the ability of clients to manage cash flow and make periodic contributions (important for loan repayment)
- Help to build up the asset base of clients.

However, compulsory savings are often perceived (rightly) by clients as a "fee" they must pay to participate and gain access to credit. Generally, compulsory savings cannot be withdrawn by members while they have a loan outstanding. In this way, savings act as a form of collateral. Clients are thus not able to use their savings

---

Box 3.7 Caisses Villageoises, Pays Dogon, Mali

THE CAISSES VILLAGEOISES WERE ESTABLISHED IN PAYS Dogon, Mali, in 1996. There are now 55 such self-managed village banks. The caisses mobilize savings from their members, who are men and women from the village or neighboring villages. Deposits are used for on-lending to members according to the decisions made by the village credit committee.

By December 31, 1996, the Caisses Villageoises had mobilized $320,000. The average outstanding deposit was $94, equivalent to 38 percent of GDP per capita. Each village bank set its own interest rates based on its experience with traditional village groups providing loans to their members or informal sources of financial services. In 1996 the nominal interest rate on deposits was on average 21 percent;, with an inflation rate averaging 7 percent, the real rate was 14 percent. Such a high level of interest was required because the caisses operate in an environment in which money is very scarce, due to minimal production of cash crops in the area and irregular amounts of excess grain for trade.

Traditionally, farmers prefer to save in livestock or invest their savings in their small businesses.

Even with high interest rates, relatively few members save with a caisse. Of the 21,500 members of the Caisses Villageoises, fewer than 20 percent used a deposit account during the course of 1996. As a result, the volume of the loan applications exceeds the amount of mobilized savings. The caisses have been borrowing from the National Agriculture Bank since 1989 to satisfy their clients' needs. However, the amount an individual caisse can borrow is a function of the amount of savings it has mobilized (one and a half to two times this amount can be borrowed from the National Agriculture Bank). In this way, the incentive to mobilize savings remains high for the caisse and members feel a significant sense of ownership, since their deposits are what determines its growth. As of December 1996 the volume of deposits to the volume of loans outstanding was 41 percent.

Source: Contributed by Cecile Fruman, Sustainable Banking with the Poor Project, World Bank.

---

until their loan is repaid. In some cases compulsory savings cannot be withdrawn until the borrower actually withdraws his or her membership from the MFI. This sometimes results in the borrowing by clients of loan amounts that are in fact less than their accumulated savings. However, many MFIs are now beginning to realize the unfairness of this practice and are allowing their clients and members to withdraw their compulsory savings if they do not have a loan outstanding or if a certain amount of savings is still held by the MFI. (Compulsory savings are discussed further in chapter 5.)

VOLUNTARY SAVINGS. As the name suggests, voluntary savings are not an obligatory part of accessing credit services. Voluntary savings services are provided to both borrowers and nonborrowers who can deposit or withdraw according to their needs. (Although sometimes savers must be members of the MFI, at other times savings are available to the general public.) Interest rates paid range from relatively low to slightly higher than those offered by formal financial institutions. The provision of savings services offers advantages such as consumption smoothing for the clients and a stable source of funds for the MFI.

The requirement of compulsory savings and the mobilization of voluntary savings reflect two very different philosophies (CGAP 1997). The former assumes that the poor must be taught to save and that they need to learn financial discipline. The latter assumes that the working poor already save and that what is required are institutions and services appropriate to their needs. Microfinance clients may not feel comfortable putting voluntary savings in compulsory savings accounts or even in other accounts with the same MFI. Because they often cannot withdraw the compulsory savings until their loan is repaid (or until after a number of years), they fear that they may also not have easy access to their voluntary savings. Consequently, MFIs should always clearly separate compulsory and voluntary savings services.

There are three conditions that must exist for an MFI to consider mobilizing voluntary savings (CGAP 1997):

- An enabling environment, including appropriate legal and regulatory frameworks, a reasonable level of political stability, and suitable demographic conditions
- Adequate and effective supervisory capabilities to protect depositors
- Consistently good management of the MFI's funds. The MFI should be financially solvent with a high rate of loan recovery.

Requirements for effective voluntary savings mobilization include (Yaron, Benjamin, and Piprek 1997):

- A high level of client confidence in the institution (a sense of safety)
- A positive real deposit interest rate (which will require positive real on-lending interest rates)
- Flexibility and diversity of savings instruments
- Security
- Easy access to deposits for clients
- Easy access to the MFI (either through its branch network or through mobile banking officers)
- MFI staff incentives linked to savings mobilization.

The provision of savings services by an MFI can contribute to improved financial intermediation by (Yaron, Benjamin, and Piprek 1997):

- Providing clients with a secure place to keep their savings, smooth consumption patterns, hedge against risk, and accumulate assets while earning higher real returns than they might by saving in the household or saving in kind
- Enhancing clients' perception of "ownership" of a MFI and thus potentially their commitment to repaying loans to the MFI
- Encouraging the MFI to intensify efforts to collect loans due to market pressures from depositors (especially if they lose confidence in the MFI)
- Providing a source of funds for the MFI, which can contribute to improved loan outreach, increased autonomy from governments and donors, and reduced dependence on subsidies.

Savings mobilization is not always feasible or desirable for MFIs: the administrative complexities and costs associated with mobilizing savings—especially small amounts—may be prohibitive. Institutions may also find it difficult to comply with prudential regulations that apply to deposit-taking institutions.

Furthermore, the volatility of microfinance loan portfolios may put deposits at unusually high risk if the MFI uses savings to fund unsafe lending operations. In addition, MFIs that offer voluntary saving services must have greater liquidity to meet unexpected increases in savings withdrawals. The provision of savings services creates a fundamentally different institution than one that provides only credit. Caution must be taken when deciding to introduce savings.

Insurance

MFIs are beginning to experiment with other financial products and services such as insurance, credit cards, and payment services. Many group lending programs offer an insurance or guarantee scheme. A typical example is Grameen Bank. Each member is required to contribute 1 percent of the loan amount to an insurance fund. In case of the death of a client this fund is used to repay the loan and provide the deceased client's family with the means to cover burial costs.

Insurance is a product that will likely be offered more extensively in the future by MFIs, because there is growing demand among their clients for health or loan insurance in case of death or loss of assets. The Self-Employed Women's' Association in Gujarat, India, provides a good example of an MFI that is meeting the insurance service needs of its clients (box 3.8).

Credit Cards and Smart Cards

Among the other services that some MFIs are beginning to offer are credit cards and smart cards.

CREDIT CARDS. These cards allow borrowers to access a line of credit if and when they need it. Credit cards are used when a purchase is made (assuming the supplier of the goods accepts the credit card) or when access to cash is desired (the card is sometimes called a "debit card" if the client is accessing his or her own savings).

The use of credit cards is still very new in the field of microfinance; only a few examples are known. Credit cards can only be used when adequate infrastructure is in place within the formal financial sector. For example, some credit cards provide access to cash through automated teller machines. If there is not a wide network of such machines and if retailers are not willing to accept credit cards, then the cards' usefulness is limited.

Credit cards do offer considerable advantages to both clients and MFIs. Credit cards can:

- Minimize administrative and operating costs
- Streamline operations
- Provide an ongoing line of credit to borrowers, enabling them to supplement their cash flow according to their needs.

A recent example of an MFI that provides its low-income clients with credit cards is the Association for the Development of Microenterprises (box 3.9).

Box 3.8 Self-Employed Women's Association Insurance

THE SELF-EMPLOYED WOMEN'S ASSOCIATION (SEWA) IS THE mother institution of a network of interrelated organizations. It began in 1972 as a trade union of self-employed women in Ahmedabad in the state of Gujarat, India. The association is active in three areas: organizing women into unions; establishing alternative economic organizations in the form of cooperatives; and providing services such as banking, housing, and child care.

The association's bank was established in 1974 to provide banking and insurance services. It acts as manager of the insurance scheme run by the Self-Employed Women's Association for its members. The insurance services are actually offered by the Life Insurance Corporation of India and the United India Insurance Company, supplemented by a special type of insurance for women workers offered by the association. The bank acts as an intermediary, packaging insurance services for its

members and helping women to apply for and settle insurance claims.

Every member who wishes to purchase insurance is given two options: pay a 60 rupee premium each year and receive all benefits or make a one-time fixed deposit of 500 rupees in the association's bank. The interest on the fixed deposit is used to pay the annual premium. For members who opt for the fixed deposit scheme, the association will also provide them with a 300 rupee maternity benefit paid through its bank.

The bank does not charge its own members or the association's members for this service and does not receive any commission from the insurance companies. However, in exchange for managing these services on behalf of the association, it receives an annual sum of 100,000 rupees. In addition, the association also pays the salaries of staff responsible for administering the insurance schemes.

Source: Biswas and Mahajan 1997.

SMART CARDS. The Swazi Business Growth Trust in the Kingdom of Swaziland provides its clients with *smart cards,* which are similar to credit cards but are generally not available for use in retail outlets (box 3.10). Smart cards contain a memory chip that contains information about a client's available line of credit with a lending institution.

Box 3.9 The Association for the Development of Microenterprises' MasterCard

IN MAY 1996 THE ASSOCIATION FOR THE DEVELOPMENT of Microenterprises (ADEMI) and the Banco Popular Dominicano, the largest private commercial bank in the Dominican Republic, launched the ADEMI MasterCard. In addition to the usual uses of the card at purchasing outlets, clients can withdraw cash at 45 Banco Popular branches and 60 automated teller machines. To qualify for the card clients must have operated their businesses for at least one year, have monthly incomes of at least 3,000 pesos (about US$230), have borrowed at least 3,000 pesos from ADEMI, and have a good repayment record. The association aims to reach 5,000 cardholders in the first year. It calls the MasterCard initiative a further step in building trust with owners of microenterprises and enhancing their status.

Source: Contributed by McDonald Benjamin, East Asia and Pacific Region Financial Sector and Development Unit, World Bank.

Payment Services

In traditional banks payment services include check cashing and check writing privileges for customers who maintain deposits (Caskey 1994). In this sense the banks' payment services are bundled with their savings services. MFIs may offer similar payment services either with their savings services (if applicable) or separately for a fee. If payment services are bundled with savings services, the MFI can pay an artificially low interest rate on customer deposit accounts to cover the cost of those services. Otherwise, a fee is charged to cover these costs, which include personnel, infrastructure, and insurance costs. Fees can be based on a percentage of the amount of the check or they can be a flat minimum fee with additional charges for first-time clients. Moreover, because the MFI advances funds on checks that must subsequently be cleared through the banking system, it incurs interest expenses on the funds advanced and runs the risk that some cashed checks will be uncollectible due to insufficient funds or fraud. MFIs, therefore, must have a relationship with at least one bank to clear the checks being cashed.

In addition to check cashing and check writing privileges, payment services include the transfer and remittance of funds from one area to another. Microfinance clients often need transfer services, however, the amounts

---

Box 3.10 *Swazi Business Growth Trust Smart Cards*

SMART CARDS ARE A NEW FINANCIAL TECHNOLOGY PIONEERED by the Growth Trust Corporation, a for-profit affiliate of Swazi Business Growth Trust, with the assistance of Development Alternatives, Inc. and the U.S. Agency for International Development.

Commercial banks in Swaziland are not interested in providing financial services to trust customers due to the high transaction costs of servicing these small businesses. The Growth Trust Corporation was thus established to provide financial services in the form of housing loans and small business loans. To minimize administrative and operating costs, the corporation introduced the smart card. Each customer is issued a smart card with a memory chip on its surface containing information about the amount of the line of credit the client has obtained. Commercial banks are

provided with the equipment to read the cards, and Swazi Business Growth Trust clients can draw funds and make repayments at various commercial bank branches in Swaziland. A smart card transaction takes a fraction of the time of a regular teller transaction. The Growth Trust Corporation holds a line of credit with participating banks and collects transaction information from the banks at the end of the day.

Smart cards enable the trust to monitor disbursements and repayments easily. The trust plans to move the smart card network on line in commercial banks once the Swazi telephone system allows. Commercial banks are willing to provide this service free of charge because the trust is a nonprofit organization and targets a different, low-income clientele.

Source: McLean and Gamser 1995.

---

that formal financial institutions require to make a transfer may be beyond the limits of the client. Without transfer services clients may be forced to carry (relatively) large amounts of money with them, thus incurring unnecessary risks. To offer payment services MFIs must have an extensive branch network or relationships with one or more banks (box 3.11). This is often difficult to achieve.

Few MFIs are currently offering these services, but it is anticipated that in the future more and more will recognize a demand for payment services and will boost their ability to cover the costs associated with such services.

Social Intermediation

For individuals whose social and economic disadvantages place them "beyond the frontier" of formal finance (Von Pischke 1991), successful financial intermediation is often accompanied by social intermediation. Social intermediation prepares marginalized groups or *individuals* to enter into solid business relationships with MFIs.[2]

Evidence has shown that it is easier to establish sustainable financial intermediation systems with the poor in societies that encourage cooperative efforts through local clubs, temple associations, or work groups—in other words, societies with high levels of social capital.

Box 3.11 *Demand for Payment Services at the Fédération des Caisses d'Epargne et de Crédit Agricole Mutuel, Benin*

THE FÉDÉRATION DES CAISSES D'EPARGNE ET DE CRÉDIT Agricole Mutuel (FECECAM) has the largest outreach of any financial institution in Benin, with 64 local branches, many in remote areas. For this reason there is widespread pressure on the bank to offer payment services, since its extensive network offers a unique opportunity to transfer funds from the capital city, Cotonou, to some very distant villages. The demand for payment services comes from a variety of actors. Member clients are interested because this service would help them receive remittances or transfer money to relatives. Government

and donors who work closely with farmers or poor communities are also interested, because they would be able to transfer subsidy payments.

For now the federation does not have the management capability to offer payment services. In addition, Article 24 of the regulatory framework for credit unions (known as the PARMEC or Programme d'appui à la réglementation des Mutuelles d'épargne et de Crédit law) does not allow these institutions to transfer funds or offer checks which strongly limits the possibility of offering payment services.

Source: Fruman 1997.

Perhaps more than any other economic transaction, financial intermediation depends on social capital, because it depends on trust between the borrower and the lender. Where neither traditional systems nor modern institutions provide a basis for trust, financial intermediation systems are difficult to establish.

Social intermediation can thus be understood as the process of building the human and social capital required for sustainable financial intermediation with the poor.

MFIs that provide social intermediation services most often do so through groups, but some also work with individuals. The following discussion focuses primarily on group-based social intermediation, including approaches that lend directly to groups and those that lend to individual members of groups. Loosely defined, "groups" include small solidarity groups (such as those found in ACCION and Grameen lending models) as well as large credit-unions or caisses villageois. Where relevant, individual-based social intermediation services are also discussed.

Group social intermediation is defined as the effort to *build the institutional capacity of groups and invest in the human resources of their members,* so that they can begin to function more on their own with less help from outside. This aspect of social intermediation responds to the growing awareness that some of the poor—especially those in remote, sparsely populated areas or where levels of social capital are low—are not ready for sustainable financial intermediation without first receiving some capacity-building assistance.

There is a range of capacity-building that can take place with social intermediation. Some MFIs simply focus on developing group cohesiveness to ensure that members continue to guarantee each other's loans and benefit as much as possible from networking and the empowerment that comes from being part of a group. Other MFIs seek to develop a parallel financial system whereby the group actually takes over the financial intermediation process (box 3.12). This often happens with the group first managing its own internal savings funds and then later taking on the lending risk and banking duties associated with on-lending external funds. This aspect of social intermediation mostly involves training group members in participatory management, accounting, and basic financial management skills and helping groups to establish a good record-keeping system. This often requires initial subsidies similar to the time-bound subsidies required for financial intermediation (figure 3.2).

Ultimately, it is the groups' cohesiveness and self-management capacity that enables them to lower the costs of financial intermediation by reducing default through peer pressure—and consequently to lower the transaction costs that MFIs incur in dealing with many small borrowers and savers (Bennett, Hunte, and Goldberg 1995).

However, not all social intermediation results in the formation of groups, nor is it always provided by the

---

Box 3.12 Village Banks: An Example of a Parallel System

STARTED IN 1985 AS AN EXPERIMENT IN COMMUNITY DEVELopment with a program for women's savings and credit in Costa Rica, the village banking model has become an increasingly popular model for providing poor women with access to financial services. FINCA, CARE, Catholic Relief Services, Freedom From Hunger, and a host of local nongovernmental organizations (NGOs) have begun to implement village banks throughout Latin America, Africa, and Asia. The Small Enterprise Education and Promotion Network (SEEP) recently reported that there are "over 3,000 banks associated with SEEP members and their partners serving close to 34,000 members, 92 percent of whom are women. Average loan sizes are $80 and the collective portfolio stands at approximately $8.5 million."

Source: Bennett 1997.

The model usually establishes a parallel system managed by elected leaders, although there are an increasing number of cases of village banks initiating relationships with formal sector financial institutions or federating into apex organizations. The village bank provides a joint liability system for its 25 to 50 members and also acts as a secure savings facility. Individual members accumulate savings, which eventually become their own source of investment capital.

The "rules of the game" for membership—meeting attendance, savings, credit, and nonfinancial services—are developed by the women themselves, usually with guidance from an NGO field worker. Enforcement of credit contracts is the responsibility of the leaders, with member support. (For more information on village banking, see appendix 1.)

---

2. This section is based on writings by Lynn Bennett between 1994 and 1997.

Figure 3.2 Group Social Intermediation

Social intermediation	**Financial intermediation**
Building self-reliant groups by training group members in: • Participatory management • Accounting skills • Basic financial and management skills	Sustainable delivery of: • Credit • Savings • Insurance • Other financial services

Timebound subsidy

• "Infant industry" approach to develop local-level human resources and institutional capacity

Timebound subsidy

• For coverage of operational shortfalls
• For loan-fund capital (no interest rate subsidies)

Source: Bennett 1997.

same institution that provides the financial intermediation. In West Africa NGOs or other local organizations (public or private) visit remote villages where access to financial services is limited to develop awareness among individual village members of available services. They help individuals open accounts and manage their funds, and generally increase their level of self-confidence when dealing with financial institutions. Social intermediation services for individuals can be provided by the MFI itself or by other organizations attempting to link low-income clients with the formal financial sector.

Agence de Financement des Initiatives de Base, a Benin Social Fund, provides a good example (box 3.13).

Enterprise Development Services

MFIs adopting an integrated approach often provide some type of enterprise development services (some MFIs refer to these services as business development services, nonfinancial services, or assistance).[3] If these services are not offered directly by the MFI, there may be a number of other public and private institutions that provide enterprise development services within the systems framework to which the MFI's clients have access.

Enterprise development services include a wide range of nonfinancial interventions, including:

• Marketing and technology services

Box 3.13 Social Intermediation in a Social Fund in Benin

AGENCE DE FINANCEMENT DES INITIATIVES DE BASE IS A social fund in Benin supported by the World Bank and Deutsche Gesellschaft für Technische Zusammenarbeit. Its goal is to help alleviate poverty through infrastructure development, capacity building of communities and NGOs, and social intermediation. Given the dozens of microfinance institutions or providers in Benin, many of which are performing well, the social fund has chosen not to engage in financial intermediation. Instead, it has focused on helping the existing institutions expand their outreach to the poorer segments of the population. To do

that, it has relied on NGOs that work with small entrepreneurs in the most remote villages or poor communities, helping them to understand the principles according to which the existing MFIs function and then linking them to the MFI of their choice. The NGOs also convey to the MFIs the messages they hear in the village, so that the MFIs can better adapt their services and products to the specific demand of this target clientele. This role of social intermediation played by the NGOs should lead to increased financial intermediation for the underserved population in Benin.

Source: Contributed by Cecile Fruman, Sustainable Banking with the Poor Project, World Bank

---

3. This section and appendix 2 were written by Thomas Dichter, Sustainable Banking with the Poor Project, World Bank.

Box 3.14 Business Skills Training

Box 3.14 Business Skills Training

FUNDACION CARVAJAL IN COLOMBIA PROVIDES SHORT practical courses in a range of accounting, marketing, and management topics adapted to microenterprise needs.

Empretec in Ghana provides a two-tiered management training course for microenterprise operators who exhibit specific entrepreneurial characteristics and are willing to adopt new management attitudes and tools.

Source: Contributed by Thomas Dichter, Sustainable Banking with the Poor Project, World Bank.

- Business training (box 3.14)
- Production training
- Subsector analysis and interventions.

The most common *providers* of enterprise development services to date have been:

- NGOs running microfinance projects with integrated approaches
- Training institutes
- Networks
- Universities
- Private firms (training companies, bilateral aid agency subcontractors)
- Producer groups (or chambers of commerce)
- Government agencies (small business assistance, export promotion bureaus)
- Informal networks providing production training through apprenticeships.

Studies sponsored by the U.S. Agency for International Development in the late 1980s found that enterprise development service programs could be divided into:

- *Enterprise formation* programs, offering training in sector-specific skills such as weaving as well as training for persons who might start up such businesses
- *Enterprise transformation* programs, providing technical assistance, training, and technology to help existing microenterprises make a quantitative and qualitative leap in terms of scale of production and marketing.

An additional distinction is between *direct* and *indirect* services, which has to do with the interaction between the provider of services and the enterprises (box 3.15). Direct services are those that bring the client in contact with the provider. Indirect services are those that benefit the client without such direct contact, as in policy-level interventions.

All enterprise development services have as their goal the improved performance of the business at hand, which in turn improves the financial condition of the owner or operator. In a sense, enterprise development services are a residual or catch-all category—they can be almost everything except financial services. As a result, they are a far broader and more complex arena in which to work than credit and savings (box 3.16).

Some experts suggest that enterprise development services be provided by a different institution than the one providing financial services. However, if an MFI chooses to provide such services, they should be clearly separated from other activities and accounted for separately. Furthermore, enterprise development services

Box 3.15 Direct and Indirect Business Advisory Services

THE BUSINESS WOMEN'S ASSOCIATION OF SWAZILAND visits clients' workshops on a regular basis to provide basic management advice for a fee (direct services).

Alternatively, the carpenters association in Ouagadougou, Burkina Faso, developed a promotional brochure to increase the number and size of contracts with small and medium-size firms and government agencies (indirect services).

Source: Contributed by Thomas Dichter, Sustainable Banking with the Poor Project, World Bank.

Box 3.16 Cattle Dealers in Mali

IN PAYS DOGON, MALI, AN MFI PROVIDING ENTERPRISE development services helped to organize a gathering with cattle dealers, where they identified their main need as a reliable means of transportation to move cattle from the villages to the towns. They decided to call a second meeting and invite some of the local truck owners to discuss the problems and identify solutions. As a result, the cattle dealers started sharing truck loads to reduce costs. They also began to pressure the truck owners to provide timely and high-quality transportation services.

Source: Contributed by Cecile Fruman, Sustainable Banking with the Poor Project, World Bank.

should never be a requirement for obtaining financial services.

They should also be fee-based. While full cost recovery may not be possible, the goal should be to generate as much revenue as possible to cover the costs of delivering the services. This is why some traditional providers (such as government agencies) have been in this arena—they know that enterprise development services must be subsidized. The services will almost always involve some type of subsidy, which has to be external to the enterprises unless it is provided by groups of enterprises that devote a portion of their profits to keeping the services going. Even private firms (or bilateral aid agency subcontractors) and universities usually provide enterprise development services under grants from foundations and governments.

Direct services to enterprises (such as entrepreneurship and business skills training), the organization of microenterprises into clusters, and so on require sensitivity on the part of the provider to the circumstances of poor people, a capacity to stick with and work for long periods in poor communities, and dedication to helping the poor. These characteristics are usually found among people who work in NGOs.

In general, enterprise development services are somewhat problematic, because even though the payoff can be great, it is difficult to judge either the impact or the performance of the service provider itself. Enterprise development services projects do not generally involve money as a commodity, but rather the transfer of knowledge in the form of skills, information, research, and analysis. The returns to the client as a result of this new knowledge are difficult to assess. Likewise, because the client cannot measure the value of "knowledge" at the "point of purchase," paying its full cost to the provider is rarely possible.

Certain studies have questioned the value of enterprise development services in the following areas:

- *Impact.* Some studies have shown that in many cases there is little difference in profits and efficiency between those microenterprises that received credit alone and those that received an integrated enterprise development services and credit package.
- *Cost and impact.* According to Rhyne and Holt (1994), "these [enterprise development service] programs tend to fall into one of two patterns. Either they have provided generic services to large numbers,

with little impact on the businesses; or they have provided closely tailored assistance to a few enterprises, at high cost per beneficiary."

- *Outreach.* A common complaint about enterprise development services is that women's access to these services is limited. A study by the United Nations Development Fund for Women in 1993 found that only 11 percent of government-sponsored business training slots went to women, due to time conflicts between their work and household responsibilities, the location (often distant from the village or slum), and bias in some formal training institutions against working with women clients.

The main response to these doubts is that enterprise development services approaches are highly varied, and to date only a few of many possibilities have been tried. It is premature to conclude that these services have little impact or have inherent limits in terms of outreach. Nor are there enough cases in which enterprise development services are provided exclusively rather than as part of an integrated package. However, they are likely most valuable for larger microenterprises, since smaller ones are often engaged in traditional activities that people know how to operate already. There is a high cost involved in providing enterprise development services directly to individual enterprises, but if the assisted business grows and creates significant employment, the long-term payoffs can outweigh the initial cost. The dissenting views mentioned above refer only to the direct provision of enterprise development services and do not take into account the potential high returns accruing to indirect provision.

There has been little documentation of the results and outcomes of enterprise development services because these services often have been part of integrated approaches. And unlike financial services, the wide range of approaches and strategies possible under the rubric of enterprise development services means that there are fewer agreed techniques to be learned and adapted by MFIs wishing to take this approach.

Whether an MFI provides enterprise development services depends on its goals, vision, and ability to attract donor funds to subsidize the costs. (See appendix 2 for more information about enterprise development services.)

Social Services

While social services such as health, nutrition, education, and literacy training are often provided by the state, a local NGO (with or without assistance from an international NGO), or a community organization, some MFIs have chosen to provide social services in addition to financial intermediation (box 3.17). In this way, they are able to take advantage of contact with clients during loan disbursement and repayment.

Box 3.17 Who Offers Social Services?

A RECENT WORLD BANK SURVEY EXAMINED THE ARRAY of financial and nonfinancial services offered by more than 200 microfinance institutions around the world.

Analysis of the types of institutions that offer social services showed that nongovernmental organizations (NGOs) were more active in providing services and training relating to health, nutrition, education, and group formation. This trend was particularly pronounced in Asia. Credit unions tended to have more of a financial focus than NGOs did but were also quite involved in literacy and vocational training. Banks and savings banks were more narrowly focused on financial services, as shown in the ratio of social staff to financial staff in the figure.

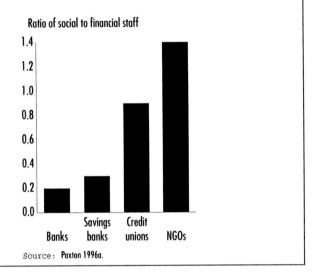

Ratio of social to financial staff

Source: Paxton 1996a.

Box 3.18 Freedom From Hunger—Providing Nutrition Training with Microfinance

FREEDOM FROM HUNGER IS AN INTERNATIONAL NON-governmental organization (NGO) based in Davis, California, with operations in Latin America, Africa, and Asia. It believes that microfinance services are unlikely to relieve most of the burdens of poverty without important economic, social, medical, and nutritional changes in participants' behavior.

Their basic premise is that very poor people—especially women in rural areas—face tremendous obstacles to becoming good financial services clients. The reasons include social isolation, lack of self-confidence, limited entrepreneurial experience, and major health and nutritional problems. When the goal is to provide credit for the alleviation of an entire family's poverty, these clients need more than credit alone. They need educational services that specifically address these obstacles and that provide a framework for solutions.

Freedom From Hunger utilizes the "credit with education" village banking model—group-based lending to the poor that cost effectively uses the regular group meetings

for educational as well as financial purposes. The organization believes that group-based lending models have social as well as economic potential and that this dual potential must be realized to have an impact on poverty. By helping the poor to manage their own self-help groups successfully and use credit to increase their incomes and begin saving, these programs engage in vital activities that improve confidence, self-esteem, and control over one's environment.

In credit with education programs, a part of each regular meeting is set aside for a learning session. Initially, a member of the program staff (usually a moderately educated person from the local area) facilitates each learning session. Village bank members identify the poverty-related problems they confront in their daily lives and become motivated to develop and use solutions that are appropriate to the location. The topics addressed in learning sessions range from village bank management to the basic economics of microenterprise to the improvement of the health and nutrition of women and children.

(Box continues on next page.)

Box 3.18 Freedom From Hunger—Providing Nutrition Training with Microfinance (Continued)

Freedom From Hunger is committed to achieving full recovery of operating and financial costs with interest revenue from loans to village banks. However, Freedom From Hunger and other credit with education practitioners (Catholic Relief Services, Katalysis, Plan International, and World Relief, among others) differ in their attitudes toward covering the costs of education with revenue from credit operations. Some have separate field agents to provide financial services and educational services to the same village bank. They regard education as a social service that can and should be subsidized by grants or government taxes and they also believe that the skills required for delivering effective education and financial services are too many and too varied for a single field agent. Other practitioners try to minimize the marginal cost of education by training and supporting each field agent to provide both financial and

education services to the same village bank. These practitioners limit the number, scope, and time allocation for topics to be addressed, maintaining that the marginal cost of education is low enough for reasonable interest charges to cover the costs of both financial and educational services. They also believe that the marginal cost of education can be legitimately charged to the village banks, because it makes the members better financial service clients by improving their family survival skills, productivity, and management skills.

Practitioners of credit with education believe that there may also be a cost to *not* providing education, such as epidemic outbreaks, loan growth stagnation, and member dropout due to illness of children. Comparison studies are currently going on to determine the impact of credit with education programs.

Source: Freedom From Hunger 1996.

As in the case of enterprise development services, the delivery and management of social services should be kept as distinct as possible from the delivery and management of financial intermediation services. This does not mean that social services cannot be provided during group meetings, but they must be clearly identified as separate from credit and savings services. Furthermore, it is not reasonable to expect that revenue generated from financial intermediation will always cover the costs of delivering social services. Rather, the delivery of social services will most likely require ongoing subsidies. MFIs that choose to provide social services must be clear about the costs incurred and must ensure that the donors supporting the MFI understand the implications of providing these services.

Freedom From Hunger provides an example of an international NGO that provides social services in conjunction with financial intermediation (box 3.18).

Appendix 1. Microfinance Approaches

The following pages provide information on some of the most well-known microfinance approaches. The approaches presented are:
- Individual lending
- Grameen Bank solidarity lending

- Latin American solidarity group lending
- Village banking
- Self-reliant village banks.

While microfinance approaches generally include some specific product design issues, a primary means of differentiating one approach from another is in the choice of products and services provided and the manner in which provision is made. Any approach must be based on the target market and its demand for financial intermediation, as well as other products, contextual factors in the country, and the objectives and institutional structure of the MFI. These approaches do not operate in isolation. Many of them rely on other institutions (either public or private) to provide additional services so that the targeted clients can effectively utilize financial services.

The Grameen Trust supports replicators of the Grameen Bank model around the world with funding and technical assistance. However, the Grameen Trust will only support MFIs that replicate *exactly* the model for their first two years as it is implemented in Bangladesh. Grameen believes that their model is successful because of *all* of its elements and that if some are rejected or changed, the MFI might fail. After two years of operations replicators are allowed to introduce changes if they feel that some elements must be adapted to the local context.

Box A3.1.1 Training for Replicators in West Africa

IN WEST AFRICA AN INNOVATIVE TRAINING CYCLE HAS been set up for African replicators (Itinéraire de Formation-Diffusion). The total cycle lasts for seven months, during which time replicators receive a month of formal training and spend four months on three different MFI sites, where they participate fully in the institution's activities. During the last three months, the trainees design their own MFI, drawing on the experience they have acquired in the field and the knowledge they have of their home market. With such a process the newly established MFIs can become a synthesis of several successful programs. After the initial training the replicators receive ongoing technical assistance and follow-up from the model programs.

Source: Contributed by Cecile Fruman, Sustainable Banking with the Poor Project, World Bank.

Other practitioners are strongly in favor of *adaptation.* They believe that there is no single model appropriate for all situations and that every model must be adapted to the local context to fit local needs. This requires that MFIs be flexible and creative. ACCION has been successful in adapting their solidarity group lending model to varying contexts.

Individual Lending

Individual lending is defined as the provision of credit to individuals who are not members of a group that is jointly responsible for loan repayment. Individual lending requires frequent and close contact with individual clients to provide credit products tailored to the specific needs of the business. It is most successful for larger, urban-based, production-oriented businesses and for clients who have some form of collateral or a willing cosigner. In rural areas, individual lending can also be successful with small farmers.

METHOD. Clients are individuals working in the informal sector who need working capital and credit for fixed assets. Credit officers usually work with a relatively small number of clients (between 60 and 140) and develop close relationships with them over the years, often providing minimal technical assistance. Loan amounts and terms are based on careful analysis by the credit officer.

Interest rates are higher than formal sector loans but lower than informal sector loans. Most MFIs require some form of collateral or cosignatories. Compulsory savings usually are not required.

Detailed financial analysis and projections are often included with the loan application. The amount and terms are negotiated with the client and the credit officer's supervisor or other credit officers. Documentation is required, including a loan contract; details regarding the clients references; if applicable, a form signed by the cosigner and his or her personal information; and legal deeds to assets being pledged and credit history. Credit officers are often recruited from the community so that they can base their analysis on their knowledge of the client's creditworthiness (character-based lending).

The loan is usually disbursed at the branch office. A visit is often made to the client's place of business to verify that the client has made the purchases specified in the loan contract. Periodic payments are made at the branch or through preapproved payments.

PRODUCTS. Loan sizes can vary from US$100 to US$3,000 with terms between six months and five years. Savings may or may not be provided depending on the institutional structure of the MFI. Training and technical assistance may be provided by credit officers; sometimes training is provided on a per-fee-basis or is mandatory.

SIGNIFICANT EXAMPLES. These include ADEMI in the Dominican Republic; Caja Municipales in Peru; Bank Rakyat Indonesia; Agence de Credit pour l'Enterprise Privée in Senegal; Alexandria Business Association in Egypt; Self-Employed Women's Association in India; Fédération des Caisses d'Epargne et de Crédit Agricole Mutuel in Benin; and Caja Social in Colombia.

APPROPRIATE CLIENTS. Clients are urban enterprises or small farmers, including both men and women, and may be medium-income small businesses, microbusinesses, and production enterprises.

Grameen Solidarity Group Lending

This lending model was developed by the Grameen Bank of Bangladesh to serve rural, landless women wishing to finance income-generating activities. This model is prevalent mostly in Asia but has been replicated in other contexts. Grameen Trust has more than 40 replicators in Asia, Africa, and Latin America.

METHOD. Peer groups of five unrelated members are self-formed and incorporated into village "centers" of up to eight peer groups. Attendance at weekly meetings and weekly savings contributions, group fund contributions, and insurance payments are mandatory. Savings must be contributed for four to eight weeks prior to receiving a loan and must continue for the duration of the loan term. The group fund is managed by the group and may be lent out within the group. Group members mutually guarantee each other's loans and are held legally responsible for repayment by other members. No further loans are available if all members do not repay their loans on time. No collateral is required. Mandatory weekly meetings include self-esteem building activities and discipline enforcement.

Loans are made to individuals within the group by the local credit officer at the weekly meetings. However, only two members receive loans initially. After a period of successful repayment, two more members receive loans. The final member receives her loan after another period of successful repayment. Grameen typically provides precredit orientation but minimal technical assistance. Loan appraisal is performed by group members and center leaders. Branch staff verify information and make periodic visits to client businesses. Credit officers usually carry between 200 and 300 clients.

PRODUCTS. Credit is for six months to one year and payments are made weekly. Loan amounts are usually from US$100 to US$300. Interest rates are 20 percent a year. Savings are compulsory.

SIGNIFICANT EXAMPLES. These include Grameen Bank and Bangladesh Rural Advancement Committee in Bangladesh; Tulay sa Pag-Unlad, Inc. and Project Dungganon in the Philippines; Sahel Action in Burkina Faso; and Vietnam Women's Union.

APPROPRIATE CLIENTELE. Clients are from rural or urban (densely populated) areas and are usually (although not exclusively) women from low-income groups (means tests are applied to ensure outreach to the very poor) pursuing income-generating activities.

Latin American Solidarity Group Lending

The solidarity group lending model makes loans to individual members in groups of four to seven. The members cross-guarantee each other's loans to replace traditional collateral. Clients are commonly female market vendors who receive very small, short-term working capital loans. This model was developed by ACCION International in Latin America and has been adapted by many MFIs.

METHOD. Customers are typically informal sector microbusinesses, such as merchants or traders who need small amounts of working capital. Group members collectively guarantee loan repayment, and access to subsequent loans is dependent on successful repayment by all group members. Payments are made weekly at the program office. The model also incorporates minimal technical assistance to the borrowers, such as training and organization building. Credit officers generally work with between 200 and 400 clients and do not normally get to know their clients very well. Loan approval is by the credit officers based on minimal economic analysis of each loan request. Loan disbursement is made to the group leader at the branch office, who immediately distributes to each individual member. Credit officers make brief, occasional visits to individual clients.

Group members normally receive equal loan amounts, with some flexibility provided for subsequent loans. Loan amounts and terms are gradually increased once clients demonstrate the ability to take on larger amounts of debt. Loan applications are simple and are reviewed quickly. Savings are usually required but are often deducted from the loan amount at the time of disbursement rather than requiring the clients to save prior to receiving a loan. Savings serve primarily as a compensating balance, guaranteeing a portion of the loan amount.

PRODUCTS. Initial loan amounts are generally between US$100 and US$200. Subsequent loans have no upper limit. Interest rates are often quite high and service fees are also charged. Savings are usually required as a portion of the loan; some institutions encourage establishing intragroup emergency funds to serve as a safety net. Very few voluntary savings products are offered.

SIGNIFICANT EXAMPLES. These include ACCION affiliates: PRODEM, BancoSol Bolivia; Asociación Grupos

Solidarios de Colombia; and Genesis and PROSEM in Guatemala.

APPROPRIATE CLIENTELE. Clients are mostly urban and include both men and women who have small to medium incomes (microbusinesses, merchants, or traders).

Village Banking

Village banks are community-managed credit and savings associations established to provide access to financial services in rural areas, build a community self-help group, and help members accumulate savings (Otero and Rhyne 1994). The model was developed in the mid-1980s by the Foundation for International Community Assistance (FINCA). Membership in a village bank usually ranges from 30 to 50 people, most of whom are women. Membership is based on self-selection. The bank is financed by internal mobilization of members' funds as well as loans provided by the MFI.

METHOD. A village bank consists of its membership and a management committee, which receives training from the sponsoring MFI. The sponsoring MFI lends seed capital (external account) to the bank, which then lends on the money to its members. All members sign the loan agreement to offer a collective guarantee. The loan amount to the village bank is based on an aggregate of all individual members' loan requests. Although the amount varies between countries, first loans are typically short term (four to six months) and are small amounts ($50), to be repaid in weekly installments. The amount of the second loan is determined by the savings a member has accumulated during the first loan period through weekly contributions. The methodology anticipates that the members will save a minimum of 20 percent of the loan amount per cycle (internal account). Loans from the internal account (member savings, interest earnings) set their own terms, which are generally shorter, and their own interest rates, which are generally much higher. Loans to the village banks are generally provided in a series of fixed cycles, usually 10 to 12 months each, with lump-sum payments at the end of each cycle. Subsequent loan amounts are linked to the aggregate amount saved by individual bank members. Village banks have a high degree of democratic control and independence.

Regular weekly or monthly meetings are held to collect savings deposits, disburse loans, attend to administrative issues, and, if applicable, continue training with the MFI officer.

PRODUCTS. Members' savings are tied to loan amounts and are used to finance new loans or collective income-generating activities. No interest is paid on savings. However, members receive a share from the bank's relending or investment profits. The dividend distributed is directly proportional to the amount of savings each individual has contributed to the bank.

Loans have commercial rates of interest (1 to 3 percent per month) and higher rates if from an internal account. Some banks have broadened service delivery to include education about agricultural innovations, nutrition, and health.

SIGNIFICANT EXAMPLES. These include FINCA in Mexico and Costa Rica; CARE in Guatemala; Save The Children in El Salvador; Freedom From Hunger in Thailand, Burkina Faso, Bolivia, Mali, and Ghana; and Catholic Relief Services in Thailand and Benin. The original model has been adapted in a variety of ways. In FINCA in Costa Rica committee members take on the tasks of bank teller and manager. Catholic Relief Services works through local NGOs. Freedom From Hunger in West Africa works directly with credit unions in order to help them increase their membership among women. Its clients graduate to the credit union.

APPROPRIATE CLIENTELE. Clients are usually from rural or sparsely populated but sufficiently cohesive areas. They have very low incomes but with savings capacity, and are predominantly women (although the program is also adequate for men or mixed groups).

Self-Reliant Village Banks (Savings and Loans Associations)

Self-reliant village banks are established and managed by rural village communities. They differ from village banks in that they cater to the needs of the village as a whole, not just a group of 30 to 50 people. This model was developed by a French NGO, the Centre for International Development and Research, in the mid-1980s.

METHOD. The supporting program identifies villages where social cohesion is strong and the desire to set up a village bank is clearly expressed. The villagers—men and women together—determine the organization and rules of their bank. They elect a management and credit committee and two or three managers. Self-reliant village banks mobilize savings and extend short-term loans to villagers on an individual basis. The sponsoring program does not provide lines of credit. The bank must rely on its savings mobilization.

After a year or two the village banks build up an informal network or association in which they discuss current issues and try to solve their difficulties. The association acts as intermediary and negotiates lines of credit with local banks, usually an agriculture development bank. This links the village banks to the formal financial sector. Because management is highly decentralized, central services are limited to internal control and auditing, specific training, and representation. These services are paid for by the village banks, which guarantees the financial sustainability of the model.

PRODUCTS. These include savings, current accounts, and term deposits. Loans are short-term, working-capital loans. There is no direct link between loan amounts and a member's savings capacity; interest rates are set by each village according to its experience with traditional savings and loans associations. The more remote the area, the higher the interest rate tends to be, because the opportunity cost of money is high. Loans are paid in one installment. Loans are individual and collateral is necessary, but above all it is village trust and social pressure that ensure high repayment rates. Management committees, managers, and members all receive extensive training. Some programs also provide technical assistance to microentrepreneurs who are starting up a business.

SIGNIFICANT EXAMPLES. These include Caisses Villageoises d'Epargne et de Crédit Autogérées in Mali (Pays Dogon), Burkina Faso, Madagascar, The Gambia (Village Savings and Credit Associations or VISACA), São Tomé, and Cameroon.

APPROPRIATE CLIENTELE. Clients are in rural areas and include both men and women with low to medium incomes and some savings capacity.

Appendix 2. Matching Enterprise Development Services to Demand

Designing appropriate enterprise development services requires an understanding of the many systems (cultural, legal, political, macroeconomic, local, marketplace) within which microenterprises operate. Microentrepreneurs and small business operators may be less aware than their larger counterparts are of the degree to which those systems can impinge upon their business activity.

One can visualize these contexts as a series of concentric circles, with the person operating the business at the center (figure A3.2.1).

Circle 1. The Business Operator

The enterprise owner's self is the first context in which he or she operates. Each individual brings his or her own circumstances, energies, character, skills, and ideas to the enterprise. At this level, constraints on the success of the business often have to do with intangibles such as the presence of or lack of confidence, tenacity, resourcefulness, ambition, adaptability, and the capacity to learn. Likewise, the business operator's level of basic skills (literacy and numeracy) and their applications in the business (book-

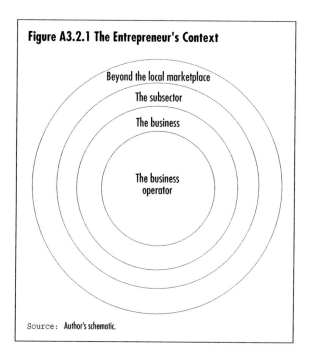

Figure A3.2.1 The Entrepreneur's Context

Beyond the local marketplace

The subsector

The business

The business operator

Source: Author's schematic.

keeping, being able to read the maintenance instructions on a machine) will obviously make a difference. Some of these needs are addressed through the provision of social intermediation or social services.

Beyond the entrepreneur's self is the realm of knowledge and skills that are *directly related to the conduct of business*. On the cusp of the second circle (the business itself) the emphasis is still on the knowledge possessed by the operator. Business skills training aimed at imparting basics such as bookkeeping and record keeping usually involves fairly generic skills and thus lends itself to classroom teaching.

For start-up businesses an enterprise development service provider can introduce concepts of the market and courses that provide opportunities for practice in bookkeeping and accounting, legal issues (registration), business planning, marketing, and pricing, as well as customer orientation.

A program could, for example, help a woman shopkeeper devise an inventory system and a simple worksheet to monitor operating costs. She also could maintain a book that lists those products her clients ask for that she does not currently sell.

It is very important to know which entrepreneurs have a chance to become successful. Accordingly, some tests of commitment and ambition can be imposed. One methods is to have people pay or agree to pay later a portion of their profits to the service provider. Another is to not offer the service until a certain level of business activity has been reached.

It is also important to differentiate between skills that can successfully be imparted by teaching (the generic business skills discussed above) and those that need to be imparted one-on-one in the business setting (see below).

Circle 2. The Business Itself

The second concentric circle surrounding the entrepreneur is the business itself. This is where all operations take place in the enterprise, from buying inputs to making and selling the product or service. At this level the problems and constraints encountered begin to have as much to do with forces external to the operator as they do with the operator's knowledge.

Enterprise development services provided directly to the business tend to be less generic in nature and more custom-tailored. Thus the cost of providing service rises.

At this level the service provider has to understand what the product or service is, how it is produced, what technology is used, what human labor is involved, and what the inputs are. For example, if a tailor requires zippers or buttons, how are they supplied and how are they inventoried, if at all? If storage is required, how is that made available? Is time being lost because regular machinery maintenance is not scheduled properly or because parts that wear out on a predictable basis are not stocked in anticipation of need? What about the employees or other human input that the business depends on? Are they family members? Are they paid? How are they paid? Do they stay on? Or do they leave to become competitors?

Can production be improved by changing the flow of work itself or by changing the physical organization of the work space? Is there waste that can be eliminated or reduced? Would changes in the timing of production or selling make a positive difference in the owner's bottom line?

Many changes that can be made within the enterprise need to be brought to the attention of the entrepreneur by an outsider. That outsider can be an "expert" or advisor working for the enterprise development service provider or a colleague in the same type of business.

The many methods used in enterprise development services at the business level range from on-site visits by a regular business advisor to the creation of local walk-in business advisory service offices and enterprise clusters or industry networks. They may, even in the case of literate urban entrepreneurs, include advice that comes in printed form or that entrepreneurs can learn themselves, for example, by going through a stock set of questions that provide them with the equivalent of an "outsider's viewpoint."

The more one moves away from one-on-one *direct* enterprise development services to *indirect* service provision the more likely it is that costs per client will go down. But in the case of indirect service provision, outcomes similar to those possible with direct service cannot be automatically achieved. Indirect services at the business level can also include industrial estates and business incubators. These can be set up on a commodity subsector basis, that is, by concentrating enterprises that are in the same or related subsector (for example, woodworking) or that share the trait of being start-ups. The first benefit is that start-ups share the costs of receiving subsidies to cover the costs of infrastructure and basic services such as electricity, water, storage space, and machinery. By concentrating businesses in the same place, enterprises also benefit from external economies—the emergence of suppliers who provide raw materials and components at a bulk price, new and second hand machinery and parts, and the emergence of or access to a pool of workers with sector-specific skills.

Sometimes the industrial estate or business incubator provides intangible but equally important benefits to start-ups by enabling the entrepreneurs to speak with each other informally. This often builds confidence and fosters the discovery of new solutions to problems. More tangibly, as start-ups mature and business grows, subcontracting arrangements within the incubator often develop.

Unfortunately, industrial estates and business incubators have often failed. Many microenterprise operators try to avoid regulation and taxation, and they often see the visibility involved in moving to an industrial estate or incubator as disincentives. Microenterprises often depend on walk-in clients, so moving out of low-income neighborhoods can mean losing customers. These are problems that can be solved by paying more attention to the location of such incubators and estates. Overall, the problems with these failed efforts often have had more to do with the fact that they have been started by government agencies without careful preparation, proper incentives for government workers, or the participation of the eventual users in their planning.

Circle 3. The Subsector

All businesses operate in the context of other businesses in the same subsector and sellers and suppliers of inputs and services to the subsector. A subsector is identified by its final product and includes all firms engaged in the supply of raw materials, production, and distribution of the product (Haggeblade and Gamser 1991). Subsector analysis describes the economic system of the businesses related to the final product and involves the provision of both financial and nonfinancial services. A subsector is defined as the full array of businesses involved in making and selling a product or group of products, from initial input suppliers to final retailers. Typical areas of intervention include technology development, skill training, collective marketing or purchasing of inputs, and, in some cases, policy advocacy (Rhyne and Holt 1994). Examples of subsectors that MFIs have developed are dairy, wool, sericulture, palm oil, and fisheries.

The subsector approach emphasizes (Rhyne and Holt 1994, 33):

- *Market access.* The subsector approach aims to identify both the growing portions of subsector markets and the barriers that must be overcome if small enterprises are to gain access to those growth markets.
- *Leverage.* The approach aims for cost effectiveness by identifying interventions that can affect large numbers of enterprises at one time, often through indirect rather than one-on-one mechanisms.
- *Releasing constraints.* Many of the most important constraints it addresses are highly industry specific and thus are missed by "generic" enterprise development.

Subsector analysis requires versatility in design and flexible access to a wide range of skills. Institutions that identify subsector analysis as a means of intervention will need to consider many issues.

Common constraints at the subsector level are:

- Rising competition, as low barriers to entry allow new microenterprises into the marketplace
- Space for the market's physical infrastructure, including warehousing
- The imposition of fees or solicitation of bribes by local authorities
- Transport availability, reliability, and cost
- Input availability, if a commodity that the enterprise needs for production is not available regularly
- Lack of appropriate technology
- Limits (permanent, cyclical, seasonal) in customer purchasing power
- Lack of product diversity
- Dominance by middlemen.

For example, the structure of ownership of transport may be something a group of enterprises could correct if assisted by an enterprise development service provider. A U.S. NGO working in rural Zaire in the mid-1980s helped local farmers pool resources to form a shareholder-owned trucking company, which served producers who were unable to make money because they faced exorbitant transport fees. The service provider undertook the legal work involved in setting up this company and helped to put together the finance plan for the first vehicle.

Often the way things are purchased is a constraint on efficiency. For example, in the second-hand clothing business in much of Africa the quality of the bales varies randomly. The buyer does not know what is in the bale and cannot look inside before purchasing it.

Accordingly, the buyer is often reluctant to pool-purchase bales with other sellers. However, if an enterprise development service provider were to come up with a way of decreasing this risk (for example, by pooling purchases and then creating a secondary distribution channel whereby the contents of each repackaged bale *would* be known), this constraint could be overcome.

Inputs are often a major problem, as are parts or the sourcing of equipment. People may not know of available alternative sources.

Technology itself is often a constraint. New technologies can be developed that are custom-tailored to a specific level of the subsector. Pricing can also be a constraint. In some subsectors, particularly retail petty trade in the urban developing world, price can be the only feature differentiating adjacent sellers (personality traits of the sellers excepted). The goods are likely to be the same, and as one seller is literally six inches away from the next, location is not a factor. And yet price itself cannot vary much, if at all. By studying the supply of the commodity traded (shoes, for example) and the nature of its wholesaling, it may be possible to form a buyers' coop through which petty traders can reduce the price they pay and thus pass on that savings to the consumer (although this competitive advantage may be short-lived).

The timing of production of some commodities affects price. Retail traders in fresh foods are often at the mercy of the agricultural production cycle and do not know how to balance the relationship between their supply and the customers' demand. Storage or value added (such as through drying) give the seller an edge on price.

EXPANSION OF THE RANGE OF SUPPLIERS AND CUSTOMERS. This can be done by clustering and networking as well as by creating intermediaries or associations. Indirect options in which the enterprise development service provider can help are the organization of trade fairs, collective promotional efforts, trade coops, showroom and exhibition space, industrial estates, business incubation, and so forth. Pooling employees or temporarily exchanging employees can loosen constraints in the labor market, and enterprise development service providers can act as brokers for subcontracting between and among enterprises.

NETWORKING AND ENTREPRENEURS CLUBS. Cross-visits and other forms of network clustering or industrial net-

works can change the parameters of the market. Encouraging entrepreneurs to work together and to combine strengths is essential for the development of microenterprises. Cooperation between firms, mutual learning, and collective innovation can often expand a microenterprise's chances of increasing its market share and profits. Some examples:

- Sharing information on markets or suppliers
- Setting up joint cooperatives
- Bidding on contracts together
- Sharing costs of holding a stand at a fair or market
- Reducing costs of warehousing by splitting a facility.

MARKET INFRASTRUCTURE IMPROVEMENT. The World Bank's Southwest China Poverty Reduction Project includes construction of farmers' markets to improve the links between low-income household producers in poor counties in mountainous southwest China and transport companies from booming markets on the south China coast.

Circle 4. Beyond the Local Marketplace

The last of the concentric circles surrounding the individual microentrepreneur is the largest and furthest away from his or her enterprise. Here at the macro level the forces exerting constraints on the enterprise are indeed large. These can be at the country level, the regional level, and even the world trade level. They extend beyond the marketplace and economic forces in general to include:

- National social and political forces (corruption, instability, tribal rivalries, the admission or exclusion of nonnative traders, investors, and suppliers) and geopolitical forces (for example, the end of the influence of cold war politics on Africa).
- Regulatory and policy forces and constraints. Laws may work for or against a sector (or subsector) or for only one channel in a particular sector and against another channel in the same sector. Likewise, laws affect the way in which lenders operate (the presence of a thorough and reliable collateral law will affect the nature of lending throughout the financial sector). Licensing requirements for businesses and taxation can be important constraints.
- Macro-level market forces, such as the dynamism or weakness of other exporters of the same commodity

> ### Box A3.2.1   Policy Dialogue in El Salvador
>
> IN THE MID-1980S A U.S. NONGOVERNMENTAL ORGANIZA-
> tion working with subsector studies in El Salvador identi-
> fied a government policy that inadvertently created import
> competition to rural small enterprises making henequen
> fibre rope. The government simply was not aware that
> domestic needs for cheap rope could be met with domestic
> production. After this study was brought to the attention of
> the government through "policy dialogue," import regula-
> tions were changed to favor local producers. The initially
> high cost of undertaking the studies proved to be amortized
> quickly once the lot of many local producers improved.
>
> *Source:* Contributed by Thomas Dichter, Sustainable Banking
> with the Poor Project, World Bank.

in other countries (for example, Ghana was a major
exporter of palm oil until surpassed by Malaysia) or
the availability of uniform containers in a country for
the micro-level retailers (in Kenya, for example, the
production and selling of honey in the late 1980s was
negatively affected by the lack of readily available,
uniformly sized small containers).

- National and global labor market forces, including
  changes in migrant labor patterns (for example,
  Filipinos are no longer going to Saudi Arabia to work,
  thus changing the nature of competition in the start-up
  microenterprise arena in the Philippines); the nature of
  the workers' prior education, especially in technical
  skill areas; or the influence of cultural factors on people's willingness to take certain kinds of jobs.
- Contiguous financial sector constraints and enablers,
  such as a viable insurance industry that can price
  insurance at a rate affordable for small businesses
  investing in capital equipment or vehicles.

In general, the constraints that are the furthest away
are the hardest for entrepreneurs to do anything about
and can be the most binding. They are the forces that
set limits and that may ultimately keep the transformation of the microenterprises in a given sector from taking place. The enterprise development service provider
must understand these constraints even though they are
the hardest and most expensive to study, requiring a special capacity to analyze large forces and an investment in
rigorous research. Once conclusions about these macro-
level constraints are drawn, implementing real solutions

is also difficult and requires not just technical ability but
often political skill as well.

Although there have been very few enterprise development service providers who have operated at this
level of intervention, the payoffs and multiplier effects
can, in theory, be great. A service provider working in
this way is clearly providing an indirect service to enterprises, which the individual entrepreneur and even
groups of individuals banding together cannot provide
for themselves.

The enterprise development service provider can
undertake studies of the sector to identify hidden constraints that are invisible to the individual entrepreneur or
that the entrepreneur knows about but cannot change
without help.

Sources and Further Reading

Bennett, Lynn. 1993. "Developing Sustainable Financial Systems
    for the Poor: Where Subsidies Can Help and Where They
    Can Hurt." Talking notes for the World Bank AGRAP
    Seminar on Rural Finance, May 26, Washington, D.C.

———. 1994. "The Necessity—and the Dangers—of
    Combining Social and Financial Intermediation to Reach
    the Poor." Paper presented at a conference on Financial
    Services and the Poor at the Brookings Institution,
    September 28–30, Washington, D.C.

———. 1997. "A Systems Approach to Social and Financial
    Intermediation with the Poor." Paper presented at the
    Banking with the Poor Network/World Bank Asia Regional
    Conference on Sustainable Banking with the Poor,
    November 3–7, Bangkok.

Bennett, L., P. Hunte, and M. Goldberg. 1995. "Group-
    Based Financial Systems: Exploring the Links between
    Performance and Participation." World Bank, Asia
    Technical Department, Washington, D.C.

Biswas, Arun, and Vijay Mahajan. 1997. "SEWA Bank." Case
    Study for the Sustainable Banking with the Poor Project,
    World Bank, Washington, D.C.

Bratton, M. 1986. "Financing Smallholder Production: A
    Comparison of Individual and Group Credit Schemes in
    Zimbabwe." *Public Administration and Development (UK)* 6
    (April/June): 115–32.

Caskey, John P. 1994. "Fringe Banking—Check-Cashing
    Outlets, Pawnshops, and the Poor." Russel Sage Foun-
    dation, New York.

Committee of Donor Agencies for Small Enterprise
    Development. 1998. "Business Development Service for

SMEs: Preliminary Guidelines for Donor-Funded Interventions." Private Sector Development, World Bank, Washington, D.C.

CGAP (Consultative Group to Assist the Poorest). 1997. "Introducing Savings in Microcredit Institutions: When and How?" Focus Note 8. World Bank, Washington, D.C.

Freedom From Hunger. 1996. "The Case for Credit with Education." Credit with Education Learning Exchange Secretariat, Davis, California.

Fruman, Cecile. 1997. "FECECAM–Benin." Case Study for the Sustainable Banking with the Poor Project, World Bank, Washington, D.C.

Goldmark, Lara, Sira Berte, and Sergio Campos. 1997. "Preliminary Survey Results and Case Studies on Business Development Services for Microentrepreneurs." Inter-American Development Bank, Social Programs and Sustainable Development Department, Microenterprise Unit, Washington, D.C.

Haggeblade, J., and M. Gamser. 1991. "A Field Manual for Subsector Practitioners." GEMINI Technical Note. U.S. Agency for International Development, Washington, D.C.

Huppi, M., and Gershon Feder. 1990. "The Role of Groups and Credit Cooperatives in Rural Lending." *World Bank Research Observer (International)* 5 (2): 187–204.

Krahnen, Jan Pieter, and Reinhard H. Schmidt. 1994. *Development Finance as Institution Building: A New Approach to Poverty-Oriented Lending.* Boulder, Colo.: Westview Press.

Ledgerwood, Joanna, and Jill Burnett. 1995. "Individual Micro-Lending Research Project: A Case Study Review—ADEMI." Calmeadow, Toronto, Canada.

McLean, Doug, and Matt Gamser. 1995. "Hi-Tech at the Frontier: Reducing the Transaction Cost of Lending in Swaziland with the Smart Card." Seminar Abstract 5,

Sustainable Banking with the Poor Project, World Bank, Washington, D.C.

Nelson, Candace, Barbara McNelly, Kathleen Stack, and Lawrence Yanovitch. 1995. *Village Banking: The State of Practice.* The SEEP Network. New York: Pact Publications.

Otero, Maria, and Elizabeth Rhyne. 1994. *The New World of Microenterprise Finance: Building Healthy Financial Institutions for the Poor.* West Hartford, Conn.: Kumarian Press.

Paxton, Julia. 1996a. "A Worldwide Inventory of Microfinance Institutions." World Bank, Sustainable Banking with the Poor Project, Washington, D.C.

———. 1996b. "Determinants of Successful Group Loan Repayment: An Application to Burkina Faso." Ph.D. diss., Department of Agricultural Economics and Rural Sociology, Ohio State University, Columbia.

Puhazhendhi, V. 1995. "Transaction Costs of Lending to the Rural Poor: Non-Governmental Organizations and Self-help Groups of the Poor as Intermediaries for Banks in India." Foundation for Development Cooperation, Brisbane, Australia.

Rhyne E., and S. Holt. 1994. "Women in Finance and Enterprise Development." Education and Social Policy Discussion Paper 40. World Bank, Washington, D.C.

Von Pischke, J.D. 1991. *Finance at the Frontier: Debt Capacity and the Role of Credit in the Private Economy.* World Bank, Economic Development Institute. Washington, D.C.

Waterfield, Charles, and Ann Duval. 1996. *CARE Savings and Credit Sourcebook.* Atlanta, Ga.: CARE.

Women's World Banking. 1996. *Resource Guide to Business Development Service Providers.* New York.

Yaron, Jacob, McDonald Benjamin, and Gerda Piprek. 1997. "Rural Finance Issues, Design and Best Practices." World Bank, Agriculture and Natural Resources Department, Washington, D.C.

CHAPTER FOUR

The Institution

In chapter 3 we introduced the "Systems Framework" in which different institutions can be involved in providing the services demanded by low-income clients. In this chapter the focus is on the primary institution that provides financial services, its institutional structure, and its capacity to meet the demands of its clients.

The majority of MFIs are created as nongovernmental organizations (NGOs). However, as the field of microfinance develops, the focus is changing from the delivery of credit services to a true process of financial intermediation, including the provision of savings and other financial services demanded by the working poor. Furthermore, the shrinking resource base (donor funds) to support the ever-increasing demand implies that MFIs will eventually need to support themselves. Accompanying this change of perspective is a better understanding of the implications of institutional structure for achieving the ends of greater service, scale, and sustainability.

Many MFIs are now beginning to look at the advantages and disadvantages of different institutional structures. This chapter examines the range of institutional types that are appropriate for microfinance and for meeting the objectives of MFIs, including formal, semi-formal, and informal structures. It also addresses other institutional issues, including:

- Institutional growth and transformation
- Ownership and governance
- The accessing of new sources of funding
- Institutional capacity.

Most MFIs have established or are establishing *partnerships* with other development agencies, such as governments, donors, and international NGOs. When deciding whom to cooperate with, the objectives of both the MFI and the potential development partner must be considered. Partnerships affect the structure of the MFI, its funding sources, and its activities. The first section of this chapter gives an overview of why institutions (and partner institutions) are important and outlines the various institutional types. The remaining sections focus on the institutional issues that arise as MFIs grow and expand their operations.

This chapter will be of interest to donors or consultants who are examining or evaluating MFIs and to practitioners who are considering transforming their institutional structure, examining issues of governance, or developing new funding sources. Practitioners, donors, and international NGOs in the process of selecting partner institutions will also find this chapter interesting.

The Importance of Institutions

An institution is a collection of assets—human, financial, and others—combined to perform activities such as granting loans and taking deposits overtime.[1] A one-time activity such as a "project" is not an institution. Thus by its very nature an institution has a function and a certain permanence. However, when one looks at specific providers of financial intermediation to low-income women and men in a given country, one can easily see differences in the degree to which they really are institutions, that is, the degree to

---

1. This section and the following section on institutional types were written by Reinhardt Schmidt, Internationale Projekt Consult (IPC) GmbH.

which they have a well-defined function and are set up and run to perform their function on a permanent basis. Clearly, permanence is important. Poor men and women need permanent and reliable access to savings and credit facilities, and only stable institutions can assure permanence.

Attributes of a Good Institution

A good institution has three attributes:
1. It provides services to the relevant target group.
- *Appropriate services* include the offering of loans that match client demand. This refers to loan size and maturity, collateral requirements, and the procedures applied in granting loans and ensuring repayment. A good MFI must have or be willing to adopt an appropriate credit technology, which will enable quality services to be designed and distributed so that they are attractive and accessible to the target group.
- *The scope of services* must be consistent with the situation of the clientele. In some cases, simply offering loans of a specific type may be all that is needed; in others, an array of different loan types may be necessary, or it may be more important to offer deposit and payment transfer facilities or a combination of all these services.
- *Prices* that the clients have to pay for the services of the institution are *not* generally a point of major importance, according to practical experience. However, low *transaction costs* for clients, a high degree of deposit *liquidity,* and *rapid availability* of loans are extremely important features for a target-group-oriented institution to provide.
2. Its activities and offered services are not only demanded but also have some identifiable positive impact on the lives of the customers.
3. It is strong, financially sound, and stable.

Because the people who belong to the target group need a reliable supply of financial services—that is, access to credit facilities—and an institution to which they can entrust their deposits, it is of paramount importance that the MFI be a stable or sustainable institution or at least be clearly on the way to becoming one.

Stability has, first and foremost, a financial dimension. A stable institution is one whose existence and function is not threatened by a lack of funds for making necessary payments; it must be solvent at any given moment and also in the foreseeable future. In addition, a sustainable institution must be able to maintain or *expand its scale of operations.* This is important for two reasons. One is that only a growing institution can meet the demand that its clientele typically exhibits. The other is that many development finance institutions that cater to poor clients are so small that the unit costs of their operations are too high. Growth is an efficient way to reduce costs.

Experts sometimes claim that an MFI should not depend on external support but rather should be *subsidy independent.* This requires that the revenues from its operations be sufficient to cover all of its costs, including loan losses, the opportunity cost of equity, and the full, inflation-adjusted cost of debt. This is a requirement that any mature institution must meet, just like any commercial business. However, in most practical cases the real question is not whether an MFI is already financially self-sufficient—most of them are not—but rather, to what extent their costs exceed their revenues and whether and how fast their dependence on external support decreases over time. An MFI must be able and determined to make visible progress toward financial self-sufficiency.

Not all aspects of stability can be readily expressed in numbers. One such aspect is *organizational stability.* A sound MFI must have an organizational and ownership structure that helps to ensure its stability both in a financial sense and with respect to its target group. One cannot call an institution stable if it simply turns away from its original target group of poor clients as soon as it starts to grow and become more efficient and professional. This temptation is great, as poor people are not the most profitable target group or the easiest to deal with. Therefore it is all the more important that an MFI have an ownership and governance structure—that is, a division of roles between the management and the board of directors or the supervisory board—that prevents the institution from "drifting away into social irrelevance."

The Importance of Partner Institutions

Most MFIs, with the possible exception of some commercial banks, work with one or more development agencies or partners. These development agencies may be international NGOs, governments, or donors that provide technical assistance, funding, and training to the MFI itself rather than the MFI's clients. (While some partner institutions may in fact provide services directly to the clients of an MFI, here we are considering partners that help to develop the ability of an MFI to provide financial intermediation.)

Table 4.1 Key Characteristics of a Strong Microfinance Institution

Key areas	Characteristics
Vision	■ A mission statement that defines the target market and services offered and is endorsed by management and staff. ■ A strong commitment by management to pursuing microfinance as a potentially profitable market niche (in terms of people and funds). ■ A business plan stating how to reach specific strategic objectives in three to five years.
Financial services and delivery methods	■ Simple financial services adapted to the local context and in high demand by the clients described in the mission statement. ■ Decentralization of client selection and financial service delivery.
Organizational structure and human resources	■ Accurate job descriptions, relevant training, and regular performance reviews. ■ A business plan spelling out training priorities and a budget allocating adequate funds for internally or externally provided training (or both). ■ Appropriate performance-based incentives offered to staff and management.
Administration and finance	■ Loan processing and other activities based on standardized practices and operational manuals and widely understood by staff. ■ Accounting systems producing accurate, timely, and transparent information as inputs to the management information system. ■ Internal and external audits carried out at regular intervals. ■ Budgets and financial projections made regularly and realistically.
Management information system	■ Systems providing timely and accurate information on key indicators that are most relevant to operations and are regularly used by staff and management in monitoring and guiding operations.
Institutional viability	■ Legal registration and compliance with supervisory requirements. ■ Clearly defined rights and responsibilities of owners, board of directors, and management. ■ Strong second level of technically trained managers.
Outreach and financial sustainability	■ Achievement of significant scale, including a large number of underserved clients (for example, the poor and women). ■ Coverage of operating and financial costs clearly progressing toward full sustainability (as demonstrated in audited financial statements and financial projections).

Source: Fruman and Isern 1996.

Both practitioners and donors should consider the importance of partnerships, because the need to strengthen local institutions and build their capacity is essential to meeting the growing demand of low-income clients.

The term "partner" does not suggest a biased relationship in which the more powerful and resourceful side imposes its will and ideas upon the other. Instead, partners discuss and jointly define objectives and ways of attaining them. In a partnership both sides have the same rights to determine what the partners can do and want to do together.

Partnerships are formed when:

"organizations seek to mutually strengthen and sustain themselves. It [the partnership] is an empowering process, which relies on trust and confidence, solidarity of vision and approach, and it acknowledges mutual contribution and equality. Both partners have complementary roles, established through negotiations and subject to change as the partnership grows and circumstances change." (Long, Daouda, and Cawley 1990, 124)

Local institutions can bring to the partnership the advantage of knowing more about local circumstances: the target group or clientele, their situation and demand for financial services, the local financial market, and the local laws and habits. Furthermore, there are ethical and political considerations that make it advisable for a foreign institution to have a local partner. Last but not least, a local partner is needed when an institution has been established and the foreign partner is planning to withdraw from the MFI and leave it in the hands of local people. The failure of thousands of development finance projects in the past demonstrates that it is necessary to have not only an institutional basis but also strong local

partners if a permanent institution with a lasting impact for low-income women and men is to be created.

Foreign partner agencies can bring funding, technical assistance, and training to the partnership. Often foreign partner agencies are familiar with microfinance "best practices" and have at their disposal information and sources to which the local partner may not readily have access.

An American international NGO, Freedom From Hunger, focuses on linking its MFI operations in Africa with local bank and credit unions. This has allowed it to focus primarily on technical assistance while creating sustainable institutions in the countries in which it works (box 4.1).

Partner selection implies cooperation, which is only possible if there is a common purpose, mutual respect and openness, and a willingness by both partners to contribute to the achievement of the common goal. Thus

---

Box 4.1 Freedom From Hunger: Partnering with Local Institutions

FREEDOM FROM HUNGER (FFH) WORKS EXTENSIVELY IN Africa with local partners. Rather than going into a country and setting up its own microfinance activity, Freedom From Hunger selects local formal financial institutions, trains them its own lending model, and provides technical advice. The organization has identified the advantages of this partnership for both parties:

- Freedom From Hunger reduces the cost of delivering services, because the local institution can often fund its own portfolio. Freedom From Hunger's expertise in financial management greatly helps in the start-up and ongoing management. The local partner offers clients access to the formal financial sector. Credit unions, as partners, bring particular advantages because they have a network of contacts, know their clients, and offer other local knowledge.

- The local partner gains access to creditworthy clients using Freedom From Hunger's model, which features a high repayment rate and group loan guarantees. The new borrowers are also savers who build the bank's loan capital and profitability. Finally, reaching out to the clients targeted by Freedom From Hunger represents an investment in the welfare of the poor from which the bank can derive public relations and marketing benefits.

Making this model work requires special attention to a variety of issues. The greatest challenge for the international NGO is finding financial partners who have an interest in the poverty and microbusiness sector and will honestly enter the relationship with a long-term commitment. It is not by

chance that Freedom From Hunger's partners are largely credit unions or development banks—institutions with a strong social or development mission. How such an approach might play out with more profit-seeking partners has not been tested.

Determinations that are of subsidiary but significant importance are:

- The financial health of the lending institution
- The source of financing for the portfolio (in some instances it is the bank or credit union, in others cases the international NGO, which may need to supplement the partner's available resources)
- The source of funding for operational costs
- The selection of staff delivering program services
- Responsibility for loan loss.

When these arrangements are worked out successfully, the international NGO can see its activities grow beyond any scale that it could have reached with its own resources; it can achieve a sustainable initiative, whether under its own control or under that of the local financial institution. In the second case it has also achieved the establishment of microfinance within the formal financial system in a way that avoids many of the difficult challenges inherent in other models. The financial services are offered under the aegis of a regulated institution that can provide security and stability to its clients, and the organization does not have to transform itself or create a new financial institution to deliver services to those it most wants to serve.

Source: SEEP Network 1996a.

there is no standard answer to the question, What makes a good local or international partner institution? It depends on who the other partner organization is, what its ideas and objectives are, what it can contribute, and the way in which it is willing to act as a partner.

Institutional Types

The following is a brief discussion of each institutional type and includes its suitability as a partner to a donor, international NGO, or government. The suitability of donors, international NGOs, and governments as partners is not discussed.

Formal institutions are defined as those that are subject not only to general laws and regulations but also to specific banking regulation and supervision. *Semiformal institutions* are those that are formal in the sense of being registered entities subject to all relevant general laws, including commercial law, but informal insofar as they are, with few exceptions, not under bank regulation and supervision. *Informal providers* (generally not referred to as institutions) are those to which neither special bank law nor general commercial law applies, and whose operations are also so informal that disputes arising from contact with them often cannot be settled by recourse to the legal system.

Formal Financial Institutions

The following are the most typical types of formal financial institutions.

PUBLIC DEVELOPMENT BANKS. Development banks are or until quite recently have been, a special type of large, centralized, government-owned bank. Most of them were set up with ample financial support from foreign and international organizations. They were created to provide financial services to strategic sectors such as agriculture or industry. Most are the product of traditional interventionist approaches, which place greater emphasis on disbursements at low, subsidized interest rates than on the quality of lending.

Their traditional clients are large businesses. In the 1970s several development banks started to offer their services to small farmers and small businesses. But because they tried to do this with the same credit tech-

---

> **Box 4.2 Types of Financial Institutions**
>
> *Formal institutions*
> - Public development banks
> - Private development banks
> - Savings banks and postal savings banks
> - Commercial banks
> - Nonbank financial intermediaries.
>
> *Semiformal institutions*
> - Credit unions
> - Multipurpose cooperatives
> - NGOs
> - (Some) self-help groups.
>
> *Informal providers*
> - (Pure) moneylenders
> - Traders, landlords, and the like (as moneylenders)
> - (Most) self-help groups
> - Rotating savings and credit associations (work groups, multipurpose self-help groups)
> - Families and friends.
>
> *Source:* Author's findings.

---

nology and organizational structures as they had used before, their success was extremely modest.

Rural development banks and specialized *small business development banks* that escaped closure during the recent wave of financial sector reforms that swept over many countries have some attractive features: almost all of them have a broad network of branches; many are by now active collectors of deposits; and quite often they are the only large institutions in rural areas to offer at least a minimum of financial services to poor clients (box 4.3).

Development banks can be considered good partners for foreign development agencies—not in the traditional sense of providing funds, but rather in improving and reshaping their organizational structures, financial management, and the way in which they design and provide their services to poorer clients. The crucial questions to be asked before undertaking such a partnership are whether there is an openness to change and a willingness to give up the ample powers that the traditional approach certainly entailed and whether a foreign organization has enough resources to support such a change if it is desired not only by the people in the bank but by relevant politicians in the country.

PRIVATE DEVELOPMENT BANKS. Private development banks are a special category of banks that exist in some

---

Box 4.3 Development Banks

DEVELOPMENT BANKS CAN LEND EITHER DIRECTLY OR through intermediaries, as shown in these examples.

Direct lending. The Bank for Agriculture and Agricultural Cooperatives (BAAC) in Thailand is a state-owned development bank created in 1966 to provide financial assistance to farmers and agriculture-related activities. Since the financial reforms of 1989 the bank's efforts have been directed predominantly at the low- to medium-income range. At first it lent mostly through agricultural cooperatives, but repayment problems led the bank to start lending directly to farmers.

Lending through intermediaries. The experience of the Banque Nationale de Développement Agricole (BNDA), a state-owned bank in Mali, is quite different. This bank ceased lending directly to clients in rural areas in the early 1990s because of very low repayment rates. Lending to vil-

lage cooperatives and groups of farmers gave better results. In more recent years the Banque Nationale has started lending to microfinance institutions, such as the *caisses villageoises*—self-managed village banks—in three regions of the country. These institutions in turn on-lend to their clients. This linkage has been extremely successful, with high repayment rates and very low costs for the bank. The bank now wishes to become directly involved in setting up self-managed village banks in other areas of the country. If its sole motivation is to channel more funds to the rural economy, this may prove to be a dangerous strategy. Indeed, the success of the caisses villageoises in Mali is based on their ownership by the villagers themselves—and this sense of ownership might be weakened if the Banque Nationale is too strongly involved.

Source: Contributed by Cecile Fruman, Sustainable Banking with the Poor Project, World Bank.

---

developing countries. Their aim is broad economic development directed to fill capital gaps in the productive sector that are considered too risky by commercial standards. They often have lower capital requirements than commercial banks and enjoy some exemptions, either in the form of tax breaks or reduced reserve requirements (box 4.4).

SAVINGS BANKS AND POSTAL SAVINGS BANKS. The legal status and ownership of savings banks varies, but they are typically not owned by the central government of their country, and they often have a mixture of public and private owners. Some, such as those in Peru, were set up and owned by municipalities; others, such as the rural banks in Ghana, are simply small local banks owned by local people.

As the name indicates, savings banks tend to emphasize savings mobilization more than other banks. Their main strength is that they are decentralized, rooted in the local community, and interested in serving local small business.

In many countries there are post office savings banks modeled on patterns imposed by former colonial powers. A typical post office savings bank operates through the counters of post offices, and therefore, has a very large network of outlets; it does not offer credit but only takes deposits and provides money transfer services. A surplus

of deposits is normally invested in government securities or simply transferred to the treasury. Most post office savings banks are part of the postal administration of their country (box 4.5).

With a few noteworthy exceptions, post office savings banks are in poor shape, both financially and operationally. Their financial situation is poor because they have to pass their net deposits on to the treasury, which often does not want to acknowledge its indebtedness to the post office savings banks. Their organizational weaknesses derive from the fact that they are managed by the postal service, which has no genuine interest in their success. This state of affairs is all the more regrettable in view of the fact that deposit facilities and money transfer services within easy reach of the majority of poor people are "basic financial needs," which other institutions tend not to provide with comparably low transaction costs.

Savings banks could be attractive partners for various kinds of microfinance activities. Their main strengths are that they are decentralized, rooted in the local community, and interested in serving local small business. Some savings banks, such as those in Peru, are among the most successful target-group-oriented financial institutions, while others may be good partners for activities aimed at restructuring the savings bank system.

COMMERCIAL BANKS. Commercial banks are formal financial institutions that focus on short- and long-term lending to established businesses. A typical commercial bank has little experience in providing financial services

---

Box 4.4 Tulay sa Pag-Unlad's Transformation into a Private Development Bank

TULAY SA PAG-UNLAD, INC. (TSPI), IN THE PHILIPPINES, determined that it would create a private development bank based on the current regulatory environment and its own institutional capacity.

- New banking regulations permit the establishment of private development banks with much lower capital requirements (US$1.7 million, as opposed to US$50 million for commercial banks). However, the new private development banks are only allowed to operate outside Metropolitan Manila, meaning that TSPI will need to consider the location of its branches carefully so as to stay close to its desired client base.
- While TSPI has managed to create a diversified product line, one of its four loan services, Sakbayan, which provides loans to tricycle and taxi drivers, is significantly stronger than the others and will become the anchor product for the bank. This product, however, has limited growth potential because taxi routes are regulated. Strengthening the other product lines is thus a priority task for TSPI.
- TSPI recognizes that it still faces some capacity-building issues, including human resource and systems development. However, the pressure to source additional loan capital and the potentially short regulatory "window of opportunity" are demanding progress toward the creation of a private development bank.

With these realities in mind, one option under consideration is a *special transitional structure*, with the new bank and the original NGO in one integrated organization with shared personnel and a unifying mission. The bank and the NGO would maintain separate financial statements and transparent intercompany transactions but would share many of the head office functions and some of the operational management. The NGO would be responsible for the Kabuhayan product aimed at the poorest people as well as those branches within Metropolitan Manila that cannot be legally transferred to the bank. The bank would be responsible for the most profitable loan products, located in those branches most ready for bank status.

The transition period would take two to three years as the bank grew and became large enough to operate within Manila and take over the rest of TSPI's branches. At that point the bank and the NGO would separate all functions and staff. The decision to merge Kabuhayan into the bank would be made at that time or later. If the conclusion was that it would never reach commercial viability, the NGO would continue with a separate head office structure. In the meantime, the unified structure provides TSPI with several clear advantages:

- It controls administrative costs.
- It avoids potential cultural conflicts between the NGO and the bank about the mission.
- It ensures coherent policies, performance measurement, and expectations.

Source: Calmeadow 1996.

Box 4.5 The Savings Bank of Madagascar

FROM 1918 TO 1985 THE POSTAL ADMINISTRATION IN Madagascar collected savings. In 1985 the Savings Bank of Madagascar (Caisse d'épargne Madagascar) was created under the financial supervision of the Ministry of Finance and the technical supervision of the Ministry of Post and Telecommunications. The Savings Bank of Madagascar began with 46 existing postal offices. In June 1996 it was operating out of 174 windows located in both main cities and remote small towns. For use of the postal outlets the bank pays the postal administration 0.8 percent on savings collected.

The Savings Bank of Madagascar provides its clients with savings services only. Clients earn interest on their savings depending on the length of time they are held. Once a year all clients give their transactions books to the bank's agency or postal office to calculate the accrued interest.

The Savings Bank of Madagascar focuses on poor clients, as evidenced by an average savings balance of less than US$32. This represents 28 percent of GDP. The total number of clients in June 1996 was 372,291, with 46 percent of them women.

Source: Galludec 1996.

to microentrepreneurs and small farmers; however, some commercial banks recently recognized that it might be beneficial to do business with these clients (box 4.6). They also understand that it might be necessary to provide services in ways that differ from the traditional commercial banking approach.

There are 12 basic principles with which banks must comply if they choose to focus part of their operations on low-income clients (Yaron, Benjamin, and Piprek 1997):
1. Ensure appropriate governance
2. Define the institution's strategies and objectives
3. Learn from the competition in the informal sector
4. Find out what services clients really want
5. Establish appropriate modes of delivery
6. Contain transaction costs
7. Cover costs with appropriate, positive on-lending interest rates
8. Customize loan terms and conditions for the target clientele
9. Monitor and maintain the quality of the assets
10. Manage and diversify risks
11. Mobilize savings resources in the market
12. Motivate staff and invest in them (with information and incentives).

Some banks choose to develop a range of services for microentrepreneurs and rural peasants and then to service them directly by going to the communities. Branch banking is the more traditional approach, with bank tellers providing services in a bank facility. A highly decentralized network of branches is necessary, which must include very small branches with minimal fixed assets, located in central villages where they can serve poor clients in nearby rural areas or in urban slums. This is the most likely approach for banks, but it is costly. Other banks may rely more on intermediaries, acting as a wholesaler rather than a retailer.

"Downscaling" is the technical term used to describe projects that aim to introduce new approaches into a commercial bank that has so far not tried to provide services to a poorer clientele. Downscaling is, for instance, the centerpiece of what the Inter-American Development Bank is practicing in its "micro global" programs in Latin America. Another example is the Russia Small Business Fund established by the European Bank for Reconstruction and Development. In both cases commercial banks are carefully selected and analyzed and, after a positive evaluation, may receive funding and tech-

---

> **Box 4.6 Caja Social: A Colombian Commercial Bank Reaching the Poor**
>
> CAJA SOCIAL, FOUNDED IN 1911 IN COLOMBIA AS THE ST. Francis Xavier Workmen's Circle and Savings Bank, is an example of a commercial bank that has a significant microfinance portfolio. Its original mandate was to promote savings among the country's poor. Its success in deposit mobilization led to an expansion of branch savings banks throughout Colombia. In 1991 Caja Social was officially transformed into a commercial bank. Its activities, overseen by the holding company, Fundacion Social, range from mortgage credit to small business loans and leasing.
>
> As of September 1995 Caja Social had 1,159,204 active savings accounts (averaging US$338) and 173,033 outstanding loans (averaging US$2,325). While Caja Social serves numerous middle-income clients, a significant portion of its business is targeted at low-income clients. Nearly 20 percent of its clients earn less than US$3,000 annually, which is 75 percent of the country's average income per economically active adult. Given the enormous scale of the bank, this translates into well over 225,000 low-income clients. In addition, the Caja has been successful in targeting female clients. Approximately 43 percent of its clients are women.
>
> While Caja Social always has maintained the objective of assisting the country's poor, it has found this market niche to be financially rewarding. In fact, it has been one of the most profitable banks in the Colombian financial system. Arrears rates remain manageable at 4.5 percent, and the bank has achieved operational and financial self-sufficiency without dependence on subsidies from either national or international organizations. Caja Social's experience has shown that banking with the poor can be sustainable and profitable.
>
> *Source:* Contributed by Julia Paxton, Sustainable Banking with the Poor Project, World Bank.

---

nical assistance to build up departments for small and micro lending.

NONBANK FINANCIAL INSTITUTIONS. In some countries special regulation has been established for nonbank financial institutions. These institutions are set up to circumvent the inability of some MFIs to meet commercial bank standards and requirements due to the nature of their lending. Examples of MFIs regulated as nonbank financial institutions are Caja de Ahorro y Prestamo Los Andes in Bolivia and Accion Comunitaria del Peru (MiBanco) (box 4.7).

Box 4.7 Caja de Ahorro y Prestamo Los Andes

CAJA DE AHORRO Y PRESTAMO LOS ANDES WAS ESTABLISHED as the first Bolivian private financial fund in 1995. Los Andes grew out of the nongovernmental microlender Pro-Credito, with the technical assistance of the private consulting firm Internationale Projekt Consult GmbH (IPC), financed by the German development agency, GTZ. The minimum capital requirement for a private financial fund is US$1 million. The majority of the total US$600,000 of paid-in capital to Los Andes came from Pro-Credito.

From its inception as Pro-Credito in 1991, the institution planned to enter the regulated financial sector. No organizational changes were implemented once it became a private financial fund. Sophisticated management information systems, which integrate data on savings and credit operations,

Source: Rock 1997.

were already in place. Consequently, Los Andes has been able to produce the required reports to the central bank and the Bolivian superintendency with few modifications.

In contrast to Los Andes, BancoSol (Banco Solidario S.A.) entered the regulated financial sector as a commercial bank in 1992, because the private financial funds did not yet exist. As a result, BancoSol became the first private commercial bank in the world dedicated solely to providing financial services to the microenterprise sector. This helps to explain why the Bolivian Superintendency of Banks is considered to be one of the most innovative in Latin America. It is making significant strides in creating a competitive financial market and is committed to opening the financial sector to microenterprises.

Finance companies or financiers are nonbank financial intermediaries that channel equity funds, retained earnings, and other borrowed capital to small, unsecured short-term loans. Finance companies are often associated with consumer credit and installment contracts. They are often not allowed to mobilize savings; however, their activities vary by their charters. For example, some are able to mobilize time deposits but not demand deposits. Their form is now being adapted in some countries to provide a regulated vehicle for microfinance with lower barriers to entry than a commercial bank (box 4.8).

Semiformal Financial Institutions

The most common types of semiformal financial institutions are financial cooperatives and financial NGOs.

CREDIT UNIONS, SAVINGS AND LOAN COOPERATIVES, AND OTHER FINANCIAL COOPERATIVES. There are a great many forms of cooperative financial institutions (often identified as *credit unions or savings and loan cooperatives*). Such institutions play a significant role in the provision of financial services to poor target groups. In several countries cooperative financial institutions are structured in accordance with the models of the American and Canadian credit union or cooperative systems. Other cooperative institutions, such as Raiffeisen (Germany), Credit Mutuel (France), Alternative Bank (Switzerland), and Triodos (Holland), are inspired by models developed in Europe.

Financial cooperatives provide savings and credit services to individual members. "They perform an active financial intermediation function, particularly mediating flows from urban and semi-urban to rural areas, and between net savers and net borrowers, while ensuring

---

Box 4.8 Accion Comunitaria del Peru

ACCION COMUNITARIA DEL PERU ORIGINALLY CONSIDERED transforming itself into a finance company (which requires a minimum capital base of US$2.7 million) or a commercial bank (which requires a minimum capital base of US$6 million.) However, the Peruvian development bank, COFIDE, proposed the formation of a new category of nonbank financial institutions to meet the financing needs of small and microenterprises. In December 1994 the superintendency issued a resolution creating a new structure called an Entidades de Desarrollo para la Pequena y Microempresa (EDPYME). As such an entity, an MFI with a minimum capital requirement of US$265,000 can access capital markets, additional bank funding, and special rediscount credit facilities from COFIDE. An EDPYME is required to maintain a loan loss reserve equivalent to 25 percent of capital, and at least 10 percent of after-tax profits must be transferred to this reserve annually. The resolution specifies that it provide financing to persons engaged in activities characterized as small or micro businesses.

Source: Montoya 1997.

that loan resources remain in the communities from which the savings were mobilized" (Magill 1994, 140).

Financial cooperatives are organized and operated according to basic cooperative principles: there are no external shareholders; the members are the owners of the institution, with each member having the right to one vote in the organization. In addition to holding shares redeemable at par, members also may deposit money with the organization or borrow from it. Membership is usually the result of some common bond among members, often through employment or membership in the same community. The policy-making leadership is drawn from the members themselves, and members volunteer or are elected for these positions. Financial cooperatives are rarely subject to banking regulation; instead, they are either unregulated or subject to the special legislation and regulation applica-

ble to cooperatives in general. In some countries specific regulations for credit unions are being developed. In the West African Economic and Monetary Union (with eight countries as members) a law for savings and loan associations was passed in 1994, placing these institutions under the supervision of the Ministry of Finance in each country.

Characteristics of financial cooperatives include:
- Clients who tend to come from low-income and lower-middle-income groups.
- Services that are almost exclusively financial in nature.
- Self-generated capital, typically without any dependence on outside funding to cover operating costs, which are generally kept low.

Individual financial cooperatives often choose to be affiliated with a national league (apex institution), which serves the following purposes: it represents the credit

---

Box 4.9 The Rehabilitation of a Credit Union in Benin

THE HISTORY OF THE FÉDERATION DES CAISSES D'ÉPARGNE et de Crédit Agricole Mutuel dates back to the 1970s. In 1975 the Caisse Nationale de Crédit Agricole, or National Agricultural Credit Bank, was established as a public development bank, followed in 1977 by the first local and regional credit unions. Over the next 10 years 99 local credit unions were created. The Caisse Nationale de Crédit Agricole then assumed the role of a national federation, taking control of the operations of the entire network and excluding the elected directors from management and control. As a result, rules and procedures were developed by the management of the bank and imposed on elected directors and members. Thus the constituencies being served were unable to voice their concerns and demands. This top-down approach proved to be highly detrimental.

The financial performance of the network slowly deteriorated, and savings were no longer secure. In November 1987 the Caisse Nationale de Crédit Agricole was liquidated. Nevertheless, a study carried out in 1988 showed that the local credit unions had continued to operate throughout the crisis and member savings had continued to grow. To strengthen the autonomy of the network, the Government of Benin decided to initiate a rehabilitation program. It emphasized the importance of the total freedom of local credit unions to define their own policies, including the choice of interest rates. The first phase of the rehabilitation program (1989-93) was developed in collaboration with the

Source: Fruman 1997.

government, members of the network, and donors that contributed funds to reimburse depositors, finance studies, and cover the operating shortfall of the network. The results of the first phase were very encouraging insofar as the project met its principal objectives: restoring the rural population's confidence in the network, strengthening management by elected directors, and improving financial discipline.

In light of the results of the first phase, particularly the enthusiasm demonstrated by the principal participants, a second phase of rehabilitation (1994-98) began. The objectives of the second phase—currently in progress—are as follows:
- Financial restructuring of the network, both to mobilize deposits for on-lending and to generate revenue to cover operational expenses
- A transfer of responsibility to elected directors through the creation of a national federation to govern network expansion, structure, and training of staff and directors
- The creation of the technical secretariat of the federation to supply specific technical support (such as training and inspection) and ensure implementation of general policies.

The second phase of rehabilitation is ongoing, but for the most part its objectives have already been met. The network's growth has greatly exceeded expectations. The transition from mere project status to that of an operational, autonomous network offering a wide array of credit and savings services is nearly complete.

unions at the national level, provides training and technical assistance to affiliated credit unions, acts as a central deposit and inter-lending facility, and, in some cases, channels resources from external donors to the national cooperative system. Contacts with foreign partners are typically handled by an apex institution. Affiliation involves purchasing share capital and paying annual dues to the national or regional apex. Membership provides the right to vote on national leadership and policies and to participate in nationally sponsored services and programs.

Savings services are a key feature for raising capital and are often tied to receiving a loan. Credit is generally delivered under the "minimalist" approach. Cooperative lending requires little collateral and is based on character references and cosigning for loans between members.

Without any doubt, there are well-functioning cooperative systems. Beyond that, the sheer number of people who are members of these systems and the aggregate amounts of deposits and loans are impressive. Nevertheless, many systems do not function as well as their basic philosophy would lead one to expect. At the same time, they are very difficult partners for foreign institutions. The reason for both of these difficulties is their structure and the mechanism, which in principle should make them work.

- The group that constitutes the organization is small enough so that members know each other well.
- The members regularly change their roles from net depositors to net borrowers and vice versa.

If these conditions are not met, a cooperative becomes unstable: the management cannot be monitored, and a structural conflict arises between borrowers (who prefer low interest rates and little pressure for repayment) and net depositors (who prefer high interest and a very cautious application of their deposits).

FINANCIAL NGOs. NGOs are the most common institutional type for MFIs. The World Bank's "Worldwide Inventory of Microfinance Institutions" found that of the 206 institutions responding to a two-page questionnaire, 150 were NGOs (Paxton 1996).

Even more than with other types of institutions, a discussion of NGOs that provide financial services has to start by emphasizing that they are indeed a very diverse group. The general definition of an NGO is based on what it is not: neither government-related nor profit-oriented. This already indicates their specific strengths,

which are the main reason that they are common institutional types for MFIs.

Financial NGOs should be distinguished from two other types of nongovernmental and not-for-profit institutions: self-help groups and cooperatives. These institutions are member-based, whereas NGOs are set up and managed not by members of the target group, but by outsiders, who are often men and women from the middle class of the country who want to support poorer people for social, ethical, and political reasons. For example, one of the first Latin American NGOs providing loans to local microentrepreneurs, a Cali-based organization called DESAP, was started and managed by a son of one of the wealthiest families in Colombia, who regarded the government's neglect of microbusiness as a serious threat to the political stability of his country.

In spite of the fact that they are not member-based, many NGOs are close to the target group, in terms of both location and understanding. An NGO set up by local business people to provide services to microentrepreneurs may indeed be better placed to respond to the needs of its clients than an institution managed by government officials or traditional bankers.

All this indicates that financial NGOs are particularly promising candidates for foreign institutions in search of a local partner. However, there are some factors that make NGOs less attractive. The weaknesses of many, though certainly not all, NGOs can be attributed to a combination of the following factors (not all of which are unique to them):

- The lack of business acumen with which some NGOs are set up and operated
- Overly ambitious aspirations with regard to their social relevance
- The limited scale of their operations, which does not permit them to benefit from elementary economies of scale
- The frequent use of donated funds or soft loans from foreign development organizations
- The influence of people who do not belong to the target group and thus are not subject to peer pressure and are not directly hurt if the institution's money is eventually lost.

All these factors can work together to create a situation in which the business and financial side of a financial NGO is not treated with as much care as it ought to be. Nonetheless, business expertise and stability are indispensable if the institution wants to have a permanent positive effect on the target group.

Another weakness of many NGOs is their lack of a longer-term perspective and strategy (or of effective business planning). The questions that a look into the future would pose are: Where will the institution stand in a few years? Will it still exist, will it collapse in the course of time, or will it survive and even prosper? How is survival possible? Will it turn away from its original target group merely to survive financially? According to available evidence and experience, for most financial NGOs to survive without losing their target-group orientation, they must first change into professional institutions and then, if desired, expand and ultimately transform their institutional structure.

Informal Financial Providers

Informal finance is probably much more important for the financial management of poor households than the provision of services by formal and semiformal financial institu-

tions. For obvious reasons, informal finance comes in many forms and not always in one that can be called a financial institution. Some agents in informal financial markets have at least some aspect of a financial institution about them. This applies to moneylenders and money collectors—known, for example, as "susu men" in Ghana—and to the millions of rotating savings and credit associations that exist and operate in many variants and under many different names in almost every country of the developing world. Self-help groups are also a type of informal (sometimes semiformal) financial institution. It seems less appropriate to apply the term "financial institution" to traders and manufacturers who provide trade credit to their customers, and such a classification is completely inappropriate for a most important source of informal finance, namely, the network of friends and family members.

A certain degree of institutionalization and functional specialization is necessary for an entity in a developing country to be a potential partner in the context of a finance-related development project. Only very few informal institutions can play the role of a local partner. This

---

Box 4.10 CARE Guatemala: The Women's Village Banking Program

CARE IS AN INTERNATIONAL NONPROFIT ORGANIZATION founded in 1946. It was created to provide assistance and development programs to the needy. In the middle to late 1980s CARE International became increasingly interested in microenterprise programs. These programs, notably microfinance, gained worldwide recognition during the 1980s, spawned in part by the success of microfinance programs such as Grameen Bank and Bank Rakyat Indonesia. While lacking expertise in this field, CARE International became interested in experimenting with microenterprise development and hired external consultants to facilitate and supervise early experiments in this area. CARE Guatemala was one of the programs selected for microenterprise development work.

While CARE Guatemala began providing health, education, and income-generating programs as early as 1959, the women's village banking program of CARE was founded in 1989. In its short history, this program has made inroads into providing microfinance services to some of the most marginalized people in Latin America. Using a village bank methodology, the program has provided loans averaging only US$170 in 1995 to some 10,000 rural women in Guatemala.

The performance of the CARE village banking program has shown steady improvement. All indicators of outreach, cost, repayment, sustainability, and profit became more favorable during 1991–95. However, the mere improvement of these figures does not necessarily indicate that the program is on a sustainable trajectory. The program is still burdened by high overhead costs and donor dependency, which, unless rectified, will prevent it from becoming sustainable.

The village banking program represents a departure from the other humanitarian programs of CARE Guatemala. For the first time a program is bringing in revenue from the very poor it serves. Like many nonprofit organizations that enter into microfinance, dual objectives pull the village banking program in two directions. Often the microfinance programs of NGOs worldwide were created to improve the lives of the poor regardless of cost, repayment, or sustainability. As programs have proliferated and donors have become more insistent on financial performance, a secondary goal of sustainability has been introduced. Given its long-standing culture of donor dependence and subsidization, the CARE village banking program has found it difficult to unilaterally reject donor assistance and insist on complete financial sustainability.

Source: Contributed by Julia Paxton, Sustainable Banking with the Poor Project, World Bank.

is regrettable because if they could be made partners, several types of informal providers of financial services might work very well, as they are certainly able to reach the target group and their permanent existence proves that they are sustainable. But many informal arrangements, such as rotating savings and credit associations, would probably only be destabilized by efforts to enlist them as partners, because the mechanisms on which they are based depend on their unfettered informality.

The important exception to be mentioned here is *self-help groups*. There are many self-help groups, consisting of self-employed women who informally support the economic activities of their members by providing mutual guarantees that facilitate their members' access to bank loans, by borrowing and lending among themselves, or by encouraging each other to save regularly (box 4.11). Yet, at the same time these groups are visible or "formal" enough to establish contact with some development agencies. There are

---

Box 4.11 The Use of Self-Help Groups in Nepal

THERE ARE MANY INTERNATIONAL NGOs AND GOVERNMENT programs in Nepal that utilize local self-help groups or savings and credit cooperatives in the provision of microfinance. They provide some or all of the following services:

- Revolving funds for on-lending
- Grants to cover operating costs, including staff and other operating expenses
- Matching funds, whereby the international NGO matches (or provides a multiple of) the amount of savings collected by the savings and credit cooperative from its members
- Technical assistance, including program development, group formation, staff and client training, and financial management.

Target Market. Many international NGOs supporting savings and credit cooperatives focus on reaching the "poorest of the poor" with financial services. In addition, many specifically target women, believing that the benefits of increased economic power will be greater for women because they are generally responsible for the health and education of their children and the welfare of the community itself. However, these organizations frequently combine the delivery of financial services with social services. This often results in lower rates of repayment, because the social services are usually delivered free of charge while financial services are not.

Methodology. In programs supported by both government and international NGOs, the savings and credit cooperatives are responsible for the delivery of financial services to clients. The cooperatives use groups for lending and savings collection. Loan sizes from the cooperatives are generally small and no physical collateral is required. Instead, group guarantees are provided. The savings and credit cooperatives, with few exceptions, provide loans for relatively short terms, generally less than one year, over half for less than six months. Loan

appraisal is generally done by the group with some guidance from the staff. Interest rates on loans to end-borrowers are between 10 and 36 percent, with the higher rates charged by nongovernment-funded programs. Some programs of international NGOs, particularly those providing microfinance as a minor activity, charge very low rates of interest, sometimes as low as 1 percent. Not surprisingly, repayment of these loans is very poor, because borrowers tend to view them as grants rather than loans.

Savings are usually compulsory and are required on a weekly or monthly basis. For the most part these savings cannot be withdrawn, resulting in significantly higher effective borrowing rates. Interest rates paid on these savings range from 0 percent to 8 percent, with the majority paying 8 percent. (Interest paid is usually simply added to the savings held.) Savings are often managed by the group itself, resulting in access to both "internal loans" (those made from the group savings) and "external loans" (those made by the cooperative). It is worth noting that interest rates on internal loans, which are set by the group, are often substantially higher than those on external loans, even within the same groups. This indicates that borrowers can pay higher rates of interest and do not require subsidized interest rates. It also indicates that the "ownership" of funds greatly influences the interest rate set on loans and the repayment of loans, in turn contributing to financial sustainability.

The success of savings and credit cooperatives providing microfinance services supported by government and international NGOs is greater than that of government-mandated programs that do not use the cooperatives. Experience over the past five years indicates that the savings and credit cooperatives can deliver financial services at a much lower cost than the government itself to reach the intended target market. However, these programs still suffer from high loan losses and inefficient management.

Source: DEPROSC and Ledgerwood 1997.

some identifiable characteristics of a good self-help group: it exhibits a high degree of coherence and strong common interests among its members; it has a democratic structure and, at the same time, a strong leadership; and empowerment of its members is an important objective.

However, development projects rarely use these groups as their main partners. Instead, some of them try to establish a network composed of various partners, including self-help groups and institutions that provide financial services to the self-help groups or their members. Only in very few exceptional cases could self-help groups of poor people with a focus on financial matters be partners in the context of projects aiming to create semiformal financial institutions such as cooperatives or NGOs.

Institutional Growth and Transformation

For the most part, MFIs are created as semiformal institutions—either as NGOs or as some form of savings and credit cooperative. Given these institutional structures, they are often limited by a lack of funding sources and the inability to provide additional products. Unless the MFI is licensed and capable of mobilizing deposits or has achieved financial sustainability and is thus able to access commercial funding sources, access is often restricted to donor funding. Furthermore, as MFIs grow the need for effective governance and the question of ownership arise.

For MFIs that are structured as formal financial institutions, that is, development or commercial banks, the issues of growth and transformation are not as significant. Generally, growth within a formal institution can be accommodated within the existing structure. Transformation is rarely an issue. An exception to this is when a commercial or development bank creates an MFI subsidiary, such as the Banco Desarrollo in Chile; however, this is a rare occurrence. Often formal institutions have the systems in place to accommodate this change.

The following discussion is adapted from SEEP Network 1996a and focuses on semiformal institutions and ways in which they manage their institutional growth. Three options are presented: maintaining the existing structure and managing growth within that structure; forming an apex institution to support the work of existing MFIs; and transforming to a new, formalized financial institution. This is followed by a dis-

cussion of governance and ownership and accessing capital markets—issues that arise as the MFI expands.

Expansion Within an Existing Structure

Depending on the objectives of the MFI and the contextual factors in the country in which it works, an NGO or cooperative may be the most appropriate institutional structure, providing the MFI can continue to grow and meet the demands of the target market. Existing structures may be most appropriate, because formalizing their institutions can require substantial capital and reserve requirements. As formal financial intermediaries, they may become subject to usury laws or other regulations that limit the MFI's ability to operate.

For example, Centro de Creditos y Capacitacion Humanistica, Integral y Sistematica para la Pequena y Microempres, a microfinance NGO in Nicaragua, wanted to expand its microlending services (see box 4.12). It considered creating a formal bank but found that the regulatory environment in Nicaragua was not suitable. This example demonstrates how local contextual factors can constrain as well as facilitate the choice of institutional structure.

Creating an Apex Institution

Some MFIs, particularly those partnering with international NGOs, may choose to create an apex institution as a means of managing growth and accessing additional funding. An apex institution is a legally registered wholesale institution that provides financial, management, and other services to retail MFIs. These apex institutions are similar to apex institutions for financial cooperatives. However, in this case the MFI or more likely its foreign partner or donor determines that a second-tier organization is required to provide wholesale funding and facilitate the exchange of information and "best practices." Rather than being member based, the apex institution is set up and owned by an external organization. Apex institutions do not provide services directly to microentrepreneurs; rather, they provide services that enable retail MFIs (primary institutions) to pool and access resources. An apex institution can:

- Provide a mechanism for more efficient allocation of resources by increasing the pool of borrowers and savers beyond the primary unit

---

Box 4.12 Using the Nongovernmental Organization as a Strategic Step in Expansion

CENTRO DE CREDITOS Y CAPACITACION HUMANISTICA, Integral y Sistematica para la Pequena y Microempres (CHISPA), a program of the NGO Mennonite Economic Development Association (MEDA), targets the poorest of the economically active in the productive, service, and commercial sectors in and around the secondary city of Masaya in Nicaragua. Established in 1991, the loan fund was valued at US$740,000, with more than 3,500 active loans in 1996. The portfolio includes solidarity groups and individual clients. Fifty-eight percent of the clients are women.

In 1996 the portfolio had a 97 percent repayment rate, a 27.5 percent nominal interest rate, a cost per dollar loaned of less than 15 cents, and a 62 percent self-sufficiency level, including financial costs, with full self-sufficiency expected by mid-1997. The program's business plan calls for scaling up to reach almost 9,000 active clients by the end of 1999, increasing the loan portfolio from US$890,000 to US$1.6 million, and developing a local institution with a legal framework that allows for credit and savings activities.

Based on these growth projections, CHISPA considered the options of forming either a bank or a credit union. While the regulatory environment for banks in Nicaragua is relatively favorable, the US$2 million paid-in capital requirement is double it's current portfolio, and to be efficient a bank should be leveraged at least four or five times. Therefore, the projected scale of operations should really be about US$8 million before contemplating a bank. There is also a legal reserve requirement on savings deposits (15 percent for Cordobas accounts and 25 percent for dollar accounts), which need to be placed in non-interest-bearing accounts at the central bank.

Banks are also required to pay a 30 percent tax on net profits or 4 percent on net worth, whichever is higher.

Credit unions are regulated by the Ministry of Labor in Nicaragua and essentially have no requirements regarding minimum capital, loan loss provisions, liquidity, legal reserves, and equity ratios. They do not pay corporate income taxes except when they pay dividends. A credit union can offer both credit and savings but cannot provide checking accounts or credit cards. They can only offer services to their own members but not the general public. However, forming a credit union would be highly risky due to the scale of operations that CHISPA has already achieved and the unpredictable outcome of board selection. Normally, credit unions are formed over a period of gradual growth based on accumulated membership shares and savings, where they all have a stake in its solvency if not its profitability.

NGOs, on the other hand, are currently neither regulated nor taxed, except by a few municipalities such as Masaya, which levies a 2 percent tax on gross profits. They can provide a range of credit services without restrictions, although they are not able to offer any type of saving accounts, checking accounts, or credit cards. However, there are plans to bring nonprofits under the supervision of the superintendency of banks within a year. If that happens, NGOs would be able to capture savings and qualify for some concessional capital currently available only to the banks.

Incorporation as an NGO either as endpoint or interim form provides CHISPA with a strong legal and organizational base to advance its mission of serving the economically active poor.

Source: Bremner 1996.

- Conduct market research and product development for the benefit of its primary institutions
- Offer innovative sources of funds, such as guarantee funds or access to a line of credit from external sources
- Serve as a source of technical assistance for improving operations, including the development of management information systems and training courses
- Act as an advocate in policy dialogue for MFIs.

The experience of apex institutions has been mixed. Apex institutions that focus on providing funds to retail MFIs, often at subsidized rates, have found limited retail capacity to absorb those funds. What MFIs most often need is not additional funding sources but

institutional capacity building. Furthermore, by providing wholesale funds in the marketplace, apex institutions remove the incentive for retail MFIs to mobilize deposits.

There are other potential weaknesses of apex institutions (SEEP Network 1996a):

- Vision and governance issues are made more complex by the number of parties involved.
- The level of commitment to expansion and self-sufficiency may vary among the members, affecting the pace of expansion and the ultimate scale achieved. The commitment to market-oriented operating principles may also vary, affecting the ability of the group to operate in an unsubsidized fashion.

- Differential growth rates among the partners can also strain their relationship, especially when their needs for resources and technical support widen dramatically.
- Monitoring and supervision are essential to good performance but are made difficult by the number of partners. If there are weaknesses in financial reporting and management at the primary level, these can adversely affect the second-tier operation.
- Unless both the primary institutions and the apex are efficient, the ultimate costs to the client can be high. There needs to be constant attention to issues of productivity and performance.

While there are many disadvantages to apex institutions, if structured appropriately and set up with clear and market-oriented objectives, they can add value and aid in the development of microfinance.

"For the most part, microfinance apex institutions provide more than just liquidity in the market. Usually the apex is set up when everyone agrees that there is a drastic shortage of retail capacity. The advertised objective of the apex is to foment the development of stronger retailers capable of reaching a much more substantial portion of the microfinance clientele." (Rosenberg 1996)

Apex institutions that focus on pooling member-mobilized funds and on-lending these funds at market rates to their members represent a far better approach than those wholesaling donor or government funds. Also, apex institutions should not be creating microfinance retailers. Rather, they are most helpful when many existing MFIs participate and benefit from doing so.

Apex institutions may also be useful in the following situations (Von Pischke 1996):

Box 4.13 Catholic Relief Services: Using the Apex Model for Expansion

CATHOLIC RELIEF SERVICES SUPPORTED THE ESTABLISHMENT of the Small Enterprise Development Company, Ltd., a finance company in Thailand, to provide financial intermediation and institutional strengthening services to its NGO and (currently five) credit union counterparts implementing the village bank methodology. The company can facilitate the use of collective savings as well as attract donors and bankers. It is expected to achieve financial self-sufficiency by 1999, when it will be managing a US$910,000 portfolio and charging a 6 to 10 percent spread. In turn, the counterparts will be lending funds to 175 village banks with almost 11,000 members.

In Indonesia Catholic Relief Services is supporting the development of formal financial services at two levels: the creation of 20 subdistrict credit banks, called Bank Perkredital Rakyats, and the formation of a national-scale limited liability company, called the Self Reliance Corporation. Catholic Relief Services' traditional target groups, the Usaha Bersamas (rural savings and credit groups), will receive financial services directly from the subdistrict credit banks. As for profit subsidiaries of Catholic Relief Services' NGO partners, the subdistrict credit banks will help them increase the clients served from 16,000 to more than 30,000 in 5 years, with loans averaging US$150. Self sufficiency of the banks is expected in 24 months. The Self Reliance Corporation will function as an Indonesian registered company and will assist with the start-up and

management of the credit banks. The corporation will seek a 51 percent equity investment in all new credit banks, with the counterparts owning between 20 and 49 percent. Revenues should enable the corporation to achieve financial self-sufficiency toward the end of the third year.

In Peru Catholic Relieve Services is assisting eight members of COPEME, a local consortium of enterprise NGOs, to form an Entidades de Desarrollo para la Pequena y Microempresa or finance company to serve the departments of Lima, Callao, Lambayeque, Arequipa, Piura, and Trujillo. Operating as a for-profit institution funded by commercial investments, the company will provide financing services enabling the partners to provide 20,000 loans, averaging between US$50 and US$200 and valued at US$425,000, by the end of three years.

Catholic Relief Services identifies four key attributes of these models:

- They are based on consistent involvement of experienced NGOs, which, in every case, remain key actors with significant decisionmaking power.
- All parties have demonstrated a willingness to experiment with new speculative models that take advantage of many regulatory innovations.
- They avoid the large capital requirements of the commercial bank form.
- Lending through diverse partners also mitigates risks associated with these transformations.

Source: SEEP Network 1996a.

- When they are lenders of last resort, not necessarily in situations of crisis but on the basis of cost. Retail lenders regard an apex institution as a good source of expensive funds and presumably use them sparingly and only for highly important and profitable programs.

- When the apex institution fills in seasonally. Agricultural-based retail lenders might want to borrow seasonally as a means of managing cash flow. Again, the funds should not have to be provided by the apex institution at anything less than commercial rates.

- When the apex institution becomes a shareholder in the retail MFIs, in the expectation that this would provide an attractive overall return. In this case the apex institution would expect to add value by providing expertise and oversight as well as funds in the form of equity and quite possibly debt.

- When retail lenders are not permitted to take deposits. Apex institutions could then play a useful role if they added value through their terms and conditions and behaved commercially.

An apex institution appears to be most successful when a critical mass of strong MFI retailers already exists and when it is focused on working with existing formal financial institutions that are "downscaling" to meet the demands of low-income clients. (For further information about apex institutions, see Gonzalez-Vega 1998.)

Creating a Formal Financial Intermediary

Recently the field of microfinance has focused on the transformation of financial NGOs into formal financial institutions. This approach involves the transfer of the NGO's or cooperative's operations to a newly created financial intermediary, while the original institution is either phased out or continues to exist alongside the new intermediary. In most cases, the original MFI's assets, staff, methodology, and systems are transferred to the new institution and adapted to meet the more rigorous requirements of a financial intermediary. Various means may be established to determine a transfer price for the assets and operations of the NGO or cooperative to the new entity. It is imperative, however, that the transfer price mechanism be transparent (box 4.14).

The rationale for developing a formal financial institution is compelling: the potential to access both savings and commercial funding may help solve an MFI's funding constraints and increase its ability to provide additional financial services to the target market. However, creating a formal financial institution also implies additional costs and restrictions as the MFI becomes regulated and supervised (see chapter 1). Capital requirements may be much higher than anticipated, and unless the MFI has reached financial self-sufficiency it will be difficult (and costly) to attract equity investors and commercial debt (see the section below on accessing capital markets). And finally, the MFI must develop the institutional capacity to manage a number of different products and services, mobilize resources (both debt and equity as well as human resources), and enhance management information systems to adhere to regulatory reporting requirements and manage additional products (see the section below on institutional capacity building). While transformation may seem like an ideal path, MFIs should consider the substantial changes that are required when transforming to a formal financial institution. They must also thoroughly examine their institutional capacity and determine if it meets the requirements for transformation (Appendix 1 provides a framework for conducting this analysis).

The costs to convert into a formal financial institution are often exceedingly high: they include feasibility and pre-start-up work, capital requirements, as well as the changes in management and systems that must be implemented. Each MFI must consider the various types of formal institutions described above and determine which one best suits their needs (box 4.15). For example, PRODEM's choice of the commercial bank model for BancoSol was due to its great leverage potential and ability to offer savings and other financial products, matched by the right combination of political and financial support. On the other hand, Accion Comunitaria del Peru and COPEME, an association of NGOs partnered with Catholic Relief Services, decided to establish finance companies in accordance with special legislation supporting these forms. Although unable to capture savings, these structures do provide regulated vehicles that have leverage potential and can begin operations with lower capital (SEEP Network 1996a).

Finally, if an NGO in the transformation process remains a separate institution, the two organizations (the NGO and new financial intermediary) must develop a working relationship that benefits both parties and that solidifies the bridge between them. Some useful bridging

Box 4.14 Transformation from a Nongovernmental Organization to Financiera Calpía

IN 1988 THE GERMAN AID INSTITUTIONS CREATED A ROTAT-
ing credit fund for the Association of Micro and Small
Entrepreneurs (AMPES) of El Salvador. The objective of this
project was to improve the supply of credit for small business
people on a lasting basis. Plans were made with the association
to create a stable and professional institution that could ultimately be transformed into a small target-group-oriented formal financial institution.

From the beginning, credit operations were organized
separately from the association's other business, both to
assure professionalism and also to limit undue personal
influence. While the association was the owner of AMPES-
Servicio Crediticio, it did not run the operations. Also, the
donor institutions insisted that the purchasing power of the
fund be maintained. Accordingly, interest rates were set at an
unusually high level (effective rates between 25 percent and
40 percent). Finally, strict lending policies were implemented and a system of financial incentives for loan officers was
created, which kept loan losses below 1 percent.

With external funding from the Inter-American
Development Bank the loan portfolio and the number of borrowers doubled every year. At the end of 1996 the number of
borrowers was around 20,000 and the loan portfolio had
grown to the equivalent of US$14 million. During this phase

of rapid growth, the fund was transformed into Financiera
Calpía, a small, strictly targeted group-oriented formal bank.
The transformation was undertaken with the full support of
the Association of Micro and Small Entrepreneurs, which,
through its Fundación Calpía, is now the main shareholder of
Financiera Calpía. The other shareholders are local and international development institutions.

Transformation and formalization were necessary for two
reasons. To satisfy the high demand for small and very small
loans, the institution needed the right to accept savings
deposits from its customers and to have access to the interbank market. And because of the challenges and dangers of
the extremely dynamic expansion of its operations, the institution needed—and wanted—the increased stability and tighter
control that the new status provides by making Calpía still
more independent from the association and putting it under
the formal control of the superintendency of banks.

Currently, Calpía is the most important specialized
lender to the small business community of El Salvador. It
has opened eight branches to date. Because of its high positive (inflation-adjusted) return on equity and its institutional
stability, other banks in the country regard it as highly credit
worthy, improving the availability of loan funds to on-lend
to the target population.

Source: Contributed by Reinhard Schmidt, Internationale Projekt Consult GmbH (IPC).

Box 4.15 Catholic Relief Services' Guatemala Development Bank

CATHOLIC RELIEF SERVICES' PARTNER IN GUATEMALA,
Cooperative Association for Western Rural Development,
is planning to establish a development bank, because its
organizing principles are more amenable than a commercial bank to the social development mission that the association supports. This mission involves:

- A focus on the very poor, the core constituency of
  Catholic Relief Services and its partners
- An emphasis on savings
- Accessibility for NGOs and popular organizations in
  terms of the initial investment requirements and
  administrative operations
- Easy replicability.

This last characteristic is seen as essential both to support rapid scale-up and to encourage diversification rather
than financial concentration.

Source: SEEP Network 1996a.

mechanisms include the following (SEEP Network
1996a):

- Overlapping directorates
- Cost sharing of head office functions, branch space,
  insurance, and so forth
- Joint resource mobilization, with the NGO attract-
  ing the social investment capital that the financial
  intermediary may not qualify for directly
- Coordinating policies for product development, target areas, and populations.

Governance and Ownership

MFIs, particularly those set up as financial NGOs, are
often formed by a visionary. These visionaries are not
usually interested in profits but rather have a social
objective to improve the lives of low-income members
of their community. Only after the MFI begins to grow
does the visionary reach the conclusion that the MFI
needs to adopt a more business-like approach. This is

often the result of limited donor funds, demands of the target market, and a general shift in the field of microfinance toward formalized institutions.

As the MFI grows and management systems are developed, the need for governance arises to ensure effective management of the MFI and, potentially, to attract people with much-needed skills (usually from the private sector). While governance does not always result in a change of *vision* for the MFI, it does establish a means of holding management accountable. Furthermore, as the MFI grows the issue of ownership becomes apparent. This is particularly important as the MFI begins to create a more formalized structure.

GOVERNANCE. (Adapted from Clarkson and Deck 1997.) Governance refers to a system of checks and balances whereby a board of directors is established to oversee the management of the MFI. The board of directors is responsible for reviewing, confirming, and approving the plans and performance of senior management and ensuring that the vision of the MFI is maintained. Management is responsible for the daily operations of putting the vision into action.

The basic responsibilities of the board are:

- *Fiduciary.* The board has the responsibility to safeguard the interests of all of the institution's stakeholders. It serves as a check and balance to ensure the MFI's investors, staff, clients, and other key stakeholders that the managers will operate in the best interest of the MFI.
- *Strategic.* The board participates in the MFI's long-term strategy by critically considering the principal risks to which the organization is exposed and approving plans presented by the management. The board does not generate corporate strategy but instead reviews management's business plans in light of the institution's mission and approves them accordingly.
- *Supervisory.* The board delegates the authority for operations to the management through the executive director or chief executive officer. The board supervises management in the execution of the approved strategic plan and evaluates the performance of management in the context of the goals and time frame outlined in the plan.
- *Management development.* The board supervises the selection, evaluation, and compensation of the senior management team. This includes succession planning for the executive. In the transition from a small, growing entrepreneurial organization to an established institution, effective governance ensures that the company survives. Governance moves an institution beyond dependency on the visionary.

The board should comprise members who have a number of different skills, including financial, legal, and managerial. In particular, representation from the private sector is important. Also, the ability to critically analyze management's plans as well as provide effective guidance is paramount when selecting a board. An MFI must define the following:

- The role of board members both within the board and with regard to external alliances
- The desired areas of expertise
- The existence of committees to oversee specific areas of operation
- Term limits for board seats
- The process for replacing board members
- The role of the executive director in selecting board members
- The optimum number of board members
- Mechanisms to evaluate the contribution of individual members.

Board members must be provided with and agree to clear and common objectives. Furthermore, it is important that members be independent from the MFI and be chosen for their expertise rather than their own interests or political agendas or those of the senior management. Board members should act in such a way that they create accountability and enable stakeholders to trust one another. Governance gives shareholders, donors, governments, and regulators confidence that managers are being appropriately supervised. Thus board members should not receive any personal or material gain other than the approved remuneration.

OWNERSHIP. (Adapted from Otero 1998.) It is the owners of the MFI that elect (or at times compose) the governing body of the institution. Owners, through their agents on the board, hold management accountable. Ownership is an important but often nebulous issue for MFIs, particularly as many are funded with donor contributions.

Neither formal financial institutions nor NGOs have owners per se. Formal MFIs have shareholders who own shares that give them a residual claim to the assets of the MFI if there is anything remaining after it has discharged all of its obligations. Shareholders have the right to vote their shares to elect board members, who in turn control the company. Having shareholders results in clear lines of accountability between the board members and the MFI.

NGOs do not generally have shareholders; rather, management usually elects the board members. This can (but does not always) result in a conflict of interest if management selects board members who will conform to the interests of senior management. Furthermore, NGO board members do not usually fulfill the board's fiduciary role by assuming responsibility for the institution's financial resources, especially those provided by donors.

As MFIs formalize their structures (that is, change from being an NGO into a formal financial institution) and begin to access funding beyond the donor community, the "owners" or those that have a financial stake in the institution can change. If the NGO remains as a separate entity, it often owns a majority of the shares of the new institution. In spite of this majority ownership, it is important that the relationship between the MFI and the NGO be kept at arm's length and include a transparent and clear system of transfer pricing.

"Owners" of formalized MFIs can generally be divided into four categories:

- NGOs
- Private investors
- Public entities
- Specialized equity funds.

All of these owners are concerned with receiving an adequate return on their investment. However, NGOs and public entities may have other priorities as well. For example, they may be concerned with a social

---

Box 4.16 BancoADEMI Ownership Structure

ON SEPTEMBER 11, 1997, THE MONETARY BOARD OF THE Dominican Republic approved a banking license for the Banco de Desarollo ADEMI, S.A. The new development bank focuses on the small and medium-size enterprise sector, making loans in the range of US$35,000 to US$300,000. BancoADEMI also offers savings facilities to the general public through time deposit accounts and financial certificates.

About 72 percent of the shares in BancoADEMI are owned by the Association for the Development of Microenterprises (ADEMI), the original NGO that spun off its small enterprise loans to the bank and continued to serve the microenterprise sector. Another 10 percent of the shares are owned by association employees and the remainder by several individuals who have been active in the development of the association.

The bank has an authorized capital of $150 million pesos, or about US$10.7 million, and an initial paid-up capital of just over $100 million pesos (US$7.1 million). With the transfer of assets from ADEMI, the new institution was projected to make a profit in its first year of operations.

Source: Benjamin and Ledgerwood 1998.

---

return or positive impact in the lives of the clients (table 4.2).

Owners may be heavily involved in the operations of the MFI or may take on a more passive role. Owners that play a more active role must have adequate skills and the ability to spend the time required. Owners are often also called upon to access additional capital, par-

---

Table 4.2 What Is at Stake for Microfinance Owners?

Nongovernmental organization	Private investors	Public entities	Specialized equity funds
Moral responsibility	Return on investment	Political concern	Return on investment
Institutional mission	Capital preservation	Entry into the field	
Return on investment	Sense of social responsibility	Return on investment	Institutional mission
Long-term concern		Good project	Long-term concern
Institutional creditability or image			

Source: Otero 1998.

ticularly equity capital. As owners they may wish to maintain their stake as the MFI grows and takes on additional capital. This implies that they also must have continued access to capital.

Accessing Capital Markets

The majority of MFIs fund their activities with donor or government funding through grants or concessional loans. However, it is becoming evident that donor funding is limited. As MFIs expand and reach a critical stage of growth, they find that they cannot sustain their growth with only donor support. Some are beginning to access capital markets. There are various ways that an MFI can access new capital, including:

- Debt accessed through guarantee funds, loans, and deposit mobilization
- Equity
- Equity investment funds
- Socially responsible mutual funds
- Securitization of the loan portfolio.

ACCESSING DEBT. For the most part it is necessary to be financially self-sufficient to access commercial sources of funds. However, with the backing of guarantees by donors or international NGOs, some MFIs, if they earn enough revenue to at least cover their cash costs, may be able to *leverage* their donor funds with commercial loans in amounts equal to the donor funds.

Guarantee funds are financial mechanisms that reduce the risk to a financial institution by ensuring repayment of some portion of a loan (adapted from Stearns 1993). Guarantee funds are used to encourage formal sector bank lending to the microenterprise sector. They can be used to guarantee a loan made by a commercial bank to an MFI, which then on-lends funds to its clients, or loans from a bank directly to microentrepreneurs. There are three types of guarantee funds that cover the risks of making loans. These risk-related design features are some of the most important determinants of the acceptance and use of a guarantee mechanism by banks. They are guarantees covering:

- A percentage of the loan principal
- A percentage of the loan principal and the interest lost
- A certain amount of the loan (say, the first 50 percent).

By reducing risk and transaction costs faced by the financial institution, guarantee funds can function as

"research and development" for commercial lenders considering entry into a new market (either lending to MFIs or directly to clients). Guarantee funds are usually designed to leverage resources. For example, a guarantee fund of US$5 million may encourage banks to lend US$10 million to microentrepreneurs, thereby leveraging the fund's resources by a factor of two to one. The more effective the guarantee mechanism the higher the leverage factor becomes (the guarantee fund backs an increasingly large loan portfolio). Ultimately, the aim is to gradually transfer the risk from the guarantee mechanism to the participating financial institutions.

For example, ACCION's Bridge Fund provides its NGO affiliates with access to commercial loans that they otherwise might not have. The Bridge Fund puts cash deposits, securities, or letters of credit with commercial banks, which in turn on-lend to the NGO affiliate at market rates. Eventually, some affiliates have been able to borrow directly without the use of the guarantee scheme.

However, the costs of guarantee schemes must be considered relative to the benefits (box 4.17). Vogel and Adams (1997) claim that there are three categories of costs that accompany loan guarantee programs: the costs of setting up the program, the costs of funding the subsidy needed to energize and sustain the program, and the additional cost incurred by the financial system of running and participating in the guarantee program. The benefits of a loan guarantee program are the additional lending induced by the transfer of part of the lender's risk to the guaranteeing organization. Both borrowers and society benefit from the increases in net income realized by borrowers. Vogel and Adams suggest that the benefits are hard to measure, because it is difficult to determine if the guarantee scheme resulted in true additionality (that is, additional lending to the target market). Furthermore, substitution can also occur whereby the bank simply transfers part or all of the qualifying portion of its existing loan portfolio to the guarantee programs or to an NGO, in this way benefiting from the subsidized guarantee program that takes borrowing clients away from other NGOs not benefiting from the subsidies.

At the very least, few guarantee schemes are financially sustainable without some form of subsidy. However, they appear to be more beneficial than direct subsidies to clients. (For further information on guarantee schemes for microenterprises see Stearns 1993, and on guarantee schemes for small and medium-size enterprises see Gudger 1997; Levitsky 1997).

As an MFI continues to expand and eventually reaches financial self-sufficiency (revenue earned covers all costs, including inflation and an imputed cost of capital; see chapter 8), its ability to leverage its equity (donor funds and retained surpluses) increases. If it becomes a formally regulated financial institution, it can achieve leverage ratios of up to 12 times its equity by borrowing directly from commercial sources or mobilizing deposits (if regulated to do so). However, mobilizing savings requires substantial changes to the MFI, which are discussed fully in chapter 6.

An MFI is ready to access commercial financing when it has built an equity base through past donor grants and has a positive net worth (see box 4.18).

MFIs can access commercial debt by borrowing directly from commercial banks or by issuing financial paper in the market place (box 4.19).

ACCESSING EQUITY. Capital markets can also be accessed by selling shares of ownership (equity) of the MFI. For this to be possible the institution must be a formal financial intermediary with shareholders. Unlike debt instruments, equity does not have a fixed yield or maturity. Rather, equity investors invest in the profitable future of the MFI and expect a share of the returns. Because the microfinance industry has not yet developed to the point where there are many investors who are aware of the potential of MFIs, it may

---

Box 4.17 Guarantee Scheme in Sri Lanka

THE GUARANTEE SCHEME IN SRI LANKA WAS STARTED IN 1979 and operated by the central bank. The scheme covered 60 percent of the loan amount and was instituted as an incentive for the commercial banks to participate in the credit line channeled through the National Development Bank, financed by the World Bank.

Between 1979 and 1995 the World Bank approved four loans for small and medium-size enterprises for a total of US$105 million. Repayment rates on the subloans given from the first two World Bank loans were low (70–73 percent), but this improved significantly to more than 90 percent in the later bank loans.

In the earlier years of operation claims were high—7 percent of guarantees claimed in 1979–80 and 13 percent in 1982–85. Substantial changes were made and claims dropped to 2 percent in 1991–95.

In 1979–96, 18,500 guarantees were given, and there were subsequently 696 claims for guarantee payment (89 rejected and 417 paid out) up to the end of 1994, for a total of US$1.36 million. Outstanding guarantees for which the central bank has a contingent liability were estimated at a maximum total claim of US$0.88 million. The actual and potential total loss on guarantees paid on bad debt was US$2.2 million. With 18,850 guarantees this was a cost to the state of US$118 per entrepreneur assisted. This amount was estimated to be more than offset by additional tax generated.

Source: Levitsky 1997.

Box 4.18 Key Measures for Accessing Commercial Financing

MFIs ARE READY TO ACCESS COMMERCIAL FINANCING IF they:

- Have perfected their service delivery methods and product design to respond to the demands of their market in a rapid and efficient way, ensuring an increased volume of operations and repeat borrowing
- Have a strong sense of mission and a sound governing structure that is free from political interference, so that they can make policy decisions that protect their financial health
- Have a management team that focuses on efficient service delivery and productivity, on profits rather than volume, and sets productivity goals and incentive schemes
- Have information systems that produce clear, accurate, timely, and relevant information for management decisionmaking and that focus on well-developed loan tracking and financial reporting systems, reporting on costs and income both on a profit-center basis and for the MFI as a whole
- Have a record of achieving high levels of financial performance, of incorporating appropriate pricing policies based on the full cost of delivering the services, and of maintaining the value of donated equity
- Maintain low levels of delinquency (well below 5 percent to 8 percent of outstanding portfolio, with loan loss rates below 2 percent) to ensure optimum income and prevent asset erosion.

Source: Clark 1997.

Box 4.19 Accessing Capital Markets by Issuing Financial Paper

ISSUING FINANCIAL PAPER REFERS TO A FORMAL IOU GIVEN by the MFI to investors in exchange for their funds. Financial paper is issued with a fixed date on which the debt will be paid (maturity) and a preestablished interest payment (yield). The financial market then evaluates the paper in terms of yield versus risk, comparing it with every other investment opportunity available. To succeed in the financial market an MFI must offer at least an equally attractive yield to alternatives that are perceived to have the same level of risk. Accordingly, for a new entrant in the market whose risk profile is unknown, a higher yield may be necessary.

Establishing the correct risk is especially important for an MFI operating in an industry that is itself unknown. For example, in 1994, when ACCION was placing paper issued by BancoSol to North American financial institutions, investors began with an expectation of returns reflecting both country and venture capital risk. While Bolivian country risk was unquestionably a relevant consideration, ACCION argued successfully that the appropriate business risk, instead of being compared to venture capital,

Source: Chu 1996b.

should reflect a methodology proven by microlending activities deployed since 1987 by BancoSol's predecessor, PRODEM. This long track record of success is evidenced by a consistent historical loss record of less than 1 percent of portfolio. On that basis the yield offered by BancoSol paper was highly attractive relative to its real rather than perceived risk.

It is not necessary to become a regulated financial institution before issuing financial paper. For example, in 1995 the ACCION affiliate in Paraguay, Fundación Paraguaya de Cooperacion y Desarrollo, as an NGO issued 350 million guaranies in debt through the Asuncion Securities Exchange.

In addition, it may not even be necessary for the issuing institutions to be 100 percent financially self-sufficient to issue paper, although it is clearly preferable, as in the case of the Grameen Bank in Bangladesh. In the debt market it is possible to find buyers as long as there is the firm expectation that the cash flow (whether generated by operations or donations) is sufficient to service the debt.

be some time before equity investors play an important role in the funding mechanisms of MFIs. However, some equity investment funds are being developed specifically to invest in growing, sustainable MFIs.

EQUITY INVESTMENT FUNDS. Equity investment funds provide equity and quasi-equity (subordinated debt) to selected organizations. ProFund is one such investment fund that was set up for the sole purpose of investing in expanding MFIs in Latin America (box 4.20). Efforts

Box 4.20 ProFund—an Equity Investment Fund for Latin America

PROFUND IS AN INVESTMENT FUND INCORPORATED IN Panama and administered from Costa Rica. It was created to support the growth of regulated and efficient financial intermediaries that serve the small business and microenterprise market in Latin America and the Caribbean. It operates on a profit basis, providing equity and quasi-equity to eligible financial institutions so that they can expand their operations on a sustainable and large-scale base. By supporting the growth of efficient intermediaries, ProFund aims to achieve superior financial returns for its investors through long-term capital appreciation of the MFIs in which it invests.

At the end of 1997 ProFund was capitalized by a group of 16 investors who have subscribed a total of more than US$22 million with 63 percent of the capital paid in

Source: ProFund Internacional 1997.

(ProFund Internacional 1996–97). ProFund's sponsors (original investors) are Calmeadow, ACCION International, FUNDES (a Swiss foundation), and Société d'Invest-issement et de Développement International (SIDI), a French NGO consortium. Other investors include the International Finance Corporation, the International Development Bank's Multilateral Investment Fund, and the Rockefeller Foundation.

By 1997 ProFund had made seven investments, with total commitments of US$12.2 million. MFIs invested in include Accion Comunitaria del Peru, Banco Empresarial (Guatemala), BancoSol (Bolivia), Banco Solidario (Ecuador), Caja de Ahorro y Prestamo Los Andes (Bolivia), Finansol (Colombia), and Servicredit (Nicaragua).

are under way to establish similar funds in Africa and Asia.

SOCIALLY RESPONSIBLE MUTUAL FUNDS. There are two types of socially responsible mutual funds: screened and shared-return funds. With *screened mutual funds,* managers screen companies for social criteria. Profits are paid to shareholders who choose to invest in these funds because they want to support socially responsible companies. *The Calvert Group* mutual fund is an example of a screened mutual fund (box 4.21).

Shared return funds are mutual funds owned by member organizations (MFIs). Shareholders agree to donate (share) a percentage of the return to the member organizations. *DEVCAP* (Development Capital Fund) is an example of a shared mutual fund owned by MFI member organizations (box 4.22).

SECURITIZATION. Securitization links microfinance institutions to capital markets by issuing corporate debentures backed by (and serviced by) the MFI's portfolio (adapted from Chu 1996a). The structure requires the creation of a single purpose corporation, which buys the microenterprise portfolio and capitalizes itself by issuing debentures into the capital market.

The purpose of creating a single purpose corporation is to acquire the microenterprise portfolios of known entities without taking on other risks. The equity of the single purpose corporation comes from the microfinance organization and its partners. The single purpose corporation uses its funds to purchase the portfolio from an MFI, which it does at a discount—that is, for less than

---

> **Box 4.22 DEVCAP—a Shared-Return Fund**
>
> DEVCAP (DEVELOPMENT CAPITAL FUND) IS A MUTUAL fund designed to provide financial returns to its investors as well as provide its members with revenue. DEVCAP represents a consortium of MFIs that invested initial capital to develop an asset base for the fund. Additional capital is provided by public investors. The assets of the fund are invested in a leading socially screened portfolio (social equity portfolio) based on the Domini Social Index, which consists of the stocks of approximately 400 U.S. companies chosen for their corporate and social responsibility as well as their financial performance. The return earned on the investments is shared between the investor and DEVCAP. The tax-deductible donation made by the investor ranges from 50 percent to 100 percent of the return earned.
>
> The return earned by DEVCAP is shared among its member MFIs. Members include Appropriate Technology International, Catholic Relief Services, Save the Children, and the Seed Capital Development Fund.
>
> *Source:* Development Capital Fund.

---

its face value. The amount of discount is based on the quality of the portfolio. For example, if the single purpose corporation purchases US$105 of portfolio for only US$100, the additional US$5 is held in a reserve to protect the corporation against any portfolio losses. This reserve amounts to roughly 5 percent of the portfolio. In this case the historic rate of default must be lower than 5 percent and likely less than 2 percent (the reserve should be greater than the historic loan loss to provide comfort for investors). In addition, the single purpose corporation has substantial equity so anyone who buys paper issued by it is highly protected.

The single purpose corporation then sells commercial paper through its financial partner, a leading brokerage firm in the local financial market. For securitization to succeed, the partner must be significant and well respected with an established network of buyers. The partner receives a management fee and an investment banking fee.

The object of securitization is to increase the availability of funds and, at the same time, reduce the cost of funds. Grameen Bank and ACCION International and its affiliate, the Fundación Ecuatoriana de Desarollo (FED) in Ecuador, are two MFIs that are either consider-

---

> **Box 4.21 The Calvert Group—a Screened Mutual Fund**
>
> ONE TO 3 PERCENT OF THE CALVERT GROUP'S ASSETS ARE invested in "high social impact" instruments such as MFIs. Eligible institutions must have loan capital of at least US$300,000 from diverse sources and demonstrate the need for more capital. The cost of borrowing by the MFIs is generally below market rates by 3 percent or 4 percent. Renewable loan terms are for one year, and the average loan amount is US$100,000. Investors risk receiving a lower return than from other mutual funds, depending on the success of the overall investment strategy of the fund.
>
> *Source:* Calvert Group.

ing or have successfully achieved securitization of their portfolios. (For an explanation of the structure that FED used for securitizing its portfolio, see Chu 1996a.)

Because both debt and equity represent a willingness to accept financial risk, the fundamental factor that determines the sustainability of access to capital markets is the institution's *credibility* as perceived by investors, whether they are lenders or shareholders. To link with capital markets MFIs must provide clear and solid answers to such critical questions of governance as (Chu 1996b):

- Can MFIs that are NGOs or have NGO owners provide financial markets with the assurance that they will make decisions with the same standards of prudence as enterprises that have traditional shareholders with commercial monies at risk?
- Will NGOs be able to resist the temptation to let nonfinancial considerations—whether lofty or base—overwhelm return considerations, because, in the absence of commercial shareholders, they are ultimately accountable only to their institutional mission?
- Can boards of directors of NGOs effectively control management?
- Will donor agencies be able to distinguish between those NGOs that can live up to the required standards and those that cannot?
- In some cases, particularly in Asia, clients become shareholders as part of the methodology. Will such atomized owners be able to participate in a meaningful way, and, if so, will the cumulative effect of minuscule portions of ownership lead to commercially sound results?
- Will NGOs that have generated their equity through grants and donations be able to exhibit the same discipline and rigor as a private investor? For example, can an institution like ACCION invest in BancoSol with funds provided by donor agencies and behave like a commercial investor?

Answers to these questions will become apparent as the field of microfinance grows and more MFIs begin to access capital markets.

Institutional Capacity Building

Regardless of institutional type and ways of managing growth, all MFIs need to periodically review their institutional capacity and consider where they might make

improvements. For more formalized institutions this may require a greater focus on client needs through improved product development and human resource management. For NGOs this may include the adoption of a formal business planning process, improved financial and productivity management, and new funding sources.

Since the purpose of this handbook is to improve the institutional capacity of MFIs, it is useful to briefly highlight the institutional capacity issues that many MFIs are facing and to identify where these issues are addressed in this and following chapters.

Institutional capacity issues include (SEEP Network 1996a):

- *Business planning.* An MFI needs to be able to translate its strategic vision into a set of operational plans based on detailed market and organizational analysis, financial projections, and profitability analyses. Appendix 2 provides an outline for business planning.
- *Product development.* An MFI must be able to diversify beyond its original credit products (usually individual, solidarity group lending, or both) into other areas such as savings, which can provide desired services to clients and accommodate their growth. An MFI must also be able to price its products on the basis of operating and financial costs and demand in the marketplace. This requires periodic review to ensure appropriate pricing. (For more on the development and pricing of credit and savings products, see chapters 5 and 6 respectively.)
- *Management information systems.* As MFIs grow one of their greatest limitations is often their management information system. It is imperative that an MFI have adequate information systems for financial and human resource management. For example, establishing an effective incentive system depends critically on the existence of a good management information system, which then allows management to track the various indicators of performance that it wants to reward. (For a more detailed discussion of management information systems, see chapter 7.)
- *Financial management.* Improvements in accounting and budgeting are often required to monitor loan portfolio quality, donor subsidies, and the growing volume of operations. Additional skills are required in:
  - The adjustment of financial statements for subsidies and inflation

- Portfolio risk management, including appropriate risk classification, loan loss provisioning, and write-offs
- Performance management, including profitability and financial viability
- Liquidity and risk management, focused on effectively administering portfolios largely based on short-term loans
- Asset and liability management, including appropriate matching of amortization periods in relation to the loan portfolio and asset management and capital budgeting processes that are inflation sensitive.

(For a discussion of financial management see chapters 8 through 10.)

Efficiency and productivity enhancement. MFIs must be able to operate in a way that best combines standardization, decentralization, and incentives to achieve the greatest output with the least cost. They must also develop systems for staff recruitment and selection, compensation, training, and motivation to support staff commitment and accountability. (For further information about efficiency and productivity enhancement see chapter 10.)

The credit unions in Guatemala present a good example of the importance of periodic reviews and a focus on institutional capacity building (box 4.23).

Appendix 1. MFI Operational Review

The following outline is from SEEP Network 1996b and was developed by Calmeadow, Toronto, Canada.

Definition

The operational review is a tool used to evaluate the institutional maturity of a microfinance organization. An operational review helps an NGO planning to transform into a self-sufficient microfinance intermediary to evaluate its readiness. This tool draws on lessons from the formal banking sector, from Calmeadow's own observations working with microfinance institutions, and from recent publications on institutional development.

Box 4.23 Credit Unions Retooled

IN MID-1987 THE U.S. AGENCY FOR INTERNATIONAL Development contracted the World Council of Credit Unions to provide technical and financial assistance to the National Credit Union Federation. During the course of the project a major restructuring of the Guatemalan credit union movement took place. New financial tools and disciplines were developed and tested in 20 community credit unions countrywide. Their use transformed the credit unions into modern, effective financial intermediaries, capable of competing in commercial financial markets.

Guatemalan credit unions had followed a traditional development model for 25 years. This model was based on the theory that the rural poor lacked the resources necessary to save and thereby fuel their development potential. International donors responded to the lack of local resources by providing the credit unions with external capital at subsidized rates for on-lending to their members. Loan sizes were based on a multiple of the amount of shares a member held in the credit union rather than on the member's repayment capacity. Shares earned very low returns, so the only purpose in saving was to access a loan. The traditional model discouraged sav-

ing, encouraged borrowing, and forced those who saved to subsidize those who borrowed. Over time, the response of many members was to find a way to borrow-out their share savings with no intention of ever repaying the loan.

In the new model created through the project, the focus was shifted from share savings to voluntary deposits with a competitive rate of return. Subsidized external financing was eliminated, and because all funding came from internally mobilized deposits, loans were priced based on market rates. Loan approvals were based on the repayment capacity of the borrower. Earnings were capitalized rather than distributed to members, so that the credit unions' capital maintained its value. The credit unions undertook a market-based, results-oriented business planning process. And finally, improved financial reporting control and evaluation was instituted through intensive training.

While the process was slow and difficult and required significant changes in the attitudes of elected leaders, employees, and the member-owners, the result was greater financial independence, stronger and safer credit union operations, and superior, member-driven financial services.

Source: Richardson, Lennon, and Branch 1993.

The Tool

The operational review provides the user with guidelines on how to evaluate a microcredit program in seven key areas: corporate governance, market and clients, credit methodology, distribution, human resource management, computerization, and financial management. Each topic includes three sections: documentation, indicators of health, and transformation issues.

How the Tool Works

The review involves a thorough documentation of the operating procedures and institutional characteristics of the organization and an evaluation of these factors against performance levels currently being achieved by leading micro-finance institutions worldwide.

An operational review takes about 2 weeks (or 10 working days) of on-site field work to gather the information required from an intermediate level organization (more than 2,000 clients). This includes collecting and synthesizing a large amount of data and materials as well as interviews with all senior managers, a comprehensive sample of other head office staff and field staff, and clients.

Two useful products can result from an operational review:
1. A detailed documentation of the organization that can be given to visitors, researchers, funders, and groups who may want to start a microcredit program and are looking for lessons from current practitioners.
2. An evaluation of the organization's readiness for rapid growth and transformation, comprising of two sections—one on institutional capacity in general and one on issues particular to transformation.

Operational Review: An Outline

1. Corporate governance
2. Markets and clients
3. Credit methodology
4. Distribution
5. Human resource management
6. Computerization
7. Financial management
   For each topic above, this outline includes three sections:
- *Documentation*—A checklist of items to be collected and documented during the review.

- *Indicators of health*—Standards against which to evaluate the organization. As we gain experience with applying the tool, these standards will become more quantitative.
- *Transformation issues*—Issues requiring thought and attention if the organization is contemplating transforming into a regulated financial intermediary.

1. CORPORATE GOVERNANCE
Documentation
- History, institutional type/incorporation, vision and goals
- Board of directors (names and professions/areas of expertise, regularity of meetings; committees of the board, term of members, and board renewal procedures)
- Managing director and senior management (names and experience; years of service)

Indicators of health
- Vision and goals clearly articulated and consistent
- Evidence of a strong sense of mission
- Board well constituted, with a mixture of financial services and other business
- Legal, marketing, fundraising, and community development skills
- Board members well informed about the global microfinance sector and committed to the vision of the organization
- Board members who are active in committees
- Depth of experience and strong leadership demonstrated by the managing director and senior management
- Strong commitment by senior management toward the vision of the organization. Sufficient breadth and depth of senior management so organization is not vulnerable to the loss of any one individual.
- A business planning process and strategic plans in place.
- If microfinance is just one activity of the organization, the financial services are run and monitored independently, unencumbered by other nonfinancial activities.

Transformation issues
- What new corporate structures are being contemplated? Do these make sense? Does transformation make sense given the institutional maturity of the organization? Is transformation being contemplated for the

right reasons or should other options be considered at this point in time?

- Will the new structure require a different mission, or is the new structure just a different vehicle for implementing the same mission? (Business versus social development mission.)
- How will ownership of the new organization be structured? Will new partners be required? What type of partners are most desirable? What combination of for-profit and not-for-profit institutions?
- Do all board members fully understand and support the goal of transformation?
- Will the board need to be reconstituted for the transformed organization?
- Do all senior managers fully understand and support the goal of transformation?

2. MARKETS AND CLIENTS
Documentation

- State of small and microenterprise sector in the country (how large? how sophisticated? how literate?)
- Barriers faced (cultural and political factors)
- Suppliers of microcredit in the country; competitors
- Target markets (size, type and subsector, gender, geographic coverage)
- Policies on client graduation
- Profile of current borrowers (size of microenterprises served; three most common activities by gender; distribution by sector: trade, manufacturing, service; proportion of new versus repeat borrowers; proportion of female borrowers)
- New product development (how done and who is accountable)

Indicators of health

- Target markets are clearly articulated; ideally only one or two primary targets. If more than one target, the different markets should work well together within one delivery structure.
- Profile of current borrowers should match the targets.
- Low client drop out rates/high renewal rates. Clients express a high level of satisfaction with the service. New clients approach the organization voluntarily.
- A strong "client service" culture is evident.
- Client and market research is conducted on a regular basis; innovation in meeting the evolving needs of clients is valued.

- New product development is viewed as a necessary and ongoing activity in the organization and accountability for product enhancements and new product development is clearly assigned to appropriate personnel.

Transformation issues

- The size of target markets should be sufficiently large to sustain a self-sufficient microfinance institution.
- Will transformation require a redefinition of the target market or a departure from the current target? Will it threaten the current market focus?

3. CREDIT METHODOLOGY
Documentation

- Product design (loan amounts (sizes), terms, and repayment frequency; pricing; interest and fees; savings products and requirements; insurance or other funds)
- Eligibility criteria (gender, age, years of experience in business, collateral, guarantors, peer groups, other collateral substitutes; legal, cultural, or other regulatory requirements)
- Credit delivery procedures (promotions, screening, orientation, group formation, applications and disbursements, repayments, renewals)
- Delinquency management (reports and monitoring; enforcement/follow-up procedures; incentives and sanctions: i) rewards for timely repayment, ii) penalties for late payment, iii) consequences of default, insurance/use of savings, policies on rescheduling, refinancing, and death of borrower)

Indicators of health

- The basic methodology appears to be well-tested and stable.
- Product design appears to suit business needs of borrowers.
- Eligibility criteria are easy to meet—not too restrictive.
- For group-based programs, group cohesion appears to be strong.
- Delivery procedures minimize inconvenience and transaction costs for client.
- Delivery procedures minimize chances for fraud.
- Branch procedures are routine/standardized and facilitate loan officer work flow—they make it easy for loan officers to conduct their work effectively.
- Strong relationship is evident between clients and loan officer.

- Delinquency management is tightly enforced. Procedures for late payment follow-up are triggered automatically after certain time periods. Loan officers not involved in collections once client is no longer negotiating in good faith. Incentives and sanctions appear to be effective. Late payments are minimal.
- Repayment/recovery rates are calculated according to international standards and are above 85% (for cumulative repayment, including arrears)
- Portfolio at risk rates are calculated according to international standards and are <10%

Transformation issues
- Will transformation require any change to the current methodology? How will this be perceived by the client?

4. DISTRIBUTION
Documentation
- Type, number, and location of field offices (diagram if desirable)
- Outreach / branching / growth strategy
- Nature and strength of relationships with related or supporting institutions that assist with operations and outreach (such as banks)

Indicators of health
- Branching strategy is clearly articulated and makes sense—urban versus rural—builds economies of scale—not too sparse
- Strong relationships with supporting institutions, that is, banks, collection agencies

Transformation issues
- How will the transformation affect relationships with other institutions? Will contracts need to be revised?

5. HUMAN RESOURCE MANAGEMENT
Documentation
- Organigram of head office and field personnel structures.
- For primary operations staff (hiring criteria and procedures, job descriptions, training program; compensation policies, incentive scheme design, other recognition and reward mechanisms).
- For head office positions (any unusual or noteworthy hiring or training policies, compensation policies, incentive scheme design, other recognition and reward mechanisms).

- Apparent culture of organization—hierarchical or participatory.
- Apparent employee satisfaction levels; turnover levels—head office and field offices.
- Existence of an employee union or association.
- Existence of an employee newsletter.
- Appraisal system.
- Promotion policies/succession planning.
- Other innovative personnel policies.

Indicators of health
- Head office size and structure that is appropriate for the size of operations currently and in the near future.
- Branch organization structure is streamlined, minimizes overhead, and does not put too much stress on managers.
- Span of control for managers is close to the ideal of five to seven direct reports each.
- Sufficient number of qualified candidates applying to advertised positions. Appropriate "incubators" for staff identified, for example, technical colleges. Time spent screening candidates is minimized. Progressive hiring policies in place (that is, gender sensitive).
- Job descriptions that are available, clearly written, and emphasize expected outputs rather than activities. No overlaps or underlaps in accountabilities between departments and individuals.
- Training materials are thorough and well designed, covering philosophy and client service concepts as well as technical skills. A period of coaching/mentoring built into the training. Training period screens out inappropriate candidates. Length and cost of training minimized.
- Compensation policies are set to attract the right caliber of staff.
- Incentive schemes are designed to reward portfolio quality as well as volume, and incentive amounts are set relative to the extra income earned through enhanced performance.
- Employees who express a high level of satisfaction with their work. Low employee turnover. No antagonistic employee unions or associations.
- Dynamic use of employee newsletter, with contributions from employees. Strong internal communications and transparency. A team spirit evident in all activities.
- Appraisal systems, promotions policies, and other policies are perceived as fair.

Transformation isues

- Will all head office and field operations go to the new institution or will some remain?
- Will split be clean or will there be complex relationships between the NGO and the new institution?
- Will head office functions be shared between institutions?
- How do staff members feel about the proposed transformation? Are they aware of it, do they understand the reasons for it, are they supportive of it? What are their biggest concerns regarding transformation?
- If the organization is being divided into two, will the same human resources policies apply to both? Will there be a differential in compensation levels? How will this be handled?

6. COMPUTERIZATION

Documentation

- Current state of automation
  - head office and field offices
  - loan portfolio system, accounting system, other systems?
- Hardware and software used, development tools used, network design
- Existence of functional specifications
- Level of staff satisfaction with current systems
- Profile and depth of information systems department
- Procedures used for auditing systems.

Indicators of health

- Degree of automation in line with size and complexity of organization, degree of automation in line with dependability of communications infrastructure in the country
- Diversification of risk—avoid dependence on a single programmer to develop and maintain the systems, and avoid dependence on one expensive firm to make small updates to the systems
- Hardware and software used should be well supported locally, development tools should be well known locally
- Apparent high level of staff satisfaction with the systems
- Strong information systems manager and department—knowledgeable, reliable, service-oriented
- Effective procedures in place for auditing systems.

Transformation issues

- What systems changes will be required to accommodate new reporting requirements for the new institution?
- Will the current system be able to handle rapid growth and increased complexity over the next 18 months?

7. FINANCIAL MANAGEMENT

Documentation

- Financial statements (when produced? when audited? how consolidated?)
- Relationship with auditors (availability of profit and cost center information and statements, availability of multiple year financial forecasting models)
- Budgeting process
- Cash flow management—cash flow forecasting, liquidity monitoring, minimizing idle cash, bank account management
- Delinquency management—repayment rates, portfolio aging, arrears aging, provision and write-off policies
- Internal controls to avoid fraud, negligence, and theft, internal audit procedures
- Sources of capital and relationship with bankers/funders, average cost of capital
- Size of equity base in relation to total assets
- Self-sufficiency management—operational efficiency, productivity, and self-sufficiency ratios.

Indicators of health

- Financial statements are produced and audited at least annually
- Statements should be produced for the financial service activities of the organization unconsolidated from any other nonfinancial activities
- Auditing firm should be respected and ideally have some financial sector experience/expertise
- Income statements and key ratios are available for each primary operating unit—branch/region/total
- A three- to five-year financial forecasting model is in place and actively used to assist with pricing and other policy setting and steer the organization toward profitability.
- An annual budgeting process is in place and is used to control expenses.
- Cash flows are well managed—liquidity problems are avoided, idle cash is minimized, and bank charges are minimized.

- Delinquency and default are closely monitored and tightly managed; appropriate provision and write-off policies are in place and properly implemented.
- Sufficient sources of loan capital are in place to fund expected growth. The average cost of capital is kept to a minimum. The relationship with banks is approached as a business relationship, not as a public relations or donations relationship. Over time, the organization is moving away from subsidized sources of funding and developing a good reputation with commercial funders.
- The equity base is sufficient in relation to overall assets and performing assets.
- Key ratios of operational efficiency, productivity, and self-sufficiency are regularly monitored and guide the decisionmaking of board and senior management. Key ratios are steadily improving, with full self-sufficiency likely to be reached within 12 to 24 months.
- Management information reports are timely, accurate, and relevant.
- Key reports include:
  - Actual payments against expected payments—for field staff
  - Client status report—for field staff
  - Bad debts report—for field staff and head office
  - Aging of arrears—for field staff and head office
  - Aging of portfolio—for head office
  - Performance indicators report—for head office and board of directors.
- Break-even analyses are available and guide decisionmaking.
- Pricing is carefully managed. Calculations are available for effective costs to the client and for effective yields to the organization. Rates are established in order to cover operating costs, loan losses, and financial costs and to achieve a profit at certain levels of operation.

Transformation issues
- How will financial statements need to be revised for the new organization(s)?
- Will new auditors need to be appointed?
- How will bank accounts and liquidity management be affected?
- How will internal audit procedures need to be changed?
- Are current subsidies in place today, due to the organization's non-profit status, which will no longer be available after transformation? How will the higher costs affect self-sufficiency levels? (consider operating cost subsidies and financial cost subsidies.)
- How should the capital structure for the new organization be designed? How much control needs to be maintained? What kind of shareholders are desirable? How much capital is required to support the new institution for the first few years of its existence? What is an optimum debt to equity ratio for the new institution?
- What will be the dividend policy for the first three to five years of the transformed institution?

Appendix 2. Manual for Elaboration of a Business Plan

The following outline is from SEEP Network 1996b and was developed by CENTRO ACCION Microempresarial, Bogota, Colombia, and ACCION International, Cambridge, Mass.

Definition

This manual provides guidelines for creating a business plan. It is divided into nine chapters, each of which covers a distinct part of a business plan, from market analysis to portfolio projections to estimating operational costs. The core chapters provide instructions for data gathering and analysis that feed directly into the construction of standard financial statements. Because the manual was written for ACCION affiliates, it focuses on planning for the expansion of credit services.

The Tool

The original tool is a 45-page manual, in spanish, with the following chapters: Institutional Analysis, Defining Market Size, Identifying the Competition, Projecting the Portfolio, Market Penetration, Financing Expansion, Operational Costs, Priority Projects, Projective Financial Statements.

The tool included here is an English summary of the manual, which highlights the main themes in each chapter and provides some examples of the many illustrative tables and charts found in the original.

How the Tool Works

The business plan is a document that explicitly establishes an institution's trajectory over a three-year period. It is the tool by which an institution's mission gets translated into measurable targets. These targets are set in function of market demand and the competition. They inform income and expense projections that take sustainability from theory to reality.

In light of its mission, an institution sets targets for the market share it will achieve by the end of the three-year planning period. Market share, defined by geographic area, translates into a certain number of branch offices and field staff, which in turn determines the institution's cost structure. From these targets, the portfolio size can be deduced, which then points to the amount of funding required. Internal coherence is then determined by combining the product pricing, the cost structure, and the financing plan to form the income statement.

The Business Plan process begins with an ACCION team (usually two people, one of whom is often the president) making a visit that includes a formal presentation of the state of the microfinance program and of its medium-term goals. The business plan tool is presented and staff learn how to apply it. This takes place over a two-day period in the presence of all members of the institution's top management and, in some cases, with the attendance of board members. While concepts related to the mission are discussed, most of the time is spent on issues, including the type and size of the market, the relative strength of the competition, setting realistic growth targets based on a number of key assumptions, and definition of a handful of priority projects that will have to be carried out if the proposed objectives are to be achieved. At the end of the two-day period, a time line for completing different drafts of the business plan is agreed upon.

Most of the work is then carried out by the affiliates themselves, over a period of two to four months. The work is divided among departments, with each manager responsible for involving his/her staff in the process to the fullest extent. As drafts of the plan are produced, they are sent to ACCION for a critical review of the assumptions and internal consistency.

The strength of the business plan lies in the way in which all elements, and every decision, have a financial implication with an impact on financial performance and the bottom line. This requires analytical rigor. It also forces

an integration of all elements of the plan, as well as functional integration of the managers who formulate and oversee it. Using a financially based planning tool helps managers adapt to changing conditions and know more precisely how their decisions will affect financial performance. The plan serves as a reference tool to clarify priorities, unify efforts, avoid contradictions and evaluate the performances of both the institution and individual employees.

Moreover, for affiliates in the ACCION network, the business plan is an essential tool in building relationships with the formal financial sector. Without a plan, financial markets will not be disposed to increase lines of credit or negotiate more favorable terms.

1. INTRODUCTION

What is business planning?

It is a process by which an organization defines a path from its current situation to where it wants to be at a determined point in the future.

How is it used?

In the course of business planning, the organization determines its destination (within a three-year horizon) and designs the road to get there. It establishes numerically defined objectives, strategies, and actions. This diagnosis helps to answer two important questions:

- Can the organization successfully travel along this path?
- What additional resources will it need and how will it secure them?

Who participates in the business planning process?

The entire management team must participate to ensure that all of the pieces of the planning puzzle fit, resulting in a consistent, coherent plan.

What are the characteristics of a successful business plan?

- Involves entire management team
- Identifies key elements that differentiate the program from other similar organizations and explain its success
- Analyzes the environment, including the market and competition
- Defines the organization's objectives
- Identifies strategies to overcome obstacles to achieving objectives
- Analyzes the financial implications of these strategies
- Translates the objectives, strategies and resources into numerical terms that are void of inconsistencies.

2. BUSINESS PLAN FORMAT

Box A4.2.1 presents a suggested format for a business plan and shows the links to financial status.

3. INSTITUTIONAL ANALYSIS

This chapter directs the reader to the elements of an institutional analysis that cover its history, mission, and comparative advantages. The institutional analysis is one of the most important parts of the business as it is the skeleton around which the rest of the plan is elaborated. Specific elements of the institutional analysis follow:

History of the institution.

Mission: The raison d'être of the enterprise, the mission statement defines the institution's values and priorities. The mission clearly defines the product and services to be offered, its target customer base and the location of this clientele.

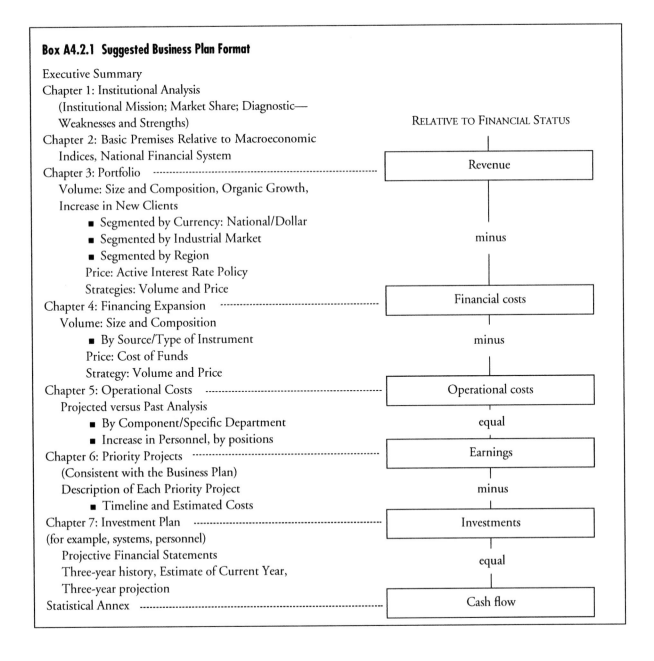

Box A4.2.1 Suggested Business Plan Format

Executive Summary
Chapter 1: Institutional Analysis
    (Institutional Mission; Market Share; Diagnostic—
    Weaknesses and Strengths)
Chapter 2: Basic Premises Relative to Macroeconomic
    Indices, National Financial System
Chapter 3: Portfolio
    Volume: Size and Composition, Organic Growth,
    Increase in New Clients
      ■ Segmented by Currency: National/Dollar
      ■ Segmented by Industrial Market
      ■ Segmented by Region
    Price: Active Interest Rate Policy
    Strategies: Volume and Price
Chapter 4: Financing Expansion
    Volume: Size and Composition
      ■ By Source/Type of Instrument
    Price: Cost of Funds
    Strategy: Volume and Price
Chapter 5: Operational Costs
    Projected versus Past Analysis
      ■ By Component/Specific Department
      ■ Increase in Personnel, by positions
Chapter 6: Priority Projects
    (Consistent with the Business Plan)
    Description of Each Priority Project
      ■ Timeline and Estimated Costs
Chapter 7: Investment Plan
(for example, systems, personnel)
    Projective Financial Statements
    Three-year history, Estimate of Current Year,
    Three-year projection
Statistical Annex

RELATIVE TO FINANCIAL STATUS

Revenue

minus

Financial costs

minus

Operational costs

equal

Earnings

minus

Investments

equal

Cash flow

In defining the mission, planners must move the mission from a concept to the articulation of its quantitative implications, which express the institution's objectives. Consequently the business plan identifies all elements necessary and sufficient to achieve those objectives and outlines the specific actions to assure that these elements are in place when they are needed.

Comparative advantage: Those characteristics that differentiate the institution from the others and explain its success.

Strengths and weaknesses (internal).

Opportunities and threats (external).

4. BASIC PREMISES

This brief section of the manual describes the general economic analysis that should be part of the business plan. This economic analysis should incorporate analysis and projections in three main areas: macroeconomics, the informal sector, and the financial system.

5. PORTFOLIO ANALYSIS AND PROJECTIONS

The projected portfolio is the "backbone" of the business plan, determining costs and income. This chapter of the manual contains six sections that offer guidelines for estimating the market, defining the competition, establishing portfolio projections, determining market penetration, classifying the portfolio, and setting interest rate policies.

Determining the market. To express an institution's mission in quantitative terms, it is necessary to define the customer base and estimate the size of the market this customer base represents. This provides a yardstick against which to measure both the reality of growth projections and progress toward achieving the stated mission.

The manual concedes that there is no one accepted, established procedure for determining market size. Given the quality and quantity of available data on the informal sector, efforts to measure it can only result in estimations drawn from available statistics, census data, sociological research and other sources. The manual does offer the following guidelines and an example of one method of estimation in box A4.2.2.

- Focus on the geographic area of operation and its potential for growth. The steps outlined in box A4.2.2 should be followed for each city or region of operation.
- Within the informal sector, define the segment of the market that is eligible for products and services that the institution provides.
- Growth projections should be based on both historical patterns and current factors such as migration, government policies relevant to the sector, and so forth.

Although only approximated, this definition of the market is extremely important because it is a vision of the business environment that must be shared by management in order to serve as a basis for decisionmaking.

Defining the competition. To position the institution in the marketplace, the following information about the competition should be collected. This information will help to identify the institution's strengths and weaknesses and influence strategies for the three-year planning horizon.

Box A4.2.2 Estimating the Market: An Example from Ecuador

Steps

1. Find the economically active population (EAP) from the most recent census data
2. Define the informal sector (for each city)
3. Estimate the percentage of the EAP that is informal
4. Estimate the percentage that is subject to credit
5. Project growth.

The case of Ecuador

1. EAP (1989 census)   38% of total population
2. Formal sector   28% of EAP registered
                              with social security
   Unemployment   13%
   Independent professionals 2%
                              43% of EAP is in the
                              formal sector

Informal sector = Total population x 38% x (1–43%)

3. We estimate that 15% of the informal sector would not be interested in credit. Of the targeted 85%, only 38% own their business and, therefore, would be candidates for loans.

   Customer base = Informal sector x 0.85 x 0.38

Source: SEEP Network 1996b.

- Who are the competitors?
- Size
- Funding sources
- Client base
- Market niche
- Marketing methods
- Portfolio size and quality
- Methodology
- How solid are they?
- Pricing
- Time to deliver service
- Marketing methods
- Numbers.

It can be helpful to construct a "Chart of Competition," placing competitors on a graph defined by interest rates and non-monetary costs. In addition to locating the institution in relation to its competitors, the graph can be used to show its movement in time.

Projecting the portfolio. Projections of portfolio growth must be made on two levels: loan volume of existing clients in the current portfolio and loan volume attributed to new clients. While the institution has the option to take new clients or not, it must attend to the needs of existing clients. (Inability to do so would trigger widespread delinquency and even default.) Additional factors to consider in projecting the portfolio include:

- Client drop-out rate
- Growth pattern of average loan size over time—influenced by average loan term, cyclical nature of demand, influence of inflation on initial loan size, and new loan products with different characteristics.

Estimating market penetration. The relationship of the portfolio projections to the estimated market for credit yields the market penetration (*MP*). Calculating the institution's market penetration serves as a reality check for the projections:

$$MP = \frac{\text{Customer base (defined in projected portfolio)}}{\text{Potential market}}$$

Classifying the portfolio. The portfolio must be disaggregated or classified by a number of factors that have an impact on cash flow and costs. These include:

- Loan size and number
- Loan maturities
- Life of the client with the program
- Indicators of portfolio quality: delinquency and default.

Interest rate policies. The final part of portfolio projections is setting the interest rate(s), which will be based on the following factors:

- Market rates (researched as part of competition analysis)
- Operating costs (explained in chapter 8).
- Financial costs (a weighted average)
- Capitalization objectives (that is, targeted level of retained earnings generated by the portfolio determined during the institutional analysis).

Although there are various methods for setting interest rates, one simple example is illustrated below:

Interest rate charged	20%
– Financing costs	10%
= Financial margin	10%
– Operating costs	5%
= Operating margin	5%
Desired margin	8%

With estimated financing and operating costs, the interest rate can be set to achieve the desired margin. In this example, the institution has not achieved its desired margin leaving it with the option to raise its interest rate or reduce costs. This is a dynamic process in which the projections and parameters will need to be adjusted to secure the desired results.

6. FINANCING EXPANSION

This chapter identifies various funding sources—their characteristics, costs, and conditions. Each is analyzed for accessibility and inherent risks. Here are two sources of funding: internal (retained earnings) and external (donations, shareholder capital, soft loans, commercial loans, and deposits). With the portfolio growth and the desired rate of capitalization established, external funding needs can be determined. Assuming multiple sources at varying cost, it is necessary to establish a weighted average of the sources to estimate the institution's financial costs. Table A4.2.1 provides a hypothetical example. The weighting factor for each funding category is the product of the proportion of the total external capital and the effective interest rate. The sum of the weights is the weighted average interest rate the organization pays on its external capital.

7. OPERATIONAL COSTS—PAST AND PROJECTED

Offices and staff by city or geographic area. Disaggregate costs by office. Personnel, the most significant cost,

Table A4.2.1 Financial Cost as a Weighted Average

Funding Source	Amount	Proportion (percent)	Interest rate (percent)	Weighted interest rate
Donations	250,000	5.0	0	0
IDB loan	500,000	10.0	1	0.001
Government loan	1,000,000	20.0	20	0.04
Bank loan	1,750,000	35.0	35	0.1225
Deposits	1,500,000	30.0	25	0.075
Total	5,000,000	100.0		0.239

Source: Fruman and Isern 1996.

should be detailed by type and number. Analyze historical performance, going back three years, including current year projections; Estimate future costs according to projections and selected productivity ratios. Every new office and additional staff must be consistent with accepted levels of productivity and fully justified in the business plan.

Productivity ratios

Clients/credit	Officer/credit officer/ employees	Portfolio credit officer
Clients/employees	Credit officer/agency	Portfolio/ employee
Clients/agency	Employees/agency	Portfolio/ agency

Personnel costs. Use historical data to estimate salaries, benefits, and annual increases.

Specific planning for new facilities or renovations. Once the number of new offices or the expansion of existing ones has been established, the process must be fully identified in the business plan, including associated projects, investments, and expenses such as legal costs, publicity, and additional maintenance.

8. PRIORITY PROJECTS

Some projects merit separate treatment in the business planning process. Examples include the introduction of savings services, the creation of a formal financial intermediary or modernization of the institution's systems. A chapter in the business plan on priority projects should outline:
Project objectives. Description, background, the problem

to be addressed, and the benefits to be gained—both qualitative and quantitative.

Costs. In addition to the impact on operating costs, the plan must account for special costs associated with these projects, such as the staff training required to operate a new system.

Timeframe for investments. A detailed plan of tasks and of the time line for their accomplishment outlines the process for purposes of control and to identify points when funds will be needed to finance the project.

Sources of financing for the project. Precise knowledge of the possible sources of funds for the project is essential to guarantee results. This involves identifying the sources, their characteristics, conditions, terms, and process by which to secure funds.

9. FINANCIAL STATEMENTS

With these projections completed, all the elements are in place to construct projected financial statements including the Balance Sheet, the Profit and Loss Statement, and the Cash Flow Statement.

Sources and Further Reading

Benjamin, McDonald, and Joanna Ledgerwood. 1998. "The Association for the Development of Microenterprises (ADEMI): 'Democratising Credit' in the Dominican Republic." Case Study for the Sustainable Banking with the Poor Project, World Bank, Washington, D.C.

Bremner, Wayne. 1996 "CHISPA." In "Institutional Structures for Micro Enterprise Finance: Implications for Sustainability and Expansion." In *Moving Forward: Emerging Strategies for Sustainability and Expansion.* The SEEP Network, New York: PACT Publications.

Calmeadow. 1996. "Planning for Institutional Transformation—Analysis of a Microfinance Organization." In *Moving Forward: Emerging Strategies for Sustainbility and Expansion.* The SEEP Network, New York: PACT Publications.

CGAP (Consultative Group to Assist the Poorest). 1998. "Apex Institutions." Occasional Paper, World Bank, Washington, D.C.

———. 1997a. "Anatomy of a Micro-finance Deal: A New Approach to Investing in Micro-Finance Institutions." Focus Note 9. World Bank, Washington, D.C.

———. 1997b. "The Challenge of Growth for Micro-Finance Institutions: The BancoSol Experience." Focus Note 6. World Bank, Washington, D.C.

———. 1997c. "Effective Governance for Micro-Finance Institutions." Focus Note 7. World Bank, Washington, D.C.

———. 1997d. "State-Owned Development Banks in Micro-Finance." Focus Note 10. World Bank, Washington, D.C.

Christen, Robert Peck. 1997. *Banking Services for the Poor: Managing for Financial Success.* Washington, D.C.: ACCION International.

Christen, Robert, Elizabeth Rhyne, and Robert Vogel. 1995. "Maximizing the Outreach of Microenterprise Finance: An Analysis of Successful Microfinance Programs." Program and Operations Assessment Report 10. U.S. Agency for International Development, Washington D.C.

Chu, Michael. 1996a. "Securitization of a Microenterprise Portfolio." In Craig Churchill, ed., *An Introduction to Key Issues in Microfinance: Supervision and Regulation, Financing Sources, Expansion of Microfinance Institutions.* Washington, D.C.: MicroFinance Network.

———. 1996b. "Reflections on Accessing Capital Markets." ACCION International summary of paper delivered at Fourth Annual MicroFinance Network Conference, November, Toronto.

Churchill, Craig, ed. 1997. *Establishing a Microfinance Industry: Governance, Best Practices, Access to Capital Markets.* Washington, D.C.: MicroFinance Network

———. ed. 1998. *Moving Microfinance Forward: Ownership, Competition, and Control of Microfinance Institutions.* Washington, D.C.: MicroFinance Network.

Clark, Heather. 1997. "When a Program is Ready to Access Commercial Funds: A Discussion for Commercial Standards." Paper prepared for the Microcredit Summit, February 3, Washington D.C.

Clarkson, Max, and Michael Deck. 1997. "Effective Governance for Micro-Finance Institutions." In Craig

Churchill, ed., *Establishing a Microfinance Industry.* Washington, D.C.: MicroFinance Network.

Development Project Service Centre (DEPROSC) and Joanna Ledgerwood. 1997. "Critical Issues in Nepal's Micro-Finance Circumstances." University of Maryland at College Park, Institutional Reform and the Informal Sector, College Park, Md.

Edgcomb, Elaine, and Jim Cawley, eds. 1993. *An Institutional Guide for Enterprise Development Organizations.* New York: PACT Publications.

Fruman, Cecile. 1997. "FEECAM—Benin." Case Study for the Sustainable Banking with the Poor Project, World Bank, Washington, D.C.

Fruman, Cecile, and Jennifer Isern. 1996. "World Bank Microfinance Training." World Bank, Washington, D.C.

Galludec, Gilles. 1996. "CGAP Appraisal Mission." World Bank, Consultative Group to Assist the Poorest, Washington, D.C.

Garber, Garter. 1997. "Private Investment as a Financing Source for Microcredit." The North South Agenda Papers 23. University of Miami, North-South Center, Miami, Fla.

Gonzalez-Vega, Claudio. 1998. "Microfinance Apex Mechanisms: Review of the Evidence and Policy Recommendations." Ohio State University, Department of Agricultural, Environmental, and Development Economics, Rural Finance Program, Columbus, Ohio.

Gudger, Michael. 1997. "Sustainability of Credit Guarantee Systems." In *SME Credit Guarantee Schemes* 4 (1 and 2): 30–33. Published for the Inter-American Development Bank by The Financier.

Holtmann, Martin, and Rochus Mommartz. 1996. *A Technical Guide for Analyzing Credit-Granting NGOs.* Saarbricken, Germany: Verlag fir Entwicklungspolitik.

Jackelen, Henry R., and Elisabeth Rhyne. 1991."Toward a More Market-Oriented Approach to Credit and Savings for the Poor." *Small Enterprise Development* 2 (4): 4–20.

Krahnen, Jan Pieter, and Reinhard H. Schmidt. 1994. *Development Finance as Institution Building: A New Approach to Poverty-oriented Banking.* Boulder, Colo.: Westview Press.

Levitsky, Jacob. 1997. "Best Practice in Credit Guarantee Schemes." In *SME Credit Guarantee Schemes.* 4 (1 and 2): 86–94. Published for the Inter-American Development Bank by The Financier.

Long, Carolyn, Daouda Diop, and James Cawley. 1990. "Report of Program Working Group." In Elaine Edgecomb and James Cawley, eds., *An Institutional Guide for Enterprise Development Organizations.* New York: PACT Publications.

Magill, John H. 1994. "Credit Unions: A Formal-Sector Alternative for Financing Microenterprise Development." In

Maria Otero and Elisabeth Rhyne, eds., *The New World of Microenterprise Finance: Building Healthy Financial Institutions for the Poor*. West Hartford, Conn.: Kumarian Press.

Montoya, Manuel. 1997. "EDPYME in Peru." In Craig Churchill, ed., *Establishing a Microfinance Industry*. Washington, D.C.: Microfinance Network.

Nataradol, Pittayapol. 1995. "Lending to Small-Scale Farmers: BAAC's Experience." Bank of Agriculture and Agricultural Cooperatives, Finance against Poverty Conference. Reading, U.K.

Otero, Maria. 1998. "Types of Owners for Microfinance Institutions." In Craig Churchill, ed., *Moving Microfinance, Forward Ownership, Competition, and Control of Microfinance Institutions*. Washington, D.C.: Microfinance Network.

Otero, Maria, and Elisabeth Rhyne, eds. 1994. *The New World of Microenterprise Finance: Building Healthy Financial Institutions for the Poor*. West Hartford, Conn.: Kumarian Press.

Paxton, Julia. 1996. "A Worldwide Inventory of Microfinance Institutions." World Bank, Sustainable Banking with the Poor Project, Washington, D.C.

ProFund Internacional. 1997. *S.A. Annual Report 1996–97*. San Jose, Costa Rica.

Rhyne, Elisabeth. 1996. "Human Resource Development: Microfinance as a Breakthrough Service." In *An Introduction to Key Issues in Microfinance*. Washington, D.C.: MicroFinance Network.

Richardson, David C., Barry L. Lennon, and Brian L. Branch. 1993. "Credit Unions Retooled: A Road Map for Financial Stabilization." World Council of Credit Unions, Madison, Wisc.

Rock, Rachel. 1997. "Regulation and Supervision Case Studies—Bolivia." In *Regulation and Supervision of Microfinance Institutions: Case Studies*. Microfinance Network Occasional Paper 2. Washington, D.C.

Rosenberg, Rich. 1996. "Comment on DevFinance Network May 15, 1996." Internet discussion group: devfinance @lists.acs.ohio-state.edu

Schmidt, Reinhard H., and Claus-Peter Zeitinger. 1994. "Critical Issues in Small and MicroBusiness Finance." Internationale Projekt Consult GmbH (IPC), Frankfurt.

SEEP (Small Enterprise Education and Promotion) Network. 1996a. *Moving Forward: Emerging Strategies for Sustainability and Expansion*. New York: PACT Publications.

———. 1996b. *Moving Forward: Tools for Sustainability and Expansion*. New York: PACT Publications.

Stearns, Katherine. 1993. "Leverage or Loss? Guarantee Funds and Microenterprises." Monograph Series 8. ACCION International, Washington, D.C.

Vogel, Robert C., and Dale Adams. "Costs and Benefits of Loan Guarantee Programs." In *SME Credit Guarantee Schemes* 4 (1 and 2): 22–29. Published for the Inter-American Development Bank by The Financier.

Von Pischke, J.D. 1991. "Finance at the Frontier: Debt Capacity and the Role of Credit in the Private Economy." World Bank, Economic Development Institute Development Studies, Washington D.C.

———. 1996. "Comment on DevFinance Network, May 14, 1996." Internet discussion group: devfinance@lists. acs.ohio-state.edu

Wesley, Glenn D., and Shell Shaver. 1996. "Credit Union Policies and Performance in Latin America." Paper presented at the 1996 Annual Meeting of the Latin American and Caribbean Economics Association, October, Mexico City.

Yaron, Jacob. 1992. *Successful Rural Finance Institutions*. World Bank Discussion Paper 150. Washington, D.C.

Yaron, Jacob, McDonald Benjamin, and Gerda Piprek. 1997. "Rural Finance Issues, Design and Best Practices." World Bank, Agriculture and Natural Resources Department, Washington, D.C.

Part II–
Designing and
Monitoring Financial
Products and Services

CHAPTER FIVE

Designing Lending Products

By definition, MFIs provide credit. Regardless of the approach selected (see chapter 4), the actual loan products need to be designed according to the demands of the target market. This involves establishing appropriate loan amounts, loan terms, collateral requirements (or substitutes), interest rates and fees, and, potentially, compulsory savings or group contribution requirements.

Successfully designed credit products that meet the needs of microentrepreneurs are a necessity for any MFI. It is important that the people who provide and evaluate lending services understand the different elements of lending products and the way in which these elements affect both borrowers and the viability of the MFI. This chapter illustrates how different design elements can result in lending products that are specifically tailored to both the target market and the capacity of the MFI.

This chapter emphasizes designing financial products to meet client needs, based on the belief that microentrepreneurs value access to financial services and act in a responsible manner if they are treated as clients rather than as beneficiaries.[1] The chapter will be of interest to practitioners who wish to modify or refine their loan products and to donors and consultants who are evaluating the credit products of MFIs, in particular their financial aspects. The appendixes to the chapter provide details on more technical topics such as setting a sustainable interest rate and calculating the effective rate on loans using the internal rate of return and taking into account varying cash flows.

Cash Patterns, Loan Terms, and Payment Frequency

This section covers credit fundamentals, including cash patterns of borrowers, loan amounts, loan terms, and repayment schedules. Underlying each topic is an emphasis on understanding the behavior and credit needs of clients.

Client Cash Patterns and Loan Amounts

To design a loan product to meet borrower needs, it is important to understand the cash patterns of borrowers. *Cash inflows* are the cash received by the business or household in the form of wages, sales revenues, loans, or gifts; *cash outflows* are the cash paid by the business or household to cover payments or purchases. Cash patterns are important insofar as they affect the debt capacity of borrowers. Lenders must ensure that borrowers have sufficient cash inflow to cover loan payments when they are due.

Some cash inflows and outflows occur on a regular basis, others at irregular intervals or on an emergency or seasonal basis. Seasonal activities can create times when the borrower generates revenues (such as after a harvest period) and times when there is no revenue (revenue may be received from other activities). However, loan terms often extend over several seasons, during which there can be gaps in revenues.

Loans should be based on the cash patterns of borrowers and designed as much as possible to enable the

---

1. Portions of this chapter are based on materials originally published in Ledgerwood (1996).

client to repay the loan without undue hardship. This helps the MFI avoid potential losses and encourages clients both to manage their funds prudently and to build up an asset base. (This does not mean that only cash flows from the specific activity being financed are considered; all cash flows are relevant.)

The appropriate loan amount is dependent on the purpose of the loan and the ability of the client to repay the loan (that is, debt capacity). When determining the debt capacity of potential clients, it is necessary to consider their cash flow as well as the degree of risk associated with this cash flow and other claims that may come before repayment of a loan to the MFI. Adjusting the debt capacity of a borrower for risk should reflect reasonable expectations about adverse conditions that may affect the borrower's enterprise. Adjustment for adversity has to reflect the lender's willingness to assume the risks of borrowers' inability to repay. The greater the MFI's capacity to assume risk, the higher the credit limits the lender can offer (Von Pischke 1991).

Often MFIs have a maximum loan size for first-time borrowers, which increases with each loan. This is designed both to reduce the risk to the MFI and to create an incentive for the clients to repay their loans (namely, the promise of a future larger loan). In addition, increasing loan sizes enable the client to develop a credit history and an understanding of the responsibilities associated with borrowing.

How Does the Loan Term Affect the Borrower's Ability to Repay?

The loan term is one of the most important variables in microfinance. It refers to the period of time during which the entire loan must be repaid. The loan term affects the repayment schedule, the revenue to the MFI, the financing costs for the client, and the ultimate suitability of the use of the loan. The closer an organization matches loan terms to its client's needs, the easier it is for the client to "carry" the loan and the more likely that payments will be made on time and in full. The following example provides three alternative loan terms with installment payments:[2]

◆ For example, a dressmaker purchases cloth and supplies every four months to benefit from bulk purchas-

ing, resulting in a four-month business cycle. Her net revenue over the four months (after purchasing supplies for 1,000 and incurring all other expenses but before loan repayment) is 1,600 (400 per month).

ALTERNATIVE 1: Four-month loan matching her business cycle. She borrows 1,000 for four months at 3 percent monthly interest, with monthly payments of 269 (calculated on the declining balance method, which is explained in detail in the section on loan pricing, below). Her total payments are then 1,076 (interest expense of 76). Revenue of 1,600 less the loan repayment of 1,076 leaves her a net income of 524.

Cash flow over the four months is as follows:

Period	Business	Loan	Net income
0	(1,000)	1,000	—
1	400	(269)	131
2	400	(269)	131
3	400	(269)	131
4	400	(269)	131
Total	600	(76)	524

In this scenario, the dressmaker has extra income to consume or reinvest as additional working capital if she chooses. The loan term is appropriately matched to her business cycle and cash flow patterns.

ALTERNATIVE 2: Two-month loan shorter than her business cycle. She borrows 1,000 for two months at 3 percent per month with monthly payments of 523 and sales of 400 per month. Total payments are 1,046 (interest expense of 46). Revenue of 1,600 less the loan repayment of 1,046 leaves 554.

Cash flow is as follows:

Period	Business	Loan	Net income
0	(1,000)	1,000	—
1	400	(523)	(123)
2	400	(523)	(123)
3	400	0	400
4	400	0	400
Total	600	(46)	554

With a two-month loan term and a four-month business cycle, the borrower does not generate enough

---

2. This loan term analysis was developed by Barbara Calvin, codirector, International Operations, Calmeadow, and was originally published in Ledgerwood (1996).

revenue in the first two months to make the loan payments. If she had no savings to begin with or no access to other income or credit to support the loan payments, she would not have been able to repay the loan.

ALTERNATIVE 3: Six-month loan longer than her business cycle. She borrows 1,000 for six months at 3 percent per month with monthly payments of 184.60 and sales of 400 per month for four months only. (Assume that because she does not have a full 1,000 built up in working capital at the end of the four months, she cannot buy more inventory at the "bulk purchase" price and thus has two months of no income While this may not always be realistic, it is presented here to illustrate the fact that in some circumstances longer loan terms are detrimental to the borrowers, particularly if they cannot access future loans until the existing loan is paid back.) Total payments are 1,107.60 (interest expense of 107.60). Revenue of 1,600 less the loan repayment of 1,107.60 leaves 492.40.

Cash flow is as follows:

Period	Business	Loan	Net income
0	(1,000)	1,000	—
1	400	(184.6)	215.4
2	400	(184.6)	215.4
3	400	(184.6)	215.4
4	400	(184.6)	215.4
5	0	(184.6)	(184.6)
6	0	(184.6)	(184.6)
Total	600	(107.6)	492.4

In this scenario the cash flow in the first four months is easier for the borrower; however, she may be tempted to spend the higher net income in the early months of the loan, resulting in potential difficulty making loan payments during the last two months. She also has less net income due to the greater amount of interest paid.

This example illustrates why 12-month loans in busy urban markets often result in delinquency and defaults toward the end of the loan term. Also, the borrower ends up being underemployed for two months, because she does not have access to credit to buy more inventory. If the loan term were shorter and she was thus able to borrow again, she could continue to be fully engaged in her business.

The preceding three alternatives demonstrate that cash flow in part determines the debt-servicing capacity of borrowers. This influences the appropriate loan terms and loan amounts, which in turn determine the debt-servicing requirements. MFIs should design the loan terms and loan amounts to meet the debt-servicing capacity of their clients.

This becomes less of a concern the more profitable the business becomes because greater revenue can potentially result in enough additional income to build up sufficient savings, so that the client no longer needs to borrow unless she or he wants to expand the business. (In such a case the MFI has successfully improved the economic position of its client and should not consider this client "drop out" to be negative or indicative of poor service or products.)

Depending on cash patterns and loan terms, clients may at times prefer to prepay their loans. *Prepayments* have two major advantages for the client.

- They can reduce both the security risk and the temptation to spend excess amounts of cash.
- They can reduce the burden of the loan installments later in the loan cycle.

Prepayments result in one clear advantage for an MFI: by having the loan repaid earlier, the MFI can revolve the loan portfolio more quickly and thereby reach more clients.

However, prepayments are difficult to monitor, and if they are significant they can disrupt the cash flow of an MFI (or its branches). This may affect the ability to accurately predict cash flow requirements. In some MFIs full loan repayment results automatically in a larger loan to the client. This may result in the MFI having reduced funds available to lend to other clients.

In addition, when interest is calculated on the declining balance, a prepayment usually includes the principal owing and any interest due up to the amount of the prepayment. This means that when loans are prepaid, less interest revenue is received than initially forecast, resulting in decreased income for the MFI (unless the funds can be immediately lent out again).

If a particular subset of borrowers (for example, market vendors) tend to prepay their loans on a regular basis, it is advisable to shorten the loan term to suit the needs of that client group. *Loan terms should be designed to minimize the need for prepayments.* This involves matching the loan term to the cash patterns both to help clients budget their cash flows and to lower the likelihood of prepayments or delinquency.

Finally, prepayments can also indicate that borrowers are receiving loans from another lender, which may be providing better service, lower interest rates, or more appropriate terms. If this is the case, the MFI needs to examine its loan products and those of other lenders.

Frequency of Loan Payments

Loan payments can be made on an installment basis (weekly, biweekly, monthly) or in a lump sum at the end of the loan term, depending on the cash patterns of the borrower. For the most part, interest and principal are paid together. However, some MFIs charge interest up front (paid at the beginning of the loan term) and principal over the term of the loan, while others collect interest periodically and the principal at the end of the loan term.

Activities that generate ongoing revenue can be designed with installment payments. In this way the client is able to repay the loan over time without having to save the loan amount (for repayment) over the term of the loan. The frequency of the loan payments depends on the needs of the client and the ability of the MFI to ensure repayment. Some moneylenders collect payments every day, particularly if their borrowers are market vendors receiving cash on a daily basis. Other lenders collect on a monthly basis, because they are not conveniently accessible to the borrower (that is, the bank branch is located far from the borrower's business). A balance must be reached between the transaction costs associated with frequent payments and the risk of default through poor cash management associated with infrequent repayments.

For seasonal activities, it may be appropriate to design the loan such that *a lump sum payment* is made once the activity is completed. Harvesting activities is a good example. (Note that other household income can be used to repay the loan in small amounts.) However, caution must be exercised with lump sum payments, particularly if there is risk that the harvest (or other seasonal activity) may fail. If when the loan is due there is no revenue being generated, the risk of default is high. Some MFIs that finance seasonal activities design their loans with installment payments so that at harvest times the borrowers keep most of their harvest revenue, because the majority of the loan has already been repaid by the end of the harvest. This works to increase the savings (assets) of borrowers.

MFIs may also combine installment loans with lump sum payments, collecting a minimal amount of the loan (for example, interest) over the loan term, with the remainder paid at the end of the harvest season (the principal).

Working Capital and Fixed Asset Loans

The amount of the loan and the appropriate loan term are affected by what the loan will be used for. There are generally two types of loans—working capital loans and fixed asset loans.

Working capital loans are for current expenditures that occur in the normal course of business. Working capital refers to the investment in current or short-term assets to be used within one year. Examples are wood purchased for carpentry, food or goods purchased for market selling, or chick feed purchased for poultry rearing. A loan made for working capital should have a loan term that matches the business cycle of the borrower (as described above). Working capital loans from MFIs are generally for two months to one year.

Fixed asset loans are those made for the purchase of assets that are used over time in the business. These assets typically have a life span of more than one year. Fixed assets are usually defined as machinery, equipment, and property. Examples of fixed assets include motorcycles, sewing machines, egg incubators, or rickshaws. Since the productive activity does not directly use up the fixed asset (that is, not sold as part of the product), its impact upon profitability is felt over a longer period of time.

A loan made for a fixed asset is generally for a larger amount and for a longer term than a working capital loan (that is, fixed asset loans do not necessarily match the business cycle). This results in higher risk for an MFI, offset somewhat if the organization takes legal title of the purchased asset as collateral. Table 5.1 provides examples of loan uses for working capital or fixed assets.

Although longer loan terms may be required for fixed asset purchases, some MFIs find that they do not need to introduce special loan products if they are relatively inexpensive and the loan can be repaid over 12 months or less.

More and more often MFIs are acknowledging the *fungibility* of money, that is, the ability at various times

Table 5.1 Examples of Loan Uses

Activity	Fixed assets	Working capital
Vendor	Food stall	Merchandise
	Refrigerator	Plastic bags
	Scale	Paper bags
Dressmaker	Sewing machine	Fabric
	Sewing table	Patterns
	Mannequin	Needles and thread
Carpenter	Saw	Lumber
	Lathe	Nails
	Sander	Sandpaper
Poultry hatchery owner	Incubator	Eggs
	Baskets	Electricity
	Wire and holder	Wrapping cloth
	Thermometer	
	Shelves	Egg sterilization

Source: Ledgerwood 1996.

to use funds borrowed for a certain activity for other household expenses. Accordingly, the purpose of the loan is not as important as the borrower's capacity to repay it.

Loan Collateral

Generally, MFIs lend to low-income clients who often have very few assets. Consequently, traditional collateral such as property, land, machinery, and other capital assets is often not available. Various innovative means of reducing the risk of loan loss have been developed, including collateral substitutes and alternative collateral.

Collateral Substitutes

One of the most common collateral substitutes is peer pressure, either on its own or jointly with group guarantees (see chapter 3). In addition, there are other frequently used forms of collateral substitute.

GROUP GUARANTEES. Many MFIs facilitate the formation of groups whose members jointly guarantee each other's loans. Guarantees are either implicit guarantees, with other group members unable to access a loan if all members are not current in their loan payments, or actual guarantees, with group members liable if other group members default on their loans.

Some MFIs require group members to contribute to a group guarantee fund, which is used if one or more borrowers fail to repay. Use of the group guarantee fund is sometimes at the discretion of the group itself and sometimes decided by the MFI. If it is used at the group's discretion, the group will often lend money from the guarantee fund to the group member who is unable to pay. The member who "borrows" from the group fund is then responsible for paying the fund back. If use of the group guarantee fund is managed by the MFI, the fund is seized to the extent of the defaulted loan, with other group members making up any shortfall. Failure to do so means that the entire group no longer has access to credit.

CHARACTER-BASED LENDING. Some MFIs lend to people based on a good reputation in the community. Prior to making a loan the credit officer visits various establishments in the community and asks about the potential client's character and behavior.

FREQUENT VISITS TO THE BUSINESS BY THE CREDIT OFFICER. Provided the branch or credit officers are within a reasonable geographical distance from their clients, frequent visits help to ensure that the client is maintaining the business and intends to repay the loan. Frequent visits also allow the credit officer to understand her or his clients' businesses and the appropriateness of the loan (amount, term, frequency of payments, and so forth). Visits also contribute to developing mutual respect between the client and the credit officer as they learn to appreciate and understand each other's commitment to their work.

RISK OF PUBLIC EMBARRASSMENT. Often clients will repay loans if they feel that they will be embarrassed in front of their family, peers, and neighbors. This would be the case if public signs, notices printed in the local newspaper, or announcements made at community meetings list borrowers who do not repay.

RISK OF JAIL OR LEGAL ACTION. Depending on the legal context in a country, some MFIs have sued or, in rare cases, even jailed clients for nonpayment. Sometimes, simply the risk of legal repercussion is enough to encourage repayment.

Alternative Forms of Collateral

There are at least three commonly used alternative forms of collateral.

COMPULSORY SAVINGS. Many MFIs require clients to hold a balance (stated as a percentage of the loan) in savings (or as contributions to group funds) for first or subsequent loans (or both). Compulsory savings differ from voluntary savings in that they are not generally available for withdrawal while a loan is outstanding. In this way compulsory savings act as a form of collateral.

By being required to set aside funds as savings, borrowers are restricted from utilizing those funds in their business activities or other income producing investments. Usually the deposit interest rate paid (if any) on the savings is lower than the return earned by the borrowers if the savings were put into their business or other investments. This results in an opportunity cost equal to the difference between what the client earns on compulsory savings and the return that could be earned otherwise.

Compulsory savings can have a positive impact on clients by smoothing out their consumption patterns and providing funds for emergencies *provided the savings are available for withdrawal by the borrower.* Most compulsory savings are available for withdrawal only at the end of the loan term, providing the loan has been repaid in full. Clients thus have additional cash flow for investment or consumption at the end of the loan term. Compulsory savings also provide a means of building assets for clients; not all MFIs view compulsory savings as strictly an alternative form of collateral.

A variation of compulsory savings required by Bank Rakyat Indonesia is for borrowers to pay additional interest each month, which is returned to them at the end of the loan provided they have made full, on-time payments each month. This is referred to as a "prompt payment incentive" and results in the borrower receiving a lump sum at the end of the loan term. This benefits the borrower and provides a concrete incentive to repay the loan on time, thus benefiting the bank as well.

Compulsory savings also provide a source of lending and investment funds for the MFI. They are generally a stable source of funds because they are illiquid (that is, savings are not generally available for withdrawal by the borrowers while their loans are outstanding). However, it is essential that the MFI act in a prudent manner when on-lending or investing client savings to ensure that the funds will be repaid and can be returned to the client in full when necessary.

ASSETS PLEDGED AT LESS THAN THE VALUE OF THE LOAN. Sometimes, regardless of the actual market value of assets owned by the borrower, the act of pledging assets (such as furniture or appliances) and the consequent realization that they can be lost (resulting in inconvenience) causes the client to repay the loan. It is important that the MFI formally seize the assets that have been pledged if the client does not repay the loan. This sends a message to other borrowers that the MFI is serious about loan repayment.

PERSONAL GUARANTEES. While microborrowers themselves do not often have the ability to guarantee their loans, they are sometimes able to enlist friends or family members to provide personal guarantees (sometimes referred to as cosigners). This means that in the event of the inability of the borrower to repay, the person who has provided a personal guarantee is responsible for repaying the loan.

Many of the foregoing collateral substitutes and alternative forms of collateral are used in combination with each other. A good example of this is offered by the Association for the Development of Microenterprises (ADEMI) in the Dominican Republic (box 5.1).

Loan Pricing

Pricing loans is an important aspect of loan product design. A balance must be reached between what clients can afford and what the lending organization needs to earn to cover all of its costs. Generally, microfinance clients are not interest-rate sensitive. That is, microentrepreneurs have not appeared to borrow more or less in reaction to an increase or decrease in interest rates. For the most part, an interest rate far above commercial bank rates is acceptable because the borrowers have such limited access to credit. However, an MFI must ensure that its operations are as efficient as possible so that undue burden is not put on its clients in the form of high interest rates and fees (box 5.1).

MFIs can determine the interest rate they need to charge on loans based on their cost structure. MFIs incur four different types of costs:

- Financing costs
- Operating costs
- Loan loss provision
- Cost of capital.

Each of these costs are discussed further in part III when adjustments to the financial statements are made and when determining the financial viability of MFIs. For specific information on how to set a *sustainable* interest rate based on the cost structure of an MFI, see appendix 1.

In general, an MFI incurs relatively low *financing costs* if it funds its loan portfolio primarily with donated funds. However, if compulsory savings (discussed above) are used to fund the loan portfolio, they can affect the

average financing costs for an MFI. Many MFIs do not pay any interest on compulsory savings, and if this is the case the cost of funds for the compulsory savings is zero. If an MFI funds its loan portfolio with borrowed money from a bank, for example, at 12 percent and with client savings at 6 percent, the higher the portion of the portfolio funded with client savings, the lower the overall cost of funding. (Note that this does not reflect the increase in operational costs, for example, for monitoring that is incurred to collect compulsory savings. This discussion only refers to the average *cost of funds* for an organization and does not include the cost of collecting compulsory savings.)

◆ For example, with a 1,000,000 loan portfolio funded by 300,000 savings (at 6 percent) and 700,000 borrowed funds (at 12 percent), the average annual cost of funds is:

$$10.2\% = \frac{(300,000 \times 6\%) + (700,000 \times 12\%)}{1,000,000}$$

If the compulsory savings component is increased to 500,000, the average cost of funds is reduced. Using the above example, with a 1,000,000 loan portfolio funded by 500,000 savings (at 6 percent) and 500,000 borrowed funds (at 12 percent), the average annual cost of funds is:

$$9\% = \frac{(500,000 \times 6\%) + (500,000 \times 12\%)}{1,000,000}$$

The opposite of this is also true. If an MFI funds its portfolio primarily with grant money for which there is no interest cost, the addition of 6 percent paid to the clients for compulsory savings increases an MFI's overall cost of funds.

Operating costs include salaries, rent, travel and transportation, administration, depreciation, and so forth. Depending on the approach selected, these costs vary between 12 percent to 30 percent of outstanding loans.

Loan loss provisions vary depending on the quality of the loan portfolio (discussed in chapter 9) and *capital costs* vary depending on the market rate of interest and the inflation rate in the country (discussed in chapter 8).

Once an MFIs' costs have been considered, there are various ways to price loans to generate the estimated revenue required. (Note that only loans that are repaid on-time and in full earn the full amount of revenue expected. This is discussed further in chapter 9.) The fol-

---

Box 5.1 The Association for the Development of Microenterprises' Collateral Requirements

THE ASSOCIATION FOR THE DEVELOPMENT OF Microenterprises (ADEMI) uses a combination of collateral and guarantors to secure its loans. All borrowers are required to sign a legal contract stating their obligation to repay funds at specified terms. Most clients also have a guarantor or cosigner who assumes full responsibility for the terms of the contract if clients are either unable or unwilling to repay loans. When feasible, borrowers are required to sign deeds for property or machinery as loan guarantees. (The association estimates that 80 percent of the deeds signed represent only 20 percent to 30 percent of the value of the loan.) In some cases, guarantors may be asked to pledge security on behalf of the borrower.

However, ADEMI strongly advocates that applicants who are unable to provide collateral not be limited in their ability to access credit. When first-time borrowers are unable to provide security, credit officers rely heavily on information as a collateral substitute. In these situations the credit officer investigates the reputation of the applicant in much the same way that an informal moneylender might. Visits are made to neighboring shops and bars and applicants may be asked to produce financial statements (when possible) or receipts for utilities or other payments. Each application is considered on a case-by-case basis.

Source: Benjamin and Ledgerwood 1998.

lowing sets out how to calculate interest rates and shows how service fees can augment interest revenue.

Calculating Interest Rates

There are several ways to calculate interest on a loan, of which two methods are most common: the declining balance method and the flat (face-value) method. Interest is generally paid over the term of the loan, although it is sometimes paid up front.

THE DECLINING BALANCE METHOD. This method calculates interest as a percentage of the amount outstanding over the loan term. Interest calculated on the declining balance means that interest is charged only on the amount that the borrower still owes. The principal amount of a one-year loan, repaid weekly through payments of principal and interest, reduces or declines every week by the amount of principal that has been repaid (table 5.2). This means that borrowers have use of less and less of the original loan each week, until at the end of one year when they have no principal remaining and have repaid the whole loan (assuming 100 percent repayment).

◆ For example, by month 6 of a 12-month loan for 1,000, the borrower will only owe approximately 500 if she or he has paid in regular weekly installments. At that point,

she or he is paying interest on only 500 rather than 1,000. (Note that with interest paid on the declining balance, a greater portion of the monthly payment is paid in interest during the early months of the loan and a greater portion of principal is paid toward the end of the loan. This results in a slightly larger amount than half of the principal remaining outstanding at the midpoint of the loan. In the example in table 5.2, in month six 524.79 is still outstanding, not 500.)

To calculate interest on the declining balance, a financial calculator is required. On most financial calculators, present value and payment must be entered with opposite signs, that is if present value is positive, payment must be negative, or vice versa. This is because one is a cash inflow and one is a cash outflow. Financial calculators allow the user to enter different loan variables as follows:

PV = Present value, or the net amount of cash disbursed to the borrower at the beginning of the loan.

i = Interest rate, which must be expressed in same time units as n below.

n = Loan term, which must equal the number of payments to be made.

PMT = Payment made each period.

◆ In the example above, a one-year loan of 1,000 with monthly payments and 20 percent interest calculat-

---

Table 5.2 Declining Balance Method

Loan amount: 1,000; 12-month loan term; monthly loan payments: 92.63; interest rate: 20 percent.

Month	Payments	Principal	Interest	Outstanding balance
0	—	—	—	1,000.00
1	92.63	75.96	16.67	924.04
2	92.63	77.23	15.40	846.79
3	92.63	78.52	14.21	768.29
4	92.63	79.83	12.81	688.46
5	92.63	81.16	11.48	607.30
6	92.63	82.51	10.12	524.79
7	92.63	83.88	8.75	440.91
8	92.63	85.28	7.35	355.63
9	92.63	86.70	5.93	268.93
10	92.63	88.15	4.49	180.78
11	92.63	89.62	3.02	91.16
12	92.63	91.16	1.53	0.00
Total	1,111.56[a]	1,000.00	111.76[a]	—

a. Difference of 0.2 is due to rounding.
Source: Ledgerwood 1996.

ed on the declining balance is computed by entering the following:

PV = –1,000 (enter as negative amount, as it is a cash outflow).

i = 20 percent a year; 1.67 percent a month.

n = 12 months.

Solve for PMT:

PMT = 92.63.

Total payments equal 1,111.56 (12 months at 92.63). Total interest is 111.56.

The declining balance method is used by most, if not all, formal financial institutions. It is considered the most appropriate method of interest calculation for MFIs as well.

THE FLAT METHOD. This method calculates interest as a percentage of the initial loan amount rather than the amount outstanding (declining) during the loan term. Using the flat method means that interest is always calculated on the total amount of the loan initially disbursed, even though periodic payments cause the outstanding principal to decline. Often, but not always, a flat rate will be stated for the term of the loan rather than as a periodic (monthly or annual) rate. If the loan term is less than 12 months, it is possible to annualize the rate by multiplying it by the number of months or

weeks in the loan term, divided by 12 or 52 respectively.

To calculate interest using the flat rate method the interest rate is simply multiplied by the initial amount of the loan. For example, if an MFI charges 20 percent interest using the flat rate method on a 1,000 loan, the interest payable is 200 (table 5.3).

It is clear that the actual amount of interest charged varies significantly depending on whether the interest is calculated on the declining balance or the flat amount. The flat method results in a much higher interest cost than the declining balance method based on the same *nominal* rate. In the example in table 5.3, interest of 200 (20 percent flat basis) is 88.44 or 80 percent greater than interest of 111.56 (20 percent declining balance).

To increase revenue some MFIs will change the interest rate calculation method from declining balance to flat rather than increase the nominal rate. This may be in reaction to usury laws imposing a maximum rate of interest that is not high enough to cover the MFI's costs. However, MFIs should realize that regardless of the nominal rate quoted, clients are well aware of how much interest they are actually paying, based on the amount due each payment period. It is important that all interest calculations be transparent.

These examples show that with all other variables the same, the amount of interest paid on a declining balance

Table 5.3 Flat Method

Loan amount: 1,000; 12-month loan term; monthly loan payments: 100; interest rate: 20 percent

Month	Payments	Principal	Interest	Outstanding balance
0	—	—	—	1,000.00
1	100	83.33	16.67	916.67
2	100	83.33	16.67	833.34
3	100	83.33	16.67	750.01
4	100	83.33	16.67	666.68
5	100	83.33	16.67	583.35
6	100	83.33	16.67	500.02
7	100	83.33	16.67	416.69
8	100	83.33	16.67	333.36
9	100	83.33	16.67	250.03
10	100	83.33	16.67	166.70
11	100	83.33	16.67	83.37
12	100	83.33	16.67	0.00
Total	1200	1,000.00	200.00	—

Source: Ledgerwood 1996.

loan is much lower than that on a loan with interest calculated on a flat basis. To compare rates of interest calculated by different methods it is necessary to determine what interest rate would be required when interest is calculated on the declining balance to earn the same nominal amount of interest earned on a loan with a flat basis calculation.

♦ In example 5.1, a 1,000 loan with 20 percent interest calculated on a declining balance for one year with monthly payments results in interest of 112 (rounded from 111.56).

The same loan with interest calculated on a flat basis results in interest of 200.

To earn interest of 200 on a loan of 1,000 with interest calculated on the declining balance, the interest rate would have to increase by 15 percentage points to 35 percent (additional interest revenue of 88):

♦ Interest on a 1,000 loan at 35 percent declining balance results in monthly payments of 99.96 for one year or a total interest cost of 200 (rounded from 199.52).

This example shows that an MFI calculating interest on the declining balance would have to increase its *nominal* interest rate substantially to earn the same revenue as an MFI calculating interest on a flat basis.

How Do Fees or Service Charges Affect the Borrower and the MFI?

In addition to charging interest, many MFIs also charge a fee or service charge when disbursing loans. Fees or service charges increase the financial costs of the loan for the borrower and revenue to the MFI. Fees are often charged as a means of increasing the yield to the lender instead of charging nominal higher interest rates.

Fees are generally charged as a percentage of the *initial* loan amount and are collected up front rather than over the term of the loan. Because fees are not calculated

on the declining balance, the effect of an increase in fees is greater than a similar increase in the nominal interest rate (if interest is calculated on the declining balance).

♦ In example 5.2, the an MFI wants to determine its future pricing policy. In doing so, it wants to calculate the effect on the borrower of an increase in the interest rate and, alternatively, an increase in the loan fee.

In example 5.1 a 20 percent interest rate (declining balance) on a 1,000 loan resulted in 112 in interest revenue. A loan fee of 3 percent on this loan would result in a fee of 30, making total revenue 142. The MFI wants to increase its rate by 5 percentage points either through the loan fee it charges (from 3 percent to 8 percent) or the interest rate it charges (from 20 percent to 25 percent declining balance). Each increase results in the following:

• A loan fee of 8 percent on a 1,000 loan results in fee revenue of 80. This represents an increase of 50 from the 3 percent fee (30).

• A interest rate of 25 percent (declining balance) on a 1,000 loan results in interest revenue of 140 (monthly payments of 95). This represents an increase of 28 from a 20 percent interest rate (112).

Total revenue collected on a 1,000 loan with 20 percent interest (declining balance) and an 8 percent fee equals 192 (112 + 80). Total revenue collected on a 1,000 loan with 25 percent interest (declining balance) and a 3 percent fee equals 170 (140 + 30).

The effect of a 5 percentage point increase in the loan fees from 3 percent to 8 percent is greater than a 5 percentage point increase in the interest rate, provided interest is calculated on the declining balance. This is because the fee is charged on the initial loan amount whereas the interest is calculated on the declining balance of the loan.

Although the interest rate may be the same *nominal* figure, the costs to the borrower—and hence the yield to the lender—vary greatly if interest is calculated on a flat basis or if fees are charged. This will be discussed further in the section below on calculating effective rates of interest.

Example 5.1

	Interest 20% declining balance	Interest 20% flat	Difference	Interest 20% flat	Interest 35% declining balance
Actual costs	112	200	88	200	200

Example 5.2

	Service fee 3%	Service fee 8%	Increase	Interest 20% declining balance	Interest 25% declining balance	Increase
Actual costs	30	80	50 (167%)	112	140	28 (25%)

Cross-Subsidization of Loans

Some MFIs choose to subsidize certain products with revenue generated by other more profitable products. This is usually time-bound in some way until the new products have reached sustainability. Cross-subsidization of loans is not very common among MFIs, because many have only one or two loan products. However, there are three significant examples, as shown in box 5.2.

Calculating Effective Rates

MFIs often speak about the "effective interest rate" on their loans. However, there are many ways in which effective rates are calculated, making it very difficult to compare institutions' rates. The effective rate of interest is a concept useful for determining whether the conditions of a loan make it more or less expensive for the borrower than another loan and whether changes in pricing policies have any effect. Because of the different loan variables and different interpretations of effective rates, a standard method of calculating the effective rate on a loan (considering all variables) is necessary to determine the true cost of borrowing for clients and the potential revenue (yield) earned by the MFI.

The effective rate of interest refers to the inclusion of all direct financial costs of a loan in one interest rate

Effective interest rates differ from nominal rates of interest by incorporating interest, fees, the interest calculation method, and other loan requirements into the financial cost of the loan. The effective rate should also include the cost of forced savings or group fund contributions by the borrower, because these are financial costs. We do not consider transaction costs (the financial and nonfinancial costs incurred by the borrower to access the loan, such as opening a bank account, transportation, child-care costs, or opportunity costs) in the calculation of the effective rate, because these can vary significantly depending on the

marketplace. However, it is important to design the delivery of credit and savings products in a way that minimizes transaction costs for both the client and the MFI.

When interest is calculated on the declining balance and there are no additional financial costs to a loan, the effective interest rate is the same as the nominal interest rate. Many MFIs, however, calculate the interest on a flat basis, charge fees as well as interest, or require borrowers to maintain savings or contribute to group funds (trust or insurance funds). The cost to the borrower is, therefore, not simply the nominal interest charged on the loan but includes other costs. Consideration must also be given to the opportunity cost of not being able to invest

---

Box 5.2 Cross-Subsidization of Loans

IN *GRAMEEN BANK* 8 PERCENT INTEREST RATES ON housing loans are subsidized by a 20 percent rate for general loans. A housing loan has eligibility criteria: a member must have received at least two general loans, she must have an excellent repayment record, and she must have utilized her loans for the purposes specified on her applications. To protect women and ensure accountability for the loan, Grameen Bank requires that women have title to the homestead land in her name.

The *Unit Desa* system in Bank Rakyat Indonesia generates a significantly higher return on average assets than the bank as a whole. This profitability makes the Unit Desa system extremely important for the bank. Indirectly, loans made to poorer clients subsidize loans made to wealthier clients at lower interest rates.

The Association for the Development of Microenterprises provides microloans and small business loans. Although the interest rate and fees charged on microloans are higher than those charged on smaller loans, some cross-subsidization still exists whereby the larger loans generate sufficient revenue to subsidize any losses resulting from the microloan portfolio.

Source: Author's findings.

the money that the borrower must pay back in regular installments (the time value of money).

Variables of microloans that influence the effective rate include:

- Nominal interest rate
- Method of interest calculation: declining balance or flat rate
- Payment of interest at the beginning of the loan (as a deduction of the amount of principal disbursed to the borrower) or over the term of the loan
- Service fees either up front or over the term of the loan
- Contribution to guarantee, insurance, or group fund
- Compulsory savings or compensating balances and the corresponding interest paid to the borrower either by the MFI or another institution (bank, credit union)
- Payment frequency
- Loan term
- Loan amount.

When all variables are expressed as a percentage of the loan amount, a change in the amount of the loan will not change the effective rate. A fee that is based in currency (such as $25 per loan application) will change the effective rate if the loan amount is changed; that is, smaller loan amounts with the same fee (in currency) result in a higher effective rate.

Calculation of the effective rate demonstrates how different loan product variables affect the overall costs and revenues of the loan. Two methods of calculating the effective rate of interest are an *estimation* method, which uses a formula that does not require a financial calculator, and the *internal rate of return* method.

Note that the estimation method does not directly take into account the time value of money and the frequency of payments, which are considered in the internal rate of return method. Although the difference may be minimal, the greater the length of the loan term and the less frequent the loan payments, the more substantial the difference will be. This is because the longer the loan is outstanding and the less frequent the payments, the greater the effect on the cost will be and hence the difference between the estimated effective cost and the internal rate of return calculation. In addition, the estimation method does not take into account compulsory savings or contributions to other funds, such as trust or insurance funds. It is presented here simply as a method for

calculating the effective rate if no financial calculator or spreadsheets are available.

Estimating the Effective Rate

If you do not have access to a financial calculator or a computer spreadsheet, you can compute an estimation of the effective rate (see Waterfield 1995). The estimation method considers the amount the borrower pays in interest and fees over the loan term. The estimation method can be used to determine the effect of the interest rate calculation method, the loan term, and the loan fee. An estimation of the effective rate is calculated as follows:

$$\text{Effective cost} = \frac{\text{Amount paid in interest and fees}}{\text{Average principal amount outstanding}}$$

Note:

$$\text{Average principal amount outstanding} = \frac{\text{(Sum of principal amounts outstanding)}}{\text{number of payments}}$$

To calculate the effective cost per period, simply divide the resulting figure by the number of periods.

As previously illustrated, the amount of interest revenue is largely affected by whether interest is calculated on a flat or declining balance basis. With all other variables the same, the effective rate for a loan with interest calculated on a declining balance basis will be lower than the effective rate for a loan with interest calculated on a flat basis.

Using an example similar to that in tables 5.2 and 5.3, the effective rate is estimated for a 1,000 loan with interest of 20 percent and a 3 percent fee, first with interest calculated on the declining balance and then with interest calculated on the flat basis.

Calculating the interest on the declining balance results in an estimated annual effective rate of 25 percent or 2.1 percent per month (table 5.4).

Calculating the interest on a flat basis results in an estimated annual effective rate of 42 percent or 3.5 percent per month (table 5.5).

With all other factors the same, the effective rate increases from 25 percent (2.1 percent per month) to 42 percent (3.5 percent per month) when the method of calculation is changed from declining balance to flat.

The effective rate also increases when the loan term is shortened if a fee is charged. This is because fees are calculated on the initial loan amount regardless of the length of the loan term. If the loan term is shortened, the same amount of

Table 5.4 Effective Rate Estimate, Declining Balance

Loan amount: 1,000; 12-month loan term; monthly loan payments: 92.63; interest rate: 20 percent; fee: 3 percent (30)

Month	Payments	Principal	Interest	Outstanding balance
0	—	—	—	1,000.00
1	92.63	75.96	16.67	924.04
2	92.63	77.23	15.40	846.79
3	92.63	78.52	14.21	768.29
4	92.63	79.83	12.81	688.46
5	92.63	81.16	11.48	607.30
6	92.63	82.51	10.12	524.79
7	92.63	83.88	8.75	440.91
8	92.63	85.28	7.35	355.63
9	92.63	86.70	5.93	268.93
10	92.63	88.15	4.49	180.78
11	92.63	89.62	3.02	91.16
12	92.63	91.16	1.53	0.00
Total	1,111.56[a]	1,000.00	111.76[a]	6,697.08

Effective rate = (111.76 + 30)/558.09* = 25% (2.1% per month)

* 6,697.08 / 12 months = 558.09

a. Difference of 0.2 is due to rounding.

Source: Ledgerwood 1996.

Table 5.5 Effective Rate Estimate, Flat Method

Loan amount: 1,000; 12-month loan term; monthly loan payments: 100; interest rate: 20 percent; fee: 3 percent (30)

Month	Payments	Principal	Interest	Outstanding balance
0	—	—	—	1,000.00
1	100	83.33	16.67	916.67
2	100	83.33	16.67	833.34
3	100	83.33	16.67	750.01
4	100	83.33	16.67	666.68
5	100	83.33	16.67	583.35
6	100	83.33	16.67	500.02
7	100	83.33	16.67	416.69
8	100	83.33	16.67	333.36
9	100	83.33	16.67	250.03
10	100	83.33	16.67	166.70
11	100	83.33	16.67	83.37
12	100	83.33	16.67	0.00
Total	1,200	1,000.00	200.00	6,500.22

Effective rate = (200 + 30)/541.69* = 42% (3.5% per month)

*6,500.22 / 12 months = 541.69

Source: Ledgerwood 1996.

money needs to be paid in a shorter amount of time, thus increasing the effective rate. (This difference is greatest when a fee is charged on a loan with interest calculated on the declining balance. This is because the shorter loan term increases the *relative* percentage of the fee to total costs.)

The effective rate can be estimated for a number of loan variables, including an increase in the loan fee and a decrease in the loan term. Table 5.6 illustrates the effect that a change in the loan fee and a change in the loan term have on the effective rate (the examples are calculated on both a flat and declining balance basis).

Note that the effect of an increase in the fee by 5 percent (to 8 percent) has the same effect (an increase of 0.8 percent per month in effective rate) whether the loan is calculated on a declining basis or flat method. This is because the fee is calculated on the initial loan amount.

Calculating the Effective Interest Rate with Compulsory Savings or Other Loan Variables

To determine the effective rate of interest considering all financial costs of a loan, including the time value of money, compulsory savings, and contributions of other funds, the internal rate of return method is used. As explained above, compulsory savings should be considered a component of the loan rather than a separate savings product. To calculate the true cost of borrowing all cost components must be considered.

The internal rate of return is defined as *the specific interest rate by which the sequence of installments must be discounted to obtain an amount equal to the initial credit amount.*

To calculate the *internal rate of return,* an understanding of *present value* is required. The concept of present value is based on the notion that 1,000 today is

worth more than 1,000 a year from now. In other words, 1,000 that is to be received a year from now has a present value of less than 1,000. How much less depends on how much can be earned if the funds are invested. This is the *time value of money* principle. The present value of 1,000 to be received any number of years in the future can be calculated as follows:

$$PV = 1 / (1 + i)^n$$

where i = the interest rate and n = the number of periods until the expected receipt of funds. To incorporate present value into the effective rate calculation, a financial calculator is required.

Note that for the purposes of calculating the effective rate, the assumption is that there are no late payments or defaulted loans (that is, that there is no credit risk—a situation that is rarely the case, but we are trying to determine the full cost to the borrower and the yield to the lender before taking risk into account). It is also assumed that the present value for the series of loan payments is equal to the rate of return that would be earned by the borrower if she reinvested the loan proceeds and paid it back all at the end of the maturity period rather than in regular installments. In doing so, we take into account the opportunity cost associated with not having the full amount of the loan for the full loan term.

Calculating the internal rate of return for each alternative involves three steps: (adapted from Rosenberg 1996) determining the actual cash flows; entering the cash flows into the calculator to determine the effective rate for the period; and multiplying or compounding the internal rate of return by the number of periods to determine the annual rate (this will be discussed further

Table 5.6 Change in Loan Fee and Loan Term Effect

Fee/term	Calculation 20% annual rate	Service fee (percent)	Loan term	Effective cost per month (percent)	Change (percent)
3% fee; 12-month term	Flat	3	12 months	3.5	
Raise fee to 8%	Flat	8	12 months	4.3	↑ 0.8
Lower term to 3 months	Flat	3	3 months	4.0	↑ 0.5
3% fee; 12-month term	Declining balance	3	12 months	2.1	
Raise fee to 8%	Declining balance	8	12 months	2.9	↑ 0.8
Lower term to 3 months	Declining balance	3	3 months	3.2	↑ 1.1

Source: Ledgerwood 1996.

in the section below dealing with the difference between effective rate and effective yield.)

To determine the effective rate by calculating the internal rate of return, the loan variables are entered into a financial calculator or computer spreadsheet (such as Lotus 1-2-3 or Excel). This analysis assumes that all cash flows are constant (that is, loan payments are the same for the entire loan term).

PV = Present value, or the net amount of cash disbursed to the borrower at the beginning of the loan.

i = Interest rate, which must be expressed in same time units as n below.

n = Loan term, which must equal the number of payments to be made.

PMT = Payment made each period.

FV = Future value, or the amount remaining after the repayment schedule is completed (zero except for loans with compulsory savings that are returned to the borrower).

To demonstrate the internal rate of return method of calculating effective rates, the rate calculation for a sample loan with six alternatives is presented to illustrate the effect of different loan variables, including:

- Flat interest calculation
- All interest paid up front
- Loan fee (service fee)
- Change in payment frequency
- Compulsory savings with interest
- Contributions to group funds (no interest).

Each of these variables is then calculated if the loan term increases.

Table 5.7 summarizes the six variables above and the corresponding effective rates for borrowing 1,000 for four months (calculations provided in appendix 2). The effect of the loan term is illustrated through calculating each variable with a six-month loan term rather than a four-month loan term (calculations not shown).

As table 5.7 shows, the effective rate (assuming the same nominal rate) is increased by all of the following variables:

- Flat interest calculation instead of declining balance calculation
- Up-front interest payments
- Loan (or service) fees
- More frequent payments
- Compulsory savings or group fund contributions.

When the loan term is extended, the *increase* in the effective rate from the base case is *greater* if interest is calculated on a flat basis (since the borrower pays 3 percent a month in interest for an additional two months), interest is paid up front, or compulsory savings or group fund contributions are required.

When the loan term is extended, the *increase* in the effective rate from the base case is *lower* if there are service fees or payments are made more frequently.

Calculating the Effective Interest Rate with Varying Cash Flows

It is also possible to calculate the effective rate using the internal rate of return method and taking into account cash flows that *vary* during the loan term. This is because the internal rate of return calculation can consider each cash flow rather than a constant stream. This would be

Table 5.7 Variables Summary

Loan variables	Effective rate, 4–month term (percent)	Effective rate, 6–month term (percent)
Base case, declining balance	36.0	36.0
Flat interest	53.3	59.3
Up-front interest payment	38.9	40.2
Loan service fee	51.4	47.1
Payment frequency	45.6	43.4
Compulsory savings	39.1	42.0
Group fund contribution	41.2	44.7

Source: Adapted from Rosenberg 1996.

useful for loans that have a grace period during the loan term or if a lump sum payment is made at the end of the loan term. For a discussion of calculating the internal rate of return on a loan with varying cash flows, see appendix 3.

How does the Effective Cost for the Borrower Differ from the Effective Yield to the Lender?

Yield refers to the revenue earned by the lender on the portfolio outstanding, including interest revenue and fees. Calculating the effective yield earned on the portfolio allows an MFI to determine if enough revenue will be generated to cover all costs, leading to financial self-sufficiency. Projecting the effective yield is also useful for forecasting revenues and determining the effect of changes in pricing policies on revenue.

The *projected* effective yield is also useful for MFIs to compare to the *actual* yield on their portfolios.

The effective yield to the lender differs from the effective cost to the borrower for two reasons:

- If there are components of the loan pricing, such as compulsory savings or fund contributions, that are not held by and hence do not result in revenue to the lender (for example, if savings are put into a commercial bank or fees are charged to the borrower by another institution, such as training fees), they are not included in the yield calculation but are included in the effective interest rate (for the borrower) calculation.

- The expected yield to the lender differs because the cost to the borrower is determined on the initial loan amount, whereas the return to the lender must be based on the average portfolio outstanding. This results in differing calculations for annualizing periodic interest rates—periodic rates are either *multiplied* by the number of periods or *compounded*.

If all elements of the loan are both costs to the borrower and revenue to the lender, then the only difference between the effective cost and the effective yield is the method used to annualize the rate.

In the examples above, for simplicity's sake we multiplied the periodic interest rate to achieve an annual rate. However, the decision to multiply or compound the periodic rate is based on whether or not the cost to the borrower or the yield to the lender is being determined.

- For the *cost to the borrower,* the internal rate of return is *compounded* by the number of payment periods in a year. The internal rate of return must be compounded rather than simply multiplied by the number of periods, because we assume that the reinvestment rate of the borrower is equal to the internal rate of return. In other words, the internal rate of return per period is the amount the borrower forgoes by repaying the loan in installments (that is, the principal amount available declines with each installment). Therefore the return earned per period if the borrower could reinvest would *compound* over time.

- For the *yield to the lender,* the per period rate is multiplied, because we assume that the revenue generated is used to cover expenses and is not reinvested (only the principal is reinvested). Therefore, the average portfolio outstanding does not increase (unless revenue exceeds expenses).

To compound the rate, the periodic internal rate of return must be stated as a decimal amount rather than as a percentage amount. To do this, the periodic internal rate of return is divided by 100. To annualize the periodic rate, the following formula is used:

$$\text{annual internal rate of return} = (1 + IRRp)^a - 1$$

where *IRRp* equals the internal rate of return per period divided by 100 and *a* equals the number of periods in a year (*a* = 12 if *p* is one month; *a* = 32 if *p* is one week).

◆ For example, a 1,000 loan, repaid in four equal monthly payments of principal and interest, with an interest rate of 36 percent per year, calculated on a flat basis results in the following internal rate of return:

$$PV = ,1000; PMT = -280; n = 4$$

Solving for *i* yields an internal rate of return of 4.69 percent.

The borrower's effective rate is 73.3 percent and the yield to the lender is closer to 56.3 percent, a difference of 17 percent (example 5.3).

The effective yield on the portfolio of an MFI is reduced by:

- The amount of delinquent (or *non-revenue-generating*) loans
- Late payments
- Low loan turnover (idle funds)
- Fraud
- Reporting errors or failures that lead to delayed collection of loans
- Prepayments if interest is calculated on the declining balance and funds remain idle.

Example 5.3

Annual rate, compounded	$(1.0469)^{12}$
	$= 1.733$
	$= (1.733) - 1 \times 100$
	$= 73.3\%$
Annual rate, multiplied	4.69×12 periods
	$= 56.3\%$

Appendix 1. How Can an MFI Set a Sustainable Rate on Its Loans?

MFIs can determine the rate necessary to charge on loans based on their cost structure. The following is one method of approximating the effective interest rate that an MFI will need to charge on its loans to cover all of its costs and thus be sustainable (adapted from Rosenberg 1996).

Note that this method assumes a mature MFI with relatively stable costs, that is, start-up costs have already been amortized and the MFI is operating at full capacity. It is understood that an MFI should not expect to break even at every point along its average cost curve. A certain scale of operations is required to break even and hence to make this method applicable.

The annualized effective yield *(R)* charged on loans is a function of five elements, each expressed as a percentage of average outstanding loan portfolio *(LP)*: administrative expenses *(AE)*, the cost of funds *(CF)*, loan losses *(LL)*, the desired capitalization rate *(K)*, and investment income *(II)*.

$$R = \frac{AE + CF + LL + K}{1 - LL} - II$$

Each variable should be expressed as a decimal fraction (percentage of average loan portfolio). For example, operating expenses of 200,000 on an average loan portfolio of 800,000 would yield a value of 0.25 for the AE rate.

Included as administrative expenses *(AE)* are all annual recurrent costs except the cost of funds and loan losses, including salaries, benefits, rent, utilities, and depreciation. Also included are the value of any donated commodities or services, such as training or technical assistance that the microfinance organization will have to pay for in the future as it grows independent of donor subsidies. Administrative expenses of efficient mature organizations tend to range between 10 and 25 percent of their average loan portfolio.

The loan loss rate *(LL)* represents the annual loss due to defaulted loans. Past loan loss experience is an important indicator of this rate. The loan loss rate may be considerably lower than the delinquency rate: the former reflects loans that must actually be written off, while the latter reflects loans that are not paid on time—many of which will eventually be recovered. Microfinance organizations with loan loss rates greater than 5 percent tend not to be viable. Many good organizations run at about 1 to 2 percent of average outstanding portfolio.

The cost of funds *(CF)* rate takes into account the actual cost of funds of the organization when it funds its portfolio with savings and commercial debt. When an MFI also benefits from concessional funding, the calculation must include an estimation of the funding costs if it were replaced with commercial debt and equity. Prior to determining the cost of funds rate, an estimation of the financial assets (excluding fixed assets) and the proportion of debt and equity to fund these assets needs to be determined, based on future funding policies. (Note that the proportion of total assets that is nonfinancial—or nonproductive—will have a large impact on the financial margin required to become sustainable.) Once this is done, two methods are suggested to determine the cost of funds:

- The estimation method: multiply the financial assets by the higher of the rate that local banks charge medium-quality commercial borrowers or the inflation rate projected for the planning period.
- The weighted average cost of capital method: based on the sources used to fund the financial assets, including *loans* to the organization, *deposits* if licensed to collect, and *equity*. (This does not consider the funding of fixed assets and cash holdings, that is, nonproductive assets. Depending on the proportion of nonproductive assets, the impact on the financial margin required may be substantial.) This method estimates the absolute amount of the annual cost of financing. For *loans* to the organization, the commercial bank lending rate to medium-quality borrowers should be used. For *deposits* mobilized by the MFI, the average local rate paid on deposits, including an adjustment for legal reserve requirements, should be used. For *equity*, the projected inflation rate should be used, because inflation represents a real annual reduction in the purchasing power of the organization's net worth. (Some experts argue in fact that a market rate for equity

should be used, because in the marketplace, equity is generally more costly than debt because of the greater risk inherent with equity. Using the inflation rate may understate the true cost of the equity.)

Calculate the total cost by adding together the costs for each class of funding. *It is important in this analysis to express the cost of funds as a percentage of the average loan portfolio, not simply as the estimated cost of debt and equity. This is because every variable in the formula above is expressed as a percentage of the average loan portfolio to provide costs on a consistent measure.*

The capitalization rate *(K)* represents the net *real* profit that the organization would like to achieve, expressed as a percentage of the average loan portfolio. Accumulating profit is important because the amount of outside funding an MFI can safely borrow is a function of the amount of its equity (leverage). Once that limit is reached, further growth requires increases in its equity base. The rate of real profit targets depends on how aggressive a microfinance organization is and its desired rate of growth. To support long-term growth, a capitalization rate of 5 to 15 percent of the average loan portfolio is suggested.

The investment income rate *(II)* is the income expected to be generated by the organizations' financial assets, excluding the loan portfolio. Some of these, such as cash, checking deposits, and legal reserves, will yield little or no interest; others, such as certificates of deposits and investments, may produce significant income. This income, expressed as a percentage of the loan portfolio, is entered as a deduction in the pricing equation.

For example, if an organization has operating expenses of 25 percent of its average loan portfolio, 23.75 percent cost of funds (stated as a percentage of its average loan portfolio), loan losses of 2 percent, a desired capitalization rate of 15 percent, and investment income of 1.5 percent, the resulting effective annual interest rate is:

$$R = \frac{AE + CF + LL + K}{1 - LL} - II$$

$$R = \frac{.25 + .2375 + .02 + .15}{1 - LL} - .015$$

$$R = 65.6$$

While this rate may seem high, the issue of what effective rate to charge depends on what the market will bear. (Also, the effective rate can be a combination of interest and fees, as discussed in the section above on effective yield). Because microentrepreneurs generally have difficulty accessing credit, economic theory predicts that on average they will be able to use each additional unit of capital more profitably than richer households or firms. Based on rates charged by moneylenders in most developing countries, relatively high interest rates do not seem to deter microclients. *The most important point to bear in mind when determining the rate to charge is the efficiency of the organization.* The purpose is to provide clients with long-term continued access to the organization, which can only be achieved if all costs are covered. If an organization is inefficient in delivering credit and consequently needs to charge substantially higher rates of interest, clients may not find value in the credit based on its price (interest and fees), and the organization will not survive.

Appendix 2. Calculating an Effective Interest Rate Using the Internal Rate of Return Method

To demonstrate the internal rate of return method of calculating effective rates, the rate calculation for a sample loan with six alternatives is presented (adapted from Rosenberg 1996). The effective rate is calculated first for a "base case" (interest calculated on the declining balance; no fees or compulsory savings). Then the effective rate is calculated to illustrate the effect of different loan variables, including:

- Flat interest calculation
- Up-front interest payments
- Loan (or service) fee
- Change in payment frequency
- Compulsory savings with interest
- Contributions to group funds (no interest).

Calculating the internal rate of return for each alternative involves three steps: determining the actual cash flows, entering the cash flows into the calculator to determine the effective rate for the period, and multiplying or compounding the internal rate of return by the number of periods to determine the annual rate.

Base Case: Declining Balance Interest

Loan amount 1,000; repaid in four equal monthly payments of principal and interest. Nominal interest rate is 36 percent a year, or 3 percent a month, calculated on the declining balance. The effective interest rate in the base case is the same as the stated nominal rate.

To compute monthly payment (note that on most financial calculators, present value and payment must be entered with opposite signs):

$$PV = -1,000; n = 4; i = 36/12 = 3$$

Solving the equation for PMT yields a monthly payment of $269.03.

Alternative 1: Flat Interest

Same as base case, except that interest is calculated on the entire loan amount (flat basis) rather than on the declining balance and is prorated over the four monthly payments.

Effective interest rate:

$$PV = 1,000; PMT = -280; n = 4$$

Solving for i yields an effective monthly rate of 4.69 percent, which is multiplied by 12 for an annual percentage rate of 56.3 percent.

Alternative 2: Up-front Interest Payments

Same as base case (interest calculated on declining balances) but all interest is charged at the beginning of the loan.

Effective interest rate:

$$PV = 923.88; PMT = -250; n = 4$$

Solving for i yields an effective monthly rate of 3.24 percent, which is multiplied by 12 for an annual percentage rate of 38.9 percent.

Alternative 3: Loan or Service Fee

Same as base case except that a 3 percent loan fee is charged up front.

Effective interest rate:

$$PV = 970; PMT = -269.03; n = 4$$

Solving for i yields an effective monthly rate of 4.29 percent, which is multiplied by 12 for an annual percentage rate of 51.4 percent.

Alternative 4: Weekly Payments

Same as base case, except that four month's worth of payments are paid in 16 weekly installments.

Effective interest rate:

$$PV = 1,000; PMT = -67.26; n = 16$$

Solving for i yields an effective weekly rate of 0.88 percent, which is multiplied by 52 for an annual percentage rate of 45.6 percent.

Alternative 5: Compulsory Savings with Interest

Same as the base case, except that as a condition of the loan the client is required to make a savings deposit of 50 along with each month's payment. The savings account yields of 1 percent per month, uncompounded, is available to the client for withdrawal at any time after the end of the loan.

(Alternatives 5 and 6 assume that the MFI receives and holds the compulsory savings and group contributions. In such a case, the yield to the organization and the cost to the client are the same. If compulsory savings are held by someone other than the MFI, such as a bank, then the amounts deposited should not enter into the computation of yield to the microfinance organization but should be included in calculating the cost to the borrower.)

Effective interest rate:

$$PV = 1,000; PMT = -319.3; n = 4; FV = 203$$

Solving for i yields an effective monthly rate of 3.26 percent, which is multiplied by 12 for an annual percentage rate of 39.1 percent.

Alternative 6: Group Fund Contribution

Same as the base case, except that as a condition of the loan the client is required to make a contribution to a group fund of 50 along with each month's payment. No interest is paid on the group fund, although it is available to the client for withdrawal at any time after the end of the loan.

Effective interest rate:

$$PV = 1,000; PMT = -319.3; n = 4; FV = 200$$

Solving for i yields an effective monthly rate of 3.43 percent, which is multiplied by 12 for an annual percentage rate of 41.2 percent.

Appendix 3. Calculating the Effective Rate with Varying Cash Flows

It is also possible to calculate the effective rate by using the internal rate of return method to take into account cash flows that vary during the loan term. This is because the internal rate of return calculation can consider each cash flow rather than a constant stream. This would be useful for loans that have a grace period at some point during the loan term or if a lump sum payment is made at the end of the loan term.

◆ For example, a 1,000 loan with interest at 36 percent per year calculated on the declining balance, a fee of 3 percent, and a loan term of six months, with a two-month grace period during the middle of the loan (resulting in four monthly payments), results in the internal rate of return shown in table A5.3.1.

To calculate this example using a financial calculator the following variables are entered:

$CFo = 970; CFj = 269.03; Nj = 2; CFj = 0; Nj = 2; CFj = 269.03; Nj = 2; i = 3$

Solve for internal rate of return (IRR).

This results in a much lower effective rate than when there was no grace period. The effective rate in this example is 36.81 percent, while a loan with a four-month loan term and no grace period would have an effective rate of 51.4. This is because the client had use of the funds for six months rather than four and paid the same amount of interest and fees as with a four-month loan.

To calculate the effective rate for a loan that is repaid in a lump sum at the end of the loan term, the interest rate for the loan term is considered the period rate and, therefore, the effective rate. However, with

Table A5.3.1 Internal Rate of Return with Varying Cash Flows (Grace Period)

Nominal annual interest rate: 36 percent; calculation method: declining balance; service fee: 3 percent of loan amount; payment frequency: monthly; loan term: six months; loan amount: 1,000

Period	Inflow	Outflow	Net flow
0	1,000	−30	970
1	—	−269	−269
2	—	−269	−269
3	—	0	0
4	—	0	0
5	—	−269	−269
6	—	−269	−269
Total	1,000	1,106	106

Internal rate of return = 3.0678 (or 36.8% annual).

Table A5.3.2 Internal Rate of Return with Varying Cash Flows (Lump Sum)

Nominal interest rate: 3 percent per month; calculation method: declining balance; service fee: 3 percent of loan amount; payment frequency: monthly (interest only); loan term: four months; loan amount: 1,000

Period	Inflow	Outflow	Net flow
0	1,000	−30	970
1	—	−19	−19
2	—	−19	−19
3	—	−19	−19
4	—	−1,019	−1,019
Total	1,000	1,106	106

Internal rate of return = 1.747 (or 21.0% annual)

loans that require the interest to be paid in installments and the principal to be paid at the end of the loan term, the internal rate of return calculation is used.

◆ For example, a 1,000 loan with interest at 3 percent per month calculated on the declining balance, a fee of 3 percent, and a loan term of four months, with interest paid monthly and the principal paid at the end of the loan term, results in the internal rate of return shown in table A5.3.2.

To calculate the above example using a financial calculator the following variables are entered:

$$CF_0 = 970; \ CF_j = 19; \ N_j = 3; \ CF_j = 1,019; \ i = 3$$

The substantially lower effective rate is a result of the borrower having use of the full amount of the principal (1,000) for the entire loan term of four months. For the MFI to earn an effective yield equal to a loan that has principal and interest paid in installments, the nominal rate would have to be increased considerably.

Sources and Further Reading

Benjamin, McDonald, and Joanna Ledgerwood. 1998. "The Association for the Development of Microenterprises (ADEMI): 'Democratising Credit' in the Dominican Republic." World Bank, Sustainable Banking with the Poor, Washington, D.C.

Ledgerwood, Joanna. 1996. *Financial Management Training for Microfinance Organizations: Finance Study Guide.* New York: PACT Publications (for Calmeadow).

Rosenberg, Rich. 1996. "Microcredit Interest Rates." CGAP Occasional Paper 1. World Bank, Consultative Group to Assist the Poorest (CGAP), Washington, D.C.

Von Pischke, J.D. 1991. *Finance at the Frontier: Debt Capacity and the Role of Credit in the Private Economy.* Washington, D.C.: World Bank, Economic Development Institute.

Waterfield, Charles. 1995. "Financial Viability Model— Facilitator's Notes." SEEP Network. New York.

Women's World Banking. 1994. "Principles and Practices of Financial Management for Microenterprise Lenders and Other Service Organizations." In *Women's World Banking Best Practice Workbook.* New York.

CHAPTER SIX

Designing Savings Products

Savings services are often not available to MFI clients for two main reasons. First, there is a mistaken belief that the poor cannot and do not save, meaning that their demand for savings products goes unheard and unnoticed. Second, due to the regulatory constraints of most MFIs, many are not legally allowed to mobilize deposits. As these reasons reinforce and perpetuate each other, deposits from the poor are formally mobilized only infrequently. Furthermore, as MFIs expand their operations, few are able to increase their outreach to a significant number of clients unless they increase their funding sources to include voluntary deposits. MFIs that depend on external sources of donated funding often concentrate on the demands of donors rather than on the demands of potential clients, especially potential savings clients (GTZ 1997a).

> "Savings mobilization is considered now to be a crucial factor in the development of sound financial markets. There are a growing number of successful savings mobilization programs in developing countries and governments and international agencies have recently become much more interested in such activities. Rural and non-wealthy households in particular have become the focus of policies to promote savings, as the myths that the poor have no margin over consumption for saving and do not respond to economic incentives are increasingly being questioned." (FAO 1995, 14)

Subsidized credit funds also contribute to the limited mobilization of savings deposits. MFIs receiving subsidized funding have little or no incentive to mobilize deposits, because they have funds available for on-lending from donors at lower rates than they would have to pay depositors. Furthermore, accessing donor funding is often less costly than developing the infrastructure required to mobilize deposits.

If an MFI is to mobilize savings effectively, there must be suitable economic and political environments in the country in which it is working. Reasonable levels of macroeconomic management and political stability are required because they affect the rate of inflation, which influences the ability of an MFI to offer savings services in a sustainable manner. In addition, an appropriate and enabling regulatory environment is necessary.

Finally, the institution itself must have established a good record of sound financial management and internal controls, which assures depositors that their funds will be safely held by the MFI.

This chapter highlights the demand for savings services and the environment in which the MFI operates, including the legal requirements for providing savings services. This activity implies a necessary development of the institutional capacity of the MFI, including its human resources, infrastructure, security, management information system, and risk management. The discussion in this chapter includes an overview of the types and pricing of savings products that MFIs provide and the costs associated with delivering savings services. Its focus is on the design of *voluntary* savings products, which are a separate and distinct product from loans and are generally accessible whether clients are borrowers or not. Voluntary savings differ from compulsory savings (discussed in the previous chapter) in that they are not a mandatory requirement for receiving a loan.

This chapter will be of primary interest to readers working with MFIs that are legally able to accept voluntary savings (or are considering creating an institutional structure that allows for the mobilization of voluntary savings). Few MFIs are currently authorized to accept voluntary deposits under current regulations, which means that there is limited experience to draw from. However, as the field matures, more donors and practitioners are realizing that there is a demand for savings services and best practices will be further developed. This chapter addresses the issues that an MFI must consider when *introducing* voluntary savings. Practitioners, consultants, and donors involved with these organizations may not be fully aware of the complexities involved in adding voluntary savings services, and the purpose of this chapter is to raise awareness of these complexities.

Demand for Savings Services

As discussed at the beginning of chapter 5, the cash flow patterns of microentrepreneurs vary. During times of excess cash flow clients need a safe and convenient way to save. When cash flow is limited these same clients need to be able to access their savings (in other words, they need a liquid form of savings).

Without access to savings services, clients often save by keeping cash in the household or investing in grain, livestock, gold, land, or other nondivisible assets. Saving in *cash* is often unsafe, particularly for women, because the male head of the household may demand that any excess money be spent. In many communities household income is shared, and if family members know that one member has money they may demand that it be given (or lent) to them. Furthermore, cash can be stolen or destroyed by fires or floods.

Saving in *hard assets* such as grain or animals does not provide safety (the animal may die), liquidity (market values may change or a market may not exist at the time of the sale), or divisibility (they cannot sell half a goat if they need only a portion of their savings). In addition, maintaining livestock, land, or grain may incur costs that add to cash flow difficulties when cash is unavailable.

Low-income clients are often unable to access savings services from traditional banks due to a limited branch network or the reluctance of banks to deal with small amounts of money. Although it has been demonstrated

that low-income clients can save substantial sums, traditional banks are not set up to collect small amounts and may not find it cost efficient to do so.

Microentrepreneurs, like other business people, save for at least five reasons (Robinson 1994):
- Consumption and for consumer durables
- Investment
- Social and religious purposes
- Retirement, ill health, or disability
- Seasonal variations in cash flow.

The people who make up the target market of most if not all MFIs need access to savings services that ensure their funds will be safe, liquid, and divisible. Savings clients are interested in three major benefits:
- *Convenience.* Clients want access to savings services without taking too much time away from their businesses.
- *Liquidity.* Clients want access to their savings when needed.

Box 6.1 Deposit Collectors in India

IN KALANNAGAR, INDIA, LOW-INCOME CLIENTS USE THE services of a "deposit collector." Each saver has a crudely printed "card" with 220 cells on it arranged in 20 columns and 11 rows. Every second day a woman collector comes to the saver's door to collect a set amount, which then fills up one cell. The saver can fill the cells up as quickly or as slowly as she likes. For example, she can deal with several cells in a day and then stop her savings for days on end. Standard "per cell" deposits are 50 paise and 1, 2, 5, and 10 rupees. As soon as all 220 cells are filled she receives the value of 200 of them. Assuming she fills in a cell every day, paying one rupee per cell, she deposits 220 rupees over 220 days (an average investment of 110 rupees). She thus pays 20 rupees to have this service. This results in a negative interest rate on her savings of approximately 30 percent (or simply, a fee of 10 percent).

These savers know very well that they are paying to save. However, they point out that despite the small expense the system is still a benefit to them, particularly if they have school fees or some other expense coming up. Saving money at home is difficult and saving a few rupees a day in a bank is inefficient because the saver must visit the branch often. Savers feel it is well worth the fee to have the service come to their door.

Source: Rutherford 1996.

■ *Security.* Clients want to be sure that their savings are safe and that the institution that collects them is stable.

For the most part, savings clients have not considered the interest earned on savings to be a priority; however, it does become a priority when resources are scarce and there are many profitable investment opportunities.

Is There an Enabling Environment?

To mobilize savings effectively, an MFI needs to be operating in a country in which the financial sector has been liberalized. This includes abolishing interest rate ceilings and foreign exchange controls, admitting new entrants into the market, as well as establishing reasonable capital requirements. Furthermore, the government must not allow unqualified institutions to mobilize public savings. Nor must is allow more institutions to mobilize savings than the supervisory body is able to supervise effectively.

Savings clients cannot be expected to have enough information to evaluate the soundness of the institution with which they save. The government must *supervise* institutions that mobilize public deposits, either directly or through an effectively managed body that it approves. This usually entails a willingness on the part of the government to modify its banking supervision so that MFIs are appropriately regulated and supervised (see chapter 1).

"Well-designed and well-delivered deposit services can simultaneously benefit households, enterprises, groups, the participating financial institutions, and the government. Good savings programs can contribute to local, regional, and national economic development and can help improve equity." (Robinson 1994, 35)

External regulations should be based on international banking standards and more specifically on international accounting principles, minimum capital requirements, techniques to reduce and diversify the risk exposure of assets, provision policies, and performance criteria (GTZ 1997a).

MFIs that are not operating in enabling environments must lobby the appropriate authorities to make the necessary changes. To do this they must familiarize themselves with international and local experience and evidence to support their arguments. They should also conduct market research on the demand for savings instruments in their own markets (CGAP 1997).

Bank Rakyat Indonesia is one of the best known cases of a state bank providing savings services to low-income clients in a sustainable manner. Bank Rakyat Indonesia has shown that microentrepreneurs utilize savings services more than credit services (box 6.2).

Legal Requirements for Offering Voluntary Savings Services

There are two major legal requirements that generally need to be fulfilled before an MFI can offer voluntary savings services: licensing and reserve requirements.

LICENSING. For the most part, an MFI needs to be licensed to collect savings. This usually means that it becomes subject to some form of regulation.

When discussing voluntary savings services, it is important to differentiate between savings services that are provided to borrowers or members and those available to the general public. Many informal or semiformal MFIs collect savings from their members and either onlend these savings or deposit them in a formal financial institution. Although some are licensed (as NGOs), they are not necessarily licensed as financial intermediaries (that is, to accept deposits) and are generally not supervised or regulated in their deposit activities.

To accept deposits from the general public, an organization *must* have a license. MFIs that are licensed as deposit-taking institutions are generally subject to some form of regulation and supervision by the country's superintendent of banks, central bank, or other government department or entity. Adhering to regulatory and supervisory requirements usually imposes additional costs on the MFI (such as reserve requirements).

Ultimately, to be licensed to accept deposits an MFI must have the financial strength and institutional capacity to do so. Determining the capacity of MFIs is the responsibility of the licensing body.

RESERVE REQUIREMENTS. Reserve requirements refer to a percentage of deposits accepted by an institution that must be held in the central bank or in a similar safe and liquid form. They are imposed by the local superintendent of banks on formalized MFIs accepting deposits to ensure that depositors' funds are both safe and accessible. By mandating a certain percentage of deposit funds as a reserve, governments restrict

---

Box 6.2 Savings Mobilization at Bank Rakyat Indonesia

IN JUNE 1983 THE INDONESIAN GOVERNMENT DEREGULATED
the financial sector to allow government banks to set their
own interest rates on most loans and deposits. At that time
TABANAS, the government's national savings program, had
been offered in Bank Rakyat Indonesia's more than 3,600
local-level banks for about a decade but had mobilized only
$17.6 million. State banks had been required to lend at 12
percent and to pay 15 percent on most deposits, providing a
negative incentive for deposit mobilization. In addition,
TABANAS, the only instrument available, limited withdrawals to twice a month, a provision that was unacceptable
to most villagers, who wanted to be sure that their savings
would be accessible whenever they were needed.

But the low savings total of the local banking system was
widely attributed not to its real causes—primarily the interest rate regulations and the poorly designed TABANAS
instrument—but to untested assumptions that villagers did
not save and that even if there were some who did, they
would not save in banks. Both assumptions were wrong.
Extensive field research in the 1980s showed—much to the
surprise of most government and Bank Rakyat Indonesia
officials—that there was vast unmet demand, both rural and
Source: Robinson 1995.

urban, for a liquid savings instrument in which both financial stocks and savings from income flows could be safely
deposited. Also, many lower-income people wanted to convert some of their nonfinancial savings into financial savings,
if these could be deposited in liquid accounts. There was also
demand for fixed deposit accounts.

As of December 31, 1995, Bank Rakyat Indonesia's primary savings product, SIMPEDES, and its urban counter-
part, SIMASKOT, accounted for 77 percent of the total
deposits in the bank's local banking system. The banking
system that mobilized $17.6 million in its first decade mobi-
lized $2.7 billion in its second decade—from the same cus-
tomers in the same banks! This spectacular change occurred
primarily because after 1983 the bank had an incentive to
mobilize savings and began to learn about its local markets.
Deposit instruments were then designed specifically to meet
different types of local demand.

With 14.5 million savings accounts as of December 31,
1995, Bank Rakyat Indonesia's local banking system provides
savings services to about 30 percent of Indonesia's households.
Households and enterprises also benefit from the expanded
volume of institutional credit financed by the savings program.

MFIs with respect to the total amount of funds available to them for on-lending.

Reserve requirements result in increased costs to
MFIs, because the amount held as reserve cannot be lent
out and thus does not earn the effective portfolio yield or
investment return rate.

Reserve requirements are often separated between primary reserves and secondary reserves. For example, in
Canada all chartered banks are required to maintain a
reserve with the central bank equal to the aggregate of 10
percent of Canadian currency demand deposits, 2 percent of Canadian currency notice deposits, 1 percent of
Canadian currency notice deposits in excess of
CDN$500 million, and 3 percent of foreign currency
deposits held in Canada by Canadian residents. This primary reserve is not interest bearing to the chartered bank.

Secondary reserves are bank reserves, which must be
maintained in prescribed interest-bearing public debt or
day loans to investment dealers in Canada, or cash.
These reserves may not be greater than 12 percent of
deposits of Canadian residents of the bank, its offices in

Canada, or any of its subsidiaries (Morris, Power, and
Varma 1986).

Reserve requirements in Indonesia are 5 percent, in
the Philippines 8 percent, and in Colombia 10 percent.
Some government banks, such as those in Thailand, are
exempt from reserve requirements, which gives them a
considerable advantage over other institutions.

Deposit Insurance

The best way to ensure the safety of deposits is to prevent the failure of the MFIs providing the deposit services. This is best done by ensuring that MFIs have
sound management and prudent lending policies and
are supported by adequate regulation and supervision.
However, most industrial countries (and many developing countries) have established deposit insurance plans
as a safety net to protect depositors should an institution
not be prudently managed. (Informal financial institutions collecting deposits are generally unable to participate in deposit insurance schemes.) Deposit insurance

guarantees a maximum nominal value of deposits to each saver (based on the amount they have deposited) if the institution collecting deposits fails. This insurance is generally government controlled and provided by an apex institution, to which each regulated deposit-taking institution pays a fee. In some countries the government also contributes funds. In all cases it is important that the government provide the necessary backup support to make the system effective (box 6.3).

Deposit insurance is established for three main reasons (FAO 1995):

- It strengthens confidence in the banking system and helps to promote deposit mobilization.
- It provides the government with a formal mechanism for dealing with failing banks.
- It ensures that small depositors are protected in the event of a bank failure.

Two of the main disadvantages of deposit insurance plans are that savers have less incentive to select stable MFIs and MFIs have less incentive to manage their organizations prudently. However, the need to protect those who deposit in MFIs is particularly important, due to the imperfect information about the MFI available to low-income clients and the lack of interest of governments in intervening and compensating savers when an MFI fails, since in most cases its failure is not likely to be seen as a threat to the financial stability of a country.

Box 6.3 Deposit Insurance in India

DEPOSIT INSURANCE IN INDIA IS IMPLEMENTED BY A PUBLIC sector agency called the Deposit Insurance and Credit Guarantee Corporation, which was set up in 1962 in the wake of the collapse of a private bank. The agency offers deposit and credit insurance to the entire banking sector in India, including cooperatives and rural banks. While credit insurance is voluntary, deposit insurance is compulsory for the banks. The Deposit Insurance and Credit Guarantee Corporation charges a premium of 5 paise per year for 100 rupees on a half-yearly basis (0.0005 percent). Each depositor is eligible for a maximum level of protection of 1 lakh (approximately US$2,565), which means practically all of the small savers are protected in India.

The scheme seems to have created a significant level of confidence among small savers, which has enabled banks to mobilize savings fairly easily, even in remote areas. While banks frequently submit claims on credit insurance, very rarely do they invoke deposit insurance, given the general financial stability in India.

Source: Shylendra 1998.

Although deposit insurance plans should include all deposit-taking institutions, including cooperatives and semiformal MFIs, it may not be appropriate to provide the same insurance for all institutions. Having separate

---

Box 6.4 Security of Deposits in the Bank for Agriculture and Agricultural Cooperatives, Thailand

THE BANK FOR AGRICULTURE AND AGRICULTURAL Cooperatives (BAAC) has operated in the rural areas of Thailand for 30 years. Originally conceived of as a vehicle for delivering low-cost credit to Thai farmers, in recent years BAAC has come to be recognized as one of the few sector-specialized government-owned rural financial institutions.

One of the important aspects of this success is the bank's impressive record in the past decade in mobilizing financial resources. It has done this through vigorous efforts to attract savings in rural areas, which finance its rapidly expanding agricultural lending portfolio.

There is no formal deposit insurance program in the Thai banking sector. However, on a case by case basis, the government has saved depositors from losing their funds by mounting rescue operations overseen by the Bank of

Source: GTZ 1997b.

Thailand. Unfortunately, this implicit guarantee approach may not be very conducive to depositor peace of mind, and it may create perverse managerial incentives for bankers if the implicit "safety net" encourages them to pursue overly risky lending operations. As a result, BAAC portfolio quality is poor.

Further financial market distortions are created when the public believes that such implicit government guarantees are operated in an uneven manner between state-owned and privately owned financial institutions. The appropriate explicit deposit guarantee framework is a risk-based deposit insurance program in which each participating financial institution (whether state-owned or privately owned) contributes an amount to the deposit insurance fund based on an independent assessment of that institution's portfolio risk.

deposit insurance funds for each major type of financial intermediary diversifies risk. For example, banks and credit union insurance funds were not affected by the savings and loan crisis in the United States, and thus insurance premiums had to be raised only for savings and loans associations (FAO 1995).

Even without the availability of deposit insurance, what seems to be most important to the saver is the reputation of the bank. Potential savers look for an established bank with a good reputation, appropriate instruments, and a convenient local outlet.

Does the MFI Have the Necessary Institutional Capacity to Mobilize Savings?

Prior to offering voluntary savings services, MFIs must ensure that they have the institutional structure that allows them to mobilize savings legally and adequate institutional capacity or the ability to develop it.[1] Institutional capacity requires that adequate governance, management, staff, and operational structures are in place to provide savings services. Furthermore, additional (and sometimes substantial) reporting requirements to the superintendent or other regulatory body imply increased personnel costs and expanded management information systems.

Ownership, governance, and organizational structures have a strong impact on client perceptions of MFIs' mobilization of savings. Moreover, the introduction of voluntary savings services implies the addition of many new customers, which in turn requires increased capacity of staff and staff training programs, management, marketing systems, infrastructure, security and internal controls, management information systems, and risk management.

Ownership and Governance

Public ownership can make an MFI seem reliable and secure, particularly if strong political support exists and political interference is minimal. Depositors know that the government will protect them in the case of a severe liquidity or solvency crisis. However, public ownership can also impose limitations on savings if subsidized credit programs exist and government intervention in pricing and customer selection prevails. MFIs must be allowed to operate free of political interference. They must not be discouraged from mobilizing savings by frequent injections of inexpensive public funds. Furthermore, if external regulation and supervision is less stringent for public than private MFIs, insufficient risk management may put depositor funds at risk (box 6.5).

Privately owned MFIs need to ensure that they both are and are perceived to be sound financial intermediaries. Relationships with well-respected individuals, families, or institutions such as a religious organization or larger holding company can help strengthen the confidence and trust of their depositors. Furthermore, MFIs that were traditionally focused only on providing credit services need to ensure that their identity is reestablished as a safe place for deposits. This will depend to a large extent on the quality of the credit services that they provide and their reputation as serious lenders who do not accept clients who default on their loans.

The *governance structure* of MFIs is crucial for ensuring appropriate financial intermediation services between savers and borrowers. MFIs that mobilize savings are likely to have a more professional governance structure, with greater representation from the private financial sector or the membership than those whose sole business is disbursing loans.

Organizational Structure

Most MFIs that mobilize savings have organizational structures that are both extensive and decentralized. A location close to deposit customers reduces transaction costs for both the MFI and its clients and is an important part of establishing a permanent relationship built on mutual trust, which is a key to successful savings mobilization.

Successful MFIs organize their branches or field offices as *profit centers* and employ a method of *transfer pricing* that ensures full-cost coverage throughout the branch network. Transfer pricing refers to the pricing of services provided by the head office to the branches on a cost-recovery basis. For example, costs incurred in the head office to manage the overall organization are prorated to the branches based on a percentage of assets (loans) or lia-

---

1. This section draws substantially from Robinson (1995) and GTZ (1997a).

Box 6.5 Ownership and Governance at the Bank for Agriculture and Agricultural Cooperatives, Thailand

THE BANK FOR AGRICULTURE AND AGRICULTURAL Cooperatives (BAAC) is governed by a board of directors appointed by the council of ministers. The board controls the policies and business operations of the bank. Its enabling legislation requires that board membership also include representatives from the prime minister's office, the Ministry of Finance, the Ministry of Agriculture and Cooperatives, and other government departments. Thus the board is mainly composed of public officials who reflect the interests of the government but lack financial enterprise acumen and experience. The composition of the board reflects the 99.7 percent government ownership of the bank.

This governance structure was inherited from earlier years when the institution acted primarily as a dispenser of financial resources received from the government and foreign

donor agencies or on behalf of the government (as in the case of mandatory commercial bank deposits). The situation has since changed; BAAC is now responsible for the stewardship and safekeeping of a large volume of resources from its new depositor-clientele.

Despite the radical change in BAAC's financial resource base, there has so far not been an adaptation of the membership of the board of directors to reflect the substantial shift in the array of the institution's stakeholders. Nor have the opportunities for ownership of the institution been modified or broadened significantly to respond to these new interests.

A change in the governance structure of the bank could make an important contribution to addressing some of the stakeholders issues that fall outside the original state-owned enterprise design concept.

Source: GTZ 1997b.

---

bilities (deposits) held at the branch. Funding costs are apportioned as well. A branch that disburses a larger volume of loans than the deposits it collects needs to receive funding from the head office (or another branch) to fund those loans. The head office (or a regional office) will act as a central funding facility to ensure that any excess deposits in one branch are "sold" to another branch to fund their loans. The branch that has excess deposits receives payment (interest revenue) for those funds, while the branch receiving them pays a fee (interest expense). If the head office determines that there is no excess funding within the system, it will then access external funding and *on-lend* it to its branches for a set price.

The transfer price charged to branches (or paid to branches for excess deposits) is set either close to the interbank lending rate or at a rate somewhat higher than the average cost of funds for the MFI. This provides incentives for branches to mobilize savings locally rather than relying on the excess liquidity of other branches within the network. It can also result in some additional revenue at the head office level to cover overheads. Transfer pricing ensures transparency and instills accountability and responsibility in the branches.

Human Resources

Once savings are introduced, the MFI becomes a true financial intermediary, and the consequences for the

institution and its human resources are considerable. Managing a financial intermediary is far more complex than managing a credit organization, especially since the size of the organization often increases rapidly. This has serious consequences if the MFI is like many that have one or two key individuals who head the organization and are personally involved in almost every aspect of operations. In particular, MFIs mobilizing deposits will be subject to much greater scrutiny and supervision by government regulators and others. The level of effective management must be greater than that of an MFI that is providing credit only.

Staff recruitment should focus on selecting staff from the local region who are familiar with customs and culture and, if applicable, the dialect spoken in the region (box 6.6). Local staff tend to instill confidence in clients and make it easier for them to communicate with the MFI. Studies have found that a strong customer orientation and service culture attitudes are crucial ingredients for successful savings mobilization (GTZ 1997a).

Significant training of both management and staff becomes imperative when introducing savings. Managers and staff need to learn how local markets operate, how to locate potential savers, and how to design instruments and services for that market. They also need to understand basic finance and the importance of an adequate spread between lending and deposit services. Often MFI staff have a social development background and may not appreciate the fact that low-income clients can and do save. While successful microlending relies on the loan officer personally understanding each client, the provision of savings services can be quite different, depending on how those savings are collected and withdrawn. The training needs of all management and staff should be assessed and delivered both initially and periodically as the MFI grows.

Marketing

MFIs providing credit services must select borrowers whom they trust to repay the loans. When collecting savings, however, it is the customers who must trust the MFI. Deposit clients must be convinced that the MFI staff is competent and honest. MFIs must actively seek out potential depositors, keeping in mind their target market. Most important, the MFI must first design its savings products appropriately and then publicize its services in locally appropriate ways.

During the market research phase, MFIs need to learn what savings services are demanded by potential clients and then incorporate this information into both product design and marketing. For example, to encourage savings mobilization Bank Rakyat Indonesia determined that savers would like the opportunity to receive gifts when they open a savings account. The bank now offers *lotter-*

ies with each of its savings products. Each month a drawing is made from the names of deposit account holders and the winners receive a gift such as a television or bicycle. Lotteries have proven to be an effective means of marketing savings services, and they have been adopted by BancoSol in Bolivia as well.

Another marketing method employed by Bank Rakyat Indonesia is the displaying of posters showing pictures of the local subbranch, its larger supervising branch, and the bank's impressive looking head office. This approach is based on the fact that savers tend to be concerned about placing their savings in what appears to be a small local bank. When the bank has a good reputation, emphasis on the relationship between the sub-branch and the larger bank is reassuring to clients.

MFIs can also establish "open door" days when clients can come in and meet staff as well as physically see the safe where the money is kept. If savers are unfamiliar with banks in general, they may derive comfort from observing a safe environment.

The design of special *trademarks* for savings products has also attracted depositors. For example, Thailand's Bank for Agriculture and Agricultural cooperatives has a savings product called "BAAC's Save to Increase your Chances," and Banco Caja Social in Colombia markets a "Grow Every Day" savings account. While special trademarks make it easier for clients to understand the particular design of each savings product, they also help to distinguish the products from those offered by a competing MFI.

Ultimately however, *word of mouth* is the best form of advertising. To ensure positive word of mouth, the service provided to depositors must be timely, considerate, and honest. Once again, client demand must ultimately be met through appropriate savings product design. A woman living in a rural area of an eastern Indonesian island who was asked what she thought about Bank Rakyat Indonesia opening a bank office there said, "If [Bank Rakyat Indonesia] opens here and provides good service, it will be wonderful for us. We need a bank." Then she said, "There is little to do here in the evenings except talk. If the bank does something good here, you can be sure that we will talk about it for years to come!" "Of course," she added, "if the bank does something bad here, we will talk about that for years to come" (Robinson 1995, 14).

Infrastructure

As previously mentioned, introducing voluntary savings products greatly alters the organization and management of an MFI. Depending on the collection method employed, some MFIs may need to develop branches close to their clients. However, this may not be necessary until the MFI reaches a certain volume of business. Alternatively, MFIs can provide "mobile banking" services, with the MFI staff traveling *to the client* to collect savings rather than having the client visit the branch. Bank Rakyat Indonesia savings officers go weekly to each village and collect savings and provide withdrawals. Mobile banking works well so long as the MFI is consistent in its scheduled visits, so that clients are assured of their ability to deposit or withdraw savings on specific days of the week.

Other MFIs enhance their branch structures to make them more convenient for their clients and more user friendly. For example, BancoSol operates primarily in urban areas (including secondary cities) where branches are relatively accessible to their clients. They modified their branches to include teller windows and a comfortable and inviting environment for savers. BancoSol also hired and trained staff specifically to manage and maintain deposit accounts.

Furthermore, convenient and flexible hours of operation that meet the needs of clients helps to make savings services more attractive.

Security and Internal Controls

As an MFI begins to offer voluntary savings services, it needs to consider the issue of security. At a minimum the MFI needs to purchase a safe to keep cash available for potential withdrawals and to minimize the risk of robbery. If the MFI collects savings through mobile banking, it should have two officers working together to minimize the risk of both fraud and robbery. Bank Rakyat Indonesia, which uses this system, has found that the community itself ensures that bank officers are not robbed, knowing that it is their money that is at risk.

MFIs need to develop internal controls to address security risk when providing voluntary savings products. There is extensive knowledge in the formal financial sector that addresses risk, including such checks and balances as dual custody of cash and combinations,

separation of duties, audit trails, and the use of fireproof vaults and drop boxes (Calvin 1995). Experts from the formal financial sector should be contracted to advise on these issues.

Management Information Systems

An appropriate and soundly operating management information system is the core of an efficient internal control and monitoring system. The management information system should be simple, transparent, and objective. An effective management information system becomes fundamentally important when savings services are introduced both for internal management and external reporting.

When designing management information systems to manage savings products, it is important to consider accuracy, reliability, and speed. There are three major goals for an information system (adapted from Calvin 1995):

- Transaction processing
- Customer service
- Management information.

To make strategic decisions about the savings products, the MFI needs the following information: number of accounts, value of accounts, and average balances; number of transactions per account; the distribution of the balances of the accounts; and the daily turnover as a percentage of balances (which may vary by season). Over time it is important to maintain a client database that allows the institution to analyze the relationship between credit and savings products and other market details.

It is increasingly important for management information systems to provide the reporting and monitoring requirements demanded by the supervisory body responsible for regulating the MFI. Systems must be designed to ensure that this information is produced regularly and that it also provides information that is beneficial to the MFI itself. (See chapter 7 for a more detailed discussion of management information systems.)

Risk Management and Treasury

The introduction of deposit-taking greatly complicates the management of assets and liabilities. In addition to meeting the reserve requirements stipulated by the regulatory authorities, it is also important to have the right amount of cash in the right branches at the right times. Poor liquidity management can seriously hamper the operational capacity of each branch. Most MFIs generating numerous small deposits have found that very small savings accounts, even those with an unlimited number of withdrawals, generally experience little turnover and therefore represent a stable liquidity cushion. Publicly owned MFIs often rely on large savings deposits from state-owned institutions or legally enforced deposits from commercial banks, which implies heightened liquidity risk if government regulations change and they lose their large depositors.

MFIs that create a central funding facility (discussed above under transfer pricing) may be better able to effectively manage their liquidity risk. (Delinquency, liquidity, and asset and liability management are discussed in chapter 10.)

Sequencing the Introduction of Savings Services

MFIs planning to introduce voluntary savings services must consider the order in which to carry out the various steps. Box 6.7 identifies six steps that an MFI should follow.

Types of Savings Products for Microentrepreneurs

Deposit instruments must be designed appropriately to meet local demand. It is crucial for an MFI to conduct market research prior to introducing savings products and to offer a good mix of products with various levels of liquidity that respond to the characteristics and financial needs of various market segments.

Box 6.7 The Sequencing of Voluntary Savings Mobilization

1. Enhance the knowledge of the MFI's board and managers about the experience of other local and international MFIs. By understanding the savings services that exist locally, MFI managers can build on existing systems.
2. Carry out market research and train staff selected for the pilot stage. Examine the regulatory environment and the institutional capacity of the MFI.
3. Conduct and evaluate a pilot project. This is a crucial step, because until the extent of demand and the costs of the different products, including labor, are known, only temporary interest rates can be set.
4. When necessary, carry out and evaluate a second set of pilot projects testing products and prices that were revised as a result of the first pilot. At the same time, hold wider staff training. During this period pay attention to planning the logistics and management information systems that will be required for the expansion of the program of deposit mobilization.
5. When the instruments, pricing, logistics, information systems, and staff training are completed, gradually expand savings mobilization throughout all branches.
6. When expansion of saving services to all branches is achieved, switch attention from the logistics of expansion to the techniques of market penetration. When well-run MFIs offer appropriate deposit facilities and services, they can quickly gain the accounts of people living or working

nearby the bank offices; this is known as "the easy money." Market penetration of the wider service area, however, requires other methods. These include the development of a systematic approach to identification of potential depositors; the implementation of a staff incentive system based on the value of deposits collected so that the staff will seek out the potential depositors rather than wait for them to come to the bank; the development of effective methods for intrabank communication; more extensive market research; a major overhaul of public relations; and massive staff training.

The sequencing outlined here may appear lengthy and cumbersome, but it is necessary for building the long-term viability of the MFI. There are often temptations to go too fast, but instituting voluntary savings mobilization too rapidly is a prime example of "haste makes waste." For example, an MFI is asking for trouble if it tries to implement its new savings program before its management information system is ready and the staff is well trained in its use. A financial institution that gets its sequencing wrong can lose its clients' trust, which in turn can lead to the loss of its reputation and eventually of its viability.

Getting the "when" and "how" of introducing voluntary savings mobilization right enables MFIs to meet local demand for savings services and provide a larger volume of microcredit, thereby increasing both outreach and profitability.

Source: Robinson 1995.

When Bank Rakyat Indonesia decided to offer voluntary savings products, it conducted an extensive study of local demand for financial services and systematically identified potential savers. The bank also looked closely at existing savings services in the informal sector and designed its products to overcome limitations and to replicate the strengths of existing services (box 6.8).

For the most part, individual voluntary savings have been found to be more successful than group savings. Most savings products for microclients include the following features (GTZ 1997a):

- The required minimum opening balances are generally low.
- A mix of liquid savings products, semiliquid savings products, and time deposits with a fixed-term structure are offered, including at least one liquid savings product with unlimited withdrawals.
- Attractive rates of interest are offered. For private MFIs this may mean rates of interest that are higher than market rates as a sort of risk premium to attract deposits, particularly if they are operating in a competitive environment. Public MFIs may be able to pay lower rates of interest based on the perceived safety of public institutions.
- Interest rates should increase with the size of the savings account to provide a financial incentive for savers to increase deposits and refrain from withdrawing.
- Conversely, savings account balances below a specified minimum are exempt from interest payments to partially compensate for the relatively higher administrative costs of small accounts.
- Some MFIs may charge fees and commissions to depositors for opening and closing accounts and for specific services related to account management, such as issuing a passbook.

There are three broad deposit groups based on the degree of liquidity: highly liquid current accounts, semiliquid savings accounts, and fixed-term deposits.

Liquid Accounts

Highly liquid deposits provide the greatest flexibility and liquidity and the lowest returns. Current accounts—or demand deposits—are deposits that allow funds to be deposited and withdrawn at any time. Frequently no interest is paid. Highly liquid accounts are difficult to manage, because they require substantial bookkeeping and are not as stable a source of funding as term deposits. Only a limited portion of demand deposits can be used to provide loans (based on reserve requirements), because the MFI must be able to service withdrawal requests at all times.

Semiliquid Accounts

Semiliquid accounts provide some liquidity and some returns. Some savings accounts are semiliquid, which means that the borrower can usually withdraw funds a limited number of times per month and deposit funds at any time. Unlike current accounts, savings accounts generally pay a nominal rate of interest, which is sometimes based on the minimum balance in the account over a given period (monthly, yearly). They begin to act like

---

Box 6.8 Bank Rakyat Indonesia Savings Instruments

AFTER A SERIES OF PILOT PROJECTS THAT BEGAN IN 1984, Bank Rakyat Indonesia introduced four savings instruments with different ratios of liquidity and returns nationwide in 1986. SIMPEDES, a savings instrument that permits an unlimited number of withdrawals, became the "flagship" of the new savings program. The SIMPEDES instrument incorporates lotteries for the depositors that were modeled loosely on Bank Dagang Bali's highly successful depositor lotteries. SIMPEDES was aimed at households, firms, and organizations that demand liquidity in combination with positive real returns. TABANAS, which provides a higher interest rate than SIMPEDES, was continued, with the withdrawal rules later liberalized. TABANAS was aimed at depositors who wanted middle levels of both liquidity and returns.

Deposito Berjangka, a fixed deposit instrument previously available from Bank Rakyat Indonesia only through its branches, was now offered as well through the bank unit in its local banking system. Deposito Berjangka is used by wealthier villagers and firms hoping to realize higher returns and also by those saving for long-term goals, such as building construction, land purchase, and children's education. Many Deposito Berjangka account holders also hold SIMPEDES accounts. The fourth instrument, Giro, a type of current account, is primarily for use by institutions that must meet special government requirements. With the exception of Giro, these deposit instruments have generally provided positive real interest rates.

Source: Robinson 1995.

term deposits if interest is paid only when a minimum balance is held in the account. This encourages the client to hold a certain amount of money in the account, which makes for easier management by the MFI.

Fixed-Term Deposits

Term deposits are savings accounts that are locked in for a specified amount of time. They provide the lowest liquidity and the highest returns. Term deposits are generally a stable source of funding for the MFI and pay a higher rate of return to the saver. Generally, the interest rate is based on the length of the term of the deposit and the expected movement in market rates. Term deposits range from a one-month term to several years; they allow the MFI to fund loans for a period of time just short of the deposit term. This makes liquidity and gap management easier for the MFI, because the funds are available for a set period of time, which is offset by reduced liquidity and increased interest-rate risk for the saver. (Gap management and interest-rate risk are discussed in chapter 10.)

The choice of products to offer must be based on the needs of the clients in the area served by the MFI. Many first-time savers will choose a highly liquid account. As they become more experienced with managing their savings, they will likely open more than one deposit account, using a semiliquid or fixed-term deposit account for longer-term savings (box 6.9).

Costs of Mobilizing Voluntary Savings

The cost of savings mobilization depends not only on internal factors such as operational efficiency, but also on external factors such as minimum reserve requirements (discussed above), tax rates, and general market conditions. Determining both internal and external costs helps to establish what rate to pay on different savings products (taking into account the market rate for deposits).

Costs include (adapted from Christen 1997):

- Setup costs
- Direct costs
- Indirect costs
- Cost of funds (paid to depositors).

Setup costs include research and development, which may include hiring outside consultants and savings experts; the printing of passbooks and other marketing

---

Box 6.9 The Choice of Savings Products in Pays Dogon, Mali

IN PAYS DOGON, A NETWORK OF 55 SELF-RELIANT AND self-managed village banks has been established. The rural communities have themselves determined the financial products that they wish their banks to offer. Both demand and term deposits are offered. The results are that term deposits are much more popular (constituting about 85 percent of total deposits) due to liquidity management, which dictates that only *term deposits* are used for lending (out of community solidarity those who are wealthy enough to save prefer to save long-term so that other people from the village can access loans); interest, which on term deposits is high (15 to 20 percent annually); and the tradition of Dogon farmers of long-term savings in kind (before the severe draughts hit the Sahel in the 1980s, they were all cattle owners, but with the loss of a majority of their herds during dry periods, these farmers are now happy to have alternative monetary savings products that offer much higher security).

Source: Contributed by Cecile Fruman, Sustainable Banking with the Poor Project, World Bank.

---

material for the initial launch; safes; computer systems, including hardware and software; as well as existing or new staff costs. These costs must all be estimated and a plan devised prior to developing the savings products.

Direct costs are those costs incurred specifically in the provision of savings services. Direct costs can be variable or fixed. Variable costs are those that are incurred per account or per transaction. They include time and materials used in opening, maintaining, and closing an account. These costs can be estimated per account based on average activity and the time taken to process the transactions in a given time period, such as a month.

Fixed direct costs are those incurred to deliver savings products that do not vary with the number of accounts (units) opened or maintained. These include salaries and ongoing training for savings officers, additional management, additional accounting personnel, branch infrastructure, and any special promotions for savings products.

Indirect costs are costs that do not relate directly to the provision of savings services but a portion of which should be charged to the savings operation by virtue of being part of the overall services provided by the organization. These include overhead (such as management), premises, general operating costs, as well as other head office and branch costs. Indirect costs are generally pro-rated based on the amount of business activity generated by savings products as opposed to other business activities (such as loans, investments, training, and so forth).

These costs can often be estimated by examining existing costs as well as in reference to other organizations providing savings services. These will vary depending on the delivery method chosen for providing savings services.

The *cost of funds* refers to the interest rate paid to depositors. The rates vary based on the liquidity of the account and the amount of time a deposit is held.

All of these cost factors must be considered when offering savings products. However, it is difficult to estimate accurately the operational costs and demand for each product and the interest rates necessary both to make the instrument attractive and the spread profitable. Pilot projects are thus imperative to estimate the costs accurately, to set appropriate interest rates, to establish suitable spreads, and to ensure that the product is designed to meet client needs. Furthermore, the incentive system of MFIs can be designed to increase staff productivity and in turn reduce administrative costs. (For a more complete treatment of the costs of savings accounts, see Christen 1997, 201–11.)

Furthermore, transaction costs incurred by deposit customers must be considered. Locating branches in densely populated areas or close to business centers where a significant number of people meet to carry out economic transactions reduces transaction costs for customers. Also, MFIs should minimize the waiting time for clients to make deposits by ensuring that enough tellers are provided, based on the number of clients and transaction volumes. Clients who are only able to visit the MFI branch during evenings or weekends should be accommodated. While these measures reduce transaction costs for clients, the administrative costs for the MFI increase. A cost-benefit analysis should be carried out to determine the best way to both lower transaction costs for clients and minimize the administrative costs for the MFI (box 6.10).

Pricing Savings Products

The interest rate paid on deposits is based on the prevailing deposit rates of similar products in similar institu-

---

> **Box 6.10 Administrative Costs for Banco Caja Social, Colombia**
>
> BANCO CAJA SOCIAL RECENTLY BEGAN COST ACCOUNTING by savings product and found that the administrative costs for an actively used traditional passbook savings account below US$10 was roughly 18 percent of the balance (without considering interest payments during the year). However, it also found that for the average savings account in 1996, administrative costs were below 1 percent of the balance. This demonstrates that while the administration of very small savings is costly, financial institutions can minimize those costs by offering a good mix of savings products and implementing cost-reducing procedures.
>
> *Source:* GTZ 1997c.

---

tions, the rate of inflation, and market supply and demand. Risk factors such as liquidity risk and interest-rate risk must also be considered based on the time period of deposits. Finally, the costs of providing voluntary savings also influences deposit pricing policies.

MFIs incur greater operational costs to administer highly liquid accounts and thus the interest rates are lower. Fixed-term deposits are priced at a higher rate, because the funds are locked in and are not available to the depositor. Thus they are of lower risk to the MFI, and as a result term deposits are a more stable source of funding than demand deposits (ignoring for the moment asset-liability management and term matching issues for the MFI and liquidity risk and interest-rate risk for the depositor, which are discussed in chapter 10).

Savings products need to be priced so that the MFI earns a spread between its savings and lending services that enables it to become profitable. Labor and other nonfinancial costs must be carefully considered when setting deposit rates. However, there are a number of unknowns at the beginning of savings mobilization. For example, a highly liquid savings account that is in high demand can be quite labor intensive and thus costly, especially if there is a large number of very small accounts. Experience to date indicates that most savers who select a liquid account are not highly sensitive to interest rates and prefer better service to higher interest. A study conducted by Ostry and Reinhart (1995) finds that the lower the income group, the less sensitive they are to interest rates paid on savings:

"A one percentage point rise in the real rate of interest should elicit a rise in the saving rate of only about two-tenths of one percentage point for the 10 poorest countries in the sample. For the wealthiest countries, by contrast, the rise in the saving rate in response to a similar change in the real interest rate is about two-thirds of a percentage point." (Ostry and Reinhart 1995, 18).

Sources and Further Reading

Calvin, Barbara. 1995. "Operational Implications of Introducing Savings Services." Paper delivered at the MicroFinance Network Conference, November 8, Cavite, Philippines.

Christen, Robert Peck. 1997. *Banking Services for the Poor: Managing for Financial Success.* Washington, D.C.: ACCION International.

CGAP (Consultative Group to Assist the Poorest). 1997. "Introducing Savings in Microcredit Institutions: When and How?" Focus Note 8. World Bank, Washington, D.C.

FAO (Food and Agriculture Organization). 1995. "Safeguarding Deposits: Learning from Experience." FAO Agricultural Services Bulletin 116. Rome.

Fruman, Cecile. 1998. "Pays Dogon, Mali" Case Study for the Sustainable Banking with the Poor Project, World Bank, Washington, D.C.

GTZ (Deutsche Gesellschaft für Technische Zusammenarbeit). 1997a. "Comparative Analysis of Savings Mobilization Strategies." CGAP (Consultative Group to Assist the Poorest) Working Group, Washington, D.C.

———. 1997b. "Comparative Analysis of Savings Mobilization Strategies—Case Study for Bank of Agriculture and Agricultural Cooperatives (BAAC), Thailand." CGAP (Consultative Group to Assist the Poorest) Working Group, Washington, D.C.

———. 1997c. "Comparative Analysis of Savings Mobilization Strategies—Case Study for Banco Caja Social (BCS), Colombia." CGAP (Consultative Group to Assist the Poorest) Working Group, Washington, D.C.

———. 1997d. "Comparative Analysis of Savings Mobilization Strategies—Case Study for Bank Rakyat Indonesia (BRI), Indonesia." CGAP (Consultative Group to Assist the Poorest) Working Group, Washington, D.C.

———. 1997e. "Comparative Analysis of Savings Mobilization Strategies—Case Study for Rural Bank of Panabo (RBP), Philippines." CGAP (Consultative Group to Assist the Poorest) Working Group, Washington, D.C.

Morris, D.D., A. Power, and D.K. Varma, eds. 1986. *1986 Guide to Financial Reporting for Canadian Banks.* Toronto, Canada: Touche Ross.

Ostry, Jonathan D., and Carmen M. Reinhart. 1995. "Saving and the Real Interest Rate in Developing Countries." *Finance & Development* 32 (December): 16–18.

Patten, H. Richard, and Jay K. Rosengard. 1991. *Progress with Profits. The Development of Rural Banking in Indonesia.* San Francisco: ICS Press.

Robinson, Marguerite. 1994. "Savings Mobilization and Microenterprise Finance: The Indonesian Experience." In Otero and Rhyne, eds., *New World of Microenterprise Finance.* West Hartford, Conn.: Kumarian Press.

———. 1995. "Introducing Savings Mobilization in Microfinance Programs: When and How?" Paper delivered at the annual meeting of the MicroFinance Network, November 8, Cavite, Philippines.

Rutherford, Stuart. 1996. "Comment on DevFinance Network, September 6, 1996." Internet discussion network, Ohio State University. Devfinance@lists.acs.ohio-state.edu

Shylendra, H.S. 1998. "Comment on DevFinance Network, March 12." Ohio State University. Devfinance@lists.acs.ohio-state.edu

Wisniwski, Sylvia. 1997. "Savings in the Context of Microfinance: Comparative Analysis of Asian Case Studies." Paper delivered at the Fourth Asia-Pacific Regional Workshop on Sustainable Banking with the Poor, November 3–7, Bangkok.

Management Information Systems

The management information system of an institution includes all the systems used for generating the information that guides management in its decisions and actions.[1] The management information system can be seen as a map of the activities that are carried out by the MFI. It monitors the operations of the institution and provides reports that reflect the information that management considers the most significant to track. Staff, management, board, funding organizations, regulators, and others rely on reports produced by the management information system to give an accurate portrait of what is occurring in the institution.

With the current trend in the microfinance community toward the significant scale-up of activities, managers of many MFIs are becoming increasingly aware of the acute need to improve their information systems. Methodological issues, staff development, and even financing are frequently not proving to be the critical constraints to growth. Rather, an institution's ability to track the status of its portfolio in a timely and accurate manner is often the most pressing need. The reliability of the systems tracking this information is in many cases the difference between success and failure of the lending and savings operations and, therefore, of the institution. More accurate, timely, and comprehensive information on operations, especially on the loan portfolio, will strengthen the management's capacity to enhance financial performance and expand client outreach.

Setting up good information systems may necessitate a significant restructuring of the institution, including the reworking of staff responsibilities (sometimes even of some staff qualifications), the redesign of work processes and information flows, the revision and rationalization of financial policies, and significant investment in computer technology. However, the benefits associated with these costs are substantial. Good information is essential for the MFI to perform in an efficient and effective manner. The better the information, the better the MFI can manage its resources.

Good information systems can:

- Improve the work of field staff, enabling them to better monitor their portfolios and provide better services to an increasing number of clients
- Enable supervisors to better monitor their areas of responsibility, pinpointing priority areas that most require attention
- Help senior management to better orchestrate the work of the entire organization and make well-informed operational and strategic decisions by regularly monitoring the health of the institution through a set of well-chosen reports and indicators.

This chapter will interest practitioners who are in the process of setting up, evaluating, or improving their management information systems. In particular, MFIs that are transforming their institutional structure or adding new products will find this chapter of interest. Donors may also wish to understand the characteristics of a good management information system for the MFIs that they are supporting.

---

1. This chapter was written by Tony Sheldon. It draws substantially on Waterfield and Ramsing (1998) and Waterfield and Sheldon (1997).

An Overview of Issues Related to Management Information Systems

At the most fundamental level, it is important to note the distinction between "data" and "information." Relevant data is generated by an institution in many forms: checks made payable to employees, suppliers, and customers; client loan repayment records; and bank withdrawals, deposits, and transfers. It is the task of a management information system to transform this "raw data" (or input) into meaningful information (or output) that can be used by the MFI in its decisionmaking.

Some MFI management information systems are manual, particularly those of MFIs just starting out. However, as MFIs expand, many of them develop computer-based management information systems requiring software programs that are designed to capture and report on the relevant information. Many of the problems in developing and implementing computer-based information systems arise from the complexity of the information to be captured and reported. The most prevalent cause of poorly performing management information systems is a lack of clarity on the part of users and systems designers about precisely what needs to be tracked and reported.

Many MFIs have spent substantial time and money developing information systems that turn out to be disappointing or unsatisfactory due to the following three factors:

- Poor identification of information needs
- Poor communication between management and systems personnel
- Unrealistic expectations about information technology.

Frequently, managers, field staff, board members, and information systems staff do not have a good sense of the complete information needs of their institution. They may be aware of many of the required reports (such as an income statement, balance sheet, or portfolio aging) and several key indicators that need to be tracked, but the precise data inputs and information outputs may be insufficiently defined. If the specifications for a management information system are poorly conceived, the system will never succeed in transforming data inputs into useful management reports.

The starting point in the development of any management information system is to determine what *information* the institution needs to make appropriate decisions and perform well (box 7.1). The key to defin-

Box 7.1 Determining the Information Needs of an MFI

IN ORDER TO DETERMINE THE INFORMATION NEEDS OF AN MFI, it is necessary to identify the users of the information and evaluate the needs of each user group.

- What key information do the users need?
- What key indicators or ratios do the users need to monitor to perform their job well?
- What additional information should the users have to be knowledgeable about the organization's performance and broader goal achievement?
- How might the users' information needs change in the future and how might those changes affect the design of the management information system ?

Source: Author's compilation.

ing information needs is to evaluate the needs of the users of that information. An integral part of this process is a consideration of how information is to be presented and what frequency and timeliness are required. In the system design stage (discussed more fully below), a focus on the specific needs of each user group, including a careful mapping of the flow of information through the institution, is essential to avoid the problem of poor identification of information needs.

Even when information needs are clearly understood and defined by users, MFI managers typically do not speak with the same vocabulary as information systems designers. The language of MFI management (for example, cost centers, portfolio aging, flat amount or declining balance interest rate calculations) is not necessarily understood in depth by systems designers. Likewise, the language of systems designers (databases, operating systems, network platforms) is not readily understood by nontechnical managers. It is crucial that the various users of the management information system not only identify their information needs but also clearly articulate them to the systems designers. The translation of user needs into the kind of specifications required to develop or maintain a management information system is comparable to a rigorous and precise translation of a text from one language to another.

Finally, unrealistic expectations about information technology by potential users also causes frustration and disappointment. A computerized management information system can serve many essential functions, but it will not function any better than the *policies and procedures* that it tracks and reports. Introducing a management information system into an MFI will not solve problems that lie in the underlying structure and work flow of the institution. As mentioned earlier, good information comes at a price; an MFI must be willing to pay that price (for ongoing data entry and maintenance as well as up-front development and purchase) if it intends to reap the benefits of a good management information system.

With good information provided in a useful form and on a timely basis, all the stakeholders in the institution—staff at all levels, clients, board members, donors, investors, regulators—can be provided with the information they need to participate productively in the activities of the MFI.

Three Areas of Management Information Systems

MFI management information systems generally fall into three main areas:

- An accounting system, with the general ledger at its core
- A credit and savings monitoring system, which captures information and provides reports about the performance of each loan disbursed, often with a savings system that monitors all transactions related to client savings
- A system designed to gather data on client impact.

Not all institutions have a management information system that covers all of these areas. The first two (general ledger and loan tracking) almost always exist in some form; however, only MFIs that accept deposits need a system to monitor savings. Client impact data is generally gathered only in an informal manner, and the "information system" that keeps track of this information is often similarly informal. In this discussion the focus is on the first two types of management information systems, particularly loan-tracking software, which is the most problematic component of an MFI's information systems.

Accounting Systems

Although the standards guiding accounting and auditing procedures vary greatly from country to country, there are almost always basic principles that determine the underlying logic of the accounting side of management information systems. Frequently, these standards are developed by a central authority (such as the Financial Accounting Standards Board in the United States) and are applied to institutions that fall within a particular area of the tax code (such as nonprofit or nongovernmental organizations [NGOs]). General ledger software programs incorporate and reflect these accounting standards and conventions. Therefore, finding an existing accounting program that performs at least the basic functions required of a microfinance institution and provides the essential accounting reports (income statement, balance sheet, and cash flow) is a relatively easy task. Management should clearly define the kinds of variations on these basic reports that it will need to oversee operations effectively, such as income statements by branches or balance sheets by funding organizations. The general ledger can then be designed to capture the relevant data and generate reports at the appropriate level of detail.

CHART OF ACCOUNTS. The core of an institution's accounting system is its general ledger. The skeleton of the general ledger is, in turn, the chart of accounts. The design of the chart of accounts reflects a number of fundamental decisions by the institution. The structure and level of detail established will determine the type of information that management will be able to access and analyze in the future. Management must be clear about its information needs and be able to reach a balance between two contrasting considerations. On the one hand, if the chart of accounts captures information at too general a level (for example, by not separating interest income from fees), the system will not provide the kind of detailed information that management needs to make informed decisions. On the other hand, if the chart of accounts is designed to capture too great a level of detail, the system will track needless amounts of data and generate information that is so disaggregated that management cannot identify and interpret trends properly. In addition, the greater the level of detail, the longer and more costly it will be to gather the data and process the information.

Nearly all MFIs make use of *key financial indicators* to monitor the status of their operations (see chapter 9). These financial indicators are based on information that is extracted at least in part from the chart of accounts. Therefore, management should determine the indicators they intend to use and make sure that the chart of accounts is structured to support the generation of those indicators.

The charts of accounts should be designed to meet the needs of management, providing the information with a degree of detail that is meaningful for managers at all levels. Donor, regulatory, and auditing requirements are usually less detailed and, therefore, can be met if management needs are met. (There are some cases, however, in which regulatory bodies will require the use of a specific chart of accounts for institutions under their jurisdiction, especially for formal financial intermediaries.)

In addition to the general ledger, low-cost software is generally available for other accounting operations, such as accounts payable, accounts receivable, and payroll. Depending on the scale and particular needs of the MFI, those additional functions can be automated in the management information system.

The following features should be sought in general ledger software packages (Women's World Banking 1994):

- A system that requires a single input of data to generate various financial reports (for example, those needed by management, auditors, and donors)
- Software that incorporates rigorous accounting standards (for example, does not accept entries that do not balance; supports accrual accounting)
- A flexible chart of accounts structure that allows the organization to track income and expenses by program, branch, funding source, and so on
- A flexible report writer that allows the organization to generate reports by program, branch, funding source, and so on
- The capacity to maintain and report on historical and budget, as well as current, financial information—a "user-friendly" design that includes clear menu layouts, good documentation, and the capacity to support networked operations, if relevant
- Reasonably priced local support, either by phone or in person (particularly during the transition and training periods)
- Relatively modest hard-disk utilization requirements.

Credit and Savings Monitoring Systems

While well-established accounting practices are reflected in general ledger software, there are currently no standards or widely accepted guidelines for the loan-tracking side of a management information system. (Here, "loan-tracking software" and "portfolio system" are used synonymously with "credit and savings monitoring system," including the capacity to track savings-related information.) As a result, each software program designed for loan tracking has its own approach to the information that is tracked, the kinds of reports that are generated, and, most important, the kinds of features that are included. Some of the key features that vary widely among loan-tracking software programs include the types of lending models supported (such as group, individual, or village banking), the methods of calculating interest and fees, the frequency and composition of loan payments, and the format of reports. Each MFI tends to have its own idiosyncratic way of structuring its credit operations, and so an MFI's loan-tracking software attempts to reflect the operational procedures and work flow of the institution.

Because there are no agreed standards for loan-tracking systems and the information to be tracked and reported is relatively complex, institutions face a number of challenges when considering how to improve the loan management component of their management information system. A portfolio system should be designed to work with all major types of financial products that are currently offered (and are likely to be offered in the future). All MFIs offer loans, which are the most complex product for the system to track. Some also offer savings accounts, time deposits, checking accounts, shares, credit cards, insurance policies, or other products. The portfolio system will need to accommodate each of these distinct products.

The system should be designed to establish distinct sets of "rules" for the different kinds of products within each major type of financial product (loans, savings, and so forth). For example, an institution may offer working capital loans, fixed asset loans, small business loans, and solidarity group loans. Each of these types of loans will have distinctly different characteristics or sets of rules. Interest rates, interest calculation methods, maximum allowable amounts and terms, definition of overdue payments, eligible collateral, and many other factors will vary among the different loan products.

Again, contrasting considerations must be balanced. The more financial products the institution offers, the more complex the portfolio system becomes. The more complex the system, the higher the cost of purchasing (or developing) the software, the higher the level of expertise needed to use and support the system, and the higher the risk of programming and data entry errors. A loan-tracking system should be full-featured enough to handle the range of existing and anticipated financial products, but not so complex as to become too difficult or expensive to develop, use, or maintain.

ASSESSING LOAN-TRACKING SOFTWARE. There are three alternative approaches to acquiring loan-tracking software:

- Purchase an "off-the-shelf" software package from either a local developer or an international supplier
- Modify an existing system, incorporating key features required for the specific MFI
- Develop a fully customized system, designed and programmed specifically for the institution.

A decision on which route to take is based largely on the scale of operations of the institution. MFIs can be categorized usefully, if simplistically, into three sizes: small, medium, and large.

Small MFIs are those with fewer than 3,000 clients that have no plans for significant expansion. These MFIs do not expect to convert into formal financial institutions or to offer a broad range of financial products. Consequently, their management information system needs are fairly basic and do not demand a rigorous and versatile portfolio system. These institutions need a relatively simple system that monitors and reports on the quality of the portfolio and can generate the information required for key management indicators.

Medium MFIs are institutions that have from 3,000 to 20,000 clients, are expanding, and offer an array of credit and savings products. These MFIs require a much more rigorous management information system with solid security features and a thorough audit trail, that handles a large volume of transactions, includes the capacity to monitor savings accounts, and will stand up to the scrutiny of banking regulators. These MFIs cannot generally afford the development of a complete, customized loan-tracking system and must, therefore, sacrifice some features and flexibility to make use of an existing package, which may be modified to meet some specific information needs.

Large MFIs exceed or intend to exceed 20,000 clients. These institutions are large enough generally to justify the substantial modification of an existing management information system—or the development of a new system—to more specifically meet their information needs. Although the costs of developing such management information

systems can easily exceed US$100,000, the increased quality of information and management control, as well as the automation of many key tasks, can lead to significant efficiencies in operations of this scale, which justify the high level of investment required.

To decide among the alternatives, the MFI should assess whether an existing software package meets a majority of its portfolio management needs. An initial assessment of software programs should include a careful review of all documentation available and, ideally, a review of any demonstration or trial versions of the software. This initial assessment should focus on major issues of compatibility among the types of financial products supported, basic interest methods supported, and so on, rather than the more technical details, such as procedures for calculating penalties, because these are sometimes difficult to determine from basic documentation. (Appendix 1 provides a summary of the most well-known software packages available.)

When areas of incompatibility are identified, they should be carefully noted for discussion with the software firm. Often incompatibilities can be addressed through undocumented features of the software and can be solved through relatively minor alterations. At other times seemingly minor incompatibilities can completely rule out the system if the necessary modifications affect its core and even extensive programming cannot resolve the issue. This level of incompatibility may lead large MFIs to decide to develop a brand new system (box 7.2).

If a particular software package passes an initial assessment (or if a decision is made to design a new system), the following *framework for loan-tracking software* can serve as a guide to a fuller evaluation of a portfolio management system. (Appendix. 2 amplifies this framework into several key considerations for each category.)

There are six aspects of loan-tracking software that should be evaluated:

- Ease of use
- Features
- Reports
- Security
- Software and hardware issues
- Technical support.

EASE OF USE. A system's value is based in part on how easy it is for staff to use. Several issues should be considered, including the "user-friendliness" of screen design

Box 7.2 Microfinance Institutions with Developed "In-House" Systems

THE ALEXANDRIA BUSINESS ASSOCIATION IN EGYPT PROVIDES individual loans to microentrepreneurs. In 1997 it had approximately 13,000 clients. The association employs the same basic software systems that it used when it started its operations seven years ago. It uses a modified off-the-shelf accounting package and a homemade portfolio system, which are not integrated. Each month the data between the two are reconciled. The Alexandria Business Association describes its accounting system as partially manual because the organization is required by Egyptian law to maintain two accounting books.

The association is in the process of decentralizing its operations. Currently, 3 of its 10 branches are decentralized, which means that there is a management information system employee in the branch who captures applications and receipts. For the other seven branches this function is fulfilled at the head office. Information between decentralized branches and the head office travels on diskette by courier; however, the Alexandria Business Association is currently accepting bids to establish a dedicated leased line. Each branch has one computer, one printer, and one uninterupted power supply (UPS) backup.

Association de Crédit et d'Epargne pour la Production (ACEP) in Senegal provides both individual and solidarity group loans. In 1997 it had about 4,000 clients. It has used the same software system since it began operations. For the accounting, payroll, and fixed assets management system it employs a modified off-the-shelf accounting software package called SAARI, which is widely used in France and in French-speaking countries. For its portfolio-tracking system the association employs a modified version of the U.S. DataEase software. The accounting and the loan-tracking systems are not integrated. For the headquarters, DataEase

Source: Waterfield 1997.

has been upgraded into a local area network (LAN) version. The association has purchased a new Windows-based system to replace the current DOS-based system very soon. Both the accounting and the loan-tracking systems are manual at the branch level. However, each of the five regional offices is equipped with a computer that processes accounting and portfolio data. In addition, each regional office has a printer and a backup power source. The information is transferred by diskette to the head office.

PRODEM is a Bolivian NGO that focuses on serving rural microentrepreneurs with financial services. In 1997 it had 28,000 clients. In 1992 PRODEM established a new data systems department. A systems manager was hired to work with four other department staff members at the national office. Together the department staff has developed a system completely in-house.

The system was designed in the environments of DOS 6.22 and LAN 3.11. The loan portfolio and accounting modules are fully integrated at the national level only. Information from these modules is exported into Excel to produce monthly performance indicators.

Under the current system the information flows between the national office and branches using a variety of systems, depending on the location. The most common method is for the loan portfolio to be sent weekly by each branch to the regional office. Typically, rural branches do not have access to management information systems. The information is consolidated at the regional office with information from all branches in the region. The regional office sends consolidated information (about loan portfolio, accounting, and administration) to the head office monthly via either fax modem or an internet link.

and data entry, the quality of program documentation and of any tutorials, the handling of errors, the availability of help screens, and so forth.

FEATURES. This category includes some of the most important aspects of the software system: user languages, setup options, loan product definitions, lending methodology issues, management of branch office information, overall accounting issues, reports, and security issues.

In the development of any software package, support for multiple-user *languages* should be incorporated into

the software design at the beginning. If an otherwise appealing software package is not available in the language required, the institution should be sure that the design of the software allows for a means of adding more languages, rather than necessitating a major revision of the program.

A robust system provides *setup options,* which require the user to input parameters that serve as the underlying structure for the system, including the widths of various data fields, the structure of client and loan account numbers, and so on. Many of these items, which may appear straightforward, can have far-ranging implications for the use of the system. For example, changing something as seemingly simple as the number of decimal places in the currency field may mean that every data screen and report format needs to be redesigned.

As mentioned previously, the *method of lending* is an area of extreme importance. There are many different lending methods in practice, and a management information system may not appropriately handle the approach used in a specific MFI. For example, to know that a system handles "solidarity group lending" does not mean that it will work for every institution employing solidarity group lending. In some MFIs each group loan is considered a single loan, whereas in other institutions each client has an "individual" loan while mutually guaranteeing the loans of other group members. The chosen management information system must support the lending approaches used by the institution.

Most MFIs define the basic parameters of their *loan product,* which determine interest rate methods, penalty calculation methods, minimum and maximum allowable loan sizes, and so on. The more parameters available, the more flexible the program will be in terms of supporting multiple lending and savings products. However, the greater complexity may imply a need for more advanced systems maintenance.

If an MFI has *branch offices,* each will need its own management information system database. The head office then needs a means by which to consolidate that data to generate reports for the institution as a whole. The management information system needs to be designed with these decentralization and consolidation requirements in mind.

A good loan portfolio package will allow for easy *transfer and reconciliation* of relevant data to the accounting system, including summary information on disbursements, repayments, interest and fee income, savings transactions, and so forth. The data for these transactions on the loan-tracking side of the management information system must tally with the comparable data on its accounting side. Some software packages feature fully integrated loan-tracking and accounting capabilities that transfer relevant data automatically; however, such systems are expensive and unnecessary for most MFIs. Most institutions need a loan-tracking system that produces a transaction report that summarizes the relevant information. This information is then reconciled with the accounting transactions on a timely basis.

REPORTS. When selecting a portfolio system, it is crucial to review the precise definitions of how information is presented to determine if the system is suitable for the institution's needs. For example, it is not sufficient to know that the system produces an "aging report" without knowing the specifics of how the aging report is structured.

The type of reports the MFI requires, as well as the format and content of those reports, depends on several factors, including the lending methodologies used, the services offered, the staffing structure, and the key indicators chosen by management. Users of reports within the MFI can be grouped into three broad categories: field staff needing day-to-day, detailed operational information; supervisors needing reports that facilitate oversight of field staff; and senior management and board members looking for more strategic information. There are also external users of reports, including auditors, regulators, donors, investors, and clients (box 7.3).

Key issues in report design include:

- *Categorization and level of detail.* Similar information may need to be presented at varying levels of aggregation (for example, portfolio quality by individual loan officer, by branch office, by region, by overall institution).
- *Frequency and timeliness.* Because the purpose of providing information is to enable staff to take constructive actions, appropriate frequency and timeliness is critical.
- *Performance indicators.* Key performance indicators that management monitors need to be generated, preferably including trend information.

SECURITY. Security features protect data, restrict user access, and limit possible fraud. Security features cannot guarantee that fraud or data loss will not occur, but they can minimize the likelihood and negative effects of such occurrences.

In general, information on computer systems should be protected against two threats:

- Purposeful attempts to gain unauthorized access to data or to certain user functions
- Data corruption from hardware, software, or power failures.

These threats imply two different types of security. The first requires securing data and user routines from unauthorized use. For example, user routines such as loan disbursement and loan repayment should not be accessible by all staff. This type of security is referred to

---

Box 7.3 Improving Reporting Formats: Experience of the Workers Bank of Jamaica

THE WORKERS BANK OF JAMAICA GREW OUT OF THE Government Savings Bank, established in 1870. The Workers Bank inherited the Post Office Banking Network, with almost 250 post office banking windows where small savers maintained accounts. By 1995 the Post Office Division had more than 95,000 small savers with more than US$10 million in deposits. That same year the bank decided to set up a microbanking unit to expand microfinance services by offering microloans through the Post Office Division.

At that time the bank was in the early stages of developing a comprehensive management information system. It determined that it needed to purchase a system that would manage its small loans and the small savings accounts in the Post Office Division until the larger management information system was fully operational. After analyzing several systems, the bank chose an internationally available system to manage its postal banking operation.

Although the system provided adequate capabilities for inputting information and making financial calculations, the bank found its standardized reports insufficient. Management was not receiving the accurate and timely information it needed about portfolio activity by loan officer, post office, and region. And neither loan officers nor managers were getting reports that would enable them to properly manage a microloan portfolio with weekly payment cycles. To help develop report formats that would better meet the bank's needs in managing its new microloan portfolio, the bank hired an independent consultant with many years of experience in computer programming and managing MFIs to advise on design.

The new reporting formats meet the needs of loan officers and managers for controlling delinquency and managing a growing microloan portfolio. They provide timely and accurate information, are easy to use, and customize information to fit the needs of users.

Source: Waterfield and Ramsing 1998.

---

as "system security" and includes such features as user passwords. The second type of threat requires frequent backup of data and a method to re-index lost or corrupted data. This type of security is called "data security."

An MFI should have as many strong security features as possible in the software. These features should extend beyond basic passwords entered by staff, which grant them access to different levels of activity, to thorough audit trails that determine who can input and change specific information in the database. In addition, a secure system should have means to prohibit tampering with the databases from outside the system.

SOFTWARE AND HARDWARE ISSUES. In evaluating loan-tracking software, a number of key technical issues must be explored. (For a more complete treatment of these software and hardware issues, see Waterfield and Ramsing 1997.) These include should the MFI run its system on a network, and if so, what kind of network is most appropriate, and which operating system should the software run on (DOS, Windows, Windows 98, or Windows NT).

There are essentially four applications of personal computer architecture for MFIs:

- Stand-alone computers
- Multiple computers in a peer-to-peer network

- Multiple computers in a server-based local area network (LAN)
- Wide-area networks that connect computers in distant locations (WAN).

Networks offer many advantages but they also add additional complexity. Many MFIs might be concerned about installing a network, considering them to be both expensive and heavily dependent on technical support. However, computer networking technology now supports simple networks requiring fairly minimal technical support.

Benefits gained from a simple peer-to-peer network are associated with information efficiency. In general, many people need access to information at the same time. In a networked system, critical information is stored on one user's computer but is available to all staff who need access to it. Networking requires more sophisticated programming techniques to ensure data integrity, so that when more than one person is accessing the same data, only one is able to modify the data at a time. While a peer-to-peer approach is not recommended for a growth-oriented MFI, it could be implemented in smaller MFIs that want the benefits of networking at minimal cost.

Growth-oriented and larger MFIs could make efficiency gains by employing a "server-based" *local area*

Box 7.4 Management Information Systems at the Association for the Development of Microenterprises, Dominican Republic

THE ASSOCIATION FOR THE DEVELOPMENT OF Microenterprises (ADEMI), one of the early prominent microcredit programs in Latin America, was also one of the first to automate its information systems. In 1984 it developed a database system that was advanced enough even to automate the printing of loan contracts and client repayment vouchers and let senior managers monitor the balance of their bank accounts directly from their desktop computers.

With technological changes and growth to more than 18,000 loans, ADEMI revamped its management information system in 1994. Nearly all the work was done in-house by an experienced management information system department. As with the earlier system, ADEMI chose to use the

more advanced UNIX operating system instead of the more common PC-based systems. The system consists of fully integrated modules for loan portfolio, savings data (only 170 time deposits), accounting, client data, payroll, and fixed assets.

The system allows all the Santo Domingo offices and the regional offices to be connected on line. Other branch offices, however, are not connected into the management information system. They send in transaction receipts every few days to the regional office, where information is input and reports are generated. These reports are then sent to the branch offices, where they are compared with independent systems used by the branches to verify the accuracy and completeness of data entry.

Source: Waterfield 1997.

---

network (LAN). A server is a personal computer with a faster processor, more memory, and more hard disk space than a typical stand-alone computer. The data to be broadly accessible is stored on the network. Network cards and cables connect the server to individual computers, enabling each user to access the information stored on the server. Security and data integrity issues are handled by the network software and by the database system.

LANs consist of computers in the same building connected by cables. Wide area networks (WANs) are computers that are connected via phone lines, so that remote offices can access and transfer data as if they were in the same place. However, WANs are beyond the technical and cost capabilities of most MFIs. For MFIs with remote branch offices, the best alternative for transferring data is by modem at the end of the day or by diskette on a weekly or monthly basis.

Most loan-tracking systems operate in DOS, which has been adequate for MFIs of all scales. There is no real restriction on the number of clients or transactions that a DOS-based system can process. Practically speaking, however, systems designed for use a few years from now will need to be redesigned to work under one of the Windows operating systems. Making a substantial investment in a DOS-based system should be done only after careful thought.

Because DOS was developed before the memory capacity of personal computers was as large as it is now,

DOS-based systems often have a problem accessing sufficient memory to run efficiently. Also, the operating speed of systems depends heavily on the programming language used, the level of hardware, the amount of memory, and, even more important, the skill level of the programmer. A system may appear to operate well initially, but after reaching a certain number of clients or accumulating a year's worth of information it may slow down unacceptably. In selecting a system, it is critical to carefully assess the future scale of activity and the capacity of each system under consideration.

SUPPORT. The role of the software provider does not end when the system is installed. There is always a need for continuing support to fix bugs, train staff, and modify the program. This need for ongoing support is the primary reason that many MFIs develop their own customized systems. They then have the in-house capacity to provide these support services, albeit at substantial cost. However, many MFIs cannot afford to have a systems designer on staff and must depend on outside support. If it is available locally, there is a good chance that the support will be reliable. However, many systems currently provide remote support, which is quite risky as well as potentially expensive. Many problems cannot be communicated and resolved quickly by e-mail, phone, or courier. Because an MFI cannot afford to have its management information system not functioning for an extended period of time, the viability of remote support should be explored carefully.

Other considerations to make in choosing loan-tracking systems include:

- Whether the system has been used internationally
- Whether the system has been in use for a sufficient amount of time to be well tested and to have reached a high level of reliability
- Whether the company supporting the system can make a strong case that it is able to support the MFI's operations (that is, provide training and technical assistance)
- Whether the system has already been used for microfinance (as opposed to commercial banking).

Client Impact Tracking Systems

Most MFIs want to track socioeconomic and impact data (that is, the number of jobs created, the number of clients moving out of poverty). However, client impact tracking is even less standardized than portfolio management and presents major challenges to MFIs looking for appropriate software packages. Virtually no off-the-shelf system for monitoring impact is currently available. Institutions that choose to monitor impact have normally selected information-gathering approaches that complement their other information collection processes. For example, they may use data already gathered in the loan application process and then keep track of this information on a spreadsheet.

One approach that is often used to track impact-related information is to incorporate the relevant data into the loan-tracking system. Special screens and reports can be designed in a customized system. However, existing software packages frequently include several "user-defined" fields in client and loan records. These can be set up to track and report on significant impact-related data.

Installing a Management Information System

Many managers do not fully comprehend the substantial process that needs to be followed when selecting and installing a management information system. The task is often much greater than typically envisioned. The interrelationship between the management information system and the entire structure and operating procedures of the institution means that in some cases the installation of a system must be done concurrently with the restructuring of the entire organization.

The following framework presents a series of overlapping steps involved in implementing a management information system.

Institutional Assessment

Before deciding on a management information system the MFI must assess the "fit" between the MFI's practices—both present and future—and the software's capabilities. As stated previously, management information systems differ not only in philosophy and approach but also in features and capabilities. Any selection process needs to begin with absolute clarity about the expected functionality of the system.

Configuration

This stage follows closely on the work done in the institutional assessment. Configuration consists primarily of:

- *The general ledger,* the basis of which is the chart of accounts. Sometimes modification of the existing chart of accounts is required to meet the redefined

---

Box 7.5 Framework for a Management Information System at Freedom From Hunger

FREEDOM FROM HUNGER, A SUCCESSFUL INTERNATIONAL NGO operating out of Davis, California, has developed a "Framework for Designing a Management Information System." The framework consists of 17 steps for designing and implementing an accounting and management information system for MFIs. Each step includes a specific list of questions and issues pertaining to each step.

The framework was developed to strengthen and streamline the accounting system of the Reseau des Caisses Populaires, Freedom From Hunger's partner in Burkina Faso. The framework may be used as an implementation or management tool to guide the user through key issues in assessing the MFI's information needs, the system alternatives available, and system implementation. The tool provides the user with a logical structure to examine the management information system needs both in the field and at headquarters. (For detailed information on the assessment framework see SEEP Network 1996.)

Source: SEEP Network 1996.

needs of the institution as well as any requirements or limitations of the software package.

- *Loan-tracking systems,* which define the various financial products, each with its own specific characteristics, such as minimum and maximum amounts, interest rate methods, the various "linkages" that the MFI uses between different accounts (such as blocking savings when a client has a loan), and treatment of delinquency.
- *The structure of branch relationships,* which determines how information will be shared and consolidated among branches.

If the initial assessment has been doing well, the configuration of the system can be handled fairly straightforwardly, provided the MFI's needs are fully compatible with the software's capabilities. If changes to the software are needed to accommodate the requirements of the MFI, then the process of software modification begins.

Software Modifications

This is potentially the most costly and time-consuming component of installing a management information system. If the software package has not been used by other MFIs or similar operating environments (such as different types of MFIs in different countries) or if the software has not previously been adapted to a wide variety of operating methodologies (for example, individual lending or group lending), there may be a need for major modifications. Extensive programming may still be required if the MFI is unwilling to compromise on its operating methods and accounting conventions, even if the software package is nearly exhaustive in functionality.

The modification process is costly and time-consuming for several reasons. The source code (or underlying logic and commands of the software) for a complex system can only be modified by a handful of people—ideally, the original programmers. Any change, no matter how minor, needs to be carefully tested and debugged, because a change in one area of the program can affect what seem to be wholly unrelated areas of the program. Program modification should only be undertaken by highly qualified programmers and only if the MFI cannot perform its essential work by using a packaged loan tracking system.

Testing

Once the software design is finalized, it is essential to run a rigorous test of the system with actual data. This testing phase serves two purposes: it allows the behavior of the system to be carefully studied, identifying any bugs or problem areas needing changes; and it allows the development of a strategy for data conversion or input of the initial data to the system.

For the general ledger, testing consists of processing sample transactions, including receipts of income, payment of checks, and journal entries. Trial balance and financial statements should be generated, with the results confirmed and presented in the formats desired by the institution.

For loan tracking, the testing phase is more complex and includes verifying that crucial procedures are handled correctly. Key questions include:

- Are repayment schedules, interest charges, penalties, and delinquencies being properly calculated?
- Does the system crash inexplicably?
- Does the network function adequately?
- Does the system allow for corrections of data entered in error?
- Are there user-friendliness issues that need to be addressed?

Data Transfer

This is another time-consuming and costly process. The volume of start-up information that must be entered can be substantial. For the portfolio system, inputting names and other data on clients as well as all outstanding balances for loans and savings accounts is extremely time consuming. At a minimum for the general ledger, opening amounts for all balance sheet accounts must be entered.

A frequently encountered problem is incompatibility between the way the previous system handled transactions and the way the new management information system treats the same transactions. For example, if delinquency is calculated even slightly differently by the two systems, the new system may calculate penalties on outstanding loans in a way not agreed to with the client.

It is often difficult to predict precisely how long or difficult this data transfer process will be, even if there has been a careful initial assessment. One way to avoid these problems is to continue to use the existing portfolio system until all outstanding loans are repaid, entering only new loans into the new system.

Training

Because a full-featured management information system is complex, implementation may require major shifts in the operational procedures of an institution, requiring extensive training at all levels of staff.

Parallel Operations

After data transfer and staff training, the new management information system is ready to be used. However, it is important to run the new system in parallel with the old system. This is essential to ensure that the new system runs reliably and generates reports that can be trusted.

During the period of parallel operation, data should be entered into both systems and the outputs carefully compared. Any discrepancies should be evaluated and accounted for. Any errors or bugs in the new system should be carefully documented and corrected.

The duration of parallel operations can vary, but it should generally last at least two months to ensure that nearly every client has come to make at least one payment and that the system has gone through two month-end closing processes. Once management is satisfied that the new system is performing well, the old system can be discontinued, but all printouts and data files should be carefully stored for future reference (box 7.6).

Ongoing Support and Maintenance

As discussed previously, the institution's need for management information system support continues once the system is installed. The cost of support will depend on how stable and reliable the system is and will normally decline as the MFI grows more experienced with it and thus more capable of resolving problems.

There are two important lessons that can be gleaned from the experience of MFIs in installing management information systems:

- An institution should be content with the essentials. An MFI should not seek a management information

---

> ### Box 7.6 Running Parallel Operations in the Fédération des Caisses d'Epargne et de Crédit Agricole Mutuel, Benin
>
> IN THE LOCAL CREDIT UNIONS OF THE FÉDÉRATION DES Caisses d'Epargne et de Crédit Agricole Mutuel, accounting was done manually until computers started slowly to be introduced and tested in 1993. For the first credit unions to be computerized, it was required that accounting be recorded both manually and by computer for one full year, so that the staff could become fully acquainted with the new software and procedures and so that the information systems technicians could make necessary adjustments to the software. As experience is gained by both parties, managers of the federation believe the required period for running accounting in parallel could be brought down to two months.
>
> *Source:* Contributed by Cecile Fruman, Sustainable Banking with the Poor Project, World Bank.

---

system that offers every ideal feature. The more that is demanded of a system , the more complex that system becomes and the less likely it is to work correctly and trouble free.

- An MFI should consider adapting some of its procedures to the standards of the loan-tracking system. Of course, this would ideally function the other way around: a management information system would be capable of implementing every aspect of an institution's policies and procedures. However, acceptance of existing features that do not fundamentally alter the institution's goals and objectives may save thousands of dollars and months of customizing time.

Appendix 1. Overview of Commercial Management Information System Software Packages

There are no set prices for commercial management information software packages.[1] Pricing depends on specific conditions in each installation, such as the scale of the MFI, the extent of customization, and the availability of local technicians who the software firm can call on. None of the commercial firms referenced

---

1. This appendix is excerpted from Waterfield (1997).

in this overview provided a set price; however, price ranges and typical contract prices have been included where possible.

IPC Banking System

The IPC banking system was developed over seven years by IPC Consulting for use in MFIs participating in long-term technical assistance contracts and has never been installed independent of a technical assistance contract. The system is currently used in Albania, Bolivia, Brazil, Colombia, Costa Rica, El Salvador, Paraguay, Russia, Uganda, and Ukraine.

The system runs in DOS on stand-alone PCs and Novell or Windows networks. It contains modules for loan monitoring, savings, fixed deposit, and accounting. It provides extensive support of the entire lending process, starting with registration of application, support for loan application analysis, integrated generation of loan agreement and payment plan, wide range of possible payment plans, and various interest rate calculation procedures. The system supports a full range of teller-based operations, including monitoring cash and check payments, monitoring various cashiers, and a money-changing function.

IPC personnel visit on site for installation, configuration, and training. Maintenance contracts are available, which provide for software modifications and updates. The system price depends on the type of contract, the extent of modifications required, and the number of installations involved, but the minimum contract amount considered is US$50,000.

The FAO Microbanking System

FAO's Microbanker was developed over the past 10 years and is currently running in 900 installations in more than 20 countries in Asia, Africa, Latin America and the Caribbean, Eastern Europe, and some former Soviet Union republics.

The system was developed as a low-cost computer software alternative for the automation of banking operations for small and medium-size financial intermediaries. It runs on basic PC equipment and is flexible enough to work as a single teller, a stand-alone installation, or as a multiteller installation.

The SRTE 2.0 version of the system covers loans, savings accounts, time deposits, current accounts, customer information, and general ledger in one integrated package. EXTE, the extended version of the system, allows the introduction of substantial modifications and customization through access to parts of the source code. Institutions with procedures that differ substantially from standard systems may need to acquire this version of the software.

The purchase of the software includes a warranty support from an authorized support provider by phone, fax, or email for three months. FAO recommends that an authorized support provider also be contracted to help with installation and customization and that a contract for longer-term assistance be established with one of the support providers when the warranty period has expired.

The current price (1997) of the SRTE 2.0 is US$800 for each installation. This includes an unlimited number of users per installation, but no customization can be made, nor is any installation support available for this price. The access fee of the customizable EXTE version is US$8,000. Customization can only be done for additional fees by an authorized support provider. The cost of a contract for assistance with minor customization and configuration assistance, installation, and basic training, typically runs between US$40,000 and US$70,000, depending on the size of the MFI and the extent of the modifications.

The Reliance Credit Union Management System

This system is owned by CUSA Technologies, Inc. (CTI), and has been marketed primarily to credit unions in the United States, although the company is also working at developing an international market.

It is currently installed in over 100 locations in the United States, and installation procedures are currently under way in Puerto Rico, Central America, and Australia (26 credit unions with more than 150 branches). The system is currently available in English and Spanish. A French version is in development.

The Reliance software incorporates modules for on-line teller transactions, loan processing, mortgage lending, integrated general ledger, ATM transaction processing, credit card processing, electronic payroll processing, share draft processing, and signature and picture verification.

Technical assistance is available 12 hours per day, Monday to Saturday, by phone and Internet. CTI is currently establishing a Spanish support center (a distributor) in Puerto Rico.

System pricing is by module, by asset size, and by the number of system users. CTI was reluctant to provide any price estimates, but indicated that the system is generally priced for larger institutions.

The SiBanque System

The SiBanque system is supported by Centre International de Credit Mutuel (CICM) in France. The system is currently available in French and English, but may be translated to other languages. SiBanque is currently installed in approximately 100 offices in 8 institutions in Burundi, Cameroon, Congo, Guinea, Mali, and Senegal.

The system is set up for "front office" and "back office" transactions, is oriented toward credit union structures, and provides some configuration through the use of parameters. It is a dBase-compatible system that operates on DOS.

Since the software is not supported by a commercial software firm, the pricing situation is nonstandard. The software itself does not have a cost, but CICM requires MFI staff to be trained as a requirement prior to installation. The cost of this training is billed to the client. Maintenance is contracted for a fee negotiated with the client.

Solace for Workgroups

This system is owned by Solace, an Australian software firm, but its distribution has been licensed to Decentralized Banking Solutions (DBS), a South African firm actively marketing the software to the microfinance community. The system is currently available in English and is installed in 13 institutions in Australia, New Zealand, South Africa, and Zimbabwe.

The system runs on Windows 95, Windows NT, UNIX, and AS400 operating systems. The teller-based system supports savings, loan, checking, and equity accounts. It provides for printing of passbooks and receipts and supports audit inquiries. It can be used in a wide range of institutional settings, including networks of more than 200 users. Technical support is provided via the Internet, with potential local support through a joint venture with a local partner when business volume warrants.

Price is based on a nominal solace software purchase fee of US$3,000 per user terminal (for example, an installation requiring access to 20 computers would cost US$60,000) plus run-time costs and an annual support fee dependent upon local requirements and conditions. Annual support is often based on the number of terminals as well. A typical installation, therefore, can cost in excess of US$100,000, and at least one installation costs US$370,000, all expenses included.

Appendix 2. Criteria For Evaluating Loan Tracking Software

Ease of use	*Hardware/software issues*
Documentation	Programming language
Tutorials	Data storage format
Error handling	Network support
Help screens	Operating system
Interface	Access speed
Features	*Support*
Languages	Customization available?
Setup options	Training
Methodology issues	Cost issues
Loan product definition	
multiple loan products	*Reports*
principal repayment methods	Existing reports
monitoring methods	New reports
fund accounting of portfolio	Print preview
data disaggregation	Printers supported
interest calculations	Width of reports
fee calculations	
savings	*Security*
Branch office management and consolidation	Passwords and levels of authorization
Linkages between accounting and portfolio	Data modification
	Backup procedures
	Audit trails

Source: Developed by Waterfield and Sheldon (1997) for Women's World Banking.

Sources and Further Reading

SEEP (Small Enterprise Education and Promotion) Network. 1995. *Financial Ratio Analysis of Micro-Finance Institutions.* New York: PACT Publications.

——. 1996. *Moving Forward: Tools for Sustainability and Expansion.* New York: PACT Publications.

Waterfield, Charles. 1997. "Budgeting for New Information Systems for Mature Microfinance Organizations." Calmeadow. Toronto, Canada.

Waterfield, Charles, and Nick Ramsing. 1998. "Management Information Systems for Microfinance Institutions: A Handbook." Prepared for CGAP (Consultative Group to Assist the Poorest) by Deloitte Touche Tohmatsu International, in association with MEDA Trade & Consulting and Shorebank Advisory Services, Washington, D.C.

Waterfield, Charles, and Tony Sheldon. 1997. "Assessing and Selecting Loan Tracking Software Systems." Women's World Banking, New York.

Women's World Banking. 1994. *Principles and Practices of Financial Management.* New York.

Part III–
Measuring
Performance and
Managing Viability

CHAPTER EIGHT

Adjusting Financial Statements

To analyze the financial performance of MFIs properly, it is necessary to ensure that their financial statements are consistent with generally accepted accounting principles. Due to the structure of many microfinance institutions and their initial reliance on donor funding, adjustments to balance sheets and income statements are often needed before the financial performance can be analyzed (see chapter 9). There are generally two types of adjustments required: those that are necessary to adhere to proper accounting standards, which are often neglected in MFIs, and those that restate financial results to reflect more accurately the full financial position of the MFI.

The first type requires accounting entries that adjust an MFI's financial statements. The amount and type of adjustment required will vary with each MFI, depending on its adherence to standard accounting principles.[1] These adjustments include:

- *Accounting for loan losses and loan loss provisions.* MFIs that fail to properly consider potential or existing loan losses, understate total expenses, and overstate the value of the loan portfolio.
- *Accounting for depreciation of fixed assets.* Failing to depreciate or inaccurately depreciating fixed assets understates the true expense of operations.
- *Accounting for accrued interest and accrued interest expense.* Accruing interest revenue on delinquent loans results in higher stated revenue than actually received, thereby overstating profits, and failure to accrue interest expense on liabilities understates expenses.

The second type of adjustments do not necessarily have to be formally recorded in the MFI's financial state-

ments. This decision would be made by each MFI or reader individually. However, the following adjustments should be made (either on the financial statements or in an external spreadsheet) to reflect the unique nature of MFIs and to account for the benefit of donor financing:

- *Accounting for subsidies.* Donor funding either for loan capital to on-lend or to cover operating expenses is generally provided as either grants or concessional loans (loans with lower than market rates of interest) and therefore contains a subsidy to the MFI.
- *Accounting for inflation.* The cost of inflation results in a loss in the real value of equity and other balance sheet accounts.

These adjustments are needed to assess the MFI in an accurate and meaningful manner and to allow for comparisons among institutions to some extent.

Finally, MFIs may wish to restate their financial statements in "constant currency terms," particularly if they are operating in a highly inflationary environment. This means expressing the financial results in *real* rather than *nominal* terms by converting financial data from previous year nominal values (in local currency) to constant, present-year values. This permits year-over-year comparisons and performance trend analysis.

This chapter presents the reasons that adjustments should be made, ways to determine the appropriate amount of adjustments, and ways to make them. Examples of adjusted financial statements for subsidies and inflation are provided in the appendixes. This chapter will be of interest primarily to practitioners or consultants evaluating MFIs. To make the most use of this chapter, it is necessary to have some understanding of

---

1. Portions of this chapter are based on material originally published in Ledgerwood 1996.

accounting and financial analysis. Readers who are not familiar with financial statements may wish to provide this chapter to the financial manager of an MFI or a financial consultant who is working with the MFI. (For basic instruction in accounting and the creation of financial statements, see Ledgerwood and Moloney 1996.)

Accounting Adjustments

Among the adjustments that are often needed before the financial performance of an MFI can be analyzed are accounting entries that adjust an MFI's financial statements so that they adhere to proper accounting standards. These adjustments include accounting for loan losses, accounting for depreciation of fixed assets, and accounting for accrued interest and accrued interest expense.

Accounting for Loan Losses

Accounting for loan losses is an important element of MFI financial management and one of the most poorly managed. To accurately reflect the financial performance of an MFI, it is necessary to determine how much of the portfolio is generating revenue and how much is likely to be unrecoverable. This is done by examining the quality of the loan portfolio, creating a loan loss reserve, and periodically writing off loans.

Many MFIs do not like to make loan loss reserves because they are anxious to report their expenses as low as possible and do not want to admit (to donors or others) that some of the loans they have made are not performing. Further, many MFIs choose to maintain bad loans on the books because they feel that if they were to write off a loan, all efforts to collect it would stop. Initially, MFIs may avoid accounting for loans losses, but as MFIs mature and their exponential growth slows down, the problem becomes more significant. Carrying loans on the books that have little or no chance of being repaid overstates the assets on the balance sheet and results in a lower-than-expected yield on assets (this is reflected in lower revenue than expected based on the effective yield calculation detailed in chapter 5). Furthermore, accurately accounting for loan losses on a periodic basis saves the MFI from taking a large loss (and a consequent increase in expenses) all at one time for loans that were made over a period of years (Stearns 1991). Loan losses should be recorded close to the period in which the loan was made.

In order to accurately account for loan losses, the first step is to determine the quality of the loan portfolio. This is done by referring to the "portfolio report" (table 8.1).

THE PORTFOLIO REPORT. One of the most important monitoring tools of an MFI is its portfolio report, which provides information on the *quality* of the loan portfolio and the size of the lending activities. Since the loan portfolio is most often the MFI's largest asset and, therefore, its main revenue-generating asset, ensuring accurate and timely reporting of the portfolio is crucial to the financial management of an MFI.

Table 8.1 Sample Portfolio Report

Portfolio data	1995	1994	1993
Total value of loans disbursed during the period	160,000	130,000	88,000
Total number of loans disbursed during the period	1,600	1,300	1,100
Number of active borrowers (end of period)	1,800	1,550	1,320
Portfolio outstanding (end of period)	84,000	70,000	52,000
Average outstanding balance of loans	75,000	61,000	45,000
Value of payments in arrears (end of period)	7,000	9,000	10,000
Value of outstanding balance of loans in arrears	18,000	20,000	20,000
Value of loans written off during the period	500	3,000	0
Average initial loan size	100	100	80
Average loan term (months)	12	12	12
Average number of credit officers during the period	6	6	4

Source: SEEP Network and Calmeadow 1995

Portfolio outstanding refers to *the principal amount of loans outstanding*. Projected interest is not usually considered part of the portfolio. Principal outstanding is an asset for an MFI; interest contributes to the income of an MFI and is recorded as revenue.

Readers should note that some MFIs *capitalize* (record as an asset on the balance sheet) the interest revenue expected when the loan is disbursed (particularly if they are operating with British accounting standards) or when the loan term has ended and an outstanding balance is still remaining. For the purposes of this handbook, we assume that interest is not recorded until received. However, those readers working with MFIs that do capitalize interest revenue should be aware that this results in higher total assets than if the MFI did not capitalize interest payments and affects the way in which loan payments are recorded for accounting purposes.

When a loan payment is received, if interest has *not* been capitalized, interest revenue is recorded on the income statement as an increase in revenue, and the principal repaid is recorded on the balance sheet as a reduction in loans outstanding (asset). For MFIs that capitalize interest, the entire loan payment amount is recorded as a reduction in the loan portfolio, since interest revenue was recorded (on the income statement) when the loan was made (see the section on accounting for accrued interest and accrued interest expenses below).

Both the "value of payments in arrears" and the "value of outstanding balance of loans in arrears" refer to loans that have an amount that has come due and has not been received. The "value of payments in arrears" includes only the amount that has come due and not been received, while the "value of outstanding balance of loans in arrears" includes the total amount of loans outstanding, including the amount that has not yet become due, of loans that have an amount in arrears. This is commonly referred to as the "portfolio at risk."

Note that the terms "arrears," "late payments," "overdue," "past due," "delinquent," and "default" are often used interchangeably. Generally, loans that are "in arrears, past-due, and overdue" have become due and have not been paid. These are also referred to as delinquent loans (that is, "this loan is delinquent" means it has an amount that is owing—is in arrears, past due, overdue—and has not been paid). To say that loans are in *default* is also referring to delinquent loans, but most often to loans that have been or are about to be written off (discussed below). Defaulted loans are often called such if there is little hope of ever receiving payment.

Some MFIs determine that a loan is delinquent if no payment was received on the due date. However, many loans are paid within a few days of the due date, and other MFIs allow a short period for late payments and do not consider a loan delinquent until one or two weeks or payment periods have passed.

Some MFIs fail to consider the amount of *time* a loan is in arrears and base the likelihood of default (loan loss) more on the *term* of the loan—in other words, a loan is reported as overdue when the loan term ends, rather than after a certain period of time in which no payments have been received. This handbook does not take into account whether or not the loan term has ended. Any loan that has an amount in arrears is considered delinquent, based on the number of days it has been in arrears.

MFIs must also determine whether or not they consider the entire outstanding balance of loans that have an amount in arrears (portfolio at risk) to be delinquent or just the amount that has become due and has not been received. Generally, MFIs should consider the entire outstanding amount as delinquent, because this is the amount that is actually at risk (that is, if the borrower has missed a payment, chances are he or she may miss more payments or will simply stop repaying the loan all together).

A *delinquent* loan becomes a *defaulted* loan when the chance of recovery becomes minimal. Defaulted loans result in loan write-offs. Write-offs should be considered after a certain period of time has passed and the loan has not been repaid. The decision to write off a loan and the timing of doing so are based on the policies of the MFI. Some MFIs choose to write loans off relatively quickly so that their balance sheets do not reflect basically worthless assets. Others choose not to write off loans as long as there is a remote possibility of collecting the loan. Regardless of when write-offs take place, it is important that an MFI have an adequate loan loss reserve (discussed below) so that the net value of loans stated on the balance sheet accurately reflects the amount of revenue-generating assets.

Based on an analysis of the quality of the loan portfolio, managers can determine what percentage of the loans is likely to default. To reflect this risk and the corresponding true value of the loan portfolio accurately, it is necessary to create a balance sheet account called the "loan loss reserve."

LOAN LOSS RESERVE. A loan loss reserve is an account that represents the amount of outstanding principal that is not expected to be recovered by an MFI. It is the amount "reserved" to cover losses of the loan portfolio. The loan loss reserve is recorded as a *negative* (or contra) asset on the balance sheet. The loan loss reserve *reduces* the net portfolio outstanding. (Some MFIs record the loan loss reserve as a liability. The net effect is the same.)

The amount of the loan loss reserve should be based on historical information regarding loan defaults and the amount of time loans have been delinquent. Past performance of delinquent loans is the most important indicator for predicting future performance.

To determine an adequate loan loss reserve, an *aging analysis* should be performed periodically (monthly or quarterly). Aging analysis refers simply to the classification of delinquent loans into the periods of time that they have been in arrears. Loan portfolios are aged using categories such as 1–30 days, 31–60 days, 61–90 days, 91–120 days, and more than 120 days. *The choice of aging category depends on the frequency of payments and the loan terms of the MFI.* Generally, the categories should be based on one or two payment periods (weekly, biweekly, monthly, and so on).

In the aging analysis, the entire outstanding balance of the loan that is in arrears (portfolio at risk) is considered.

The purpose of calculating an *aged* portfolio at risk is that it allows MFIs to estimate the required loan loss reserve. The longer a loan has been delinquent, the greater the likelihood of default and, therefore, the greater the need for a loan loss reserve. Aged portfolio at risk reports should be compared over time with previous reports to determine if the portfolio at risk is increasing or decreasing and to determine if new policies implemented to control delinquencies are working. This is particularly important if the portfolio is growing rapidly, because recording a large number of new loans can hide a delinquency problem (that is, the overall loan quality can appear good because a large portion of loans may not have become due).

Once an aging analysis has been completed, the loan loss reserve is established based on the likelihood of loan recovery for each aging category. (The loan loss reserve as a percentage of loans outstanding may be regulated in some countries, which would be applicable if the MFI is regulated as a formal financial institution.) For example, if approximately 10 percent of loans that are past due less than 30 days have historically defaulted, a provision of 10 percent should be created. If 50 percent of loans that are past due greater than 30 days but less than 90 days have historically defaulted, a 50 percent provision should be created (table 8.2).

Once the loan loss reserve is calculated, it is then necessary to compare it to the existing loan loss reserve (if there is one) on the balance sheet and determine if it needs to be increased. Increases in loan loss reserves are made by creating a *loan loss provision.*

LOAN LOSS PROVISION. The loan loss provision is the amount expensed in a period to increase the loan loss reserve to an adequate level to cover expected defaults of the loan portfolio. It is based on the difference between the required loan loss reserve and the current outstanding loan loss reserve.

Table 8.2 Sample Loan Loss Reserve Calculation, December 31, 1995

	(A) Number of loans past due	(B) Portfolio at risk (outstanding balance)	(C) Loan loss reserve (%)	(D) Loan loss reserve ($) (B) x (C)
1–30 days past due	200	8,750	10	875
31–60 days past due	75	5,000	50	2,500
61–90 days past due	60	2,500	75	1,875
90–120 days past due	15	1,100	100	1,100
> 120 days past due	10	650	100	650
Total	360	18,000	—	7,000

Source: SEEP Network and Calmeadow 1995.

To make the adjustment, the first time a loan loss reserve is created, a loan loss provision is recorded on the *income statement* as an expense (debit) in an amount equal to the required loan loss reserve. The loan loss reserve is then recorded on the balance sheet as a negative asset (credit). This reduces the net outstanding loan portfolio. Subsequent loan loss provisions are recorded on the income statement in the amount necessary to increase the loan loss reserve to its required level. Once debited on the income statement, the amount is added (credited) to the existing loan loss reserve on the balance sheet. Note that the loan loss provision is a *noncash expense* and does not affect the cash flow of an MFI.

RECORDING LOAN WRITE-OFFS. Once it has been determined that the likelihood of a particular loan being repaid is remote (the borrower has died, left the area, or simply will not pay), a write-off occurs. Write-offs are only an accounting entry; they do not mean that loan recovery should not continue to be pursued if it makes economic sense. Writing off a loan does not mean the organization has relinquished its legal claim to recover the loan.

To make the adjustment, actual loan losses or write-offs are reflected on the balance sheet only and do not affect the income statement when they occur. Write-offs reduce the "loan loss reserve" and the "outstanding loan portfolio" by equal amounts. (If the loan loss reserve has been recorded as a liability, it is reduced when loans are written off.) The resulting effect is to leave the net portfolio on the balance sheet unchanged because the reserve has already been made (and expensed as a loan loss provision). When making a write-off, a reduction in the loan loss reserve (which is a negative asset) is recorded as a debit. The write-off is offset by a reduction (credit) of the outstanding loan portfolio.

If the loan loss reserve is too low relative to the value of loans to be written off, then the loan loss reserve needs to be increased by making an additional loan loss provision on the income statement.

If a loan that was previously written off is *recovered* (in other words, the borrower has repaid the loan) then the full amount recovered is recorded as *revenue* (credit) on the income statement. This is because the principal amount written off was recorded as an expense (through the loan loss provision that created the loan loss reserve), and, therefore, if recovered it is recorded as revenue and not as a decrease in outstanding loan portfolio (assets). The outstanding loan portfolio is not

---

Box 8.1 The Impact of Failure to Write Off Bad Debt

MFIs OFTEN FAIL TO WRITE OFF BAD LOANS BECAUSE OF legal restrictions or the desire to show exaggerated profits or a high portfolio amount. When bad debts are not written off, reported loan recovery performance may be severely distorted. The calculation below provides an example of the type of distortion that can arise when a bad debt is not written off but rather carried over as part of the outstanding loan portfolio. Loan-collection performance should be measured as follows: loan collection over the amount falling due during the reported year net of accumulated "old" bad debt that occurred in the past and, therefore, should have been written off. Instead, it is often measured as loan collection over disbursed (the amount falling due plus the cumulative total of previous years' bad debt).

Assume that the MFI lends 100 units of currency every year of which 10 are never collected and never written off. The denominator (disbursed) consequently increases by 10 units annually, resulting in a misleading deterioration of the recovery ratio while actual performance has remained constant—at a 90 percent annual collection ratio.

Ratio	Year 1	Year 2	Year 3	...	Year 10
$\dfrac{\text{Repaid}}{\text{Disbursed}}$	$\dfrac{90}{100} = 90\%$	$\dfrac{90}{10 + 100} = 82\%$	$\dfrac{90}{(10 \times 2) + 100} = 75\%$	...	$\dfrac{90}{(10 \times 9) + 100} = 47\%$

This illustration proves the futility of overreliance on the repayment rate as an adequate test for collection performance. The absence of write-offs makes this financial ratio inaccurate in portraying the actual collection performance.

Source: Yaron 1994.

affected because the loan amount was already removed from the balance sheet when the write-off occurred. The offsetting entry (debit) is an increase in assets, usually cash.

To determine if a write-off has taken place, it is necessary to have the previous year's closing balance sheet, this year's closing balance sheet, and this year's income statement. The first step is to determine the difference between the amount of the loan loss reserve in the previous year and the amount of the loan loss reserve this year. This amount should equal the amount of the loan loss provision for this year. If it does not, the difference is the amount of write-off taken in the current year.

◆ For example, the financial statements (not shown) for the sample MFI portfolio report in table 8.1 showed a loan loss reserve of 5,000 on the balance sheet at the end of 1994, a loan loss reserve of 7,000 on the balance sheet at the end of 1995, and a loan loss provision on the income statement in 1995 of 2,500. Adding the 1995 loan loss provision (2,500) to the 1994 loan loss reserve (5,000) should result in a loan loss reserve for 1995 of 7,500. Since it is not 7,500 but only 7,000, a write-off of 500 must have occurred. This can be verified by looking at the sample portfolio report in table 8.1.

Note that write-offs reduce the amount of portfolio at risk. MFIs that wish to report a healthy portfolio (or minimal portfolio at risk) may choose to write off loans more frequently than they should. The decision on when to write off a loan should be based on a sound policy established and agreed to by the board members of an MFI.

Accounting for Depreciation of Fixed Assets

Many MFIs depreciate fixed assets according to generally accepted accounting principles. However, some do not. If in an analysis of an MFI's financial statements there does not appear to be an operating account (expense) called depreciation on the income statement, or if the account seems too large or too small relative to the amount of fixed assets on the balance sheet, it is necessary to adjust the financial statements and depreciate each capital asset by the appropriate amount for the number of years that the MFI has owned it.

When a fixed asset such as a piece of machinery or a motorcycle is purchased, there is a limited time that it will be useful (that is, able to contribute to the generation of revenue). Depreciation expense is the accounting term used to allocate and charge the cost of this usefulness to the accounting periods that benefit from the use of the asset. Depreciation is *an annual expense that is determined by estimating the useful life of each asset.* Like the loan loss provision, depreciation is a non-cash expense and does not affect the cash flow of the MFI.

To make the adjustment, when a fixed asset is first purchased, it is recorded on the balance sheet at the current value or price. When a depreciation expense (debit) is recorded on the income statement, it is offset by a negative asset (credit) on the balance sheet called *accumulated depreciation.* This offsets the gross property and equipment reducing the net fixed assets. Accumulated depreciation represents a decrease in the value to property and equipment that is used up during each accounting period. (Accumulated depreciation is similar to the loan loss reserve in that both serve to reduce the value of specific assets on the balance sheet.)

◆ For example, when an MFI purchases a motorcycle, it estimates its useful life for a number of years. Recording depreciation on the motorcycle is a process of allocating the period cost to the accounting periods that benefit from its use. If the useful life is estimated at, say, five years, then depreciation would be recorded for each of the five years. This results in a reduced book value of the motorcycle on the MFI's balance sheet.

There are two primary methods of recording depreciation: the straight-line method and the declining balance method. The *straight-line method* allocates an equal share of an asset's total depreciation to each accounting period. This is calculated by taking the cost of the asset and dividing it by the estimated number of accounting periods in the asset's useful life. The result is the amount of depreciation to be recorded each period.

◆ In the example above, if the motorcycle costs 5,500, has an estimated useful life of five years, and has an estimated value of 500 at the end of the five years (salvage value), its depreciation per year calculated by the straight-line method is 1,000, as follows:

$$\frac{\text{Cost} - \text{salvage value}}{\text{Service life in years}}$$

$$\frac{5,500 - 500}{5}$$

$$= 1,000 \text{ depreciation per year}$$

The declining balance method refers to depreciating a fixed percentage of the cost of the asset each year. The percentage value is calculated on the remaining undepreciated cost at the beginning of each year.

◆ In the example, if the motorcycle is depreciated on a declining balance basis at 20 percent a year, the first year's depreciation would be 1,100 (5,500 x 20%). In the second year the depreciation would be based on the reduced amount of 4,400. Twenty percent of 4,400 is 880, which is the depreciation expense for year 2. This continues until the asset is either fully depreciated or sold:

Year	Beginning value	Depreciation (at 20 percent a year)	Ending value
1	5,500	1,100	4,400
2	4,400	880	3,520
3	3,520	704	2,816
4	2,816	563	2,253
5	2,253	451	1,802

If a depreciated asset is sold for an amount greater than its recorded book value (that is, its cost net of depreciation), then the book value is reduced to zero and the difference is recorded as revenue on the income statement.

Many countries set standards for depreciation by classifying assets into different categories and setting the rate and method for depreciating each class. This is referred to as the *capital cost allowance*.

Accounting for Accrued Interest and Accrued Interest Expense

The last adjustment that may be required to adjust the financial statements of MFIs is an adjustment for accrued interest revenue and accrued interest expense on liabilities.

ADJUSTING FOR ACCRUED INTEREST REVENUE. Recording interest that has not been received is referred to as *accruing* interest revenue. Based on the assumption that the interest will be received at a later date, accrued interest is recorded as revenue and as an asset under *accrued interest* or *interest receivable*. (Had the interest revenue been received, it would be recorded as revenue [credit] and as cash [debit]. With accrued interest, the debit entry [increase in assets] is to interest receivable rather than to cash.)

MFIs vary substantially in their treatment of accrued interest revenue. Some only accrue interest revenue when the loan term has ended with a portion of the loan still outstanding. Others accrue interest revenue during the term of the loan when payments become due but are not received. Still others record the entire loan principal and interest revenue at the time of loan disbursement as an asset (referred to as *capitalizing* interest as mentioned above) either as part of the loan portfolio or in a separate asset account. Many MFIs do not accrue interest revenue at all. The decision of whether or not to accrue interest revenue and, if so, when, must be determined by each MFI based on its accounting standards.

Two adjustments may be required for accrued interest revenue. If an MFI does not accrue interest revenue at all and makes loans that have relatively infrequent interest payments (quarterly, biannually, or as a lump sum at the end of the loan term), it should accrue interest revenue at the time financial statements are produced. (MFIs that have weekly or biweekly payments need not necessarily accrue interest revenue; it is more conservative not to and may not be material enough to consider.) Interest revenue is accrued by determining how much interest revenue has been earned but not yet become due (the number of days since the last interest payment that the loans have been outstanding times the daily interest rate) and recording this amount as revenue (credit) and debiting the asset account accrued interest.

The second adjustment for accrued interest revenue is to reflect the amount of revenue that an MFI is unlikely to receive due to delinquent loans. MFIs that accrue interest on delinquent loans overstate both the value of their assets and their revenue and should make an adjustment to remove the accrued interest.

If an MFI has accrued interest on loans that have little chance of being repaid, it is necessary to make an adjustment to the financial statements. To make this adjustment, the amount of accrued interest on delinquent loans is deducted on the balance sheet by crediting the asset where it was recorded initially (outstanding loan portfolio or interest receivable) and reversed on the

Box 8.2 *Cash and Accrual Accounting for Microfinance Institutions*

SOME MFIS ACCRUE INTEREST REVENUE WHEREAS OTHERS account for it on a cash basis. MFIs that accrue interest revenue account for it as earned whether or not it has come due and been paid. This is standard practice in the banking industry; however, banks have to stop accruing interest once a loan is past due more than 90 days (nonperforming loans).

Most MFIs account for interest revenue more conservatively, on a cash basis. They treat interest as income only after it is actually received. In institutions that do not grow, the difference between the two systems does not entail a great difference in the final results presented at year end. If payment frequency is high (for example, weekly) then there is little difference between the two systems: in the case of weekly payments, the closing balance done on a cash basis would fail to reflect only a week's worth of interest income. Likewise, the final results under the two systems are not widely different in institutions that are not growing: under a cash accounting system in a no-growth program, the *omission* of earned but unpaid interest is approximately balanced by the *inclusion* of cash interest income earned in the prior period but received in the present period.

In MFIs where growth is strong and payments are less frequent, the results produced by cash and accrual accounting can be substantially different. MFIs should eventually move toward the banking industry practice of accruing interest. However, many MFIs do not have the computing power to do accrual accounting, and they should not necessarily acquire it only for this purpose.

Source: Christen 1997.

position of the MFI as of that date. When MFIs borrow from external sources (concessional or commercial loans or client savings or both) to fund their assets, they incur a liability. Liabilities carry financing charges that are paid periodically. At year-end it is likely that the MFI will owe interest on borrowed funds for the period from the last loan or interest payment to the day the year ends. The financial statements will need to be adjusted to reflect this financing expense that has been incurred but not yet paid. This is referred to as accrued interest expense. If interest owed is not accrued, the MFI's financing costs at the end of the year are understated, its profitability is overstated, and its liabilities are understated.

To accrue interest expense, the amount of interest owing as of the date the balance sheet is created is debited on the income statement as a financing cost and credited as a liability on the balance sheet in the accrued interest expense account.

♦ For example, an MFI borrows 10,000 on January 1 at an annual interest rate of 5 percent with interest due once a year on January 1 and the principal due at the end of five years. If its year-end is December 31, it will have had the loan for one year less a day when it closes its balance sheet. However, it will not have paid any interest yet, as interest is not due until January 1. To properly reflect this interest expense, the MFI should debit its income statement to include 500 in interest expense (financing costs) and credit its accrued interest expense account (liability) 500.

Adjusting for Subsidies and Inflation

Unlike the three adjustments described above, which reflect proper accounting procedures, the following adjustments may or may not be required to adhere to proper accounting procedures, depending on which country the MFI is operating in. However, adjustments for both subsidies and inflation should be made to accurately determine the true financial viability of an MFI. Some readers may wish to make these adjustments separately from the adjusted financial statements described above.

The following describes why adjustments for subsidies and inflation should be made and how to make actual accounting entries to the financial statements. (Adjusted financial statements are provided in appendixes 1 and 2.)

income statement by decreasing interest revenue (debit). This adjustment correctly states the true financial position of the MFI.

♦ For example, if an MFI has accrued interest of 500 in the interest receivable account on a loan that has been overdue for more than a year, it should decrease interest revenue by 500 and decrease interest receivable by 500 to correctly state its revenue and assets.

The best practice for MFIs is not to accrue interest revenue on delinquent loans at all.

ADJUSTING FOR ACCRUED INTEREST EXPENSE. When a fiscal year ends, the balance sheet should reflect the financial

Accounting for Subsidies

Unlike traditional financial intermediaries that fund their loans with voluntary savings and other debt, many MFIs fund their loan portfolios (assets) primarily with donated equity or concessional loans (liabilities). Concessional loans, donated funds for operations (including indirect subsidies—such as reserve requirement exemptions or government assumption of loan losses or foreign exchange losses—or "in-kind" donations—such as free office space, equipment, or training provided by governments or donors), and donated equity are all considered subsidies for MFIs.

Yaron (1992) shows that standard accounting measures of profitability are not valid for analyzing the performance of institutions receiving subsidies. Accounting profits are simply the sum of profits (or losses) and subsidies received. For example, if an MFI receives a grant to cover operating shortfalls and records it as revenue, its net income will be overstated. In this case a highly subsidized MFI appears more profitable than a better-performing, subsidy-free MFI.

It is, therefore, necessary to separate out and adjust the financial statements for any subsidies to determine the financial performance of an MFI as if it were operating with market debt and equity rather than donor funds. In addition, as an MFI matures, it will likely find it necessary to replace grants and concessional loans with market rate debt (or equity) and would thus need to determine its financial viability if it were to borrow commercial funds.

To some extent, these adjustments also allow for comparison among MFIs, because it puts all MFIs on equal ground analytically, as if they were all operating with commercially available third-party funds (Christen 1997).

It is important to note that while the adjustments for subsidies may ultimately be entered on the MFI's financial statements, they do not represent actual cash outflows. Subsidy adjustments are calculated for analysis purposes only to accurately assess the institution, its subsidy dependence, and the risk that it would face if subsidies were eliminated.

There are three types of subsidies typically received by MFIs:

- Funds donated to cover operational costs and donations in-kind
- Concessional loans
- Donated equity.

To make subsidy adjustments, it is necessary first to determine the value of the subsidy and then record accounting entries. For concessional loans and donated equity, it is also necessary to determine the appropriate "cost of funds" to apply to the subsidies.

Adjustments for subsidies result in a change in the net income reported on the income statement equal to the value of the subsidies; that is, subsidy adjustments result in increased expenses, which lower the net income. Subsidy adjustments do not, however, ultimately change the totals on the balance sheet, because a new capital account is created to reflect the increase in equity necessary to compensate for the effect of the subsidies, which offsets the lower retained earnings. Audited financial statements may reflect the effect of direct donations (grants to cover operating expenses) to the MFI but would not likely be adjusted for implicit subsidies (in-kind donations or concessional loans).

DONATIONS TO COVER OPERATIONAL COSTS AND DONATIONS IN KIND. Funds donated to cover operational costs are a direct subsidy to the MFI. The value of the subsidy is, therefore, equal to the amount donated to cover expenses incurred in the period reported. Some donations are provided to cover operating shortfalls over a period greater than one year. Only the amount "spent" in the year is recorded on the income statement as revenue. Any amount still to be used in subsequent years remains as a liability on the balance sheet (referred to as deferred revenue). This occurs because, theoretically, if an MFI stopped operations in the middle of a multiyear operating grant, they would have to return the unused donation to the donor. Therefore, the unused amount is considered a liability.

Donated funds for operations should be reported on the income statement separately from revenue generated by lending and investment activities to accurately report the earned revenue of the MFI. These funds should be deducted from revenue or net income prior to any financial performance analysis, because they do not represent revenue earned from operations. (Note that any costs incurred to obtain donor funds—"fundraising costs"—should also be separated from other operating expenses, because the benefit of receiving the funds is not included.)

In-kind donations such as free office space or staff training constitute a subsidy to the MFI and should be recorded as an expense on the income statement. This accurately reflects the true level of expenses that would be incurred if the MFI were to operate without in-kind donations.

To make the adjustment, if an MFI has recorded donations to cover operational costs on the income statement as revenue earned, the amount should be reported below the net income line, resulting in a reduction in operational revenue and, therefore, a reduction in the amount transferred to the balance sheet as current year net surplus (deficit). An offsetting credit entry is made to the balance sheet in the accumulated capital—subsidies account (equity).

Similarly, the market value of donations in kind is debited on the income statement (an increase in expenses) and offset in the same equity account on the balance sheet: accumulated capital—subsidies.

◆ For example, in the sample financial statements in appendix 1, a donation of 950 was received for operations (assume no donations in kind were received). The income statement is adjusted to reflect a reduction in profits of 950 (debit) and a credit of 950 to the accumulated capital account on the balance sheet is made.

CONCESSIONAL LOANS. Concessional loans are loans received by the MFI with lower than market rates of interest. Concessional loans result in a subsidy equal to the value of the concessional loans times the commercial or market rate, less the amount of interest paid.

$$\text{Subsidy} = [(\text{concessional loans} \times \text{market rate}) - \text{amount of interest paid}]$$

The actual financing costs of concessional loans are netted out in this calculation because they are captured in the recorded financing costs on the income statement (as an actual cash outflow or accrued interest payable).

To determine the appropriate market rate (cost of funds) to apply, it is best to choose the form of funding that the MFI would most reasonably be able to obtain if it were to replace donor funds with market funds. Suggested market rates include:

- Local prime rate for commercial loans (adjusted upward for a potential risk premium due to the perceived risk of MFIs)
- 90-day certificate of deposit rate (adjusted for risk)
- Interbank lending rate (adjusted for risk)
- Average deposit rate at commercial banks (adjusted upward to account for the additional operating costs

incurred to collect deposits and the added cost of reserve requirements on deposits).

- Inflation rate plus 3 to 5 percentage points per year (particularly if the prime rate is negative in relation to inflation).

MFIs may wish to select the same market rate for all types of concessional debt, or they may choose different rates, depending on what form of funding might replace each subsidy. This must be decided by each MFI based on the existing forms of debt and equity available and the ability to access different types of debt and equity.

Adjustments must be made to both the balance sheet and the income statement. The amount of the subsidy is entered as an increase to equity (credit) under the *accumulated capital—subsidies* account and as an increase in financial costs (debit).

◆ For example, in the sample financial statements in appendix 1, concessional funds outstanding at the end of the year were 30,000. If we assume that the interest paid for the year on the 30,000 concessional loan was 900 and the market rate was 10 percent, then the subsidy would equal 2,100 [(30,000 * 10%) – 900].

The subsidy can also be determined by calculating the average rate of interest paid on the concessional loans. For example, if we assume that the average interest rate paid on those funds was 3 percent and the market rate for commercial loans is 10 percent, the annual subsidy is equal to (30,000 x 7%) or 2,100.

To make this adjustment on the balance sheet, 2,100 is entered in the capital accumulation account (credit), which increases equity. To offset this entry, an adjustment has to be made to the income statement. The amount of the subsidy is entered as an increase in financial costs (debit) of 2,100, which in turn reduces the profit of the MFI. When this reduced profit is transferred to the balance sheet, the net equity changes result in no change to the totals on the balance sheet.

FUNDS DONATED FOR LOAN CAPITAL (EQUITY). Funds donated for loan capital are often treated as equity by MFIs and, therefore, are not always considered when adjusting for subsidies, since these funds are not usually included on the income statement as revenue. (Note that some MFIs do record donations for loan fund capital on the income statement, which then "flow through" to the balance sheet. If this is the case, an adjustment similar to the one made for funds donated for operations should be made.)

Funds donated for loan capital are reported on the balance sheet as an increase in equity (sometimes referred to as loan fund capital) and an increase in assets (either as cash, loan portfolio outstanding, or investments, depending on how the MFI chooses to use the funds).

Donations for loan fund capital differ from donations for operations in that the total amount received is meant to be used to fund assets rather than to cover expenses incurred. Some analysts would suggest that, therefore, no *subsidy* adjustment needs to be made for funds donated for loan capital. Furthermore, donors are not normally looking for any return on their funds (as a normal equity investor would), nor are they expecting to receive the funds back. What they are interested in is the ability of the MFI to maintain the real value of the donated funds, relative to inflation, so that it can continue to provide access to credit for the target group. Therefore, the argument goes that donations for loan fund capital need only be adjusted for inflation, *not* for subsidies.

On the other hand, if an MFI did not receive donations for loan capital, it would have to either borrow (debt) or receive investor funds (equity). Both debt and equity have associated costs. The cost of debt is reflected as financing costs. The cost of equity is normally the return required by investors (either through dividends or capital gains). Equity in formal financial institutions is often more "expensive" than debt, because the risk of loss is higher and, therefore, the return demanded is higher. It can be argued, therefore, that MFIs receiving donations for loan fund capital should make a subsidy adjustment to reflect the market cost of equity (or debt, depending on which one the MFI might use to replace donor funds).

Hence, adjusting for the effects of funds donated for loan fund capital poses two possibilities:

- Adjust for the rate of inflation (inflation adjustment)
- Adjust using the market rate for commercial debt or equity (subsidy adjustment).

To adjust donations for loan fund capital for the effect of *inflation*, an adjustment is made to equity as discussed below.

To reflect the *subsidy* on donations for loan fund capital based on market rates, a similar calculation to the adjustment for concessional loans is made. A market rate is chosen and simply multiplied by the amount donated.

The resulting figure is then recorded as an expense (financing costs) on the income statement and an increase is made to equity (credit) under the *accumulated capital—subsidies* account.

For the purposes of this handbook, funds donated for loan fund capital are treated as equity and are adjusted for inflation only (therefore, no example is provided in the appendix for a subsidy adjustment to funds donated for loan capital).

Accounting for Inflation

Inflation is defined as a substantial rise in prices and volume of money resulting in a decrease in the value of money. Goldschmidt and Yaron (1991) state that conventional financial statements are based on the assumption that the monetary unit is stable. Under inflationary conditions, however, the purchasing power of money declines, causing some figures of conventional financial statements to be distorted. Inflation affects the nonfinancial assets and the equity of an organization. Most liabilities are not affected, because they are repaid in a devalued currency (which is usually factored into the interest rate set by the creditor). (However, variable-rate liabilities are nonmonetary and must be adjusted in the same way as fixed assets. This will not be covered here because it becomes quite complicated; for more information see Goldschmidt and Yaron 1991.)

This section describes how to account for inflation, considering its effect on both equity and the nonfinancial assets of an MFI. (If donations for loan fund capital are included in the subsidy adjustment, it is double-counting to calculate an inflation adjustment for these funds as well. Adjusting other equity and nonfinancial assets for inflation may, however, still be required.)

To adjust for inflation, two accounts must be considered:

- The revaluation of nonfinancial assets
- The cost of inflation on the real value of equity.

Nonfinancial assets include fixed assets such as land, buildings, and equipment. Fixed assets, particularly land and buildings, are assumed to increase with inflation. However, their increase is not usually recorded on an MFIs' financial statement. Thus their true value may be understated.

Since most MFIs fund their assets primarily with equity, equity must increase at a rate at least equal to the rate of inflation if the MFI is to continue funding its portfolio. (If MFIs acted as true financial intermediaries, funding their loans with deposits or liabilities rather than equity, the adjustment for inflation would be lower because they would have a higher debt-equity ratio. However, interest on debt in inflationary economies will be higher, so the more leveraged an MFI the greater the potential impact on its actual financing costs.) Most assets of an MFI are financial (loan portfolio being the largest) therefore, their value decreases with inflation (that is, MFIs receive loan payments in currency that is worth less than when the loans were made). (In addition, the value of the loan amount decreases in real terms, meaning it has less purchasing power for the client. To maintain purchasing power, the average loan size must increase.) At the same time, the price of goods and services reflected in an MFI's operating and financial costs increase with inflation. Therefore, over time an MFI's costs increase and its financial assets, on which revenue is earned, decrease in real terms. If assets do not increase in real value commensurate with the increase in costs, the MFI's revenue base will not be large enough to cover increased costs.

An MFI should adjust for inflation on an annual basis based on the prevailing inflation rate during the year, regardless of whether the level of inflation is significant, because the cumulative effect of inflation on the equity of an MFI can be substantial.

Note that similar to subsidy adjustments, unless an MFI is operating in a hyperinflationary economy, adjustments for inflation are calculated for the purpose of determining financial viability only. Inflation adjustments do not represent actual cash outflows or cash inflows. The choice of whether or not an MFI records inflation adjustments directly on their financial statements must be made by its board.

Unlike adjustments for subsidies, adjustments for inflation result in changes to both the balance sheet totals and the income statement. The balance sheet changes because fixed assets are increased to reflect the effect of inflation, and a new capital account is created to reflect the increase in nominal equity necessary to maintain the real value of equity. The income statement is affected by an increase in expenses relative to the cost of inflation.

Audited financial statements may or may not include adjustments for inflation depending on the rate of infla-

tion. As a guideline, International Accounting Standard 29 suggests that adjustments should be made if the accumulated inflation over the three-year period exceeds 100 percent (26 percent per year compounded) (Goldschmidt, Shashua, and Hillman 1986).

To calculate the cost of inflation, the following formula is used:

$$1 - (1 + \text{inflation rate})^p$$

where p = the number of periods (generally years as inflation rates are most often quoted as annual rates).

◆ For example, an annual rate of inflation of 10 percent results in a percentage loss in real terms in the value of a loan portfolio over a period of three years of 23 percent [$1 - (1 + 0.1)3$]. This means that for the portfolio to maintain its real value, it would have to grow by 23 percent over the three-year period.

REVALUATION OF ASSETS. To adjust nonfinancial assets, the nominal value needs to be increased relative to the amount of inflation. To make this adjustment, an entry is recorded as revenue (credit) (note that this is not recorded as operating income because it is not derived from normal business operations) on the income statement and an increase in fixed assets (debit) is recorded on the balance sheet. The increased revenue results in a greater amount of net income transferred to the balance sheet, which in turn keeps the balance sheet balanced although the totals have increased. (The increase on the asset side of the balance sheet equals the increase in the equity, the result of higher revenue. This increase in fixed assets would also have an impact on the annual depreciation, which would increase and, therefore, reduce income. For simplicity's sake, it is possible to ignore this factor.)

◆ For example, in the sample financial statements in appendix 2, the MFI has 4,000 in fixed assets recorded on the balance sheet. Assume that the annual rate of inflation for 1994 was 10 percent. This means that the fixed assets should be revalued at 4,400 [$4,000 + (4,000 \times 10\%)$]. An increase in revenue of 400 is entered on the income statement (credit) and an increase in assets (debit) of 400 is recorded on the balance sheet.

CALCULATION OF THE COST OF INFLATION ON EQUITY. To account for the devaluation of equity caused by inflation, the prior year's closing equity balance is multiplied by the current year's inflation rate. This is recorded as an operating expense on the income statement. An adjustment is then made to the balance sheet under the equity reserve account "inflation adjustment."

◆ For example, in the sample financial statements in appendix 2, the MFI had 33,000 in equity at the end of 1993. With an annual rate of inflation of 10 percent, the revalued equity should be 36,300 [33,000 + (33,000 x 10%)]. An increase in operating expense of 3,300 is entered on the income statement (debit) and an increase in equity (credit) of 3,300 recorded on the balance sheet in the inflation adjustment account.

Restating Financial Statements in Constant Currency Terms

Some MFIs may want to restate their financial statements in *constant currency terms* (adapted from Christen 1997). This is not considered an adjustment in the same way that financial statements are adjusted for proper accounting. Constant currency terms means that, on a year-by-year basis, financial statements are continually restated to reflect the current value of the local currency relative to inflation. Converting prior-year nominal local currency values to present-year values permits year-to-year comparisons of the real (that is, inflation-adjusted) growth or decline in key accounts such as loan portfolio or operating expenses. This conversion does not affect the financial results of the MFI, because all accounts are converted and no new costs or capital accounts are created.

To convert prior year data, the amounts are multiplied by either one plus the annual rate of inflation for each year or divided by the consumer price index (or GDP deflator) for each year. To do this, conversion factors must be calculated. For example, if the inflation rate is used, the current year (say, 1997) has a factor of one, and the conversion factor for the previous year is simply 1 plus the current year's inflation rate (for a 1997 inflation rate of 20 percent, the conversion factor would be 1.2 for 1996 financial data). For the year previous to that (1995), the conversion factor is the previous conversion factor (1.2) multiplied by 1 plus the rate of inflation for the prior year (assume a 1996 inflation rate of 30 percent so the conversion factor is 1.2 x 1.3, or 1.56), and so on. (Note that the inflation rate for the earliest year that is converted is not referenced, since the conversion factor for each year uses the inflation rate for the following year.)

To use the consumer price index or GDP deflator, the prior year's consumer price index is divided by the current year's consumer price index to arrive at the conversion factor (to convert 1996 data, if the 1996 consumer price index was 200 and the 1997 consumer price index was 174, then the conversion factor would be 1.15). Unlike the inflation method, the price index method always uses the current year's index divided by the converted year's index.

Finally, MFIs may want to convert their local-currency financial data into U.S. dollars or another foreign currency for the benefit of their donors or to compare their performance with MFIs in other countries. This is simply done by multiplying (or dividing, depending on how the exchange rate is stated) the financial data by the current year's exchange rate.

Appendix 1. Sample Financial Statements Adjusted for Subsidies

The following balance sheet represents an MFI's finan-

cial position as at December 31, 1994, with adjustments for subsidies (950 donation for operating costs and 2,100 for imputed financial costs on concessional loans).

SAMPLE BALANCE SHEET (adjusted for subsidies)

as at December 31, 1994

		1994	Adjust	1994A
ASSETS				
Cash and bank current accounts		2,500		2,500
Interest-bearing deposits		7,000		7,000
Loans outstanding				
Current		50,000		50,000
Past due		29,500		29,500
Restructured		500		500
Loans outstanding (gross)		70,000		70,000
(Loan loss reserve)		(5,000)		(5,000)
Net loans outstanding		65,000		65,000
Other current assets		1,000		1,000
TOTAL CURRENT ASSETS		75,500		75,500
Long-term investments		11,000		11,000
Property and equipment				
Cost		4,000		4,000
(Accumulated depreciation)		(300)		(300)
Net property and equipment		3,700		3,700
TOTAL LONG-TERM ASSETS		14,700		14,700
TOTAL ASSETS		90,200		90,200
LIABILITIES				
Short-term borrowings (commercial rate)		12,000		12,000
Client savings		0		0
TOTAL CURRENT LIABILITIES		12,000		12,000
Long-term debt (commercial rate)		15,000		15,000
Long-term debt (concessional rate)		30,000		30,000
Restricted or deferred revenue		0		0
TOTAL LIABILITIES		57,000		57,000
EQUITY				
Loan fund capital		33,000		33,000
Accumulated capital—financial costs	0	2,100	2,100	
Accumulated capital—donation	0	950	950	
Retained net surplus (deficit) prior years	0		0	
Current-year net surplus (deficit)		200	(2,850)	(2,850)
TOTAL EQUITY		33,200		33,200
TOTAL LIABILITIES AND EQUITY		90,200		90,200

Source for unadjusted statements: SEEP Network and Calmeadow 1995.

SAMPLE INCOME STATEMENT (adjusted for subsidies)

for the period ended December 31, 1994

	1994	Adjustment	1994A
FINANCIAL INCOME			
Interest on current and past due loans	12,000		12,000
Interest on restructured loans	50		50
Interest on investments	1,500		1,500
Loan fees and service charges	5,000		5,000
Late fees on loans	300		300
TOTAL FINANCIAL INCOME	18,850		18,850
FINANCIAL COSTS			
Interest on debt	3,500		3,500
Adjusted concessional debt	0	2,100	2,100
Interest paid on deposits	0		0
TOTAL FINANCIAL COSTS	3,500		5,600
GROSS FINANCIAL MARGIN	15,350		13,250
Provision for loan losses	3,000		3,000
NET FINANCIAL MARGIN	12,350		10,250
OPERATING EXPENSES			
Salaries and benefits	5,000		5,000
Administrative expenses	2,500		2,500
Occupancy expense	2,500		2,500
Travel	2,500		2,500
Depreciation	300		300
Other	300		300
TOTAL OPERATING EXPENSES	13,100		13,100
NET INCOME FROM OPERATIONS	(750)		(2,850)
Grant revenue for operations	950	(950)	0
EXCESS OF INCOME OVER EXPENSES	200		(2,850)

Source for unadjusted statements: SEEP Network and Calmeadow 1995.

Appendix 2. Sample Financial Statements Adjusted for Inflation

The following balance sheet represents an MFI's finan-

cial position as at December 31, 1994, with adjustments for inflation (400 for revaluation of nonfinancial assets; 3,300 for devaluation of equity).

SAMPLE BALANCE SHEET (adjusted for inflation)

as at December 31, 1994

	1994	Adjustment	1994A
ASSETS			
Cash and bank current accounts	2,500		2,500
Interest-bearing deposits	7,000		7,000
Loans outstanding			
Current	50,000		50,000
Past due	29,500		29,500
Restructured	500		500
Loans outstanding (gross)	70,000		70,000
(Loan loss reserve)	(5,000)		(5,000)
Net loans outstanding	65,000		65,000
Other current assets	1,000		1,000
TOTAL CURRENT ASSETS	75,500		75,500
Long-term investments	11,000		11,000
Property and equipment			
Cost	4,000		4,000
Revaluation of fixed assets	0	400	400
(Accumulated depreciation)	(300)		(300)
Net property and equipment	3,700		4,100
TOTAL LONG-TERM ASSETS	14,700		15,100
TOTAL ASSETS	90,200		90,600
LIABILITIES			
Short-term borrowings (commercial rate)	12,000		12,000
Client Savings	0		0
TOTAL CURRENT LIABILITIES	12,000		12,000
Long-term debt (commercial rate)	15,000		15,000
Long-term debt (concessional rate)	30,000		30,000
Restricted and deferred revenue	0		0
TOTAL LIABILITIES	57,000		57,000
EQUITY			
Loan fund capital	33,000		33,000
Inflation adjustment - equity	0	3,300	3,300
Retained net surplus (deficit) prior years	0		0
Current-year net surplus (deficit)	200	(2,700)	(2,700)
TOTAL EQUITY	33,200		33,600
TOTAL LIABILITIES AND EQUITY	90,200		90,600

Source for unadjusted statements: SEEP Network and Calmeadow 1995.

SAMPLE INCOME STATEMENT (adjusted for inflation)

for the period ended December 31, 1994

	1994	*Adjustment*	*1994A*
INCOME			
Interest on current and past due loans	12,000		12,000
Interest on restructured loans	50		50
Interest on investments	1,500		1,500
Loan fees and service charges	5,000		5,000
Late fees on loans	300		300
Revaluation of fixed assets	0	400	400
TOTAL FINANCIAL INCOME	18,850		19,250
FINANCIAL COSTS			
Interest on debt	3,500		3,500
Interest paid on deposits	0		0
TOTAL FINANCIAL COSTS	3,500		3,500
GROSS FINANCIAL MARGIN	15,350		15,750
Provision for loan losses	3,000		3,000
NET FINANCIAL MARGIN	12,350		12,750
OPERATING EXPENSES			
Salaries and benefits	5,000		5,000
Administrative expenses	2,500		2,500
Occupancy expense	2,500		2,500
Travel	2,500		2,500
Depreciation	300		300
Other	300		300
Revaluation of equity	0	3,300	3,300
TOTAL OPERATING EXPENSES	13,100		16,400
NET INCOME FROM OPERATIONS	(750)		(3,650)
Grant revenue for operations	950		950
EXCESS OF INCOME OVER EXPENSES	200		(2,700)

Source for unadjusted statements: SEEP Network and Calmeadow 1995.

Sources and Further Reading

Bartel, Margaret, Michael J. McCord, and Robin R. Bell. 1994. *Fundamentals of Accounting for Microcredit Programs.* GEMINI Technical Note 6. Development Alternatives Inc., Financial Assistance to Microenterprise Programs. Washington, D.C.: U.S. Agency for International Development.

Christen, Robert Peck. 1997. *Banking Services for the Poor: Managing for Financial Success.* Washington, D.C.: ACCION International.

Eliot, Nicola. 1996. *Basic Accounting for Credit and Savings Schemes.* London: Oxfam Basic Guides.

Goldschmidt, Yaaqov, Leon Shashua, and Jimmye S. Hillman. 1986. *The Impact of Inflation on Financial Activity in Business.* Totowa, N.J.: Rowman and Allanheld.

Goldschmidt, Yaaqov, and Jacob Yaron. 1991. "Inflation Adjustments of Financial Statements." Policy Research Working Paper 670. World Bank, Washington, D.C.

Ledgerwood, Joanna. 1996. *Financial Management Training for Microfinance Organizations: Finance Study Guide.* New York: PACT Publications (for Calmeadow).

Ledgerwood, Joanna, and Kerri Moloney. 1996. *Financial Management Training for Microfinance Organizations: Accounting Study Guide.* Toronto: Calmeadow.

SEEP (Small Enterprise Education and Promotion) Network and Calmeadow. 1995. *Financial Ratio Analysis of MicroFinance Institutions.* New York: PACT Publications.

Stearns, Katherine. 1991. *The Hidden Beast: Delinquency in Microenterprise Programs.* Washington, D.C.: ACCION International.

Yaron, Jacob. 1992. *Assessing Development Finance Institutions: A Public Interest Analysis.* World Bank Discussion Paper 174. Washington, D.C.

———. 1994. "The Assessment and Measurement of Loan Collections and Loan Recovery." World Bank, Agriculture and Natural Resources Department, Washington, D.C.

CHAPTER NINE

Performance Indicators

Effective financial management requires periodic analysis of financial performance. Performance indicators collect and restate financial data to provide useful information about the financial performance of an MFI. By calculating performance indicators, donors, practitioners, and consultants can determine the efficiency, viability, and outreach of MFI operations.

Performance indicators usually are in the form of ratios, that is, a comparison of one piece of financial data to another. Comparing ratios over a period of time is referred to as *trend analysis,* which shows whether financial performance is improving or deteriorating. In addition to trend analysis, ratios should be analyzed in the context of other ratios to determine the overall financial performance of an MFI. Calculating ratios does not in itself result in improved financial performance. However, analysis of the performance indicators (ratios) and changes to provides information that can identify potential or existing problems, which can lead to changes in policies or operations, which in turn may improve financial performance. (This is discussed further in chapter 10.)

The performance indicators presented here are organized into six areas:

- Portfolio quality
- Productivity and efficiency
- Financial viability
- Profitability
- Leverage and capital adequacy
- Scale, outreach, and growth.

Each of these performance indicators was chosen because they are useful in managing MFIs. Many of them (including financial viability, profitability, leverage and capital adequacy ratios, and scale, outreach, and growth) are also useful for external parties, such as investors or donors. There are many other useful indicators. The ones presented here are considered to be the minimum set of performance indicators that an MFI might use to guide its financial management.

This chapter presents performance indicators that provide information about different areas of MFI operations. It will be of interest to readers who are evaluating the financial performance and outreach of an MFI. Practitioners will be able to use the performance indicators to determine how well they are doing financially and to establish future performance goals. Donors or consultants can also determine whether the MFIs that they are supporting or evaluating are achieving planned results. Furthermore, donors may recognize performance indicators that are useful for the financial management of MFIs and may consequently require that those ratios be incorporated into the reports submitted by MFIs. In this way, donor reporting can also benefit MFI internal management.

A balance sheet, income statement, and portfolio report are required to construct the ratios presented in this chapter. (If the reader is not familiar with how financial statements are created, see Ledgerwood and Moloney 1996.) Performance indicators are calculated once financial statements have been adjusted to reflect generally accepted accounting principles as presented in chapter 8.

At the end of each section ratios are calculated for a three-year period using the sample financial statements and portfolio report found in appendixes 1, 2, and 3 of this chapter. Note that these sample financial statements are not adjusted for subsidies and inflation (but do accurately reflect portfolio quality, depreciation, and accrued interest and expenses) as discussed in chapter 8.

This is because, with the exception of the profitability ratios, the ratios presented here are either not affected by subsidies or inflation (portfolio quality, productivity, and efficiency ratios) or consider subsidies and inflation in the formulas (financial viability ratios). (For simplicity's sake, we have assumed that no in-kind donations were provided. Therefore, all operating costs incurred are recorded on the income statement. Donations are not included in any ratios that consider earned revenue.) For the profitability ratios only, one year of ratios is calculated using the adjusted statements from chapter 8.

Some readers may be looking for a *standard range of performance* for each of the ratios. Given the small number of MFIs that measure their financial performance taking into account the necessary adjustments, it is premature to provide ranges. As time goes on, however, more MFIs will begin to measure their performance in accordance with generally accepted accounting principles. As the number of comparative organizations increases, standard ranges will likely be established. The last section of this chapter, on performance standards and variations, provides an overview of four of the most well-known performance analysis systems currently used in the microfinance industry.

In analyses of performance indicators, there are contextual factors that must be considered, such as the geographical context (appropriate benchmarks in Latin America are not necessarily adequate for Asia and Africa), the maturity of the institution (younger institutions may be incurring expansion costs without commensurate revenue and should not be compared to mature institutions), and the varying lending approaches that are used around the world. All of these factors greatly influence performance indicators. Hence, their primary use should (for now) be for internal management of the MFI. Although both practitioners and donors will (and to some extent should) compare institutions, performance indicators must be put in the context of where and how the different MFIs are operating.

Finally, it is important to consider that the majority of these performance indicators are based on the assumption that most MFIs are primarily lending institutions. Hence, while managing liabilities is an important part of financial management, the focus here is on effective asset management. Where relevant, the effect of savings mobilization has been taken into account.[1]

Portfolio Quality

Portfolio quality ratios provide information on the percentage of nonearning assets, which in turn decrease the revenue and liquidity position of an MFI. Various ratios are used to measure portfolio quality and to provide other information about the portfolio (even though they are all referred to here as "portfolio quality" ratios). The ratios are divided into three areas:

- Repayment rates
- Portfolio quality ratios
- Loan loss ratios.

Repayment Rates

Although the repayment rate is a popular measure used by donors and MFIs, it does not in fact indicate the *quality* of the loan portfolio (that is, the amount of risk in the current outstanding portfolio). Rather, the repayment rate measures the historical *rate of loan recovery*.

Repayment rates measure the amount of payments received with respect to the amount due, whereas other ratios indicate the quality of the current outstanding portfolio (see the arrears rate and the portfolio at risk rate discussed below). This is not to say that the repayment rate is not useful—it is a good measure for monitoring repayment performance over time (if it is calculated correctly and in a consistent manner). It is also useful for projecting future cash flow, because it indicates what percentage of the amount due can be expected to be received, based on past experience.

However, MFIs should not use the repayment rate to indicate the current quality of the outstanding portfolio and are discouraged from using it as an external indicator of success or as a comparative measure with other organizations. It is only possible to compare repayment rates of different organizations (or any other ratios in fact) if they are calculated in exactly the same manner and for the same period.

Repayment rates are particularly misleading if the MFI portfolio is growing rapidly and if loan terms are

---

1. Portions of this chapter are based on material originally published in Ledgerwood (1996).

long. This is because the percentage that has become due (the numerator) compared with the amount disbursed or the amount outstanding (the denominator) is relatively low, which means that a delinquency problem, in fact, may not show up right away.

There are many variations used to calculate repayment rates, which is why it is difficult to use as an indicator of success unless the exact method of calculation is known and understood. For example, if an MFI measures the repayment rate based only on loans made in a certain period—say, the previous month—the repayment rate may be very high, even though the number of loans and the portfolio at risk in the total outstanding portfolio may also be high but are simply not included because they are loans from previous months. Some MFIs calculate the repayment rate based on the amount disbursed, while others calculate it based on the amount still outstanding. For the most part, MFIs tend to use the amount received as the numerator and the amount expected as the denominator, with some variation.

Some MFIs calculate the repayment rate as follows:

$$\text{Repayment rate} = \frac{\substack{\text{Amount received} \\ \text{(including prepayments} \\ \text{and past due amounts)}}}{\substack{\text{Amount due} \\ \text{(excluding past due amounts)}}}$$

This formula overstates the amount received by the prepayments and the amount received on past due loans (because it does not include past due amounts in the denominator). This is why repayment rates can sometimes be greater than 100 percent. This formula does not provide useful information about the ongoing performance of the portfolio and should not be used. Instead, two other formulas are suggested:

$$\text{On-time repayment rate} = \frac{\substack{\text{Collection on current amounts due} \\ \text{less prepayments}}}{\text{Total current amounts due}}$$

or

$$\substack{\text{Repayment rate} \\ \text{including past due} \\ \text{amounts}} = \frac{\substack{\text{Collection on current amounts due} \\ \text{plus past due less prepayments}}}{\substack{\text{Total current amounts due} \\ \text{plus past due amounts}}}$$

These formulas remove the effect of prepayments and show the actual rate of received payments against expected payments either on time or taking into account past due amounts.

Portfolio Quality Ratios

Three ratios are suggested here to measure portfolio quality: the *arrears rate*, the *portfolio at risk*, and the *ratio of delinquent borrowers*.

Arrears represent the amount of loan principal that has become due and has not been received. Arrears generally do not include interest; however, if the MFI records the interest owing as an asset (for more on capitalized interest see chapter 8) at the time the loan is disbursed, it should also include interest in the amount of arrears. The arrears rate provides an indication of the risk that a loan will not be repaid.

ARREARS RATE. The arrears rate is the ratio of overdue loan principal (or principal plus interest) to the portfolio outstanding:

$$\text{Arrears rate} = \frac{\text{Amount in arrears}}{\substack{\text{Portfolio outstanding} \\ \text{(including amounts past due)}}}$$

(Some organizations calculate the arrears rate as 1 minus the repayment rate. This works only if the repayment rate on the entire portfolio outstanding is considered, including past-due amounts, and not just for a certain period of loan disbursements).

The arrears rate shows how much of the loan has become due and has not been received. However, the arrears rate understates the risk to the portfolio and understates the potential severity of a delinquency problem, because it only considers payments as they become past due, not the entire amount of the loan outstanding that is actually at risk.

◆ For example, a client who borrows 1,000 for petty trading for 12 months at 15 percent interest on the declining balance must repay 90 per month (made up of approximately 83 principal and 7 interest). If she misses the first three months of payments, the amount past due is 270 (249 principal and 21 interest). Accordingly, the arrears rate would be approximately 25 percent:

$$\text{Arrears rate} = \frac{249}{1,000}$$

$$= 25\%$$

Since no payments have been received, the true amount at risk is the full amount of the loan (1,000 or 100 percent), not 249. A more conservative formula to use to calculate risk is the portfolio at risk rate.

PORTFOLIO AT RISK. The portfolio at risk refers to the outstanding balance of all loans that have an amount overdue. Portfolio at risk is different from arrears because it considers the amount in arrears plus the remaining outstanding balance of the loan.

The portfolio at risk ratio is calculated as follows:

$$\text{Portfolio at risk} = \frac{\text{Outstanding balance of loans with payments past due}}{\text{Portfolio outstanding (including amounts past due)}}$$

The portfolio at risk ratio reflects the true risk of a delinquency problem because it considers the full amount of the loan at risk—this is particularly important when the loan payments are small and loan terms are long. (Some MFIs choose to declare a loan at risk only after a specific number of days have passed since the payment became due and has not been received, based on the fact that many clients are able to make their loan payments within a few days of the due date. By calculating the portfolio at risk rate on a periodic basis, MFIs can determine whether delinquency is improving or deteriorating. Portfolio at risk can be calculated for an MFI as a whole, for a region, a branch, a credit officer, or by sector (loan purpose or geographic).

Tables 9.1 and 9.2 show the difference between the calculation of the arrears rate and the portfolio at risk for the same organization. The information in both tables is exactly the same with the exception of the aged amounts being either arrears (table 9.1) or portfolio at risk (table 9.2). Note the difference in *arrears* as a percentage of outstanding loans (6.8 percent) and the *portfolio at risk* as a percentage of outstanding loans (19.8 percent).

DELINQUENT BORROWERS. As a further indication of portfolio quality, it is useful to determine the number of borrowers who are delinquent relative to the volume of delinquent loans. If there is variation in the size of the loans disbursed, it is helpful to know whether the larger or smaller loans result in greater delinquency. If the ratio of delinquent borrowers is lower than the portfolio at risk or the arrears rate, then it is likely that larger loans are more problematic than smaller ones.

$$\text{Delinquent borrowers} = \frac{\text{Number of delinquent borrowers}}{\text{Total number of active borrowers}}$$

◆ For example, if an MFI has a portfolio at risk of 20 percent and the ratio of delinquent borrowers to total borrowers is 5 percent, it will know that the delinquency problem lies mostly with larger borrowers.

In determining the number of delinquent borrowers it is also useful to see whether more loans are becoming delinquent at the beginning of the loan cycle or toward the end.

DEFINING DELINQUENCY. The policy used by an MFI to define *delinquent loans* directly influences the portfolio

---

Box 9.1 Repayment Rates Compared with Portfolio Quality Ratios

PROJECT DUNGGANON WAS CREATED IN OCTOBER 1989 by the Negros Women for Tomorrow Foundation. It is one of the most active Grameen Bank replicators in the Philippines. As of April 1995 there was 5,953 active borrowers. Total loans outstanding was 4.4 million pesos (US$174,000) and total savings collected in the Group Fund was 3.3 million pesos.

Project Dungganon has historically recorded repayment rates ranging from 94 to 99 percent, calculated by dividing the amount received by the amount expected for each month. (The repayment rate does not include any past-due loan amounts in the denominator and does include prepayments in the numerator.) However, when further analysis of Dungganon's portfolio was completed, it was found that 32 percent or 1.5 million pesos (US$58,000) of the total outstanding loans in April 1995 was in arrears, the majority of them for more than two years.

Because the focus had been on the high repayment rate, Project Dungganon was touted as one of the most successful Grameen replicators. In fact, if it had continued to operate with such poor loan portfolio quality, it would have eventually gone out of business!

In April 1995 Project Dungganon began calculating portfolio quality ratios, realized its portfolio quality was poor, and implemented highly effective delinquency management techniques. As of August 1997 Dungganon reported a portfolio at risk of 16 percent over 30 days (yet continued to report a repayment rate of 99.4 percent). In June 1997 it wrote off 5 percent of its portfolio.

Source: Ledgerwood 1995 and discussion with Briget Helms, CGAP, World Bank.

Table 9.1 Sample Portfolio Report with Aging of Arrears

Client	Amount disbursed	Amount outstanding	Amount in arrears	Arrears rate (%)	Aging 1–30 days	31–60 days	61–90 days	91–180 days	181–365 days	> 365 days
Vincze	300,000	250,000	50,000	20.0	25,000	25,000				
Earle	390,000	211,000	38,000	18.0	13,000	13,000	12,000			
Galdo	150,000	101,000	30,000	29.7	13,000	11,000	4,000	2,000		
Feria	50,000	41,000	12,000	29.3	4,000	4,000	4,000			
Perez	78,000	64,000	64,000	100.0			5,000	14,000	45,000	
Manalo	300,000	206,000	30,000	14.6						30,000
Nelson	32,000	28,000	4,000	14.3	1,500	1,500	1,000			
Kinghorn	50,000	45,000	45,000	100.0		4,000	4,000	18,500	18,500	
Debique	100,000	84,000	25,000	29.8	5,000	5,000	5,000	10,000		
Foster	100,000	16,000	8,000	50.0	8,000					
Lalonde	257,000	60,000	60,000	100.0				12,000	48,000	
Blondheim	37,000	32,000	25,000	78.1	3,000	3,000	3,000	3,000	13,000	
Prudencio	43,000	37,000	14,000	37.4			7,000	7,000		
Current	5,600,000	4,750,000	0	0.0						
Total	7,487,000	5,925,000	405,000	6.8	64,500	66,500	45,000	66,500	124,500	38,000
					1.1%	1.1%	0.8%	1.1%	2.1%	0.6%

Note: Amount in arrears is defined as the amount that has become due and has not been received.
Total arrears as a percentage of outstanding loans 405,000/5,925,000 = 6.8%
Source: Contributed by Stefan Harpe, Calmeadow.

Table 9.2 Sample Portfolio Report with Aging of Portfolio at Risk

Client	Amount disbursed	Amount outstanding	Amount in arrears	Aging 1–30 days	31–60 days	61–90 days	91–180 days	181–365 days	> 365 days	Total
Vincze	300,000	250,000	50,000		250,000					
Earle	390,000	211,000	38,000			211,000				
Galdo	150,000	101,000	30,000				101,000			
Feria	50,000	41,000	12,000			41,000				
Perez	78,000	64,000	64,000					64,000		
Manalo	300,000	206,000	30,000						206,000	
Nelson	32,000	28,000	4,000			28,000				
Kinghorn	50,000	45,000	45,000					45,000		
Debique	100,000	84,000	25,000				84,000			
Foster	100,000	16,000	8,000	16,000						
Lalonde	257,000	60,000	60,000					60,000		
Blondheim	37,000	32,000	25,000					32,000		
Prudencio	43,000	37,000	14,000				37,000			
Current	5,600,000	4,750,000	0							
Total	7,487,000	5,925,000	405,000	16,000	250,000	280,000	222,000	201,000	206,000	1,175,000
				0.3%	4.2%	4.7%	3.7%	3.4%	3.5%	19.8%

Note: Portfolio at risk is defined as the outstanding balance of loans with an amount past due.
Total portfolio at risk as a percentage of outstanding loans 1,175,000/5,925,000 = 19.8%
Source: Contributed by Stefan Harpe, Calmeadow.

quality ratios and the determination of the MFI's level of risk. If an MFI defines past due (overdue, delinquent) only after the loan term has ended, the portfolio quality ratios will mean little. The date that a loan term ends has no relevance to the amount of time a loan is overdue. What matters is the amount of time that has passed since the borrower stopped making payments.

As discussed in chapter 8, the time at which a loan is classified as delinquent should be related to the payment frequency and the loan term. Obviously, when comparing institutions it is important to determine how each classifies delinquent loans.

♦ For example, an MFI's credit policy states that loans that have two weekly payments past due should be treated as delinquent—that is, the outstanding balance of loans with two weeks and more past due (loans C and D in table 9.3; loan B is not included since it only has one weekly payment overdue). If the MFI decided to consider all loans with one payment missed to be delinquent, the portfolio at risk would increase to 76 percent (3,225 divided by 4,250), even though the same loans were at risk.

If a portfolio is growing rapidly (due to an increase in the number of borrowers, an increase in average loan size, or both), using the arrears rate may understate the risk of default, because the outstanding portfolio (denominator) is growing at a faster rate than the amounts becoming due (since the outstanding portfolio grows with the total disbursed amount whereas the amount due only grows with the payments as they become due). A rapidly growing portfolio can hide a delinquency problem regardless of which portfolio quality ratios are used (Stearns 1991). MFIs should take care

to examine the quality of their loan portfolios by periodically aging the amounts past due (see chapter 8).

A similar situation occurs when loan terms are relatively long. Long loan terms result in payments (installments) that represent a relatively small percentage of the loan amount. Overdue payments can represent a small portion of the loan, yet the portfolio at risk will be very high relative to the arrears rate, because the majority of the loan outstanding is considered even though it has not become due.

If an MFI has relatively long loan terms with frequent loan installments (such as weekly), it is even more important to use the portfolio at risk rate rather than the arrears rate. Weekly payments over a long term result in relatively small payments each week. Each payment past due has a small effect on the rate of delinquency, even though the amount of risk to the portfolio might be increasing. If the 1,000 loan described above were a two-year loan, then, after two months with no payments, only 90 would be in arrears, yet the majority of the 1,000 outstanding should be considered at risk.

Portfolio quality ratios are directly affected by the write-off policy of the MFI (box 9.2). If delinquent loans continue to be maintained on the books rather than written off once it has been determined that they are unlikely to be repaid, the size of the portfolio, and hence the denominator, is overstated. However, the numerator is also greater (because it includes the delinquent loans, but the amount of delinquent loans is *proportionately* less relative to the denominator). The result is a higher portfolio at risk than for an MFI that writes loans off appropriately.

Alternatively, if loans are written off too quickly, the portfolio at risk ratio will be unrealistically low, since delinquent loans are simply taken out of the numerator

Table 9.3 Calculating Portfolio at Risk

Client	Amount disbursed	Week 1	Week 2	Week 3	Week 4	Week 5	Amount outstanding
A	1,150	25	25	25	25	25	1,025
B	1,150	25	25	–	25	25	1,050
C	1,150	25	–	–	25	25	1,075
D	1,150	25	–	–	–	25	1,100
Total							4,250

Portfolio at risk = $\frac{2,175}{4,250} \times 100 = 51\%$

Source: Ledgerwood 1996.

and denominator and the portfolio is seemingly quite healthy. However, the income statement will reflect the high amount of loan loss provisions required to make these write-offs, illustrating the high costs of loan losses.

Loan Loss Ratios

There are two loan loss ratios that can be calculated to provide an indication of the expected loan losses and the actual loan losses for an MFI. The first is the *loan loss reserve ratio* and the second, the *loan loss ratio.*

LOAN LOSS RESERVE RATIO. As discussed in chapter 8, the loan loss reserve (recorded on the balance sheet) is the cumulative amount of loan loss provisions (recorded as an expense on the income statement) minus loan write-offs. The amount of the loan loss reserve is determined based on the quality of the loan portfolio outstanding. Once the loan loss reserve has been determined, it is useful to state it as a percentage of the portfolio outstanding.

(Note that we are not measuring the loan loss *provision* in this ratio, which is a flow item. We are interested in determining, as a percentage of the average portfolio, how much is held as a reserve for future losses—a stock item. The loan loss provision ratio relates to the expense for the period and is not necessarily a good indicator of the quality of the portfolio.)

The loan loss reserve ratio shows what percentage of the loan portfolio has been *reserved* for future loan losses. By comparing this ratio over time, MFIs can determine

how well they are managing delinquency, provided they are making adequate loan loss reserves.

(Note that this ratio can be misleading if the MFI is growing at a fast rate or if loan sizes are increasing, because the denominator is likely to be growing faster than the numerator. In this case, it is recommended that the denominator used be the *average* portfolio outstanding to reflect more accurately the loans on which the loan loss reserve has been made.)

This ratio should decrease as the MFI improves its delinquency management.

$$\text{Loan loss reserve ratio} = \frac{\text{Loan loss reserve for the period}}{\text{Portfolio outstanding for the period}}$$

Loan loss reserve ratios for successful MFIs rarely exceed 5 percent.

LOAN LOSS RATIO. The loan loss ratio is calculated to determine the rate of loan losses for a specific period (usually a year). The loan loss ratio reflects only the amounts written off in a period. It provides an indication of the volume of loan losses in a period relative to the *average* portfolio outstanding.

To determine the *average* portfolio outstanding, the portfolio outstanding at the beginning of the year is added to the portfolio outstanding at the end of year, and the result is generally divided by two. Because loan write-offs generally occur on older loans, the loan loss ratio may not be as indicative of *current* loan portfolio quality as the loan loss reserve ratio. The loan loss ratio will rarely be higher than the loan loss reserve ratio because some loans on which a reserve has been made are in turn repaid and the loan loss reserve itself is usually greater than the actual write-offs.

$$\text{Loan loss ratio} = \frac{\text{Amount written off in the period}}{\text{Average portfolio outstanding for the period}}$$

The loan loss ratio can be compared over time to see if loan losses as a percentage of average outstanding portfolio are increasing or decreasing. It can also be compared to the amount of loan loss reserve to determine if the loan loss reserve is sufficient based on the amount of historical loan losses.

SAMPLE RATIOS. The portfolio quality ratios in table 9.4 were calculated using data from appendixes.

Table 9.4 Calculating Portfolio Quality Ratios

Portfolio quality ratio	Ratio	1995	1994	1993
Arrears rate	Payments in arrears/ Portfolio outstanding	8.3%	12.9%	19.2%
Portfolio at risk	Balance of loans in arrears/ Portfolio outstanding	21.4%	28.6%	38.5%
Loan loss reserve ratio	Loan loss reserve/ Portfolio outstanding	8.3%	7.1%	9.6%
Loan loss ratio	Amount written off/ Average portfolio outstanding	0.67%	4.9%	0%

Source: Ledgerwood 1996; appendixes 1–3.

♦ Most of the portfolio quality ratios appear to be improving (decreasing) over time. The loan loss ratio increases in 1995, which partially explains why the loan loss reserve ratio is lower in that year (write-offs reduce the loan loss reserve). In general, loan losses of more than 2 percent each year indicate a delinquency problem. This will obviously vary depending on the write-off policy established by the MFI.

Productivity and Efficiency Ratios

Productivity and efficiency ratios provide information about the rate at which MFIs generate revenue to cover their expenses. By calculating and comparing productivity and efficiency ratios over time, MFIs can determine whether they are maximizing their use of resources. Productivity refers to the volume of business that is generated (output) for a given resource or asset (input). Efficiency refers to the cost per unit of output.

Both productivity and efficiency ratios can be used to compare performance over time and to measure improvements in an MFI's operations. By tracking the performance of the MFI as a whole, well-performing branches, credit officers, or other operating units, an MFI can begin to determine the "optimum" relationships between key operating factors. If applicable, branch managers can compare their branches to other branches and determine where they might need to reduce costs to increase profitability.

Productivity Ratios

Several ratios are suggested to analyze the productivity of an MFI. These ratios focus on the productivity of the credit officers, because they are the primary generators of revenue. The ratios include:

- Number of active borrowers per credit officer
- Portfolio outstanding per credit officer
- Total amount disbursed in the period per credit officer.

For MFIs that mobilize deposits, productivity ratios can also be calculated for staff involved in collecting savings. These ratios are similar to those above and include:

- Number of active depositors per savings officer
- Deposits outstanding per savings officer
- Total amount of savings collected in the period per savings officer.

To calculate productivity ratios, current financial statements and a portfolio report (or savings report if applicable) are required. The ratios presented focus on credit officers and analyze the asset side of the balance sheet only. For MFIs wishing to analyze the productivity of their savings staff, the same principles would apply.

NUMBER OF ACTIVE LOANS PER CREDIT OFFICER. The number of active loans (or borrowers) per credit officer varies depending on the method of credit delivery and whether or not loans are made to individuals, to individuals as group members, or to groups. For each MFI there is an optimal number of clients that each credit officer can manage effectively. While salary costs may appear lower when credit officers carry a large number of clients, too many clients may result in higher loan losses, which can more than offset lower administrative costs.

When comparing this ratio with other MFIs (or between different branches or different lending products within the same MFI), it is necessary to take into account the average loan term because this greatly affects the number of borrowers a credit officer can maintain. If loan terms are relatively long, a credit officer need not spend as much time processing renewals as she would if the loan terms were shorter. If this is the case, a credit officer should in theory be able to carry more active borrowers than a credit officer working with shorter loan terms (assuming all other factors are the same). (Note: *average* amounts in both the numerator and denominator are used.)

AVERAGE PORTFOLIO OUTSTANDING PER CREDIT OFFICER. The size of the average portfolio outstanding per credit officer will vary depending on the loan sizes, the maturity of the MFI's clients, and the optimal number of active loans per credit officer. This ratio is useful primarily for the internal management of productivity and must be used cautiously (if at all) when comparing productivity to other MFIs.

If a credit officer is with an MFI over a long period of time, the number of active borrowers and portfolio outstanding should increase to an optimal level, at which point growth in the number of active borrowers that the credit officer manages should be minimized. (Note: *average* amounts in both the numerator and denominator are used.)

AMOUNT DISBURSED PER PERIOD PER CREDIT OFFICER. In accounting terms, the amount disbursed by a credit officer is a *flow* item (cash flow item) whereas the amount outstanding is a *stock* item (balance sheet item). It is

important to differentiate between the two because there are specific costs associated with both stock and flow items. The average portfolio outstanding ratio measures the stock (portfolio outstanding). This ratio measures the flow of loan disbursements.

As clients take out additional loans, both the portfolio outstanding and the total amount disbursed per credit officer should increase, provided the clients require larger loan amounts or the MFI is operating in an inflationary environment.

SAMPLE RATIOS. Table 9.5 calculates productivity ratios for the three-year period using data from the appendixes. (Because this sample MFI does not collect deposits, productivity ratios are not calculated for savings staff.)
◆ These ratios show a generally positive trend. As determined from the sample portfolio report, two additional credit officers were hired in 1994. This affected all of the ratios, particularly the total amount disbursed per credit officer in 1994. By 1995 all of the ratios had improved, indicating increased productivity.

Efficiency Ratios

Efficiency ratios measure the cost of providing services (loans) to generate revenue. These are referred to as operating costs and should include neither financing costs nor loan loss provisions. Total operating costs can be stated as a percentage of three amounts to measure the efficiency of the MFI: the average portfolio outstanding (or average performing assets or total assets—if an MFI is licensed to mobilize deposits, it is appropriate to measure operating costs against total assets; if the MFI only provides credit services, operating costs are primarily related to the administering of the loan portfolio and hence should be mea-

Table 9.5 Calculating Productivity Ratios

Productivity ratio	Ratio	1995	1994	1993
Average number of active loans per credit officer	Average number of active loans/ Average number of credit officers	279	239	271
Average portfolio per credit officer	Average value of loans outstanding/ Average number of credit officers	12,500	10,167	11,250
Total amount disbursed per period per credit officer	Total amount disbursed/ Average number of credit officers	26,667	12,667	22,000

Source: Ledgerwood 1996; appendixes 1–3.

sured against the average portfolio outstanding) per unit of currency lent, or per loan made.

For a more detailed analysis, operating costs can also be broken down to measure the efficiency of specific cost elements such as salaries and benefits, occupational expenses such as rent and utilities, or travel. Since salaries and benefits generally make up the largest portion of operating costs, the ratio of salaries and benefits to the average portfolio outstanding is often calculated, as well as the average credit officer salary with the country's per capita GDP. Other breakdowns are not be presented here but can be easily calculated depending on the objectives of the analyst.

For MFIs that mobilize deposits, efficiency ratios will be somewhat lower because additional operating costs are incurred to collect deposits. Therefore, efficiency ratios of MFIs that collect deposits should not be compared to MFIs that do not collect deposits. This analysis focuses only on the credit operations.

In analyzing the credit operations of an MFI, two key factors influence the level of activity and hence operating costs and efficiency: the turnover of the loan portfolio and the average loan size (Bartel, McCord, and Bell 1995). The impact of these two factors and the corresponding efficiency of operations can be analyzed by looking at operating costs as a percentage of portfolio outstanding and at the costs associated with lending on a per unit of currency basis or a per loan basis.

OPERATING COST RATIO. The operating cost ratio provides an indication of the efficiency of the lending operations (sometimes referred to as the *efficiency indicator*). This ratio is affected by increasing or decreasing operational costs relative to the average portfolio.

$$\text{Operating cost ratio} = \frac{\text{Operating costs}}{\text{Average portfolio outstanding}}$$

Successful MFIs tend to have operating cost ratios of between 13 and 21 percent of their average loan portfolios and between 5 and 16 percent of their average total assets (Christen and others 1995).

SALARIES AND BENEFITS TO AVERAGE PORTFOLIO OUTSTANDING. Many successful MFIs have salaries and benefits running between 4 percent and 16 percent of average portfolio outstanding (Christen and others 1995). This

varies depending on the model, the density of the population, and the salary level in the country.

$$\begin{array}{c}\text{Salaries and benfits}\\\text{to average portfolio}\\\text{outstanding ratio}\end{array} = \frac{\text{Salaries and benfits}}{\text{Average portfolio outstanding}}$$

AVERAGE CREDIT OFFICER SALARY AS A MULTIPLE OF PER CAPITA GDP. The average credit officer salary as a multiple of per capita GDP is an effective ratio to determine the appropriateness of salary levels relative to the economic level of activity in the country. This ratio can be compared to similar organizations operating in the same environment.

$$\begin{array}{c}\text{Average credit officer salary}\\\text{as a multiple of per capita GDP}\end{array} = \frac{\text{Per capita GDP}}{\text{Average credit officer salary}}$$

COST PER UNIT OF CURRENCY LENT. The cost per unit of currency lent ratio highlights the impact of the turnover of the loan portfolio on operating costs. The lower the ratio, the higher the efficiency. This ratio is most useful to calculate and compare over time to see if costs are decreasing or increasing. However, it can sometimes be misleading. For example, while operating costs may increase, even though the size of the portfolio remains the same, the cost per dollar lent may actually decrease. This would happen if more short-term loans were made during the period and. therefore, the turnover of the portfolio was higher. Although the ratio would be reduced, it does not necessarily indicate increased efficiency.

$$\begin{array}{c}\text{Cost per unit of}\\\text{currency lent}\end{array} = \frac{\text{Operating costs for the period}}{\text{Total amount disbursed in the period}}$$

COST PER LOAN MADE. The cost per loan made ratio provides an indication of the cost of providing loans based on the number of loans made. Both this ratio and the cost per unit of currency lent need to be looked at over time to determine whether operating costs are increasing or decreasing relative to the number of loans made, indicating the degree of efficiency. As an MFI matures, these ratios should decrease.

$$\text{Cost per loan} = \frac{\text{Operating costs for the period}}{\text{Total number of loans made in the period}}$$

It is difficult to compare efficiency ratios among MFIs because the average loan size and loan term are so significant in these calculations. For example, MFIs that make relatively large loans will have lower cost per unit

Table 9.6 Calculating Efficiency Ratios

Efficiency ratio	Ratio	1995	1994	1993
Operating costs	Operating costs/ Average portfolio outstanding	19.1	21.5	24.2
Salaries as a percentage of average portfolio outstanding	Salaries and benefits/ Average portfolio outstanding	7.8	8.2	8.9
Cost per unit of currency lent	Operating costs/ Total amount disbursed	0.09	0.10	0.12
Cost per loan made	Operating costs/ Total number of loans made	8.94	10.08	9.91

Source: Ledgerwood 1996; appendixes 1–3.

of currency lent or cost per loan made ratios than those of MFIs that make very small loans. Furthermore, lending to groups usually reduces costs relative to lending directly to individuals. The specific lending model that each MFI employs makes a large difference to the results of efficiency ratios. Thus these ratios are most useful for internal financial management.

SAMPLE RATIOS. The efficiency ratios in table 9.6 were calculated using the sample financial statements provided in the appendixes. The average credit officer salary as a multiple of per capita GDP is not calculated here because the GDP is not known. However, the average credit officer salary as a multiple of per capita GDP for successful MFIs ranged from a low multiple of one to three times GDP to as high of 18 to 21 times GDP (Christen and others 1995).

◆ These ratios all decrease over time, indicating the increased efficiency of the MFI. The amount disbursed and the average portfolio outstanding appear to be growing at a greater rate than costs, which is good. This should be the case for an MFI that is expanding and developing greater efficiencies in its operations.

Financial Viability

Financial viability refers to the ability of an MFI to cover its costs with earned revenue. To be financially viable, an MFI cannot rely on donor funding to subsidize its operations. To determine financial viability, self-sufficiency indicators are calculated. There are usually two levels of

self-sufficiency against which MFIs are measured: *operational self-sufficiency* and *financial self-sufficiency*. If an organization is not financially self-sufficient, the subsidy-dependence index can be calculated to determine the rate at which the MFIs interest rate needs to be increased to cover the same level of costs with the same revenue base (loan portfolio).

Revenue is generated when the assets of an MFI are invested or put to productive use. Expenses are incurred to earn that revenue. To determine financial viability, revenue (yield) is compared to total expenses. If revenue is greater than expenses, the MFI is self-sufficient. It is important to note that only *operating* revenue (from credit and savings operations and investments) should be considered when determining financial viability or self-sufficiency. Donated revenue or revenue from other operations such as training should not be included, because the purpose is only to determine the viability of credit and savings operations.

Expenses incurred by MFIs can be separated into four distinct groups: financing costs, loan loss provisions, operating expenses, and the cost of capital. (Note that self-sufficiency can be determined by stating total revenue and the four expense categories as a percentage of average assets—either total assets, performing assets, or portfolio outstanding. For further information see SEEP Network and Calmeadow 1995.) The first three groups are actual expenses that MFIs incur (although some expenses such as loan loss provisions and depreciation are noncash items), while the last expense is an *adjusted* cost that all MFIs must consider (unless the MFI pays dividends, which would be an actual cost).

In the example in chapter 8, various adjustments were made to ensure that the MFI's financial statements adequately reflected total expenses. Adjustments were made to reflect the cost of poor loan portfolio quality, depreciation of fixed assets, and accrued interest revenue and interest expense. Further adjustments were made to reflect the benefit of subsidies received and the cost of inflation. In making these adjustments, a *cost of capital* was adjusted on the equity of the MFI. That is, the equity was adjusted to reflect the benefit of donations and concessional loans and the cost of inflation. Thus in the adjusted financial statements all four costs are clearly recorded. For unadjusted statements, however, an adjusted cost of capital must be calculated. This is described below.

For the purposes of this section, *nonadjusted* financial statements are used to demonstrate the difference between operational and financial self-sufficiency by providing a formula to *impute* the cost of capital. This is provided for those readers who do not choose to adjust their financial statements directly for inflation and subsidies. If, in fact, the MFI's financial statements *are* adjusted, then a cost of capital need not be imputed, and both the operational and financial self-sufficiency formulas can be calculated using the adjusted figures.

Financial *Spread*

True financial intermediaries mobilize deposits from members, from the general public, (or both). They then lend these funds to their clients. They normally pay a rate of interest to the depositors and charge a higher rate of interest to the borrowers (or earn a greater rate on investments). The difference between these two rates of interest is what is referred to as "spread" (sometimes referred to as gross financial margin if all operating revenue is included).

In the case of MFIs, which may or may not be mobilizing deposits from the public, *spread* refers to the difference between the yield earned on the outstanding portfolio and the average cost of funds (whether the funds be deposits, concessional loans, or commercial loans). Spread is what is available to cover the remaining three costs that an MFI incurs: operating costs, loan loss provisions, and the cost of capital. Spread is usually stated as a percentage of portfolio outstanding (or alternatively, if return on investments is included in the yield calculation, average performing assets can be used as the denominator).

If the portfolio is funded with debt (liabilities), then the average cost of the debt is subtracted from the average yield on the portfolio to determine the spread.

If the entire portfolio is funded with equity or donated funds, then the spread is equal to the portfolio yield. (This is not to say that there is no "cost" for equity; in fact, equity is generally more *expensive* than debt, because equity investors are taking a higher risk than those lending money since they have no guaranteed rate of return, which debt holders have in the form of interest. However, when discussing spread, this term refers only to the difference between the cost of debt [liabilities] and the interest rate earned. The cost of equity is considered after a net profit is made and transferred to the balance sheet; for most MFIs, no cost is ever really determined. Rather, the return on equity is calculated and compared with other investment choices. See the discussion of profitability below).

The formula for calculating spread is:

$$\text{Spread} = \frac{\text{Interest and fee revenue} - \text{financing costs}}{\text{Average loan portfolio}}$$

or if investment income is included:

$$\frac{\text{Spread (gross}}{\text{financial margin)}} = \frac{\text{Operating revenue} - \text{financing costs}}{\text{Average performing assets}}$$

From here the loan loss provision (expense item) can be subtracted from the spread, which results in the net financial margin and then the operating costs (operating cost ratio as discussed above), which results in the net margin (SEEP Network and Calmeadow 1995).

Two Levels of Self-Sufficiency

As the microfinance industry matures, the definition of self-sufficiency has begun to narrow. A few years ago people spoke about three (or four) levels of self-sufficiency that an MFI should progressively aim to achieve. Some analysts considered an MFI to be operationally self-sufficient (level one) if the revenue it generated from operations covered its operating costs, including loan loss provisions. Reaching level two meant that an MFI generated enough revenue to cover financing costs, operating expenses, and loan loss provisions. Level three (financial self-sufficiency) referred to revenue that covered nonfinancial and financial expenses calculated on a commercial basis—"profit without subsidy" (Christen and others 1995).

Currently, most people in the microfinance industry refer to only two levels of self-sufficiency: *operational self-sufficiency* and *financial self-sufficiency*. However, the definition of operational self-sufficiency varies among different MFIs and donors. The difference centers on the inclusion of financing costs. Whereas actual financing costs used to be included only in levels two and three (as above), some analysts include them in calculating both operational and financial self-sufficiency and some only in calculating financial self-sufficiency.

OPERATIONAL SELF-SUFFICIENCY. Some MFIs define operational self-sufficiency as generating enough operating revenue to cover operating expenses, financing costs, and the provision for loan losses.

$$\text{(i)   Operational self-sufficiency} = \frac{\text{Operating income}}{\substack{\text{Operating expenses} + \text{financing costs} \\ + \text{provision for loan losses}}}$$

Operational self-sufficiency thus indicates whether or not enough revenue has been earned to cover the MFI's direct costs, excluding the (adjusted) cost of capital but including any actual financing costs incurred.

Other MFIs argue that operational self-sufficiency should not include financing costs, because not all MFIs incur financing costs equally, which thus makes the comparison of self-sufficiency ratios between institutions less relevant. Some MFIs fund all of their loans with grants or concessional loans and do not need to borrow funds—or collect savings—and thus either do not incur any financing costs or incur minimal costs. Other MFIs, as they move progressively toward financial viability, are able to access concessional or commercial borrowings and thus incur financing costs. However, all MFIs incur operating expenses and the cost of making loan loss provisions, and they should be measured on the management of these costs alone. Furthermore, MFIs should not be penalized for accessing commercial funding sources (through the inclusion of financing costs in the formula), nor should MFIs that are able to finance all of their loans with donor funds be rewarded.

$$\text{(ii)   Operational self-sufficiency} = \frac{\text{Operating income}}{\substack{\text{Operating expenses} \\ + \text{provision for loan losses}}}$$

The choice of which formula to use is personal, because both are correct. However, it is important that when comparing institutions, the analyst determine that the same formula has been used, because no standard definition has yet been established.

Regardless of which formula is used, if an MFI does not reach operational self-sufficiency, eventually its equity (loan-fund capital) will be reduced by losses (unless additional grants can be raised to cover operating shortfalls). This means that there will be a smaller amount of funds to loan to borrowers, (which could lead to closing the MFI once the funds run out). To increase its self-sufficiency, the MFI must either increase its yield (return on assets) or decrease its expenses (financing costs, provision for loan losses, or operating costs).

FINANCIAL SELF-SUFFICIENCY. Financial self-sufficiency indicates whether or not enough revenue has been earned to cover both direct costs, including financing costs, provisions for loan losses, and operating expenses, and indirect costs, including the *adjusted cost of capital.*

The adjusted cost of capital is considered to be the cost of maintaining the value of the equity relative to inflation (or the market rate of equity) and the cost of accessing commercial rate liabilities rather than concessional loans. This was discussed and detailed adjustments were made in chapter 8, and so the adjusted cost of capital will be discussed here only briefly.

Many MFIs fund their loans with donated funds (equity) and thus to continue funding their loan portfolio, they need to generate enough revenue to increase their equity to keep pace with inflation. (If the MFI was to operate with borrowed funds, the financing costs in the income statement would capture the costs of debt and the cost of inflation, because inflation only affects equity and not liabilities. Liabilities are priced by the lender to cover the cost of inflation, because the borrower—in this case, the MFI—repays the loan in the future with inflated currency. If it turns out that the rate of inflation is greater than the rate of interest on the loan, the lender loses money, not the MFI.) Furthermore, many MFIs also access concessional funding (quasi-equity) at below-market rates. Consideration must be given to this subsidy and an additional cost of funds included, based on the MFI accessing commercial loans. Theoretically, this puts all MFIs on a somewhat level playing field regardless of their funding structures (although this will vary depending on the degree to which the MFI is leveraged).

The formula for the adjusted cost of capital is as follows:

$$\text{Cost of capital} = [(\text{Inflation rate} \times (\text{average equity} - \text{average fixed assets}))] \\ + [(\text{average funding liabilites} \times \text{market rate of debt}) \\ - \text{actual financing costs}]$$

The first half of the formula quantifies the impact of inflation on equity. (Some analysts and MFIs may wish to use a market rate of equity rather than inflation, based on the fact that if the MFI was to have equity investors they would demand a return greater than the rate of inflation.) Fixed assets are subtracted based on the assumption that property and buildings generally hold their value relative to inflation. The second half of the formula quantifies the cost of the MFI if it were to access commercial debt rather than concessional debt. Average amounts are used throughout to account for the fact that the MFI may have grown (or cut back) during the year.

This cost of capital formula relates directly to the adjustments to equity for inflation and subsidies calculated in chapter 8. If adjusted financial statements are used, no adjusted cost of capital is required to calculate the financial self-sufficiency.

Once the adjusted cost of capital is determined, the financial self-sufficiency ratio can be calculated:

$$\frac{\text{Financial}}{\text{self-sufficiency}} = \frac{\text{Operating income}}{\text{Operating expenses} + \text{financing costs} \\ + \text{provision for loan losses} \\ + \text{cost of capital}}$$

The "cost of capital" in the formula relates to the adjustments that were made to equity for subsidies and inflation in chapter 8 (other subsidy adjustments for in-kind donations and operating grants are included in the adjusted operating expenses).

This ratio relates to the bottom line of the income statement after adjustments for grants or concessional loans and inflation. Unless at least 100 percent financial self-sufficiency is reached, the provision of financial services in the long-term is undermined by the continued necessity to rely on donor funds.

Ideally, MFIs move progressively toward achieving operational self-sufficiency first and then financial self-sufficiency. Often, as an MFI matures, it experiences increas-ing financing costs as it accesses market-rate funding, decreasing provisions for loan losses as it manages its delinquency, and decreasing operating costs as it becomes more efficient. (Financing costs are affected by changes in the cost of funds and the mix between debt and equity [grants, donations, and retained earnings] in the MFI's funding structure. An increase in the interest paid by an MFI or an increase in the debt portion of the portfolio funding (relative to donated equity) will increase financing costs). Each of these changes affects the achievement of self-sufficiency.

SAMPLE RATIOS. Table 9.7 calculates viability ratios for the three-year period using data from appendixes 1 and 2 (financial self-sufficiency for 1993 is not calculated because we need 1992 figures to calculate the imputed cost of capital). In this example, the operational self-sufficiency formula includes financing costs. (Note that the sample financial statements are *unadjusted* because the cost of capital is captured in the financial self-sufficiency formula.)

◆ With the exception of the spread, these ratios show an increasing trend, which is good. The spread decreases, which is quite common with MFIs that begin to access less grant funding and more concessional or commercial debt, thus increasing their financing costs. For long-term viability, this sample MFI will have to earn additional revenue or reduce its costs, because it has not yet achieved financial self-sufficiency.

Subsidy Dependence Index

A third and final way to determine the financial viability of an MFI is to calculate its *subsidy dependence index* (SDI). The subsidy dependence index measures the degree to which an MFI relies on subsidies for its continued operations. The subsidy dependence index was developed by Jacob Yaron at the World Bank (1992a) to calculate the extent to which an MFI requires subsidy to earn a return equal to the opportunity cost of capital.

The subsidy dependence index is expressed as a ratio that indicates the percentage increase required in the on-lending interest rate to completely eliminate all subsidies received in a given year.[2] (Alternatively, the MFI could reduce its operating or financing costs when possible.) The subsidy dependence index is calculated using an MFI's *unadjusted* financial statements to determine the true value of the subsidies. The subsidy dependence

Table 9.7 Calculating Viability Ratios

Viability ratio	Ratio	1995	1994	1993
Spread	(Interest and fee revenue – financing costs)/ Average portfolio outstanding[a]	23.1%	22.7%	26.7%
Operational self-sufficiency	Operating income/(Operating costs + financing costs + loan loss provisions)	104.9%	96.2%	79.5%
Financial self-sufficiency	Operating income/(Operating costs + financing costs + loan loss provisions + cost of capital)	84.0%	82.1%	n/a

a. Assumes for 1994 and 1995 that the inflation rate was 8 percent and the commercial rate on debt was 10 percent.
Source: Ledgerwood 1996; appendixes 1 and 2.

index makes explicit the subsidy needed to keep the institution afloat, much of which is not reflected in conventional accounting reporting.

The purpose of the subsidy dependence index is similar to the financial self-sufficiency ratio and the adjustments to financial statements for subsidies and inflation in that it determines the extent to which MFIs rely on subsidies. However, one major difference between them is that the subsidy dependence index uses a market rate rather than inflation when adjusting the cost of the MFI's equity.

The objective of the subsidy dependence index is to provide a comprehensive method of assessing and measuring the overall financial costs involved in operating an MFI and quantifying its subsidy dependence. The subsidy dependence index methodology suggests moving away from overreliance on the financial profitability ratios of conventional accounting procedures in the financial analysis of MFIs.

(Although removal of subsidies received by an MFI is not always politically feasible or desirable, the measurement of any subsidy is always warranted economically and politically. This type of analysis involves taking full account of the overall social costs entailed in operating an MFI.)

The subsidy dependence index is instrumental in:
- Placing the total amount of subsidies received by an MFI in the context of its activity level, represented by interest earned on its loan portfolio (similar to calculations of effective protection, domestic resource cost, or job-creating cost)
- Tracking an MFI's subsidy dependence over time
- Comparing the subsidy dependence of MFIs providing similar services to a similar clientele
- Providing the notion of a "matching grant" by measuring the value of subsidy as a percentage of interest earned in the marketplace.

Calculating the subsidy dependence index involves aggregating all the subsidies received by an MFI. The total amount of the subsidy is then measured against the MFI's on-lending interest rate multiplied by its average annual loan portfolio (because lending is the prime activity of a supply-led MFI). Measuring an MFI's annual subsidies as a percentage of its interest income yields the percentage by which interest income would have to increase to replace the subsidies and provides data on the percentage points by which the MFI's on-lending interest rate would have to increase to eliminate the need for subsidies. As with any other financial measurement tool, however, the subsidy dependence index is only as accurate as the data used to compute it (see box 9.3).

Common subsidies include:
- Concessional central bank rediscounting facilities
- Donated equity
- Assumption of foreign exchange losses on loan by the state
- Direct transfer to cover specific costs or negative cash flows
- Exemption from reserve requirements.

A subsidy dependence index of zero means that an MFI has achieved financial self-sufficiency as described

---

2. This discussion of the subsidy dependence index is adapted from Yaron, Benjamin, and Piprek (1997).

Box 9.3 Computation of the Subsidy Dependence Index

THE AMOUNT OF THE ANNUAL SUBSIDY RECEIVED BY AN MFI is defined as the subsidy dependence index (SDI):

$$SDI = \frac{\text{Total annual subsidies received } (S)}{\text{Average annual interest income } (LP * i)}$$

$$= \frac{A(m-c) + [(E*m) - p] + K}{(LP * i)}$$

where:

A = MFI concessional borrowed funds outstanding (annual average)

m = Interest rate that the MFI would be assumed to pay for borrowed funds if access to borrowed concessional funds were eliminated

Source: Yaron, Benjamin, and Piprek 1997.

c = Weighted average annual concessional rate of interest actually paid by the MFI on its average annual concessional borrowed funds outstanding

E = Average annual equity

P = Reported annual profit (before tax and adjusted, when necessary, for loan loss provisions, inflation, and so on)

K = The sum of all other annual subsidies received by the MFI (such as partial or complete coverage of the MFI's operational costs by the state)

LP = Average annual outstanding loan portfolio of the MFI

i = Weighted average on-lending interest rate earned on the MFI loan portfolio

$$i = \frac{\text{Annual interest earned}}{\text{Average annual loan portfolio}}$$

---

above. A subsidy dependence index of 100 percent indicates that a doubling of the average on-lending interest rate is required if subsidies are to be eliminated. Similarly, a subsidy dependence index of 200 percent indicates that a threefold increase in the on-lending interest rate is required to compensate for the subsidy elimination. A negative subsidy dependence index indicates that an MFI not only fully achieved self-sustainability, but that its annual profits, minus its capital (equity) charged at the approximate market interest rate, exceeded the total annual value of subsidies, if subsidies were received by the MFI. A negative subsidy dependence index also implies that the MFI could have lowered its average on-lending interest rate while simultaneously eliminating any subsidies received in the same year.

Four factors are critical for reducing or eliminating subsidy dependence: adequate on-lending rates, high rates of loan collection, savings mobilization, and control of administrative costs. (Active savings mobilization helps to ensure a continuous source of funds for an MFI. An increase over time in the ratio of the *total value of voluntary savings to the loan portfolio* will indicate the extent to which an MFI has been successful in replacing concessional funds from donors (or the state) with savings from clients—see chapter 6.) Similarly, self-sufficiency ratios will also improve. Box 9.4 provides an example of CARE Guatemala's subsidy dependence index.

Profitability Ratios

Profitability ratios measure an MFI's net income in relation to the structure of its balance sheet. Profitability ratios help investors and managers determine whether they are earning an adequate return on the funds invested in the MFI. Determining profitability is quite straightforward—does the MFI earn enough revenue excluding grants and donations to make a profit? To calculate profitability ratios, profit is stated as a percentage return on assets (ROA), a return on business (ROB), and a return on equity (ROC). ("Business" refers to the result of adding assets and liabilities together and dividing by two; this ratio is useful for MFIs that fund a majority of their assets with mobilized savings.) Each of these ratios is calculated below using the adjusted financial statements (for subsidies and inflation) for 1994 from chapter 8 (see appendix 4).

For readers who would like to analyze the profitability of an MFI further, appendix 5 provides a model to decompose the return on assets into its constituent elements, including *profit margin analysis* and *asset utilization analysis*. This breakdown helps to determine the sources of profitability and to identify areas where the MFI might improve its operations and asset management from a profitability perspective. In particular, the yield on the portfolio and on the performing assets can be determined and compared with projected returns and between periods.

Box 9.4 CARE Guatemala's Subsidy Dependence Index

THE CARE VILLAGE BANKING PROGRAM IN GUATEMALA HAS recorded nearly perfect repayment rates since the program's inception. All indicators of outreach, cost, sustainability, and profit have become more favorable during 1991–95. However, the mere improvement of these figures does not necessarily indicate that the program is on a sustainable trajectory. The subsidy dependence index in 1995 was 4.77 (a dramatic improvement from the 1991 level of 28.17). In other words, interest rates would have to be increased by 4.77 percent in order to cover program costs if no subsidies existed.

The following figure compares the rapid decline of CARE Guatemala's subsidy dependence index measure to an older village banking program in Central America, FINCA Costa Rica. FINCA Costa Rica was founded in 1984, whereas CARE Guatemala was started in 1989. In comparisons of the seventh year of operation in both programs, FINCA Costa Rica's subsidy dependence index measure of 3.76 was lower than CARE Guatemala's subsidy dependence index measure of 4.77. CARE Guatemala's higher dependence on subsidies can be attributed to the fact that it serves a poorer and more uneducated clientele, offers smaller loans, has higher client training costs, and depends on grants rather than loans to finance its operations.

Village Banking Subsidy Dependence Index Measures, 1991–95

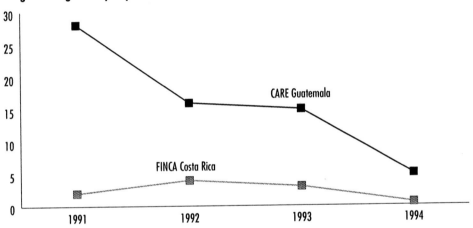

One of the main causes for the decline in the subsidy dependence index for CARE Guatemala is the gradual increase in real interest rates charged by the program. In 1991 the real interest rate charged to the Village Banks was -11.4 percent, whereas in 1995 it was 19.8 percent. In nominal terms, the interest rates swung from nearly half the commercial lending rate in 1991 to 33 percent above commercial rates in 1995. This bold interest rate policy has allowed the program to become much more sustainable, allowing for project growth while maintaining excellent repayment rates.

Despite its favorable decline in recent years, the subsidy dependence index measurement for CARE Guatemala is alarmingly high. After six years of operation, a subsidy dependence index of 4.77 indicates that the program has a long road ahead toward reaching sustainability. After six years of operation, the Grameen Bank had a subsidy dependence index measure of 1.3 in 1989.

Source: Paxton 1997.

Return on Assets Ratio

The return on assets (ROA) ratio measures the net income earned on the assets of an MFI. For calculating the return on assets, average *total* assets are used rather than performing assets, because the organization is being measured on its total financial performance, including decisions made to purchase fixed assets or invest in land and buildings (in other words, using funds that could be used for other revenue-generating investments) or invest in securities. This ratio can also be calculated using only the average outstanding portfolio or the average performing assets as the denominator to determine how specific assets are performing. (The return on portfolio ratio indicates the productivity of the lending activities only. It measures the average revenue received for every unit of currency outstanding in loans. While the return on portfolio might indicate an adequate return, if only 50 percent of the assets are represented by outstanding loans, the organization may not be performing as well as the return on portfolio ratio would indicate. The return on performing assets ratio takes into account the return earned on other investments. The return on total assets ratio shows how the MFI is performing relative to all assets, including nonproductive assets such as fixed assets or land and property.)

◆ For example, if an MFI earns 50,000 in net income and has average assets of 2,740,000 then the return on assets is 1.8 percent.

$$\text{Return on assets} = \frac{\text{Net income}}{\text{Average assets}}$$

$$= \frac{50,000}{2,740,000}$$

$$= 1.8\%$$

Factors that affect the return on assets ratio are varying loan terms, interest rates and fees, and changes in the level of delinquent payments. The split between interest income and fee income also affects this ratio if loan terms and loan amounts change (see chapter 5).

The return on assets ratio is an important indicator to analyze when pricing or loan term structures are changed (or decisions are made to purchase capital assets—see chapter 10). Analysis of this ratio will improve the ability of an MFI to determine the revenue impact of policy changes, improved delinquency management, or the addition of new products.

◆ Using the adjusted sample balance sheet and sample income statement in appendix 4 (with combined adjustments for subsidies and inflation), the following return on assets ratio for 1994 is calculated:

$$\begin{array}{l}\text{Return on assets} \\ \text{(adjusted)}\end{array} = \frac{\text{Net adjusted income}}{\text{Average total assets}}$$

$$= \frac{-5,750}{77,950}$$

$$= -7.4\%$$

(Note that for simplicity's sake, 1993 assets did not include an adjustment to fixed assets for inflation.)

With the adjustments for inflation and subsidies, this sample MFI does not earn a profit. However, if an MFI is financially sustainable (earning a profit after adjustments for subsidies and inflation), the return on assets ratio provides an indication of whether or not the MFI has the potential to generate a commercially acceptable rate of return, which would enable it to access commercial financing as well as potentially become a formal financial institution (if this is not already the case).

Most commercial financial institutions in developing countries earn return on assets ratios of less than 2 percent. Of the 11 successful MFIs studied by the U.S. Agency for International Development, the adjusted return on assets ratios in 1993 ranged from a high of 7.4 percent (LPD in Bali) to a low of –18.5 percent (Kenya Rural Enterprise Programme) (Christen and others 1995).

Return on Business Ratio

To take into account the fact that some MFIs mobilize deposits as a large part of their operations, the return on business (ROB) ratio is provided.

By summing the assets and liabilities and dividing by two, an average *business base* is provided. This is important when an MFI collects deposits due to the added operational and financing costs associated with voluntary savings. The return on business ratio accounts for the dual activity (collecting savings and loans) of its operations. Some commercial banks calculate the return on business ratio, particularly if only a small amount of their business is off-balance sheet activities (letters of credit, guarantees. and so forth).

The return on business ratio is directly affected by the capital structure of an MFI. If the majority of an MFI's assets are funded by equity, the return on business ratio will be misleading and should not be calculated. If an MFI is acting as a true financial intermediary and funding its loan portfolio with client savings, the return on business ratio may be a fairer ratio to compare with other institutions than the return on assets ratio. This is because when an MFI collects savings, it incurs additional costs. These costs are offset either completely or partially by the lower cost of funds (interest paid on client savings is generally lower than the market rate for debt, which is used for the adjusted statements). If only the return on assets ratio was considered, MFIs that mobilize deposits would be penalized by their increased operating costs. The return on business ratio mitigates this fact by including deposits in the denominator.

◆ Using the adjusted sample balance sheet and sample income statement in appendix 4, the following return on business ratio for 1994 is calculated:

$$\text{Return on business (adjusted)} = \frac{\text{Net adjusted income}}{\text{Average business base}}$$

$$= \frac{-5,570}{61,300}$$

$$= -9.4\%$$

Because the sample MFI's capital structure consists of a relatively large amount of equity (no client savings), *it is not applicable to calculate the return on business ratio.* However, ignoring the specific numbers for a moment, we can make some observations.

If the sample MFI collected savings, presumably the spread earned on its loans would more than offset the higher operational costs. The result would be a higher net adjusted income because financing costs would be lower. (This assumes that the MFI would otherwise be funding its loans with borrowed funds at commercial rates or that adjustments have been made to reflect the adjusted cost of capital.) The denominator would also be higher since liabilities would increase relative to equity. The result would be a return on business ratio much closer to the return on assets ratio. If, in fact, the return on business ratio were lower than the return on assets ratio, the MFI would have to consider whether it is profitable to mobilize savings.

Return on Equity Ratio

The return on equity (ROE) ratio provides management and investors with the rate of return earned on the invested equity. It differs from the return on assets ratio in that it measures the return on funds that are owned by the MFI (rather than total assets, which by definition includes both liabilities and equity). If the return on equity is less than the inflation rate, then the equity of the MFI is reduced each year by the difference (net of the nonmonetary assets owned by the MFI). The return on equity ratio also allows donors and investors to determine how their investment in a particular MFI compares against alternative investments. This becomes a crucial indicator when the MFI is seeking private investors.

The return on equity ratio will also vary greatly depending on the capital structure of the MFI. Those that fund their assets primarily with equity will show a lower return on equity than those that fund their assets primarily with liabilities.

◆ Using the adjusted sample balance sheet and sample income statement in appendix 4, the following return on equity for 1994 is calculated:

$$\text{Return on equity (adjusted)} = \frac{\text{Net adjusted income}}{\text{Average equity}}$$

$$= \frac{-5,570}{33,300}$$

$$= -1.7\%$$

Because the sample MFI has not earned profit, its return on equity is not particularly relevant. However, if it were to earn a profit, its return on equity ratio would still be low, because it has a larger portion of equity than most commercial financial institutions. If it were to make a profit or to increase its leverage (amount of debt relative to equity, see below), this ratio would improve.

Many commercial financial institutions target an return on equity of about 15 to 25 percent, depending on the inflation rate in the country. Of the 11 successful MFIs studied by USAID, the adjusted return on equity in 1993 ranged from a high of 32.7 percent (LPD in Bali) to a low of −18.7 percent (FINCA Costa Rica). Bank Rakyat Indonesia and CorpoSol in Colombia also recorded high ROEs of 31 percent and 22.5 percent respectively (Christen and others 1995).

Leverage and Capital Adequacy

Leverage refers to the extent to which an MFI borrows money relative to its amount of equity. In other words, it answers the question of how many additional dollars or other currency can be mobilized from commercial sources for every dollar or other currency worth of funds owned by the MFI. Leverage states the relationship of funding assets with debt versus equity.

Capital adequacy refers to the amount of capital an MFI has relative to its assets. Capital adequacy relates to leverage in terms of the adequacy of the MFI's funding structure.

The term "capital" includes the equity of an MFI and a portion of its liabilities, including subordinated debt.

(For formal financial institutions, capital is defined as equity plus *appropriations for contingencies*. Appropriations for contingencies are a reserve against unforeseen losses on loans, including off-balance sheet items such as letters of credit and guarantees.) Financial institutions generally have three types of capital:

- Invested capital, including member shares, notes payable, and investments by outsiders
- Institutional capital, including retained earnings and reserves (that is, a required amount of capital that a financial institution must set aside as regulated by the superintendent of banks or the government)
- Debt capital, including subordinated debt and loans from the central bank.

Capital serves a variety of purposes: as a source of security, stability, flexibility, and as a buffer against risk and losses. As the possibility of losses increase, the need for capital increases. This is particularly relevant for MFIs, because the borrowers or members often lack occupational and geographical diversity to help spread risk. Capital must be sufficient to cover expected and unexpected losses.

In addition, capital is required to fund losses when new services are introduced, until those services generate adequate income, or when an MFI is expanding. Expansion of the number of branches or the area covered by each branch requires substantial capital investment. The planned growth of an MFI requires capital to increase in proportion to its asset growth.

Leverage

Capital also serves as a base for borrowing. Two common sources from which MFIs borrow funds (leverage their capital base) are *bank loans* (commercial or central banks) and *client deposits*. (However, before any MFI can borrow either commercially or from its client base, it must prove that it is financially viable and that it will continue to be financially viable in the long term.) Sufficient capital encourages lenders and depositors to have confidence in the MFI relative to its ability to provide for losses and fund future growth.

An MFI's leverage is measured by calculating its debt to equity ratio. The *debt to equity ratio* states how much debt an MFI has relative to its equity.

$$\text{Debt to equity ratio} = \frac{\text{Debt}}{\text{Equity}}$$

It is important for all organizations to maintain a proper balance between debt and equity to ensure that the equity or viability of the organization is not at risk. If an MFI has a large amount of equity and very little debt, it is likely limiting its income-generating potential by not making use of external sources of debt (that is, a line of credit or a loan that can be borrowed for, say, 10 percent and on-lent to clients at 25 percent). Therefore, it may be better for the MFI to increase its liabilities, if possible, to increase its income-generating assets (its loan portfolio). (Note, however that this only considers financing costs, not operating costs or loan loss provisions. In this example, if the operating costs and loan loss provisions as a percentage of loans outstanding are greater than 15 percent—the spread—then the MFI should not borrow.) An organization must ensure that it does not take on too much debt relative to its ability to repay that debt.

The degree of leverage greatly affects the return on equity ratio of an MFI (table 9.8). An MFI that is more highly leveraged than another will have a higher return on equity, all other things being equal.

When an MFI is regulated, the degree to which it is allowed to leverage its equity is based on capital adequacy standards.

Capital Adequacy Standards

Capital adequacy means that there is a sufficient level of capital required to absorb potential losses while providing financial sustainability. The purpose of establishing and measuring capital adequacy for an MFI is to ensure the solvency of the organization based on the reasons mentioned above. For the most part, MFIs are highly capitalized due to donor funding and their inability to access commercial debt. However, this is changing, and if MFIs

Table 9.8 Effect of Leverage on Return on Equity

	MFI 1	MFI 2
Average assets	200,000	200,000
Average liabilities	100,000	150,000
Average equity	100,000	50,000
Net income	10,000	10,000
Return on equity	10%	20%

Source: Author's example.

are to reach substantial numbers of low-income clients, they will have to increase and expand their sources of funding while ensuring prudent management. Capital adequacy standards help to ensure the viability of MFIs as they increase their degree of leverage.

International standards of capital adequacy have been put forth through the Basle Agreement (as discussed in chapter 1). Capital adequacy standards require MFIs to have both a minimum nominal amount of capital and an adequate amount of capital to cover the risk of losses.

Capital adequacy is based on risk-weighted assets (as set out under the Basle Accord, which identifies different risk levels for different assets types. There are five standard risk weights ranging from 0 percent to 100 percent risk. For most MFIs, only the first category—0 percent weight; includes cash, central bank balances, and government securities, and the last category—100 percent weight; includes loans to private entities and individuals—are relevant, because MFIs do not generally have fully secured loans—50 percent weight—or off-balance sheet items.) Capital adequacy is set at 8 percent of risk-weighted assets. This means that a regulated MFI can have up to 12 times the amount of debt as equity based on the adjusted (risk-weighted) assets being funded.

Capital is also classified under the Basle Accord by different categories available for inclusion in the calculation of capital adequacy. For example, *core capital* including equity and reserves must be at least 4 percent of risk-weighted assets.

Capital adequacy is usually measured by the following ratio of *capital to risk-weighted assets:*

$$\text{Capital to risk-weighted assets} = \frac{\text{Invested capital + reserves + retained earnings}}{\text{Risk-weighted assets}}$$

This ratio should be calculated periodically to determine the level of capital adequacy of an MFI. As the MFI grows and presumably increases its leverage, this ratio will decrease over time as the organization takes advantage of increased borrowings.

Scale and Depth of Outreach Indicators

In addition to financial performance indicators, many MFIs collect data on their client base—both the *scale* of their activities (number of clients served with different types of instruments) and the *depth* of outreach (type of clients reached and their level of poverty).

A performance assessment framework introduced by Yaron (1992b) consists of two primary criteria: the level of *outreach* achieved among target clientele and *self-sustainability* of the MFI. While these do not provide a full assessment of the economic impact of the operations of an MFI, they serve as quantifiable *proxies* of the extent to which an MFI has reached its objectives, and they make transparent the social costs associated with supporting the institution (Yaron, Benjamin, and Piprek 1997). This section presents the first half of the performance assessment framework only (that is, outreach indicators; self-sustainability indicators are provided above).

The indicators of outreach are both qualitative and quantitative. They are relatively simple to collect and provide a good measure of scale of outreach and good proxies for depth of outreach (a more detailed discussion of depth of outreach is provided below). The indicators can be weighed, quantified, and prioritized according to their relevance to a particular MFI. For example, if gender does not limit access to credit, the weight attached to the number of women clients may be low or even zero (Yaron, Benjamin, and Piprek 1997).

Some of the indicators are repeated from the portfolio report presented in chapter 8 and others are mentioned in the various formulas presented above. Depending on the objectives of the MFI, additional or different indicators may be appropriate. To evaluate the successful outreach of an MFI it is useful to track these indicators over time and compare them with the stated goals of the organization (or projected figures; see box 9.5).

Although outreach often is recorded by the total number of clients served by an MFI (scale of outreach), the *depth of outreach* is a more nebulous measure. As mentioned above, the depth of outreach is proxied by average loan size or average loan size as a percentage of GDP per capita. Although useful measures, these indicators can sometimes be misleading, because the loans are for different terms and uses and may not reflect the income level of the clients. Depth of outreach can have many different meanings. If one takes the view that it refers to providing financial services to those excluded from formal financial services, then it is important to define which sectors of society have little or no access to formal finance (adapted from Paxton and Fruman 1998).

Box 9.5 Outreach Indicators

Clients and staff

Number of clients or members (percentage women)
Percentage of total target clientele serviced (current)
Number of women as percentage of total borrowers
Number of women as percentage of total depositors
Number of staff
Number of urban branches or units
Number of rural branches or units
Ratio of rural to urban branches or units
Ratio of volume of deposits to volume of outstanding loans
Mobile banking in use[a]

Loan outreach

Number of currently active borrowers
Total balance of outstanding loans
Average outstanding portfolio
Real annual average growth rate of loans outstanding
  during the past three years (in real terms)
Loan size
    Minimum
    Maximum
Average disbursed loan size
Average disbursed loan as a percentage
  of GDP per capita
Average outstanding loan size
Average outstanding loan as a percentage
  of GDP per capita
Average loan term
Nominal interest rate
Effective annual interest rate
Value of loans per staff member (per credit officer)
Number of loans per staff member (per credit officer)

Savings outreach

Total balance of voluntary savings accounts
Total annual average savings as a percentage
  of annual average outstanding loan portfolio
Number of current voluntary savings clients
Value of average savings account
Average savings deposits as a percentage of GDP per capita
Value of savings deposits per staff member
Number of savers per staff member
Nominal deposit interest rate (per annum)

a. Mobile banking refers to mobility of staff to be in the villages
and poor neighborhoods daily or weekly, visiting borrowers,
explaining requirements to potential clients, disbursing loans,
and collecting payments.

Source: CGAP 1997; Yaron, Benjamin, and Piprek 1997.

Von Pischke (1991) describes a frontier between the formal and informal financial sectors. Those outside the frontier do not have regular access to formal financial services. In developing countries, several categories of people consistently have been underserved by financial institutions, including (but not restricted to):

- *Rural inhabitants.* Due to the high transactions costs associated with serving a widely dispersed population and the high risk associated with agriculture, formal financial intermediaries have avoided rural areas. Government-sponsored programs that offer rural credit have resulted in disappointing performance due to their reliance on subsidized interest rates, inappropriate terms and conditions, a lack of repayment enforcement, and corruption.

- *Women.* Women have been excluded from formal financial services for a variety of reasons. Perhaps foremost is a cultural bias against women. At the household level, most financial decisions are made by male heads of household, although this cultural norm is shifting gradually. In addition, women represent some of the poorest people in developing countries. Their microenterprises and petty trade do not have sufficient scale to interest formal financial intermediaries. Finally, literacy requirements have barred some illiterate women from obtaining formal financial services. Female clients have been targeted by MFIs not only because of their exclusion from formal finance, but also because women spend a greater percentage of their share of household income on food, children's clothes, education, and health than men do, as demonstrated in several studies (for example, Hopkins, Levin, and Haddad 1994).

- *The poor.* Formal financial intermediaries experience relatively high transaction costs when dealing with very poor people because of the very small size of each transaction. For instance, the cost of offering savings facilities to clients who make frequent microdeposits can be quite high. The same applies for very small loans that require a similar bureaucracy as larger loans in formal financial institutions but capture very little rent, resulting in losses.

- *The uneducated.* People who cannot read and write face an obvious obstacle to obtaining financial services that require any type of written application or paperwork. MFIs have served the illiterate by adopting innovative techniques, including oral training and screening, pictorial training, group guarantees, and the use of thumbprint signatures.

Obviously, many people excluded from formal finance fall into more than one of these categories and thus a correlation exists between these four outreach indicators. To compare MFI clients with the population of the country on average, depth of outreach diamonds provide a simple, intuitive measure of the types of clients being served by a MFI. Box 9.6 illustrates this technique using data from credit-first and savings-first MFIs in Sub-Saharan Africa.

Performance Standards and Variations

There is a multitude of performance indicators that an MFI might use to analyze its financial performance. The ones presented in this chapter have been drawn from a number of institutions, both semiformal and formal. To date, there is no standard set of ratios to use nor standard ranges of performance for the microfinance industry. However, there are currently several efforts under way to establish a set of worldwide micro-

finance performance standards (Saltzman, Rock, and Salinger 1998):

- ACCION recently developed and made public its CAMEL system.
- The Private Sector Initiatives Corporation is developing a rating agency.
- CGAP and the World Bank are funding the *MicroBanking Financial Review*.
- DFID–Department for International Development (UK) is funding the development of the BASE Kenya "Micro Finance Institution Monitoring and Analysis System."
- USAID funded the PEARLS rating system as used by the World Council of Credit Unions (WOCCU).

In addition, various guides have been developed, including the Small Enterprise Education and Promotion Network's *Financial Ratio Analysis of Micro-Finance Institutions*, CGAP's *Management Information Systems for Microfinance Institutions*, and the Inter-American Development Bank's *Technical Guide for the Analysis of Microenterprise Finance Institutions*.

An overview of four of the most well-known approaches and of the ratios used is provided in boxes 9.7–9.10.

Box 9.6 Depth of Outreach Diamonds

IN ORDER TO ANALYZE THE DEGREE TO WHICH CREDIT-FIRST
and savings-first financial institutions serve rural, female,
poor, and illiterate clients, depth of outreach diamonds
were constructed. These diamonds examine these four outreach indicators of credit-first and savings-first institutions
in comparison to the overall country averages.

The diamonds present a simple graphic representation
of the four outreach indicators. Three of the variables
(urban, male, and literate) are percentages calculated on a 0
to 1 scale. Rather than using GDP per capita as a measure
of country-level income, the alternative measure of GDP
divided by the economically active population was used.
This measure was normalized to one for the country average. The income of the clients was put on the same scale by
dividing the average income of the clients by the country-
level income. Using this approach, smaller diamonds reflect
a greater depth of outreach.

The outreach diamonds illustrate an average of the sav-
ings-led institutions in the first diamond and the credit-led
institutions in the second diamond. The country averages
give a general benchmark for comparison for the savings-
first and credit-first averages. Upon first glance, one notices
that the credit-first diamond generally is smaller than the
country average diamond, representing a deep outreach,
while the savings-first diamond has a roughly similar area
to the country average diamond. This finding parallels a
similar study performed on Latin American microfinance
institutions.

Upon further examination, more specific details of outreach are revealed. Among the savings-first institutions, the
average clients tend to be more literate and male than the
country average. Many credit unions have a predominantly
male membership, although more female members have
joined African credit unions in recent years. In addition,
credit unions have been active in literacy training in Africa.
On average, credit-first membership is slightly poorer and
much more rural than the country averages.

In contrast, the outreach diamond for credit-first institutions shows an entirely different clientele. On average, the
credit-first programs target a more urban, female, illiterate
clientele than the country average. Urban market women
represent a large percentage of credit-first clients. The
incomes of these clients is nearly one half the average income
per economically active worker in the country. In this
respect, it is clear that the credit-first programs have a significant outreach to underserved portions of the community.

Source: Paxton and Fruman 1998.

Outreach of Savings-First and Credit-First Institutions

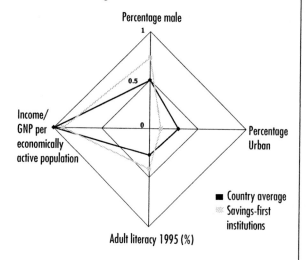

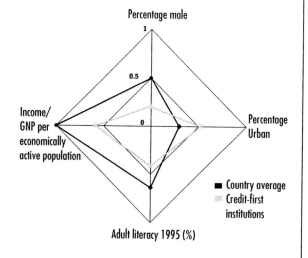

Box 9.7 CAMEL System, ACCION

THE CAMEL SYSTEM ANALYZES THE FIVE TRADITIONAL aspects considered to be most important in the operation of a financial intermediary. These five areas reflect the financial condition and general operational strength of the MFI and are briefly summarized below.

C—Capital adequacy. The capital position of the institution and its capacity to support growth of the loan portfolio as well as a potential deterioration in assets are assessed. The CAMEL analysis looks at the institution's ability to raise additional equity in the case of losses and its ability and policies to establish reserves against the inherent risk in its operations.

$$\text{Leverage} = \frac{\text{Risk assets}}{\text{Equity}}$$

$$\text{Reserve adequacy} = \frac{\text{Actual loan loss reserve}}{\text{CAMEL adjusted loan loss reserve}}$$

A—Asset quality. The overall quality of the loan portfolio and other assets, including infrastructure (for example, office location and environment), is examined. This requires analyzing the level of portfolio at risk and write-offs, as well as the appropriateness of the portfolio classification system, collection procedures, and write-off policies.

$$\text{Portfolio at risk} = \frac{\text{Past due loan balance} > 30 \text{ days} + \text{legal recovery}}{\text{Active loan portfolio}}$$

$$\text{Write-offs} = \frac{\text{Net write-offs}}{\text{Active loan portfolio of the relevant period}}$$

M—Management. Human resource policy, the general management of the institution, management information systems, internal control and auditing, and strategic planning and budgeting are examined as distinct areas that reflect the overall quality of management.

E—Earnings. The key components of revenues and expenses are analyzed, including the level of operational efficiency and the institution's interest rate policy as well as the overall results as measured by return on equity (ROE) and return on assets (ROA).

$$\text{Return on equity} = \frac{\text{Net income from operations}}{\text{Average equity}}$$

$$\text{Operational efficiency} = \frac{\text{Operational expenses}}{\text{Average loan portfolio}}$$

$$\text{Return on assets} = \frac{\text{Net income from operations}}{\text{Average assets}}$$

L—Liquidity. This component of the analysis looks at the institution's ability to project funding needs in general and credit demand in particular. The liability structure of the institution, as well as the productivity of its current assets, is also an important aspect of the overall assessment of an institution's liquidity management.

$$\text{Productivity of other current assets} = \frac{1 - \text{interest income earned cash and near-cash}}{[(\text{average monthly cash} + \text{near-cash} - \text{liquidity cushion}) * (\text{average 6 month CD rate})] + (\text{liquidity cushion} \times \text{average savings rate})}$$

Source: Saltzman, Rock, and Salinger 1998.

Box 9.8 Financial Ratio Analysis for Microfinance Institutions, Small Enterprise Education and Promotion Network

THIS GUIDE SETS OUT A FRAMEWORK FOR ANALYZING THE financial condition of an MFI. The framework is divided into three groups, each of which comprises a set of ratios.

The first group of ratios analyzes the *financial sustainability* of the MFI—or the ability of an MFI to meet the needs of its clientele without reliance on external assistance.

$$\text{Return on performing assets} = \frac{\text{Financial income}}{\text{Average performing assets}}$$

$$\text{Financial cost ratio} = \frac{\text{Financial costs}}{\text{Average performing assets}}$$

$$\text{Loan loss provision ratio} = \frac{\text{Loan loss provisions}}{\text{Average performing assets}}$$

$$\text{Operating cost ratio} = \frac{\text{Operating expenses}}{\text{Average performing assets}}$$

$$\text{Adjusted cost of capital} = \frac{\begin{array}{c}[(\text{Inflation} \times (\text{net worth} \\ - \text{net fixed assets})] \\ + [(\text{inflation} - \text{interest rate paid}) \\ \times \text{concessional loans}]\end{array}}{\text{Average performing assets}}$$

$$\text{Donations and grants ratio} = \frac{\text{Donations and grants}}{\text{Average performing assets}}$$

$$\text{Operating self-sufficiency} = \frac{\text{Financial income}}{\begin{array}{c}\text{Financial + operating costs} \\ + \text{loan loss provision}\end{array}}$$

$$\text{Financial self-sufficiency} = \frac{\text{Financial income}}{\begin{array}{c}\text{Financial + operating costs} \\ + \text{provision + cost of capital}\end{array}}$$

The second group of ratios analyzes *financial efficiency*. MFIs must be concerned with serving as many people as possible with their resources.

$$\text{Cost per unit of money lent} = \frac{\text{Operating costs}}{\text{Total amount disbursed}}$$

$$\text{Cost per loan made} = \frac{\text{Operating costs}}{\text{Number of loans made}}$$

$$\begin{array}{c}\text{Number of active borrowers} \\ \text{per credit officer}\end{array} = \frac{\text{Average number of active borrowers}}{\text{Average number of credit officers}}$$

$$\text{Portfolio per credit officer} = \frac{\text{Average number of loans outstanding}}{\begin{array}{c}\text{Financial + operating costs} \\ + \text{loan loss provision}\end{array}}$$

The third group of ratios helps MFIs monitor their *portfolio quality*. If the quality of the portfolio is poor, the MFI cannot continue to operate in the long term.

$$\text{Portfolio in arrears} = \frac{\text{Payments in arrears}}{\text{Value of loans outstanding}}$$

$$\text{Portfolio at risk} = \frac{\text{Balance of loans in arrears}}{\text{Value of loans outstanding}}$$

$$\text{Loan loss ratio} = \frac{\text{Amount written off}}{\text{Average loans outstanding}}$$

$$\text{Reserve ratio} = \frac{\text{Loan loss reserve}}{\text{Value of loans outstanding}}$$

Source: SEEP Network and Calmeadow 1995.

Box 9.9 PEARLS System, World Council of Credit Unions

PERLAS OR PEARLS IS A SYSTEM OF 39 FINANCIAL RATIOS that the World Council of Credit Unions (WOCCU) uses worldwide to monitor the performance of credit unions. It was originally designed and implemented with Guatemalan credit unions in the late 1980s.

The WOCCU now uses it to create a universal financial language that each credit union can speak and understand, to generate comparative credit union rankings, and to provide the framework for a supervisory unit at the second tier. Each ratio has a standard target or goal that each credit union should strive to achieve.

A brief description of the PEARLS system and some of the key ratios are provided.

P—Protection (5 ratios). Refers to adequate protection of assets. Protection is measured by comparing the adequacy of the provisions for loan losses against the amount of delinquent loans. Protection was deemed adequate if a credit union had sufficient provisions to cover 100 percent of all loans delinquent for more than 12 months and 35 percent of all loans delinquent for 1–12 months.

E—Effective financial structure (8 ratios). Determines growth potential, earnings capacity, and overall financial strength. Ratios measure assets, liabilities, and capital, and their associated targets constitute an ideal structure for credit unions.

Net loans/total assets	(Goal 60%–80%)
Liquid investments/total assets	(Goal maximum 20%)
Fixed assets/total assets	(Goal maximum 5%)
Savings and deposits/total assets	(Target 70%–80%)
External borrowing/total assets	(Goal 0%)
Reserves and retained earnings/ total assets	(Minimum 8%)

A—Asset quality (3 ratios). Ratios measure the impact of assets that do not generate income.

Portfolio at risk > 30 days/ total loans	(Goal is < 5%; maximum 10%)
Nonearning assets/ total assets	(Maximum 7%)

R—Rates of return and costs (12 ratios). Disaggregates the essential components of net earnings (by investment) to help management calculate investment yields and evaluate operating expenses. The results more clearly indicate whether the credit union is earning and paying market rate on its assets, liabilities, and capital.

Operating expenses/ average assets	(Goal < 10%)
Net income/ average assets	(Sufficient to maintain capital ratio of > 8%)
Return to members on shares	(Goal > inflation rate)

L—Liquidity (4 ratios). Reveal if the credit union is administering its cash to meet deposit withdrawal requests and liquidity reserve requirements, while minimizing the amount of idle funds.

Liquidity reserve/ withdrawable savings	(Goal 10% minimum)

S—Signs of growth (7 ratios). Measures both financial and membership growth. By comparing asset growth to other key areas, it is possible to detect changes in the balance sheet structure that could have a positive or negative impact on earnings. Growth of institutional capital is the best indicator of profitability and success, particularly if it is proportionately greater than the growth in assets.

Source: Evans 1997.

Box 9.10 Tracking Performance through Indicators, Consultative Group to Assist the Poorest

IN ITS PUBLICATION *MANAGEMENT INFORMATION SYSTEMS for Microfinance Institutions* CGAP put forth a list of indicators oriented toward the needs of managers of MFIs. The indicators are divided into six broad groups. Fifteen of the indicators are considered by the group as key for both managers of MFIs and such external users as donors, investors, and regulators. Key indicators are presented in capital letters.

Portfolio quality indicators
Portfolio at risk, two or more payments
LOAN LOSS RESERVE RATIO
LOAN WRITE-OFF RATIO
LOAN RESCHEDULING RATIO

Profitability indicators
ADJUSTED RETURN ON ASSETS
Adjusted return on equity
Return on assets
Return on equity
Financial sustainability

Financial solvency indicators
Equity multiplier
Quick ratio
Gap ratio
Net interest margin
Currency gap ratio
Currency gap risk
Real effective interest rate

Growth indicators
ANNUAL GROWTH IN PORTFOLIO
ANNUAL GROWTH IN BORROWERS
Annual growth in savings
Annual growth in depositors

Productivity indictors
ACTIVE BORROWERS PER LOAN OFFICER
Active borrower groups per loan officer
NET LOAN PORTFOLIO PER LOAN OFFICER
Active clients per branch
Net loan portfolio per branch
Savings per branch
YIELD GAP
Yield on performing assets
YIELD ON PORTFOLIO
Loan officers as a percentage of staff
OPERATING COST RATIO
Average cost of debt
Average group size
Head officer overhead share

Outreach indicators
NUMBER OF ACTIVE CLIENTS
Percentage of female clients
Number of active savers
Value of all savings accounts
Median savings account balance
Number of active borrowers
VALUE OF NET OUTSTANDING LOAN PORTFOLIO
DROPOUT RATE
Median size of first loans
MEDIAN OUTSTANDING LOAN BALANCE
Percentage of loans to targeted group

Source: Waterfield and Ramsing 1998.

Appendix 1. Sample Balance Sheet

BALANCE SHEET

as at December 31, 1995

	1995	1994	1993
ASSETS			
Cash and bank current accounts	5,000	2,500	5,000
Interest-bearing deposits	8,000	7,000	2,000
Loans outstanding			
Current	66,000	50,000	32,000
Past-due	17,000	29,500	20,000
Restructured	1,000	500	0
Loans outstanding (gross)	84,000	70,000	52,000
(Loan loss reserve)	(7,000)	(5,000)	(5,000)
Net loans outstanding	77,000	65,000	47,000
Other current assets	500	1,000	500
TOTAL CURRENT ASSETS	90,500	75,500	54,500
Long-term investments	12,500	11,000	8,000
Property and equipment			
Cost	4,000	4,000	3,000
(Accumulated depreciation)	(700)	(300)	(200)
Net property and equipment	3,300	3,700	2,800
TOTAL LONG-TERM ASSETS	15,800	14,700	10,800
TOTAL ASSETS	106,300	90,200	65,300
LIABILITIES			
Short-term borrowings (commercial rate)	18,000	12,000	6,000
Client savings	0	0	0
TOTAL CURRENT LIABILITIES	18,000	12,000	6,000
Long-term debt (commercial rate)	12,000	15,000	7,500
Long-term debt (concessional rate)	35,000	30,000	18,800
Restricted or deferred revenue	0	0	0
TOTAL LIABILITIES	65,000	57,000	32,300
EQUITY			
Loan fund capital	40,100	33,000	33,000
Retained net surplus (deficit) prior years	200	0	0
Current-year net surplus (deficit)	1,000	200	0
TOTAL EQUITY	41,300	33,200	33,000
TOTAL LIABILITIES AND EQUITY	106,300	90,200	65,300

Source: Ledgerwood 1996.

Appendix. 2 Sample Income Statement

STATEMENT OF INCOME AND EXPENDITURE

For the period ending December 31, 1995

	1995	1994	1993
FINANCIAL INCOME			
Interest on current and past due loans	15,400	12,000	9,000
Interest on restructured loans	100	50	0
Interest on investments	500	1,500	400
Loan fees and service charges	5,300	5,000	3,850
Late fees on loans	200	300	350
TOTAL FINANCIAL INCOME	21,500	18,850	13,600
FINANCIAL COSTS			
Interest on debt	3,700	3,500	1,200
Interest paid on deposits	0	0	0
TOTAL FINANCIAL COSTS	3,700	3,500	1,200
GROSS FINANCIAL MARGIN	17,800	15,350	12,400
Provision for loan losses	2,500	3,000	5,000
NET FINANCIAL MARGIN	15,300	12,350	7,400
OPERATING EXPENSES			
Salaries and benefits	6,000	5,000	4,000
Administrative expenses	2,600	2,500	2,300
Occupancy expense	2,500	2,500	2,150
Travel	2,500	2,500	2,000
Depreciation	400	300	200
Other	300	300	250
TOTAL OPERATING EXPENSES	14,300	13,100	10,900
NET INCOME FROM OPERATIONS	1,000	(750)	(3,500)
Grant revenue for operations	0	950	3,500
EXCESS OF INCOME OVER EXPENSES	1,000	200	0

Source: Ledgerwood 1996.

Appendix 3. Sample Portfolio Report

PORTFOLIO REPORT

Portfolio data	1995	1994	1993
Total value of loans disbursed during the period	160,000	130,000	88,000
Total number of loans disbursed during the period	1,600	1,300	1,100
Number of active borrowers (end of period)	1,800	1,550	1,320
Average number of active borrowers	1,675	1,435	1,085
Value of loans outstanding (end of period)	84,000	70,000	52,000
Average outstanding balance of loans	75,000	61,000	45,000
Value of payments in arrears (end of period)	7,000	9,000	10,000
Value of outstanding balances of loans in arrears (end of period)	18,000	20,000	20,000
Value of loans written off during the period	500	3,000	0
Average initial loan size	100	100	80
Average loan term (months)	12	12	12
Average number of credit officers during the period	6	6	4

Days past due	(A) Number of loans past due	(B) Outstanding balance of loans past due	(C) Loan loss reserve (%)	(D) Loan loss reserve ($) (B) x (C)
1–30	200	8,750	10	875
31–60	75	5,000	50	2,500
61–90	60	2,500	75	1,875
90–120	15	1,100	100	1,100
> 120	10	650	100	650
	360	18,000		7,000

Appendix 4. Adjusted Sample Financial Statements (Combined)

The following balance sheet represents an MFI's financial position as at December 31, 1994, with ad-justments for inflation (400 for revaluation of non-financial assets and 3,300 for devaluation of equity) and subsidies (950 donation for operating costs and 2,100 for adjusted financial costs on concessional loans).

BALANCE SHEET (adjusted)
as at December 31, 1994

	1994	Adjust	1994A
ASSETS			
Cash and bank current accounts	2,500		2,500
Interest-bearing deposits	7,000		7,000
Loans outstanding			
Current	50,000		50,000
Past due	29,500		29,500
Restructured	500		500
Loans outstanding (gross)	70,000		70,000
(Loan loss reserve)	(5,000)		(5,000)
Net loans outstanding	65,000		65,000
Other current assets	1,000		1,000
TOTAL CURRENT ASSETS	75,500		75,500
Long-term investments	11,000		11,000
Property and equipment			
Cost	4,000		4,000
Revaluation of fixed assets		400	*400*
(Accumulated depreciation)	(300)		(300)
Net property and equipment	3,700		**4,100**
TOTAL LONG-TERM ASSETS	14,700		**15,100**
TOTAL ASSETS	90,200		**90,600**
LIABILITIES			
Short-term borrowings (commercial rate)	12,000		12,000
Client savings	0		0
TOTAL CURRENT LIABILITIES	12,000		12,000
Long-term debt (commercial rate)	15,000		15,000
Long-term debt (concessional rate)	30,000		30,000
Restricted or deferred revenue	0		0
TOTAL LIABILITIES	57,000		57,000
EQUITY			
Loan fund capital	33,000		33,000
Inflation adjustment—equity		3,300	*3,300*
Accumulated capital—financial costs		2,100	*2,100*
Accumulated capital—donation		950	*950*
Retained net surplus (deficit) prior years	0		0
Current-year net surplus (deficit)	200		(5,750)
TOTAL EQUITY	33,200		33,600
TOTAL LIABILITIES AND EQUITY	90,200		90,600

Source for unadjusted statements: SEEP Network and Calmeadow 1995.

INCOME STATEMENT (adjusted)

for the period ended December 31, 1994

	1994	Adjustment	1994A
FINANCIAL INCOME:			
Interest on current and/past due loans	12,000		12,000
Interest on restructured loans	50		50
Interest on investments	1,500		1,500
Loan fees or service charges	5,000		5,000
Late fees on loans	300		300
Revaluation of fixed assets		*400*	*400*
TOTAL FINANCIAL INCOME	18,850		**19,250**
FINANCIAL COSTS			
Interest on debt	3,500		3,500
Adjusted concessional debt		*2,100*	*2,100*
Interest paid on deposits	0		0
TOTAL FINANCIAL COSTS	3,500		5,600
GROSS FINANCIAL MARGIN	15,350		13,650
Provision for loan losses	3,000		3,000
NET FINANCIAL MARGIN	12,350		**10,650**
OPERATING EXPENSES			
Salaries and benefits	5,000		5,000
Administrative expenses	2,500		2,500
Occupancy expense	2,500		2,500
Travel	2,500		2,500
Depreciation	300		300
Other	300		300
Revaluation of equity		*3,300*	*3,300*
TOTAL OPERATING EXPENSES	13,100		**16,400**
NET INCOME FROM OPERATIONS	(750)		(5,750)
Grant revenue for operations	950	(950)	0
EXCESS OF INCOME OVER EXPENSES	**200**		**(5,750)**

Source for unadjusted statements: SEEP Network and Calmeadow 1995.

Appendix 5. Analyzing an MFI's Return on Assets

To further analyze the financial performance of an MFI, it is useful to decompose the return on assets ratio into two components: the *profit margin* and *asset utilization*.[3] The profit margin looks at profits relative to total revenue earned. This can then be further broken down into the four costs incurred by an MFI stated as a percentage of total revenue. (Alternatively, these costs can be stated as a percentage of total assets, performing assets, or portfolio and compared with the yield [revenue] earned on these assets. For further information see SEEP Network

and Calmeadow 1995.) Asset utilization examines the revenue per dollar (or other currency) of total assets. This is further broken down into interest income per dollar of assets and noninterest income per dollar of assets to provide an indication of where the revenue is earned based on where the assets are invested (loan portfolio versus other investments).

When analyzing an MFI, it is useful to break down the profit margin and asset utilization into a series of ratios that relate each item to total income or total assets. In this way, it is possible to examine the source of the major portion of the MFI's revenue and the funding sources. For example, the adjusted financial

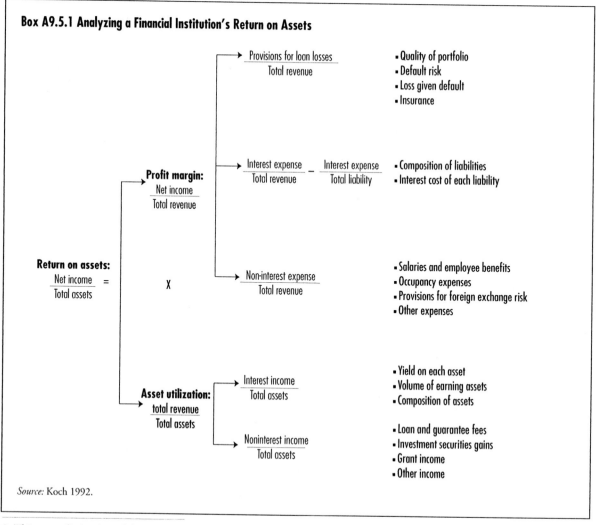

Box A9.5.1 Analyzing a Financial Institution's Return on Assets

Source: Koch 1992.

---

3. This appendix is adapted from Benjamin and Ledgerwood (1998).

statements of the sample MFI in appendixes 1 and 2 for 1994 are broken down as shown in table A9.5.1.

This breakdown shows clearly the sources of revenue for an MFI, the way it invests its assets, and the way it funds those assets. This, in turn, can be compared with other MFIs or formal financial institutions to potentially improve the financial management of the MFI. For example, if it is discovered that the MFI has a large portion—say, 20 percent—of its assets in nonrevenue-generating assets (such as cash or bank current accounts), it would be necessary to ensure that the portion of nonrevenue-generating assets be reduced.

Rather than carry out a detailed return on assets analysis on the sample MFI (since it does not make a profit once the adjustments are made), the following examines a real-life MFI and its profitability through an analysis of the return on assets.

Analysis of the Return on Assets of the Association for the Development of Microenterprises, 1996

(Excerpt from Benjamin and Ledgerwood 1998.)

Although the Association for the Development of Microenterprises (ADEMI) is a nonprofit institution, it has earned remarkable surpluses on its equity. The return on equity (excluding grants) ranged from 30 to 45 percent in the past three years, compared to around 25 percent for commercial banks in the Dominican Republic. The return on assets for the past five years has ranged between 13 percent and 20 percent, far exceeding most commercial bank return on assets ratios of 1 percent to 2 percent.

In 1996 ADEMI enjoyed a profit margin of 44 percent, up from the 35 percent to 40 percent range that has prevailed since 1992. ADEMI has achieved this both by containing costs and bad debts, and by generating substantial revenues. For example, in 1994, ADEMI's ratio of total revenues to total assets was 37 percent, compared to 18 percent for Banco Popular, which is widely regarded as one of the best-managed banks in the Dominican Republic, and under 10 percent for U.S. banks.

While the profit margin has been rising, the asset utilization ratio has been declining fairly rapidly, due to declining market rates and major shifts in the composition of the portfolio. In particular, it has fallen by 20 percentage point since the inception of small- and medium-scale lending, which ADEMI began in 1992 (in addition to its microlending). Taken together, this explains the decline in ADEMI's return on assets over the past five years (see table A9.5.2).

BOOSTING PROFITS BY ENSURING PORTFOLIO QUALITY. This is the key area in which ADEMI and other successful MFIs have excelled relative to unsuccessful lenders. ADEMI's

---

Table A9.5.1 Breakdown of a Microfinance Institution's Profit Margin and Asset Utilization

Profit margin	1994 (percent)
Total income	100
Interest revenue—loans	65
Interest revenue—investments	8
Loan fees	28
Other income (revaluation of fixed assets)	2
Expenses	130
Financing costs (adjusted)	29
Provision for loan losses	16
Operating expenses (adjusted)	85.2
Salaries and benefits	26
Revaluation of equity	17
Net income	−30

Asset utilization	1994 (percent)
Total assets	100
Cash and bank current accounts	3
Interest-bearing deposits	8
Loans outstanding—gross	77
Loans outstanding—net	72
Other assets	1
Long-term investments	12
Net property and equipment	5
Total liabilities and equity	100
Short-term debt	13
Long-term debt—commercial	17
Long-term debt—concessional	33
Total liabilities	63
Loan fund capital—equity and retained earnings	30
Accumulated capital—financial costs and donations	3
Inflation adjustment—equity	4
Total equity	37%

Source: Benjamin and Ledgerwood 1998.

Table A9.5.2 Analysis of ADEMI's Return on Assets

Overall return	1984	1986	1988	1990	1992	1994	1996
Return on equity	46.7	70.0	29.2	55.3	46.9	33.5	31.0
Equity/assets	45.5	35.3	30.9	32.3	43.0	41.5	44.1
Return on assets	21.2	24.7	9.0	17.9	20.2	13.9	13.7
Return on equity excluding grants	−55.8	−14.2	20.7	44.5	45.4	33.5	30.3
Return on assets excluding grants	−25.4	−5.0	6.4	14.4	19.5	13.9	13.4
Profit margin							
Net income/total revenue	28.6	44.7	22.6	37.9	38.2	37.1	43.7
Expense/total revenue	5.0	1.5	7.8	12.9	19.5	21.2	11.2
Interest expense/debt	10.1	1.3	4.7	9.6	19.9	14.3	6.7
Loan loss provision/total revenue	3.6	5.4	5.0	5.3	6.0	6.3	6.2
Noninterest expense/total revenue	62.8	48.5	64.7	43.9	36.3	35.4	38.9
Asset utilization							
Total revenue/total assets	74.2	55.3	40.0	47.1	52.8	37.4	31.3
Interest income/total assets	27.6	25.6	35.5	41.2	48.0	34.5	28.2
Interest income/loan portfolio	35.2	44.0	46.6	54.7	62.4	43.3	38.0
Noninterest income/total assets	46.6	29.7	4.5	5.9	4.8	2.9	3.0

Source: Benjamin and Ledgerwood 1998.

success is due in large part to the introduction, in 1987, of performance-based incentives for its credit officers. Since then, arrears have remained below 10 percent of the loan portfolio and have been reduced to under 6 percent in 1995 and 1996. Overall, ADEMI has managed to maintain a historic loss ratio of less than 2 percent.

BOOSTING PROFITS BY CONTAINING NONINTEREST EXPENSES. Non-interest expenses as a share of total income, excluding grants, have fallen every single year since ADEMI's inception, from 63 percent in 1984, to 44 percent in 1990, to 35 percent in 1994, until 1996 when they rose again to around 39 percent. As a share of total assets, ADEMI's noninterest expenses continued to decline to 3 percent in 1996 from 6 percent in 1990.

BOOSTING THE PROFIT MARGIN BY CONTAINING INTEREST EXPENSES. ADEMI has maintained a low debt:equity ratio. This has never risen above 2.5:1. In recent years it has hovered around 1.3:1 compared with an average of 10:1 in the Dominican banking system. By generating vast profits and ploughing them back into its operations, ADEMI has held total borrowings below 70 percent of its net loan portfolio in recent years and thus substantial-

ly reduced interest expenses. Second, ADEMI has continually substituted, to the extent possible, lower cost funding (long-term, low-interest loans, grants, and "loans from clients") for the relatively expensive funding it received from the Banco Popular and FONDOMICRO (USAID-sponsored apex lender) in earlier years.

UTILIZING ASSETS TO GENERATE INTEREST INCOME. ADEMI's loan portfolio grew by an average of 46 percent a year during the 1990s and now exceeds that of the majority of banks in the Dominican Republic. In recent years ADEMI's loan portfolio accounted for 76 percent to 80 percent of assets. Only in 1996 did the portfolio decline to 70 percent of assets as ADEMI took an unusually liquid position with cash and bank deposits more than doubling to 17 percent of assets. However, since 1992 interest rates in the Dominican economy have declined. At the same time ADEMI began making small business loans at much lower rates than its micro loans. The result has been a drop in ADEMI's interest income over its loan portfolio from 62 percent to 32 percent between 1992 and 1996.

UTILIZING ASSETS TO GENERATE NONINTEREST INCOME. Noninterest income in ADEMI's case consists of premia on life insurance policies, which are mandatory for unsecured microenterprise loans and are assessed at a rate of 28 basis points per peso lent, income from disposition of acquired assets, fee income from Banco Popular related to the ADEMI MasterCard, and income from grants. (While ADEMI charges up-front fees on loans, these are classified under interest income.) Since 1992 there has been only one year in which grants accounted for more than 1.2 percent of total revenue. While other noninterest income has grown slightly as a share of total income, rising to around nine percent by 1996, it has declined relative to total assets, from 4.2 percent in 1992 to 2.7 percent in 1996.

Sources and Further Reading

Bartel, Margaret, Michael J. McCord, and Robin R. Bell. 1995. *Financial Management Ratios I: Analyzing Profitability in Microcredit Programs.* GEMINI Technical Note 7. Financial Assistance to Microenterprise Programs: Development Alternatives Inc. Washington, D.C.: USAID.

Benjamin, McDonald, and Joanna Ledgerwood. 1998. "The Association for the Development of Microenterprises (ADEMI): 'Democratising Credit' in the Dominican Republic." Case Study for the Sustainable Banking with the Poor Project, World Bank, Washington, D.C.

Christen, Robert, Elisabeth Rhyne, Robert Vogel, and Cressida McKean. 1995. *Maximizing the Outreach of Microenterprise Finance: An Analysis of Successful Microfinance Programs.* Program and Operations Assessment Report 10. U.S. Agency for International Development, Washington, D.C.

CGAP (Consultative Group to Assist the Poorest). 1997. *Format for Appraisal of Micro-Finance Institutions.* World Bank, Washington, D.C.

Evans, AnnaCor. 1997. "PEARLS: A Tool for Financial Stabilization, Monitoring, and Evaluation." *NEXUS Newsletter* 38. Small Enterprise Education and Promotion Network, New York.

Koch, Timothy. 1992. *Bank Management.* 2d ed. Chicago: Dryden Press.

Ledgerwood, Joanna. 1995. "Philippines Poverty Strategy Report: Access to Credit for the Poor." World Bank, East Asia Country Department, Washington, D.C.

Ledgerwood, Joanna. 1996. *Financial Management Training for Microfinance Organizations: Finance Study Guide.* New York: PACT Publications (for Calmeadow).

Ledgerwood, Joanna, and Kerri Moloney. 1996. *Financial Management Training for Microfinance Organizations:*

Accounting Study Guide. New York: PACT Publications (for Calmeadow).

Paxton, Julia. 1997. "Guatemala CARE Village Banks Project." Case Study for the Sustainable Banking with the Poor Project, World Bank, Washington, D.C.

Paxton, Julia, and Carlos Cuevas. 1997. "Outreach and Sustainability of Member-Based Rural Financial Intermediaries." Sustainable Banking with the Poor Project, World Bank, Washington, D.C.

Paxton, Julia, and Cecile Fruman. 1998. "Outreach and Sustainability of Savings-First vs. Credit-First Financial Institutions: A Comparative Analysis of Eight Microfinance Institutions in Africa." Sustainable Banking with the Poor Project, World Bank, Washington, D.C.

Saltzman, Sonia B., Rachel Rock, and Darcy Salinger. 1998. *Performance and Standards in Microfinance: ACCION's Experience with the CAMEL Instrument. Discussion Document 7.* Washington, D.C.: ACCION International.

SEEP (Small Enterprise Education and Promotion) Network and Calmeadow. 1995. *Financial Ratio Analysis of Micro-Finance Institutions.* New York: PACT Publications.

Stearns, Katherine. 1991. *The Hidden Beast: Delinquency in Microenterprise Programs.* Washington, D.C.: ACCION International.

Vogel, Robert C. 1988. "Measurement of Loan Repayment Performance: Basic Considerations and Major Issues." World Bank, Economic Development Institute, Washington, D.C.

Von Pischke, J.D. 1991. *Finance at the Frontier: Debt Capacity and the Role of Credit in the Private Economy.* Washington, D.C.: World Bank, Economic Development Institute.

———. 1994. "Measuring the Performance of Small Enterprise Lenders." Paper prepared for a conference on Financial Services and the Poor, Brookings Institution, September 28–30, Washington, D.C.

Waterfield, Charles, and Nick Ramsing. 1998. "Management Information Systems for Microfinance Institutions: A Handbook." Prepared for the Consultative Group to Assist the Poorest by Deloitte Touche Tohmatsu International in association with MEDA Trade & Consulting and Shorebank Advisory Services, Washington, D.C.

Yaron, Jacob. 1992a. *Assessing Development Finance Institutions: A Public Interest Analysis.* World Bank Discussion Paper 174. Washington, D.C.

———. 1992b. *Successful Rural Finance Institutions.* World Bank Discussion Paper 150. Washington, D.C.

Yaron, Jacob, McDonald P. Benjamin Jr., and Gerda L. Piprek. 1997. *Rural Finance: Issues, Design, and Best Practices.* Environmentally and Socially Sustainable Development Studies and Monographs Series 14. Washington, D.C.: World Bank.

CHAPTER TEN

Performance Management

The effective financial management of an MFI requires an understanding of how various operational issues affect financial performance. The performance indicators presented in chapter 9 provide a means of analyzing the financial performance of an MFI and determining the improvements that might be required. This chapter offers information on effectively managing the financial and operational aspects of an MFI to improve performance.

It addresses three main areas of performance management:

- Delinquency
- Productivity and efficiency
- Risk, including liquidity and interest rate risk, foreign exchange risk, and operating risk (credit risk is discussed under delinquency management).

Much of the focus in this chapter is on controlling costs and increasing revenue. Profitability and financial viability are not discussed here, because financial viability is a result of dealing successfully with *all* of the issues discussed in parts II and III of this handbook. Specifically, once MFIs have determined appropriate demand, they must then develop and price their products (chapters 5 and 6), create effective and useful management information systems (chapter 7), produce accurate and timely financial statements (chapter 8), calculate appropriate and relevant performance indicators (chapter 9), and effectively manage delinquency, productivity, liquidity risk, interest rate risk, and operating risk (chapter 10). Thus this chapter, while not directly addressing financial viability issues, does address the financial management issues that ultimately affect financial viability.

Effective performance management is of concern primarily to practitioners and consultants, because it is they who must implement or advise on effective financial management tools and policies. Donors will be interested in this chapter to the extent that they must ensure that the MFIs they support are moving toward developing management practices that will result in financial sustainability.[1]

Delinquency Management

Delinquent loans play a critical role in an MFI's *expenses, cash flow, revenue, and profitability.*

Additional efforts to collect delinquent loans usually mean additional *expenses* for closer monitoring, more frequent visits to borrowers, more extensive analysis of the portfolio, legal fees for pursuing seriously delinquent borrowers, and so forth. The more time, effort, and resources that are put into controlling delinquency, the less there are available for the MFI to reach new borrowers and expand services or outreach.

Delinquency can result in a slower turnover of the loan portfolio and an inability to pay expenses due to reduced *cash flow.* If loan principal is not recovered at the scheduled time, loans to other borrowers cannot be made, and payment of some expenses may also have to be delayed. Also, with reduced cash flow, the MFI may be unable to make timely repayment of borrowed funds or meet the demand for savings withdrawals.

Delinquent loans also result in postponed or lost interest *revenue.* To determine the amount of postponed revenue resulting from delinquent loans, the

1. Portions of this chapter are based on material originally published in Ledgerwood (1996).

interest received in a given period is compared with the expected revenue in the period. This is done by multiplying the effective yield by the average portfolio outstanding in the period and comparing the result with interest received.

$$\text{Expected revenue for the period} = \frac{\text{Period of effective yield}}{\text{x amount outstanding during the period}}$$

The difference between the amount actually received in the period and the expected revenue is the amount of postponed or lost revenue for the period.

The Effect of Delinquency on an MFI's Profitability

Clearly, the profitability of an MFI is affected if interest revenue is not received on delinquent loans. However, the most significant effect on profitability occurs when the loan principal is not repaid and loan loss provisions must be made. For every loan lost, many additional new loans must be made to generate enough revenue to replace the lost loan capital. In other words, when a loan is not recovered, the entire principal (and if capitalized, the interest) must be expensed through a loan loss provision. This greatly affects the profitability of the MFI and consequently the amount transferred to the balance sheet as equity. If the MFI records a net loss, the equity is reduced, resulting in fewer funds available to finance additional loans. If operations are to continue, the equity will have to be increased at least to its level before the loss was recorded. Since investors or donors are not likely to be willing to invest in the long term in an MFI that is losing money, the MFI must work toward generating enough income net of expenses to replace the lost capital (equity). Note that even if loans are funded with debt, the debt still needs to be repaid regardless of whether or not the loans (assets) made to borrowers are repaid to the MFI. If not enough revenue is generated to repay the debt, then equity will be reduced.

◆ For example, a 3,000 loan with a 46-week term, weekly payments, and an interest rate of 15 percent flat (a flat interest rate is used here for demonstration purposes only—it is not intended to suggest that this is the best way to price a loan—see chapter 5) becomes delinquent after 14 weeks of payments. To make up for lost principal and interest, 16 additional loans of 1,000 must be made (table 10.1).

However, this example only takes into account the gross revenue of 150 earned per 1,000 loan. It does not consider any operating or financing costs associated with the loan.

To accurately determine the full cost of replacing lost loan principal, the variable costs associated with disbursing and managing a loan must be taken into account. To do this, the annual contribution margin is calculated by reducing the revenue per 1,000 outstanding by the variable costs per 1,000 outstanding (variable costs include the cost of funds, operating costs, and provisions). This presents a much more accurate analysis of the costs of delinquency by determining the total costs to the MFI of replacing the lost principal (table 10.2).

Note the substantial increase in the number of loans (40 versus 16) required when the variable costs associated with disbursing and managing loans are considered. This emphasizes the significant cost that delinquency

Table 10.1 Cost of Delinquency, Example 1

Item	Calculation
Initial loan amount	3,000
Loan term	46 weeks
Weekly payment	75
Payments received	14 weeks (1,050)
Payments overdue	32 weeks (2,400)
Total lost revenue and principal	= 2,400
Lost revenue	= 312
Lost principal	= 2,088
Revenue earned per 1,000 loan for 46 weeks	= 150
Number of loans required to earn lost principal	$= \dfrac{\text{Lost principal}}{\text{Revenue per loan}}$
	$= \dfrac{2,088}{150}$
	= 14 loans of 1,000
Number of loans required to earn lost revenue and principal	$= \dfrac{\text{Lost revenue and principal}}{\text{Revenue per loan}}$
	$= \dfrac{2,400}{150}$
	= 16 loans of 1,000

Source: Ledgerwood 1996.

Table 10.2 Cost of Delinquency, Example 2

Item	Calculation
Initial loan amount	3,000
Loan term	46 weeks
Weekly payment	75
Payments received	14 weeks (1,050)
Payments overdue	32 weeks (2,400)
Total lost revenue and principal	= 2,400
Lost revenue	= 312
Lost principal	= 2,088
Revenue earned per 1,000 loan for 46 weeks	= 150
Variable costs per 1,000	= 90
Contribution margin outstanding	= 60

Number of loans required
to earn lost principal [a]

$$= \frac{\text{Lost principal}}{\text{Contribution margin per 1,000}}$$

$$= \frac{2,088}{60}$$

$$= 35 \text{ loans of } 1,000$$

Number of loans required
to earn lost revenue
and principal

$$= \frac{\text{Lost interest and principal}}{\text{Revenue per loan}}$$

$$= \frac{2,400}{60}$$

$$= 40 \text{ loans of } 1,000$$

a. Taking into account variable costs of disbursing and managing loans outstanding.
Source: Ledgerwood 1996.

has for an MFI both in terms of revenue and lost capital as well as additional expenses incurred to both make new loans and attempt to recover delinquent loans.

Controlling Delinquency

Delinquency management requires a comprehensive review of the lending methods, operational procedures, and institutional image of the MFI. Delinquency is often a result of poorly designed loan products and delivery mechanisms. There are six essential elements to managing delinquency (Ledgerwood 1996):

■ *The credit service must be valued by clients.* The main reason that clients repay a loan is that they want to receive a subsequent and larger loan. This incentive is not effective unless the clients value the loan service. Therefore, the loan product should suit the clients' needs, the delivery process should be convenient, and the clients should be made to feel that the MFI respects and cares about them.

■ *Clients must be screened carefully.* The borrower selection process should as much as possible weed out unreliable borrowers or entrepreneurs whose activities will not enable them to repay a loan. Once borrowers are selected, it is important that they receive loans structured in such a way as to enable them to repay in accordance with their repayment capacity.

■ *Field staff and clients must understand that late payments are not acceptable.* An MFI's image as a lending institution rather than a social development organization is very important. Borrowers must clearly understand that in accepting a loan they agree to a financial contract that must be respected by repaying the loan according to the payment schedule. Some MFIs charge a late payment penalty after a certain number of days have passed without payment. There is evidence to show that this works well in discouraging late payments, but if clients are substantially late with their payments, an accumulating penalty could result in too great an additional cost and may cause them to default on their loans altogether. (A maximum late penalty such as one month's interest avoids this problem.) Others MFIs, such as Bank Rakyat Indonesia, charge a higher rate of monthly interest and return a portion of it if the client repays the entire loan on time. Clients are thus encouraged to repay their loans as agreed and receive a lump sum payment at the end of the loan term to invest as they wish. This is similar to the compulsory savings required by many MFIs but is designed as an on-time payment incentive rather than as a means of obtaining credit. Often MFIs encourage on-time repayments by offering successively larger loans to borrowers who repay promptly.

■ *MFIs need accurate and timely management information systems.* Staff must be able to quickly identify borrowers who are delinquent through a management information system that accurately reports and monitors loan repayments. The easier it is for field staff to figure out whose payments are due and when and who is late and by how much the more time they can spend with borrowers. Credit officers should review their portfolios daily to see which borrowers are behind in their payments.

■ *Delinquency needs effective follow-up procedures.* Once a delinquent borrower is identified, MFI staff must immediately follow up with the borrower to communicate the message that delinquency is unacceptable. It is crucially important that other borrowers see and understand the consequences of delinquency, so that they do not begin to miss payments (the domino effect). Follow-up procedures may involve getting the group or village leaders to put pressure on the borrower, visiting the client, repossessing an asset, or publicly announcing (for example, through the newspaper, signs on the borrowers home, or hiring someone to sit in front of the borrowers' house) that the borrower is delinquent. Furthermore, MFIs should schedule weekly staff meetings to discuss problem loans and decide on the correct action. Sometimes, depending on the context in which the MFI is working, delinquent loans are passed on to a collection agency or police are brought in and criminal charges are pressed.

■ *The consequences of loan default must be sufficiently unappealing to clients.* These consequences could include no further access to loans (for borrowers or the entire group), a bad credit rating, collection of collateral, legal action, visits by debt collectors, penalties, and public announcements.

Ultimately, MFIs should understand that delinquency is not usually the result of borrowers who *cannot* pay. More often it is the result of borrowers who *will not pay.* Borrowers who respect and value the services offered by an MFI and understand that delinquency is not tolerated will repay their loans. Those who view the MFI as providing a charitable service will not repay their loans. Box 10.1 provides steps to take when an MFI has a delinquency problem.

Table 10.3 outlines some of the costs and benefits to borrowers of on-time and late or no payments.

Rescheduling or Refinancing Loans

When a client is unable to repay a loan due to illness, disaster, mismanagement, or some other crisis, it may be appropriate to reschedule or refinance the loan. Rescheduling a loan refers to extending the loan term or changing the payment schedule, or both. Refinancing a loan refers to providing an amount of loan funds in addition to the original loan amount. This allows clients to begin making the loan payments again and, it is hoped, to continue payments until the loan is paid in full.

Box 10.1 Fifteen Steps to Take in a Delinquency Crisis

1. *Review credit policies and operations* for their compliance with basic principles and methodology.
2. *Evaluate* the extent to which loan officers are complying with a sound methodology; look for deviations.
3. *Design an incentives system* that will maintain the type of performance sought by the program.
4. *Lay off loan officers and other field staff* who have particularly poor performance and who will most likely reject the manner of improving performance.
5. *Separate the poorest loans* from the rest and give them to a specialized collections department. Leave loan officers with an acceptable level of delinquency.
6. *Review your information system* to ensure that it gives you adequate management information for day-to-day control of operations and implementation of incentives systems.
7. *Lay out* the reviewed policies and operational procedures along with an incentives system to field staff.
8. *Set deadlines* for improving performance and achieving incentives.

9. *Set up ex-post control capacity* to measure refinancing requests, delinquent accounts, and a sample of on-time accounts against new policies.
10. *Review the performance of new versus old loans* after about six months under new policies. If it is satisfactory, proceed with the following steps. If not, repeat prior steps from the beginning.
11. Judiciously *refinance* some clients who have a genuine potential to repay loans.
12. *Write off* the major number of loans that are more than six months late. Continue collection efforts through a specialized department (in those cases where the money involved is significant).
13. *Promote strong growth* both in amounts and numbers of clients.
14. *Move clients* out who have had poor records as they pay off their loans.
15. *Remove loan officers* who continue to perform poorly or who drag down the entire concept.

Source: Economics Institute 1996.

Table 10.3 On-Time and Late or No Payments

	On-time payments	Late or no payments
Benefits	■ Probability of immediate, larger follow-up loans ■ Development of positive credit history ■ Positive reputation among peers ■ Access to training, savings, or other programs and advice from credit officers ■ Awards or prizes for timely payment	■ Maintenance of capital (or portion) from loan in business ■ Lower expenses if interest payments not made ■ Fewer or no trips to branch to make payments (lower transaction costs) ■ Lower transaction costs for attending meetings
Costs	■ Payment of interest and capital of current loan ■ Time and transportation costs (transaction costs) to make payments	■ Loss of access to other program services ■ Delay of future loans or loss of access to future loans ■ Possible legal action and costs ■ Frequent visits by credit officers ■ Pressure from group members

Source: Stearns 1991b.

◆ For example, a client borrowed money to engage in trading. She has consistently repaid her loan on time and is now on her fourth consecutive loan. Recently she become ill and has had to forgo her trading activities for the time being while using her savings to pay for health care. However, she is recovering and will eventually be able to resume her income-generating activities. In this case, the MFI may be justified in rescheduling this client's loan to incorporate a period in which no payments are required, but interest continues to accumulate. This would result in a longer-loan term and in additional interest costs to the client (and, therefore, continued revenue to the MFI for the amount outstanding). In this way, no revenue is lost—assuming the borrower resumes the loan repayment and pays in full with interest. If interest is calculated on a flat basis upfront, the MFI might consider levying an additional fee to make up for lost revenue on the loan (because the loan has been rescheduled, it is outstanding for a longer period and, therefore, should generate more revenue).

Alternatively, the MFI might consider lending the client an additional amount (that is, refinancing the loan) to enable her to continue to make loan payments and pay for some of her health care costs. This would only be done if the MFI felt that without refi-

nancing the borrower would never be able to repay the loan because she would not be able to continue with her business. Refinancing is generally more risky than rescheduling and should be done only with extreme caution.

MFIs should be cautioned against rescheduling or refinancing loans. While it is ultimately done to encourage repayment of loans, it is risky and must only be carried out under extreme circumstances. Furthermore, it affects the reported quality of the loan portfolio and the cash flow of the MFI.

Rescheduling or refinancing loans reduces the arrears in a portfolio by converting a delinquent loan into one that appears to be a healthy loan. This happens even though the risk has not necessarily been reduced. In fact, the risk may be higher due to the rescheduling or refinancing. MFIs should ensure that they monitor all rescheduled or refinanced loans separately from the rest of the portfolio and with additional care. They should not be reported as *healthy* loans in the portfolio.

When loans are rescheduled, previously expected cash inflows from the loan repayment do not occur. If many loans are rescheduled, the MFI may run into liquidity problems, which may mean that loan disbursement must be reduced or stopped. This in turn leads to delinquency problems. (Effective liquidity management is discussed below.)

Productivity and Efficiency Management

Productivity and efficiency management involve both maximizing revenue and minimizing costs relative to the volume of business produced and managed. Productivity management includes ensuring that staff is accountable for its activities, given the right incentives for productive and efficient performance, and provided with timely and useful management information. Efficiency management focuses on managing and reducing costs where possible.

Improving Staff Productivity

Due to the nature of microlending, the main responsibility for effective outreach and loan repayment rests with the credit officer. (Note that the productivity of savings officers can also be encouraged with incentive schemes, recognition, and so on. For simplicity's sake only credit officers are discussed here, although the same discussion is relevant for savings officers who focus on savings

accounts rather than outstanding loans.) It is therefore necessary to ensure that credit officers are both motivated and held appropriately accountable for managing and cultivating their portfolios.

Productivity is affected by the choice of lending model and delivery mechanisms as well as by the target client group. These variables affect both the volume of loans outstanding and the number of clients per credit officer (for how to calculate these ratios, see chapter 9) (box 10.2).

AVERAGE PORTFOLIO OUTSTANDING AND THE NUMBER OF CLIENTS PER CREDIT OFFICER. The volume of loans outstanding is very much a function of the target group chosen and the lending methodology. Productivity can be improved by larger portfolios achieved through larger loan sizes or by a larger number of clients per credit officer.

Larger loan sizes must be balanced against the demands of the target group and its ability to absorb and manage a greater amount of debt. Increased loan sizes that result in a greater amount of delinquent loans or an exclusion of the target client group may increase productivity but would not improve overall financial viability or achieve the stated mission of the MFI. "Increased loan

---

Box 10.2 Unusual Gains in Efficiency at Women's World Banking, Cali, Colombia

AN EXAMPLE OF AN NGO THAT ACHIEVED UNUSUAL SUC-CESS in its efforts to reduce costs, work toward financial self-sufficiency, and, at the same time, provide more and better services to its target population is the affiliate of the Women's World Banking network based in Cali, Colombia.

Women's World Banking (WWB) Cali was founded in the early 1980s. Its objective was to provide credit and other services to underprivileged people, mostly women, from the city of Cali and the surrounding area. In 1991 WWB Cali was still strongly dependent on external support and the efficiency of its credit operation was not satisfactory. Operating costs were high and outreach was poor. In this situation, the decision was taken to restructure the organization with the help of foreign donors and consultants. One element of the reform program was to discontinue all nonfinancial services, a second was to make a determined effort to introduce a new lending methodology, and the third element was to undertake a massive training effort.

The results of the reform were impressive. Within four years the number of outstanding loans increased more than tenfold, from 529 to 5,343 (as of December 1995). The loan portfolio grew by a factor of almost 15. Thus average loan size did not increase much, and the target group was not altered. The processing time for a loan application decreased sharply, as did arrears and loan delinquency rates.

Even more important for the financial sustainability was the marked increase in productivity. The average number of loans outstanding per credit officer at the end of 1995 stood at 314, as opposed to 88 loans at the end of 1991. This gain was achieved through a standardized and consistent lending policy, strict monitoring, and intensive use of computers. All of this was reflected in the continuous decline of the rate of administrative costs as a percentage of the loan portfolio. In 1991 this rate had been 35 percent. At the end of 1995 it had been reduced to 20 percent. In combination with a declining rate of loan losses, the efficiency gain now enables WWB Cali to be financially viable without having to charge an excessively high interest rate.

Source: Contributed by Reinhard Schmidt, Internationale Projekt Consult GmbH (IPC).

sizes can be beneficial if they reflect the release of previous funding constraints, the growth of the enterprises of existing clients, and a gradual expansion of the range of clients served to increase financial viability" (Rhyne and Rotblatt 1994, 48).

Increasing the number of clients per credit officer is an effective way to improve an MFI's efficiency and productivity. However, each MFI has an optimal number of clients per credit officer, based on credit methodology and average loan terms. Credit officers of MFIs that utilize group-lending models with relatively long loan terms can usually carry a larger number of clients than credit officers of MFIs who make individual loans with shorter loan terms. This is because credit officers need to spend less time with clients if the loan terms are longer. Also, group lending can transfer some of the administrative tasks to the group, thereby reducing overall costs.

Increasing the number of clients per credit officer must be balanced with the credit officer's ability to provide an adequate level of services to clients and to maintain the quality of the loan portfolios. Incentive schemes, when designed correctly, work to encourage credit officers to achieve the optimal number of clients and productivity levels.

While most people working in microfinance are motivated by the benefits of working with low-income clients and the ability to "make a difference," the bottom line for many employees is also recognition and monetary compensation.

Nobody knows a microfinance client better than the credit officer. He or she is the one who visits clients regularly, understands their business, and is in a position to make the best decisions about their financing needs and the ability of the MFI to meet those needs. For credit officers to be accountable and responsible for their portfolios, they need to have considerable autonomy and decisionmaking authority. The degree of autonomy must be commensurate with the degree of responsibility for portfolio performance, the ability to increase salary, or recognition. Well-defined and well-planned incentive schemes help to create strong credit officers and good clients.

INCENTIVE SCHEMES. A well-designed incentive scheme rewards staff behavior that benefits the MFI and punishes behavior that results in increased risk or losses for the MFI. Incentive schemes generally work (that is,

whatever is rewarded is usually what will occur more frequently). Therefore, it is imperative that management understand what type of behavior will lead to which results, so that it can design the incentive scheme in such a way that the MFI's productivity and profitability will increase. It is also important to bear in mind the effect that different incentive schemes will have on clients and their needs. If the service level suffers in response to the introduction of incentive schemes, eventually the MFI may lose productivity as the number of clients decreases.

Incentive schemes can include any combination of the following factors:

- Monetary rewards
- Promotions
- Additional holidays
- Recognition in the form of ceremonies or certificates
- Additional training
- Increased bonuses
- Bicycles, motorcycles, or vehicles.

When designing incentive schemes, the following questions must be answered:

- Who will qualify? All staff? Field staff only?
- What will the incentives be based on? Portfolio size? Quality? Profitability?
- How often will they be calculated and paid out? Monthly? Quarterly?
- How will the size of the pool and distribution be determined?

Incentive schemes for lending should feature *quality* as well as *volume* measurements. For example, if an MFI wants to increase the number of clients as well as the average loan balance of its clients, it must first determine whether there is adequate demand in the areas where they work and ensure that the clients need (and are able to repay) larger loans. Once this has been established, the MFI can design an incentive scheme to pay bonuses to credit officers for portfolios greater than a certain size and for an increased client base over a specific time period. This *must* be balanced with an additional incentive that measures the loan portfolio quality. Many MFIs have set out to increase loan disbursements at the risk of severely increasing loan delinquency.

Alternatively, if the MFI wants to ensure that the loan sizes remain under a certain level (to focus on their target market), incentive schemes can be designed to reward credit officers for the *number* of clients and the *quality* of the loan portfolio as opposed to the size of their portfolios. In this way, credit officers are encourage to add new clients rather than simply increase loan sizes. Finally, MFIs may want to encourage repeat borrowers over new borrowers. This can also be built into an incentive scheme.

Incentive schemes can be designed to encourage and reward any or *all* of the following results (although all incentive schemes should include portfolio quality):

- Portfolio growth, both in terms of number of clients and total portfolio outstanding
- Client retention, based on number of repeat loans
- Increased number of new clients
- Portfolio quality, through portfolio at risk-aging analyses
- Increased number of clients or groups (if applicable)
- Training of clients and clients or groups (if applicable)
- Training of new credit officers.

The Association for the Development of Micro-enterprises (ADEMI) provides an excellent example of an effective incentive scheme (box 10.3).

Incentive schemes can be designed for individuals, branches, or departments as a whole, depending on the activities and responsibilities of each individual and the shared responsibilities within a branch or department. If no one individual has the ability to directly influence productivity, an incentive scheme designed to reward individuals would not be appropriate. This might be the case if an MFI collects savings at the branch and disburses loans in the field. An incentive scheme that rewards increased savings mobilization by individual staff members may not be appropriate, because savings deposits collected in a branch are not generally related to the activities of one staff member. However, credit officers responsible for loan disbursements and collections could be rewarded individually for excellence in managing their loan portfolios.

Incentive schemes based on field staff performance can also provide incentives to management and support staff. This is done by paying management and support staff a percentage based on the performance of their staff or coworkers. Tulay Sa Pag-Unlad, Inc. in the Philippines provides a good example of an incentive scheme that is designed to reward management and support staff as well as credit officers (box 10.4).

Prior to implementing an incentive scheme, the MFI should ensure that all eligible staff begin at the same level,

---

Box 10.3 Performance Incentives at the Association for the Development of Microenterprises, Dominican Republic

AT THE ASSOCIATION FOR THE DEVELOPMENT OF Microenterprises (ADEMI), credit officers receive a base salary plus a bonus based on the performance of their portfolio. Through the bonus system they can increase their basic monthly salary by up to 50 percent. The base salary is set for the first three months (the probationary period), and it then increases incrementally per month after they reach 100 clients. The amount of the bonus is determined by the arrears rate, the number of active microenterprises, the size of their portfolio, and the total amount disbursed in the month. The most important category in the incentive scheme is the arrears rate, whereby an additional bonus is given for every 1 percent reduction of the arrears rate below 8 percent.

All staff members receive substantial Christmas and year-end bonuses of between three and eight months salary. They also receive insurance coverage in the event of an accident or death, can participate in a pension plan, and have access to subsidized employee loans for housing or consumption. In addition, all staff receive severance payments whether they quit or are fired.

In addition to financial incentives, credit officers are given promotions to provide further recognition. ADEMI tries to retain its credit officers over the long term, recognizing that they have substantial influence over the profitability of the organization.

Source: Ledgerwood and Burnett 1995.

---

because a more mature credit officer or branch may have significantly more clients than a new officer or a new branch. Also, credit officers may have inherited portfolios that are performing well (or poorly) through no effort of their own. Finally, particular branches may inherently perform better due to their geographic location or the level of business activity and market potential in their area.

Incentive schemes must be transparent to all staff members. An incentive scheme that is secretive may result in more problems than no incentive scheme at all. Furthermore, to be effective incentive schemes must be achievable and capable of making a tangible difference to staff members.

MANAGEMENT INFORMATION SYSTEMS. One of the most important elements of effective delinquency manage-

---

Box 10.4 Performance Incentive Schemes at Tulay Sa Pag-Unlad, Inc., the Philippines

CREDIT OFFICER PAY AT TULAY SA PAG-UNLAD, INC. (TSPI) IS supplemented by a comprehensive incentive scheme based on past due amounts and outstanding loan volumes. The incentive scheme was introduced in January 1995 and is calculated as follows for the three loan products handled in their urban branches:

	Sakbayan (tricycle loans)	Individual	Solidarity groups
Number of groups	Minimum 20 groups at the end of the month	Minimum 25 borrowers at the end of the month	Minimum 12 groups at the end of month
Outstanding loans	Outstanding loans must have increased from previous month and must achieve 75 percent of cumulative quarterly targets (5 groups every 3 months); full capacity at 40 groups	Outstanding loans must have increased from previous month and must achieve 75 percent of quarterly targets (2 borrowers per month); full capacity at 75 borrowers	Outstanding loans must have increased from previous month and must achieve 75 percent of quarterly targets (2 new groups per month; renewals valued at 50 percent of target); full capacity at 60 groups
Repayment rate	At least 98 percent	At least 96 percent	At least 98 percent
Monthly incentive increase	Ranges from P1,000 (20 groups; 98 percent repayment) to P10,000 (50 groups; 100 percent repayment)	Ranges from P500 (25 borrowers; 98 percent repayment) to P7,000 (71 groups; 100 percent repayment)	Ranges from P1,000 (12 groups; 98 percent repayment) to P7,000 (57 groups; 100 percent repayment)

Branch managers receive incentives based on the incentives received by their credit officers and the overall repayment rate of the branch at the end of the month. The branch must achieve a minimum repayment rate of 98 percent and achieve the monthly target at least twice during the quarter. If the accounts processed exceed the targets two out of three months, branch managers receive twice their monthly salary in the quar-ter. If targets are achieved in all three months, branch managers receive three times their monthly salary in the quarter.

Area managers also receive incentives each quarter if all their branches have attained a 98 percent repayment rate and achieved the monthly targets at least twice during the quar-ter. The incentive structure for area managers is the same as that for branch managers.

Source: Ledgerwood and Harpe 1995.

---

ment is useful and timely management information. Credit officers need information about their clients on a daily basis to ensure that loan repayment is taking place. For credit officers to achieve their goals and benefit from an incentive structure that rewards the quality of their loan portfolios, they must be aware as soon as possible of any delinquent loans. Effective management of delinquency requires immediate follow-up. If possible, credit officers should receive daily or weekly reports of their clients' activity (box 10.5).

Managing Costs

Efficiency management refers to managing costs per unit of output. The nature of microfinance lending (small loans and a client base that is potentially difficult to access) works against maintaining a low-cost structure. Furthermore, as more MFIs reduce their reliance on donor funding and access commercial funding, their "spread" (the difference between financing costs and revenue generated by lending funds, which must cover administrative costs, loan losses, and adjusted capital

Box 10.5 Credit Officer Reports at the Association for the Development of Microenterprises

THE ASSOCIATION FOR THE DEVELOPMENT OF Microenterprises (ADEMI) provides its credit officers with daily reports of the loan activity in their portfolios. These reports are physically placed on each credit officer's desk before they arrive in the morning so that they can plan to visit delinquent borrowers or concentrate on new loan disbursements. The daily reports also provide information about the end of the loan term for each client, enabling the credit officers to visit clients whose loan terms are nearly over so they can help them apply for a new loan, if necessary, before their old term ends. In this way clients have continued access to credit (assuming they have repaid previous and existing loans on time).

Source: Ledgerwood and Burnett 1995.

- Standardization of systems and policies
- Management information systems.

TOTAL SALARY COSTS. Salaries are generally the largest component of operating costs. As a percentage of total administrative expenses, salary costs ranged from 48 percent to 75 percent in the 11 MFIs identified by Christen and others (1995). Salary costs are affected by the general level of salaries in the country in which the MFI operates and the quality of staff hired. The decision about whether to hire highly educated staff is related to the objectives of the MFI and the specific tasks required of the credit officers.

Salaries can be based to a great extent on monetary incentive schemes, thereby ensuring that average salaries are related to the revenue generated on the loan portfolio.

DECENTRALIZED DECISIONMAKING. Most successful MFIs have fairly decentralized operational structures (see Christen 1997). Due to the relatively homogenous nature of microfinance loans (small loan sizes, common delivery methods), loan approvals can usually be relegated to the credit officers (or the borrower group, if applicable), with final decisions on larger loan amounts made by the credit manager, usually at the branch level. Decentralized loan approval processes reduce operating costs, decrease waiting time for clients, and enhance the accountability of the credit officers.

Treating branches as *profit centers* rather than simply administrative units and providing them with the decisionmaking authority to manage productivity and efficiency generally results in overall improved efficiency for the MFI. Decentralizing day-to-day decisionmaking to the branches or units is an effective way to increase efficiency and make the branches responsible for managing costs.

The transfer of cost reporting from the MFI to its branches is commensurate with decentralized decisionmaking. Operating costs, provisions for loan losses, subsidy adjustments, depreciation, and all other costs should be accounted for at the branch or unit level and measured against the revenue generated by the branch. In addition, some MFIs transfer overhead (or head office) costs to the branches, which ensures full-cost coverage throughout the network. Transferred costs are prorated on a cost-recovery basis on a percentage of assets (loans) or liabilities (deposits) held at each branch.

Furthermore, many MFIs access funding (either commercially or through donors) at the wholesale level and

costs—see chapter 9) will decrease. This implies a need to emphasize the efficiency of operations, particularly as MFIs grow to reach significant levels of outreach. Also, as more and more MFIs enter the field, competition will gradually force interest rates down, further decreasing MFI spreads. In light of this it is imperative that MFIs effectively manage their costs.

As mentioned in chapter 9, MFIs incur four types of costs: financing costs, provisions for loan losses, operational or administrative costs, and adjusted costs of capital. Financing costs and adjusted capital costs are to a great extent a function of the marketplace in which the MFI operates. The management of loan losses has already been discussed under delinquency management. Efficiency indicators measure an MFI's operational costs relative to its assets, and this discussion focuses on managing these operational costs.

Operating efficiency improves as an MFI matures and reaches a certain optimum economy of scale. Operating cost ratios (operating costs relative to outstanding loans) will thus be higher for newer MFIs. This is why it is difficult to compare efficiency indicators with other MFIs or financial intermediaries. For the internal management of operating efficiency, MFIs can focus on the following aspects of their operations and compare them over time to measure improvements:

- Total salary costs
- Decentralized decisionmaking

Box 10.6 Transfer Pricing at Bank Rakyat Indonesia and Grameen Bank in Bangladesh

BANK RAKYAT INDONESIA AND GRAMEEN BANK OFFER TWO methods of transfer pricing that can help implement policies and influence the funding structure and operational efficiency of MFIs.

Bank Rakyat Indonesia retains the ability to adjust the relative emphasis of the system as a whole on credit versus savings through the mechanism of transfer pricing. The transfer price is the rate that Bank Rakyat Indonesia branches pay to the units for deposits. It determines the profitability to the units of generating savings. Because the KUPEDES (loan product) lending rate is fixed, adjusting the transfer price can change the relative emphasis units give to savings and credit. If the transfer price is set very low (only slightly above the rate paid to depositors), units receive so little spread on savings collections that they must earn all of their income from lending. In 1991, when the Indonesian financial system experienced a liquidity squeeze, Bank Rakyat Indonesia set the transfer price very high, so that the rate received for placing funds internally neared the rate received on loans. This encouraged the units to generate savings and turn them over to the main branches, where the return would be higher than if they put them into loans (and thus incurred the costs associated with lending). Accordingly, the growth rate of the lending program halted at that time. The transfer price for units to borrow from the main branches

can be similarly manipulated. At present the transfer price is set low to provide maximum incentives to lend, and lending levels are beginning to increase again.

The profit-center concept is also applied at Grameen Bank. Grameen branches receive their lending funds by using the mandatory savings deposits that they hold (on which they pay 8.5 percent) and by borrowing from the head office at 12 percent for general loans (less for housing loans). This price is set by Grameen to reflect a market-relevant cost of funds (though it is higher than Grameen's actual cost of funds), to cover headquarters expenses and to encourage branches to control costs and generate savings. It should be noted that the profitability of retail units in any MFI is not the same as overall system profitability, because transfer prices are set expressly to give a policy signal and do not necessarily reflect true costs directly. For example, at Grameen a 2 percent transfer price for housing loans affords branches a spread of 6 percent, thereby applying appropriate incentives for efficiency by branches, which must strive to keep their costs within that spread. However, because Grameen uses subsidized funds for housing loans, the loans do not contribute to Grameen's overall financial self-sufficiency. This is an example of the way that Grameen manages to combine the continued use of selected subsidies with a strong drive for efficiency.

Source: Rhyne and Rotblatt 1994.

then transfer funds to the individual branches or retail units for on-lending. The costs associated with these funds (actual financing costs or imputed capital costs) should be transferred to the branches. This is referred to as *transfer pricing* and is common in many MFIs and commercial financial institutions (discussed briefly in chapter 6). Similarly, some MFIs' retail branches mobilize savings and transfer these funds to the head office. They should receive a transfer price for these funds.

Transfer pricing sets a "cost of funds" on funds transferred from the head office to the branches and on funds transferred from the branches to the head office. Funds transferred from the head office should be fixed at a rate above the rate paid by the branches on voluntary savings (if applicable) to encourage savings mobilization (that is, if branches are assessed on their ability to keep costs low, they are better off mobilizing savings at a lower cost of funds than "borrowing" from the head office). The transfer price should also take into account the additional

operational costs incurred to mobilize savings and should consequently be higher. Funds transferred to the head office should be priced at a market rate lower than that paid by the MFI's borrowers and above the rate paid to voluntary savers (that is, branches should be encouraged to lend out excess funds to earn more revenue rather than just transfer funds to the head office).

Usually only one transfer price is established between the branches and the head office, regardless of which office is "lending" the funds. This rate should generally equal the commercial market rate of debt (which is usually lower than the interest rate on loans to borrowers but higher than the rate paid on voluntary savings). It may include a small spread for the head office or the branch to cover their costs of mobilizing those funds (whether through savings or commercial debt). Note that transfer pricing does not result in a transfer of cash. Rather, it is an accounting entry that ultimately nets to zero in the consolidated MFI statements.

◆ For example, assume an MFI accesses commercial funds at a cost of 10 percent a year and it mobilizes savings at a cost of 5 percent per year. Within its branch network there will be some branches that mobilize more savings than the amount of loans they disburse. Other branches will disburse a greater amount of loans than the amount of savings collected. For the branch that has excess funds (more savings than loans), it *lends* these funds to the head office and receives a transfer price for them (probably close to 10 percent). The branch that requires funds (more loans than savings) borrows funds from head office at the transfer price.

STANDARDIZED SYSTEMS AND POLICIES. Highly standardized systems and policies in MFIs contribute to overall efficiency. The functions of each staff member must be clearly defined, and daily and weekly schedules of activities should be made routine in all branches. A high level of standardization is essential for an MFI to monitor performance, expand outreach, and achieve operational efficiency. Regular procedures also enable clients to arrange their schedules around the policies of the MFI.

Standardized procedures also benefit an MFI that is growing rapidly or help when staff is transferred to different branches. However, procedures must also allow for some autonomy at the branch level, particularly when they are treated as profit centers. Core activities such as credit and savings should be highly standardized, whereas client visits, involvement in the community, and other initiatives may be less so.

Box 10.7 Standardization at Grameen Bank

GRAMEEN BANK DIRECTS CREDIT OFFICERS TO TAKE THE initiative in reducing rural poverty in any way they can, and this leads to a proliferation of small local activities and experiments. Grameen's client centers provide a vehicle for local initiatives because the centers often decide to make collective investments or carry out ongoing activities such as starting informal schools. However, even at Grameen such activities do not detract from the core business of providing credit, and each Grameen branch carries out its credit operations in a standard way. A general conclusion is that local variation beyond a certain tolerance is not compatible with scale.

Source: Rhyne and Rotblatt 1994.

MANAGEMENT INFORMATION SYSTEMS. (see chapter 7 and Christen 1997). Effective management information systems are essential for an MFI to control its costs and manage efficiency. Timely and accurate information must be available to management to manage productivity at the branch or unit level and at the overall MFI level. Good information systems must be built on good administrative systems and procedures.

The importance of information to calculate key indicators has been emphasized in previous sections of this handbook. In addition to financial management information, "supervisors and policymakers need a full range of supporting information, and frontline staff need information to manage their own daily activities" (Rhyne and Rotblatt 1994, 59).

Risk Management

Risk management is one of the most important areas of financial management for MFIs. Risk management can be broadly grouped under asset and liability management and operating risk management.

Asset and Liability Management

Asset and liability management refers to the financial risk management of a financial institution. Generally, any action to increase the expected returns of an MFI will also increase its risk structure. Asset and liability management (ALM) involves understanding those risk and return tradeoffs and making them clear so that the board of directors and senior management can make informed business judgments about the best course for the MFI.

ALM manages the structure of an MFI's balance sheet and the risks and returns inherent in this structure. Most narrowly defined, asset and liability management refers to spread management or the maintenance of a positive spread between the interest rate on earning assets and the interest cost of funds.

Since many MFIs do not act as true financial intermediaries (by providing loans and collecting savings), they may not be overly concerned with asset and liability management. However, as time goes on, ALM will become more important as the availability of donor funds declines and MFIs take on more commercial debt.

In formal financial institutions asset and liability management is normally carried out by a committee, because it involves both operations management and treasury activities. This committee is commonly referred to as the asset and liability committee or ALCO and it sets policies and guidelines to establish the risk tolerance of the organization. These policies are generally ratified by the board of directors. The asset and liability committee meets frequently and determines the lending organization's current position in every risk dimension while also forecasting for all future time periods. If the organization is currently or expected to be outside of its risk limits, then the asset and liability committee must make a decision as to how to correct the situation. This could involve a change in the structure of the balance sheet to ensure that the level of risk is appropriate or, less commonly, a change in the policies and guidelines of the MFI.

Most MFIs do not have the depth of financial and operational management to create a committee. Hence asset and liability management will likely be carried out by the director and the financial manager of the MFI.

The goal of asset and liability management is to maximize the risk-adjusted returns to shareholders over the long run. The major categories of asset and liability management risk that an MFI needs to consider are:

- Credit risk
- Liquidity risk
- Interest rate risk
- Foreign exchange risk.

Two other types of risk are also often cited: capital adequacy risk and fiduciary risk. "Capital adequacy risk" is something of a misnomer, because capital is a funding source, not a source of risk. However, there is an optimal capital structure for MFIs, and thus the primary risk is that capital is improperly allocated, affecting pricing policies and strategic decisions. Fiduciary risk refers to the risk that management will make imprudent decisions about the management of external resources. Beyond the discussion in chapter 9 of capital adequacy, this handbook will not discuss optimal capital structures or fiduciary risk.

Credit risk represents the potential loss resulting from the poor quality of the organization's assets, particularly its loan portfolio. Credit risk is by far the most important of risk categories and is discussed above under delinquency management.

LIQUIDITY RISK. Liquidity refers to the ability of an MFI to meet its immediate demands for cash, that is, loan disbursement, bill payments, and debt repayment. An MFI is in a liquid position if it is able to meet its current obligations as they become due. An MFI is in an illiquid position if it is unable to meet claims for funds. Liquidity risk refers to the risk of incurring additional expenses for borrowing relatively expensive short-term funds to finance an illiquid position. Liquidity management is the process of ensuring that the demand for funds is readily met without additional borrowing. The goal of liquidity management is to maintain an acceptable level of liquidity while balancing the need to earn revenue. Too much cash in a branch or head office results in lost income, since idle cash does not earn any revenue but does incur a cost of funds. Too little cash results in missed loan disbursement opportunities, delayed bill payments, or higher borrowing costs for the MFI (overdraft charges).

Liquidity management and cash flow management are often used interchangeably. In fact, liquidity management includes the management of not only cash but also other short-term assets and short-term liabilities.

Cash flow management refers to the timing of cash flows to ensure that cash coming in (cash inflow) is equal to or greater than cash going out (cash outflow). Cash flow analysis identifies the amount of cash needed for daily operations as well as idle funds that can be used for investment or loans. The purpose of cash flow management is to maintain an adequate level of cash both in the branches (if applicable) and at the head office. This is done by accurately forecasting cash needs.

An effective cash management program ensures that:

- Policies are set for minimum and maximum cash levels
- Cash needs are forecast
- Cash budgets are continuously updated
- Surplus funds are invested or disbursed as loans
- Cash is available for savings withdrawals and loans.

Various ratios can be calculated to help determine the appropriate level of cash flow. Three are presented here: the idle funds ratio, the liquidity ratio, and the current ratio.

The idle funds ratio deals with funds that an MFI has but that are not earning any revenue or are earning less revenue than what could be earned if they were lent out to borrowers.

$$\text{Idle funds ratio} = \frac{\text{Cash} + \text{near cash}}{\text{Total outstanding portfolio}}$$

Near-cash refers to noninterest-bearing deposits and deposits that earn a very low rate of interest and have a maturity of three months or less (term deposits, investment certificates). Near-cash is so called because generally the money is highly liquid (that is, available on demand).

The denominator used in this formula could also be total assets or total performing assets, depending on the structure of the MFI (that is, it may have a large amount of assets in investments). It is important, however, to use the same denominator consistently over time.

A certain amount of idle funds is necessary in an MFI. However, too great an amount will affect the overall return on assets.

By calculating the *liquidity ratio,* the MFI can determine if there is enough cash available for disbursements and also whether there is too much idle cash.

$$\text{Liquidity ratio} = \frac{\text{Cash} + \text{expected cash inflows in the period}}{\text{Anticipated cash outflows in the period}}$$

The liquidity ratio should always be greater than one.

The accuracy of the liquidity ratio is dependent on the accuracy of the projections of cash receipts and disbursements.

To forecast cash requirements an MFI must calculate its anticipated cash receipts and anticipated cash disbursements. A *cash forecast* is then created showing the cash inflows and cash outflows expected over a period of time. The cash forecast:

- Identifies periods in which there might be a shortage of cash or a large cash requirement
- Identifies periods in which there is likely to be an excess of cash

- Enables the organization or branch to plan smooth cash flow
- Helps prevent the accumulation over time of excess funds.

The first task in forecasting cash requirements is to select a period of time to be covered. If cash flows are expected to be stable, then the cash forecast can be for a longer term. If cash flows are uncertain, a shorter period should be selected. For an MFI a cash forecast should be created on a monthly basis. Cash flow may be affected by the season or the time of year (such as holidays). Therefore, monthly cash forecasts will show the fluctuation of cash requirements from month to month.

Only actual cash items are included in a cash forecast. Noncash items, such as depreciation, provisions for loan losses, or subsidy and inflation adjustments, do not affect cash flow. Cash items for an MFI typically include:

- *Cash inflows*—loan repayment, interest and fee revenue, client savings, bank interest, sale of investments, and cash received from donors or other debtors
- *Cash outflows*—loan disbursement, debt repayment, fixed asset purchases, investments, and operating expenses such as transportation costs, salaries, benefits, supply purchases, training materials, rent, and utilities.

When forecasting the cash flow for a branch of an MFI, a potential cash inflow to consider is funds received from the head office. Conversely, a potential cash outflow would be funds returned to the head office. Note that the rate received for transferring funds to the head office or receiving funds from the head office (the transfer price) is not a cash flow item and should not be included when forecasting cash flows.

Table 10.4 Branch Cash Flow Forecasts

Opening cash at beginning of the month (A)	Loan payments due (including interest) (B)	On-time repayment rate (percent) (C)	Expected loan payments (D)	Expected delinquant loan recovery (E)	Expected loan fees collected (F)
January 1					
50,000	600,000	65	390,000	12,000	9,000
February 1					
50,000	400,000	75	300,000	4,000	8,250
March 1					
50,000	375,000	95	356,250	7,000	10,500

Note: At the beginning of each month the maximum cash per branch is 50,000. Net cash = (A + D + E + F + G) − (H + I + J + K).
Source: Ledgerwood 1996.

The cash flow forecast begins with credit officers determining the amount of loan disbursements are expected in the month and the amount of loan repayments expected. A shortage of funds requires additional borrowing or donations, delayed payment of debt or expenses, or, in the case of a branch, a request to the head office for additional funds. Note that a shortage of cash should never result in delayed disbursement of loans. The incentive of continued access to credit contributes largely to the on-time repayment of loans. In this sense, liquidity risk for MFIs ultimately may be reflected in increased loan delinquency in addition to the potential increase in the cost of funds.

If there are *excess funds,* a decision must be made on whether to hold the funds in short-term investments, repay short-term debt, or, in the case of a branch, return the funds to the head office. Some idle funds should be held at all times to compensate for late loan repayments or to pay for emergencies (or, if voluntary savings are collected, to meet demands for withdrawal). The amount of cash held needs to be balanced with the loss of revenue experienced when holding idle funds. If an MFI has a number of branches, the head office will usually determine the appropriate amount of idle funds to be held at each branch. Note that if there is a network of branches, all branch forecasts (or cash requirements) need to be consolidated to result in a cash flow forecast for the MFI as a whole.

It is important that the cash flow forecast consider the recovery rate on loans. This will vary for each MFI and within each branch. For example, if loan repayments due are 100,000 but the branch historically experiences a 90 percent repayment rate, then estimated loan repayments

(cash inflow) must be adjusted to 90,000. Table 10.4 provides a sample branch cash flow forecast.

By calculating the net cash at the end of each month, it is possible to determine how much cash the branch will return to the head office or request from it

The final ratio presented to manage liquidity risk is the *current ratio.* The current ratio is commonly used by commercial financial institutions and is sometimes referred to as the *liquidity adequacy ratio.*

$$\text{Current ratio} = \frac{\text{Current assets}}{\text{Current liabilities}}$$

The current ratio demonstrates the ability of the MFI to make debt-service payments and calculates the degree of coverage provided by short-term assets. In the Christen and others (1995) study current ratios for the most successful MFIs ranged between 1:1 and 5:1.

Some MFIs manage liquidity by establishing a line of credit, that is, by managing the liability side of the balance sheet rather than the asset side (such as cash flow). In this way costs are incurred only when the credit line is used. This method of liabilities management is only available to MFIs that have proven their ability to manage their financial performance and have thus been able to establish a relationship with a commercial bank.

INTEREST RATE RISK. Interest rate risk is the most conventional asset and liability management topic. Interest rate risk arises when interest rates on assets and interest rates on liabilities (which fund the assets) are mismatched, both in rates and terms. Interest rate risk occurs after assets and liabilities have been priced or loans have been

Expected savings collected (G)	Expected loan disbursements (H)	Expected payments fixed costs (I)	Expected payments variable costs (J)	Expected savings withdrawal (K)	Net cash (L)
15,000	300,000	50,000	30,000	0	96,000
13,750	275,000	50,000	27,000	5,000	19,000
17,500	350,000	50,000	33,000	0	8,250

booked. It should not be confused with pricing loans to cover the MFI's costs and expected returns.

Interest rate risk is particularly a problem for MFIs operating in countries with unpredictable inflation rates, which directly affects interest rates on debt. If the inflation rate rises, the interest rate set on loans will not be high enough to offset the effects of inflation. An MFI's ability to adjust interest rates on its loans is determined by the degree to which short-term liabilities are used to fund longer-term loans within the portfolio; in other words, short-term liabilities may be *repriced* before the MFI is able to change the interest rates on its loans (assets), reducing spread (Bartel, McCord, and Bell 1995). Interest rate risk is primarily of concern to MFIs that mobilize deposits or have relatively long loan terms (of greater than one year).

Interest rate risk analysis begins with two main questions:

- What is the *amount* of funds at risk for a given shift in interest rates?
- What is the *timing* of the cash flow changes that will be experienced for a given interest rate shift?

It is important to know how large the effect of a change in interest rates will be in present value terms and when the effect will be felt.

To determine the amount of funds at risk for a given shift in interest rates, it is necessary to look at the different assets and liabilities of an MFI. Not all assets or liabilities behave the same given a percentage change in interest rates. This is referred to as *interest rate sensitivity.* MFI clients are generally *not* interest rate sensitive. Given the lack of alternatives for credit or savings services in the informal sector, a percentage change in interest rates (either credit or savings) will not greatly influence their behavior. What is important is the availability, quality, and convenience of services. (Alternatively, time deposits and larger loans are provided to more sophisticated clients who are generally more interest rate sensitive. However, based on the premise that microfinance serves lower-income clients, we can assume that interest rate sensitivity is for the most part less important to managing interest rate risk than responding to the timing of any cash flow shifts.)

For the timing of cash flow shifts, there are two techniques in general use. They are *gap analysis* and *simulation modeling.* Only gap analysis is presented here, because simulation modeling involves very sophisticated techniques not appropriate for most MFIs at this time. Gap analysis

refers to determining the *gap* between rate-sensitive assets and rate-sensitive liabilities. Rate-sensitive assets or liabilities are those that mature or can be priced either upward or downward over the next few months (Christen 1997). Gap analysis allows for managers to manage their gap position based on their expectations of future interest rate changes (see appendix 1 for more information).

While gap analysis may seem unnecessary for most MFIs, it will become more important as more MFIs mature and begin to take on different types of funding, such as voluntary deposits or commercial debt. Gap positions will have to be managed effectively to maintain (or achieve) financial sustainability. Again, as with most financial self-sufficiency issues, gap analysis will become more common for MFIs as donor funding decreases and they begin to take on more liabilities.

FOREIGN EXCHANGE RISK. Most MFIs are exposed to foreign exchange risk if they receive donor or investment funds in other than their local currency or if they hold cash or other investments in foreign currency. The devaluation or revaluation of these assets and liabilities acts the same way as interest rates in exposing the MFI to potential gain or loss. Managing this risk can influence the profitability of an MFI.

Managing foreign exchange risk refers to measuring traditional currency mismatches by the maturity of the mismatch. However, most often MFIs only need to worry about foreign exchange risk if they must repay loans (to donors or commercial sources) in a foreign currency that they have converted to local currency (either immediately or as needed) and, therefore, on which they are earning revenue in local currency. This means that funds that are received in one currency and lent out in another must be managed to reduce potential losses when they are converted back to the foreign currency. This can be done through gap analysis similar to that done for interest rate risk, except that this measurement is of currency mismatches rather than maturity mismatches.

Operating Risk Management

Operating risk refers to the risk of losses or unexpected expenses associated with fraud, inefficiency, errors, and unforeseen contingencies. Clear and transparent operational guidelines and policies help to reduce all types of operating risk, including errors. Unforeseen contingencies can be minimized through experience. Operational guidelines should be reviewed (although not too frequently, because staff may be operating under older guidelines if not properly informed) and revised periodically. Annual external audits can also contribute to the reduction of operating risk.

REDUCING THE LIKELIHOOD OF FRAUD. The decentralized nature of microfinance activities lends itself to fraud. Common types of fraud are fictitious loans, claiming borrowers have not repaid when they have, accepting savings contributions without recording them, or disbursing smaller loan amounts than recorded (box 10.8).

Controlling fraud is difficult in MFIs. Four aspects are crucial for successful fraud control: market pricing, adequate salaries for credit officers, simplicity of operations, and accountability and transparency (Hook 1995).

Below-market pricing invites bribes to MFI employees who make loan decisions. At low rates, the borrower can afford to pay a bribe and still benefit from taking the loan. Artificially low rates also invite borrowers to on-lend the funds at higher rates, often to the intended target market.

Credit officers who do not feel that they are earning an *adequate salary* will be more apt to commit fraud as a means of supplementing their low salaries, either through taking bribes or creating fictitious loans.

The more *standardized* the credit operations, the fewer opportunities for individual negotiation of terms and the fewer opportunities for fraud.

The accounting system must be developed in a *decentralized* manner so that management can see clearly what lending and recovery is taking place at the credit officer level. An effective way to control fraud is to do periodic audits of branches' and credit officers' records. These audits should include a review of operational procedures and periodic visits to clients to verify recorded information. Further control measures are established with an effective and timely management information system.

Box 10.9 lists the internal controls and operational issues the Mennonite Economic Development Association (MEDA) identified in response to an incident of fraud that seriously undermined one of its credit operations.

AUDITING MICROFINANCE INSTITUTIONS. Audits are performed to verify that the financial statements of an MFI fairly reflect its performance. There are a number of people interested in external audits, including the management of the MFI, the board, donors, lenders, investors, and regulators. Auditors should review the accounting system and the loan-tracking system. Most particularly, external audits should verify the quality of the loan portfolio, including loan loss provisioning and write-off policies.

Although most large MFIs are externally audited each year, most auditors are not familiar with microfinance and there are few procedures in place for auditing MFIs.

Box 10.8 Institution Vulnerability to Fraud

THERE ARE SEVERAL FEATURES THAT MAKE MFIS MORE vulnerable to fraud:

- A *weak information system* exposes the institution to fraudulent practices. If an MFI cannot detect instances of delinquency at the loan officer level, it could have significant problems with fraud.
- A *change in the information system* is a time of particular vulnerability. To protect against fraud when an institution introduces a new computer system, it is common practice to run the old and new system in tandem until both have been audited.
- *Weak or nonexistent internal control procedures* create an environment in which fraud can be prevalent. Many MFIs do not have an internal audit function and their external

auditors do not even visit branches, much less confirm client balances.

- MFIs are vulnerable when they have *high employee turnover* at management, administrative, or loan officer levels.
- If the organization offers *multiple loan products* or if its products are not standardized, staff and clients have an opportunity to negotiate mutually beneficial arrangements.
- If *loan officers handle cash* and if clients do not understand the importance of demanding an official receipt, the MFI is extremely vulnerable to wide-scale petty fraud.
- When an MFI experiences *rapid growth,* it is difficult to cultivate the depth of integrity that is required among staff members and for internal control practices to keep pace.

Source: Valenzuela 1998.

Box 10.9 Fraud Control at Mennonite Economic Development Association

THE MENNONITE ECONOMIC DEVELOPMENT ASSOCIATION
(MEDA) recently enforced the following policies to control
fraud:

- Checks never written to cash
- Payments only to the cashier
- Complete documentation of clients
- Adherence to the defined lending methodology
- Regular internal and external audits
- Accountability of loan officers for the performance of
  their portfolios
- Accurate and timely reporting
- Reliable client-tracking database
- Monthly reconciliation of portfolio records and the
  accounting system.

MEDA also identified the following organizational and
management lessons that help in controlling fraud:

- *Entrench the vision.* Carefully recruit and check references; provide training complemented by modeling and testing.
- *Control growth.* Begin with a pilot program; put an early emphasis on operations, not institutional development; do not scale up until *everything* is working; have the courage to say no and to shut the funding tap periodically.
- *Make sure management stays close to operations.* Encourage an open management environment; avoid distance management; ensure management structure demands accountability for results; demand timely and accurate reports; monitor, monitor, monitor.
- *Understand your clients.* Use pilot phases to test methodology; ensure staff knows the impact on clients' businesses.

Source: Contributed by Allan Sauder, Mennonite Economic Development Association.

"External auditors in traditional finance have a
much easier job than those dealing with MFIs,
because the most crucial measure of financial
health—the quality of assets—has a number of
internal procedures and cross-checks that allow
for external verification and validation. The lack
of collateral in microfinance throws auditing off
balance. The financial assets of an MFI are not
backed by the type of assets or security with
which an auditor feels comfortable." (Jackelen
1998, 57)

There are four possible ways for auditors to make up
for the lack of collateral common in microfinance
(Jackelen 1998):

- *Procedural audit.* This audit should make sure that
  loan applications and loan analysis were done correctly, loan sizes and terms comply with MFI policies, loans were approved by the proper people, legal
  documents were properly signed and notarized and
  kept in the appropriate place, and delinquency management timing and procedures are correctly followed. These items cannot be checked simply by
  looking at documents. Auditors need to observe the
  procedures in action to assess whether they were followed properly.
- *Portfolio quality.* Portfolio reports need to be reconciled with client information. The main issues are

the actual amounts outstanding and the accuracy of
the portfolio classification. In addition, refinanced or
restructured loans must be looked at carefully.

- *Client sampling.* Auditors need to verify information
  with a statistical sampling of clients. This requires
  physically visiting the clients and having them volunteer their account balances.
- *Industry benchmarking and trend analysis.* The microfinance industry needs established standards or
  benchmarks to allow auditors to compare the performance of one MFI with that of another. Auditors
  should also complete a trend analysis on the portfolio quality. This analysis will demonstrate that even
  though loans of MFIs are often unsecured, they can
  be safe.

Appendix 1. Gap Analysis

The concept of gap analysis is relatively simple. Each
asset and liability category is classified according to the
time that it will be repriced and is then placed in a
grouping called a time bucket. Time buckets refer to the
time that assets or liabilities mature, generally grouped in
three-month to one-year intervals.

In microfinance organizations, the assets are frequently
short-term (loans, term deposits, and so on) while the lia-

bilities are frequently long term (concessional loans, compulsory deposits). This results in a *funds gap*. A funds gap is defined as assets minus liabilities within each time bucket. The *gap ratio* is assets divided by liabilities in each time bucket. A funds gap or gap ratio of zero means that the MFI has exactly matched the maturity of its assets and that of its liabilities. This match, however, is difficult to achieve based on the balance sheet structure of most MFIs.

Gap positions are measured for each time bucket using the following formula:

$$\text{Cumulative gap to total assets ratio} = \frac{\substack{\text{Assets maturing (or eligible for repricing)} \\ \text{within one year} - \text{liabilities maturing} \\ \text{(or eligible for repricing) within one year}}}{\text{Total Assets}}$$

An acceptable level for this ratio depends on the average loan term, terms of the liabilities, and expectations about the movement of interest rates (Bartel, McCord, and Bell 1995). If the gap ratio is greater than one, it is referred to as a positive gap or asset-sensitive position. This means that there are more interest rate sensitive assets for a particular time period than liabilities. If an MFI expects interest rates to rise, it will likely maintain a positive short-term gap. However, if interest rates decline, both assets and liabilities will be repriced at a lower rate when the time period ends. Because there are fewer *repriced liabilities* to fund the *repriced assets*, the result is increased risk (that is, the lower repriced assets will be funded in part with higher liabilities that have not yet been repriced).

On the other hand, if the gap ratio is less than one or if there is a negative gap, a liability-sensitive position results. If interest rates decline, risk is reduced because the lower-priced liabilities will be funding more assets that are still priced at the higher rate. If an MFI anticipates declining interest rates, it will maintain negative short-term gaps, which allow more liabilities to reprice relative to assets.

Sources and Further Reading

Bartel, Margaret, Michael J. McCord, and Robin R. Bell. 1995. *Financial Management Ratios II: Analyzing for Quality and Soundness in Microcredit Programs.* GEMINI Technical Note 8. Financial Assistance to Microenterprise Programs, Development Alternatives Inc. Washington, D.C.: U.S. Agency for International Development.

Christen, Robert Peck. 1997. *Banking Services for the Poor: Managing for Financial Success.* Washington, D.C.: ACCION International.

Christen, Robert, Elisabeth Rhyne, Robert Vogel, and Cressida McKean. 1995. *Maximizing the Outreach of Microenterprise Finance: An Analysis of Successful Microfinance Programs.* Program and Operations Assessment Report 10. Washington, D.C.: U.S. Agency for International Development.

Churchill, Craig, ed. 1998. *Moving Microfinance Forward: Ownership, Competition, and Control of Microfinance Institutions.* Washington, D.C.: MicroFinance Network.

Economics Institute. 1996. "Managing the Delinquency Crisis." Microfinance Training Program, Boulder, Colo.

Fitzgerald, Thomas M. 1997. "Risk Management." Comptroller of the Currency, Administrator of National Banks, Washington, D.C.

Flaming, Mark. 1994. *Technical Guide for the Analysis of Micoenterprise Finance Institutions.* Washington, D.C.: Inter-American Development Bank.

Hook, Richard. 1995. "Controlling Fraud in Microfinance Programs." Microenterprise Development Brief 6. U.S. Agency for International Development, Washington, D.C.

Jackelen, Henry. 1998. "Auditing: The Missing Dimension in Microfinance." In Craig Churchill, ed., *Moving Microfinance Forward: Ownership, Competition, and Control of Microfinance Institutions.* Washington, D.C.: MicroFinance Network.

Ledgerwood, Joanna. 1996. *Financial Management Training for Microfinance Organizations: Finance Study Guide.* New York: PACT Publications (for Calmeadow).

Ledgerwood, Joanna, and Jill Burnett. 1995. *ADEMI Case Study.* Calmeadow, Toronto, Canada.

Ledgerwood, Joanna, and Stefan Harpe. 1995. "Tulay Sa Pag-Unlad." Calmeadow, Toronto, Canada.

Mommartz, R., and M. Holtman. 1996. *Technical Guide for Analyzing the Efficiency of Credit Granting NGOs.* Saarbrücken, Germany: Verlag fur Entwicklungspolitik Saarbrücken.

Morris, D.D., A. Power, and D.K. Varma, eds. 1986. *Guide to Financial Reporting for Canadian Banks.* Ottawa, Canada: Touche Ross.

Rhyne, Elisabeth, and Linda S. Rotblatt. 1994. "What Makes Them Tick? Exploring the Anatomy of Major Microenterprise Finance Organizations." Monograph 9. Washington, D.C.: ACCION International.

Stearns, Katherine. 1991a. *The Hidden Beast: Delinquency in Microenterprise Programs.* Washington, D.C.: ACCION International.

———. 1991b. "Methods for Managing Delinquency." GEMINI Technical Report. Development Alternatives, Inc., Bethesda, Md.

Uyemura, Dennis G., and Donald R. van Deventer. 1993. *Financial Risk Management in Banking: The Theory and Application of Asset and Liability Management.* Bankline, Salem, Mass: Bank Administration Institute Foundation.

Valenzuela, Liza. 1998. "Overview on Microfinance Fraud." In Craig Churchill, ed., *Moving Microfinance Forward: Ownership, Competition, and Control of Microfinance Institutions.* Washington, D.C.: MicroFinance Network.

Glossary

Glossary

Adjusted cost of capital: the cost of maintaining the value of the equity relative to inflation (or the market rate of equity) and accessing commercial rate liabilities rather than concessional loans.

Apex institution: a legally registered wholesale institution that provides financial, management, and other services to retail MFIs.

Arrears: the amount of loan principal (or principal plus interest) that has become due and has not been received by the MFI.

Arrears rate: the amount of overdue loan principal (or principal plus interest) divided by the portfolio outstanding.

Asset utilization: provides an indication of where revenue is earned based on where the assets are invested.

Asset and liability management: the financial risk management of a financial institution, particularly regarding the structure of its balance sheet and the risks and returns inherent in this structure.

CAMEL: a system to analyze the five traditional aspects considered to be most important in the operation of a financial intermediary. These five areas reflect the financial condition and general operational strength of an MFI and include capital adequacy, asset quality, management, earnings, and liquidity.

Capital: invested funds in the form of member shares, notes payable, and investments by outsiders. Institutional capital is capital in the form of retained earnings and reserves.

Capital adequacy: the amount of capital an MFI has relative to assets, indicating a sufficient level of capital to absorb potential losses while ensuring financial sustainability.

Capitalize: record as an asset on the balance sheet to be depreciated in the future (through a depreciation expense on the income statement).

Cash flow analysis: identification of the cash flows of an MFI relative to the amount of cash needed for operations and the amount of funds available for investment.

Cash inflows: cash received by the business or household in the form of wages, sales revenues, loans, or gifts.

Cash outflows: cash paid by the business or household to cover payments or purchases.

Cash management: the timing of cash flows to ensure that cash coming in (cash inflow) is equal to or greater than cash going out (cash outflow).

Collateral: traditionally, property, land, machinery, and other fixed assets. Alternative forms of collateral include group guarantees, compulsory savings, nominal assets, and personal guarantees.

Concessional loans: loans with rates of interest lower than the market rates.

Covariance risk: the risk that exists if the majority of clients are active in the same economic sector—that is, if they are all traders in the same area or manufacturers of the same products.

Cosigner: a person who agrees to be legally responsible for a loan but has not usually received a loan of her or his own from the MFI.

Credit: borrowed funds with specified terms for repayment.

Credit unions: see **Financial cooperatives.**

Current ratio: a ratio indicating the ability of an MFI to make debt-service payments—that is the degree of coverage provided by short-term assets. (Also called the **liquidity adequacy ratio.**)

Declining balance method: a method of calculating interest as a percentage of the amount outstanding over the loan term.

Debt: monies borrowed by the MFI to fund its assets.

Debt capacity: the ability of a client (or an MFI) to repay borrowed funds.

Depth of outreach activities: the poverty level of clients reached by an MFI. (See also **scale of outreach**.)

Depreciation: an annual expense determined by estimating the useful life of each asset.

DEVCAP: a shared mutual fund designed to provide financial returns to its investors and to member microfinance institutions.

Direct targeting: the allocation of a specific amount of funds to provide credit to a particular sector of the economy or population.

Econometrics: an analytical technique applying statistical methods to economic problems.

Efficiency indicator: see **operating cost ratio**.

Efficiency management: the management of costs per unit of output.

Enterprise development services: nonfinancial services for microentrepreneurs, including business training, marketing and technology services, skills development, and subsector analysis.

Financial cooperatives: member-owned financial institutions that have no external shareholders, with each member having the right to one vote in the organization. Members may deposit money with the organization or borrow from it, or both.

Financial intermediation: the provision of financial products and services, such as savings, credit, insurance, credit cards, and payment systems.

Financial regulation: the body of principles, rules, standards, and compliance procedures that apply to financial institutions.

Financial supervision: the examination and monitoring of organizations for compliance with financial regulation.

Financial viability: the ability of an MFI to cover its costs with earned revenue.

Fixed assets: machinery, equipment, and property (for example, motorcycles, sewing machines, egg incubators, or rickshaws).

Fixed asset loans: loans made for the purchase of assets that are used over time in the business.

Flat method: a method for calculating interest as a percentage of the initial loan amount rather than as the amount outstanding during the term of the loan.

Formal institutions: financial institutions that are subject not only to general laws and regulations but also to specific banking regulation and supervision.

Fungible: Exchangeable, replaceable. For example, fungible money is money intended for purpose x that may be used for purpose y.

Gap analysis: a determination of the gap between rate-sensitive assets and rate-sensitive liabilities.

Group-based lending: lending involving the formation of groups of people who have a common wish to access financial services; often includes group guarantees.

Group social intermediation: assistance in building the capacity of groups and investing in the human resources of their members so that they can begin to function on their own.

Idle funds: funds held by an MFI that are not earning any revenue or are earning less revenue than could be earned if they were lent out to borrowers or invested.

Impact analysis: a determination of the outcome of an intervention.

Indirect targeting: the design of products and services for people who are beyond the frontiers of normal formal finance (rather than the mandating of specific funds for particular groups with a narrowly defined profile).

Informal providers: organizations or individuals, but generally not institutions, that are not subject to special banking laws or general commercial laws, whose operations are so "informal" that disputes arising from contact with them often cannot be settled by recourse to the legal system.

Integrated MFIs: MFIs offering financial intermediation as well as enterprise development, social, or other services.

Interest rate risk: the risk that rises when interest rates on assets and interest rates on liabilities funding the assets are mismatched in both rates and terms.

Leverage: the amount of money borrowed by an MFI relative to its amount of equity.

Liquidity: the amount of cash (or near-cash) available to an MFI relative to its demand for cash.

Liquidity adequacy ratio: see **current ratio**.

Liquidity ratio: a calculation determining whether enough cash is available for disbursements and also whether there is too much idle cash.

Liquidity risk: the risk of not having enough cash to meet demands for cash leading to additional expenses for borrowing relatively expensive short-term funds to fund an illiquid position.

Loan loss ratio: a calculation determining the rate of loan losses for a specific period (usually a year).

Loan loss reserve: the cumulative amount of loan loss provisions (recorded as an expense on the income statement) minus loan write-offs; generally recorded on the balance sheet as a negative asset.

Loan loss reserve ratio: a calculation showing the percentage of the loan portfolio that has been reserved for future loan losses.

Microfinance: the provision of financial services to low-income clients, including the self-employed. In addition to financial intermediation, some MFIs also provide social intermediation services, including help in group formation and the development of self-confidence, financial literacy, and other services.

Minimalist MFIs: MFIs offering financial intermediation only.

Monopsony: a market with a single buyer, in distinction to a monopoly, which is a market with a single seller.

Moral hazard: the incentive of an agent who holds an asset belonging to another person to endanger the value of that asset because the agent bears less than the full consequence of any loss.

Near-cash: noninterest-bearing deposits and deposits earning a very low rate of interest and having a maturity of three months or less (that is, term deposits, investment certificates). Near-cash is money that is generally highly liquid (available on demand).

Nonbank financial institutions: financial institutions that circumvent the inability of some microfinance institutions to meet commercial bank standards and requirements due to the nature of their lending.

Operating cost ratio: a calculation determining operating costs relative to outstanding loans (or performing assets); regarded as an indication of the efficiency of the lending operations. (Also called the **efficiency indicator**.)

Operating risk: the risk of losses or unexpected expenses associated with fraud, inefficiency, errors, and unforeseen contingencies.

PERLAS (or PEARLS): a system of 39 financial ratios used by the World Council of Credit Unions to monitor the performance of credit unions.

Performance indicators: ratios comparing one piece of financial data to another. (See trend analysis.)

Portfolio diversification: the avoidance by a financial institution of a portfolio that is concentrated in one geographic sector or market segment.

Portfolio at risk: the outstanding balance of all loans having an amount overdue. In distinction to arrears, portfolio at risk includes the amount in arrears plus the remaining outstanding balance of the loan.

Portfolio outstanding: the principal amount of loans outstanding in a microfinance institution.

Portfolio quality ratios: calculations providing information on the percentage of nonearning assets, which in turn decrease the revenue and liquidity position of an MFI.

Productivity: the volume of business generated (output) for a given resource or asset (input).

Productivity and efficiency ratios: calculations providing information about the rate at which an MFI generates revenue to cover expenses.

Profit margin: profits relative to total revenue earned.

ProFund: an equity investment fund that provides equity and quasi-equity (subordinated debt) to selected MFIs to support the growth of regulated and efficient financial intermediaries that serve the small business and microenterprise market in Latin America and the Caribbean.

Ratios: calculations comparing one piece of financial data to another, often referred to as performance indicators.

Refinancing a loan: providing an amount of loan funds in addition to the original loan amount.

Repayment rate: the historic rate of loan recovery, measuring the amount of payments received with respect to the amount due.

Rescheduling a loan: extending the loan term or changing the payment schedule of an existing loan.

Return on assets: a ratio measuring the net income earned on the assets of a microfinance institution.

Return on equity: a ratio measuring the return on funds that are owned by the organization.

Scale of outreach: the number of clients served by an MFI. (See also **depth of outreach**.)

Securitization: a method of linking MFIs to capital markets by issuing corporate debentures backed by (and serviced by) the MFI's portfolio.

Semiformal institutions: institutions that are formal in the sense that they are registered entities subject to all relevant general laws, including commercial law, but informal insofar as they are, with few exceptions, not subject to bank regulation and supervision.

Sharia: the Islamic law, administered by councils of advisors, that dictates which financial products and services are viewed as correct.

Social capital: those features of social organization, such as *networks*, *norms*, and *trust*, that facilitate coordination and cooperation for mutual benefit.

Social intermediation: the process of building the human and social capital required for sustainable financial intermediation for the poor.

Social services: nonfinancial services that focus on improving the well-being of microentrepreneurs.

Spread: the difference between the rate of interest paid by a financial institution to borrow money and the rate of interest charged by that institution to lend money; used to cover administrative costs, loan losses, and adjusted capital costs.

Subsidy dependence index: the percentage increase required in the on-lending interest rate to completely eliminate all subsidies received in a given year.

Target market: a group of potential clients sharing certain characteristics, tending to behave in similar ways, and likely to be attracted to a specific combination of products and services.

Transfer pricing: the practice of pricing services or funds between the head office and branches on a cost-recovery basis.

Trend analysis: the comparison of performance indicators over time.

Index

Index

Printed in the United States
42433LVS00005BA/35-40

9 780821 343067